Off-Premise Catering Management

Off-Premise Catering Management

THIRD EDITION

Chris Thomas

Bill Hansen

WILEY

Published by John Wiley & Sons, Inc., Hoboken, New Jersey.
Published simultaneously in Canada.

Library of Congress Cataloging-in-Publication Data

Thomas, Chris, 1956-
    Off-premise catering management / Chris Thomas with Bill Hansen. — 3rd ed.
        p.   cm.
    Rev. ed. of: Off-premise catering management / Bill Hansen, Chris Thomas. 2005.
    Includes bibliographical references and index.
    ISBN 978-0-470-88971-8 (cloth)
        1. Caterers and catering—Management—Handbooks, manuals, etc.   I. Hansen, Bill.   II. Hansen, Bill. Off-premise catering management.   III. Title.
TX921.H36 2013
642'.4—dc23

                                                                    2011045250

Printed in the United States of America
10 9 8 7 6 5 4 3 2

Contents

Preface

Since Bill Hansen published the first edition of *Off-Premise Catering Management* a lot has changed, in the industry and the world.

To prepare this new edition, I turned to a friend and colleague in the off-premise catering business for assistance. Maxine Turner, founder and president of Cuisine Unlimited Catering and Special Events in Salt Lake City, Utah, opened her company's doors to me. Over more than a year, I spent many days at event sites, in her company's commissary and warehouse, and assisting in every department. The Turners have grown their family-run business from a one-person (Maxine) operation in a rented school cafeteria kitchen to a world-class international off-premise catering operation with 10,000 square feet of commissary and warehouse space. Cuisine Unlimited has catered for multiple Olympic Games, the Sundance Film Festival, and other major events too numerous to list here. And Maxine isn't just a caterer—she's a force of nature, full of energy and ideas. I was fortunate that she agreed to consult on this edition of the book.

Within these pages, you will find updates on:

- Food trends galore, from the importance of local and artisan producers, to new ideas for food stations and "stand-up" dining
- "Green" facets of catering, from recyclable utensils to green wedding planning

- Beverage service, with information about off-premise bar setup and interesting cocktail ingredients, plus how to select beers and wines for events
- New technology in commercial kitchen equipment
- Federal employment laws, including immigration status and background checks
- Different service styles
- Website development and social media
- The use of catering software for budgeting and accounting

Specific websites with further information can be found on this book's companion site. Visit www.wiley.com/college/thomas for more information. I've also added end-of-chapter summaries and study questions to make the book more useful in the classroom.

An online *Instructor's Manual* with *Test Bank* accompanies this book and is available to instructors to help them effectively manage their time and enhance student-learning opportunities.

The *Test Bank* has been specifically formatted for Respondus, an easy-to-use software program for creating and managing exams that can be printed to paper or published directly to Blackboard, WebCT, Desire2Learn, eCollege, ANGEL, and other eLearning systems. Instructors who adopt this book can download the *Test Bank* for free.

A password-protected Wiley Instructor Book Companion website devoted entirely to this book (www.wiley.com/college/thomas) provides access to the online *Instructor's Manual* and the text-specific teaching resources. The *Respondus Test Bank* as well as the *PowerPoint* lecture slides are also available on the website for download.

With more than 20 years of off-premise catering expertise reflected in a single volume, this newest edition will provide you with all the guidance you need to succeed, whether you are just starting out, growing your business, or working to maintain standards of excellence for your off-premise catering business.

Ms. Chris Thomas

Acknowledgments

Any book about running a business involves extensive research on a wide variety of topics and a great deal of assistance to pull it all together. Of the many people I have worked with who added their professional flair to this draft, a few deserve special recognition. They include Cynthia Thomas and Robin Heid, who helped with the research for the chapters on human resources and marketing, respectively; bookkeeper Heather Cherry, who patiently confirmed and/or updated all the calculations for the financial chapters of the book; social media guru Dave Green; and attorneys Andre Michniak and Christopher Tinari, who reviewed portions of the human resources chapter. I also very much appreciate the work of my "ace" editor at John Wiley & Sons, Christine McKnight.

Most of all, however, I am grateful to Marvin and Maxine Turner and their sons, Aaron and Jeff. Together they own and manage Cuisine Unlimited Catering and Special Events. As mentioned in the preface, the Turners allowed me to spend time in every department of their company—asking questions, shadowing people, taking notes, and observing at numerous events. (Thanks also to their terrific executive chef, Steve Ulibarri.) As a longtime food writer, I have specialized in the restaurant and beverage businesses, for the most part. The time spent at Cuisine enabled me to mesh that knowledge with the unique aspects of off-premise catering.

And finally, to Thomas Verdos, who cooked while I wrote.

Introduction to Off-Premise Catering Management

There are more than 53,000 off-premise caterers in the United States. In fact, eight out of ten caterers working in the United States today are off-premise caterers, which means they serve food at locations away from their central food production facility. They might have a freestanding commissary, a kitchen facility used exclusively for preparing foods to be served at other locations; or they might use the kitchen of a hotel, restaurant, church, or club. In most cases, there is not a full-service, commercial kitchen facility at the location where the food is served.

Off-premise catering is both an art and a science. The art is creating foods and moods, as the caterer and client work together to turn the client's vision into reality. The science is the business of measuring money, manpower, and material. Successful off-premise caterers recognize the importance of both aspects, and are able to master the creative facets of the industry, as well as the financial challenges.

As you might imagine, catering off-premise has similarities to a football team's playing all of its games away from home, often in unfamiliar surroundings. With no home field advantage, plenty of pitfalls can emerge without thorough planning, keen organizational skills, and the ability to "punt" when necessary.

In this chapter, you will learn about:

- Differences between off-premise and on-premise catering
- Challenges faced by off-premise caterers

1

- Traits and skills required for success as an off-premise caterer
- Food-related trends that could affect catering businesses
- Ways that off-premise caterers can gauge their success

Off-premise caterers can be divided into subcategories based on their specialties, although many catering companies do all of these as needed by their clients:

- Drop-off caterers supply only the food for an event. It might be attractive trays for a party, upscale box lunches for a business meeting, or prepared desserts on contract for a restaurant. The food is prepared and packaged at the catering kitchen; any last-minute details (reheating, plating, garnishing), as well as service and cleanup, are left to others. Drop-off service can also be an extremely profitable facet of a full-service catering company.

- Hot buffet caterers provide hot foods, delivered from their commissaries in insulated containers, ready to set out and serve. They sometimes provide serving staff at an additional charge.

- Full-service caterers not only provide food, but frequently cook it to order on-site. They also provide service personnel at the event, plus all the necessary food-related equipment—china, glassware, flatware, tables and chairs, tents, and so forth. They can arrange for other services, like décor and music, as well. In short, a full-service caterer can plan an entire event, not just the food to be served there.

Off-premise catering can mean preparing thousands of box lunches for a group of conventioneers; barbecuing chicken and ribs for fans before a big college game; serving an elegant dinner for two aboard a luxury yacht; or providing food, staff, and equipment for an upscale fund-raiser with hundreds of guests.

A Realistic Look at Off-Premise Catering

On a degree of difficulty scale from one to ten, with one meaning "easy" and ten meaning "most challenging," on-premise catering is a three, and off-premise is a ten.

Off-premise caterers meet the needs of all market segments, from the low-budget customer who looks for the greatest quantity and quality for the least amount of money, to the upscale client with a more flexible budget who wants the highest level of service, the ultimate in food quality, and the finest in appointments—crystal stemware, silver-plated flatware, and luxurious linens. Between these two extremes is the midscale market segment, which requires more polish and product selection than the low-budget sector, but less than the upscale.

In off-premise catering, there is only one chance to get it right. Many events, such as wedding receptions, occur only once in a lifetime. Other events are scheduled annually, quarterly, or on a regular basis, putting the caterer in a position of always trying to top the previous event—or at least, put a new and interesting spin on it. A caterer who fails to execute all details of such an event to the satisfaction of the client will seldom have another chance.

Unfortunately for some, catering off-premise events can be like living on the brink of disaster unless the caterer is cool-headed, flexible, and experienced. Amateurs may not recognize a volatile situation until it becomes a problem, later realizing they should have seen it coming. As caterers plod their way toward the completion of an event, there are thousands of potential "land mines" that can ruin an otherwise successful affair. Some examples follow:

- Already running late for a catering delivery, the catering van driver discovers that all vehicle traffic around the party site is in gridlock. The traffic has been at a standstill for more than an hour, the police say it will be hours before the congestion can be eliminated, and the clients and their guests are anxiously awaiting dinner.

- The only freight elevator in a high-rise office building has been commandeered for the evening by moving and cleaning people, thus preventing access to the floor where a caterer is to stage an event scheduled to start in two hours.

- The wrong hot food truck is dispatched to a wedding reception. The error is not discovered until the truck has reached the reception and the bride and groom are ready for their guests to be served. It will take more than an hour to send the correct truck with the food that was ordered.

- A cook wheels a container filled with cooked prime ribs down a pier toward a yacht where the meat will be served to a group of 80 conventioneers in half an hour. Suddenly, the cook is distracted, and the prime rib container tumbles over the edge of the pier and into 40 feet of water.

- The table numbers have vanished, and the guests are ready to be seated for dinner.

- The fire marshal arrives at a party site 20 minutes before a catered event and refuses to allow guests access to the party site because the space has not been authorized for party use.

- The catering crew arrives at the party site with a van full of food, cooked to order—exactly one week early.

- A new customer places an order and asks that the caterer deliver to a home where family members and guests will have gathered prior to a funeral service. The caterer sends the food and, upon arrival, is told that the person with the checkbook is at the funeral home and is asked to please stop back in an hour for the money. The delivery person leaves without obtaining a signature. Upon returning, the delivery person finds there is no one home and no one from whom to collect payment.

- While using a garbage disposal in a client's home, the caterer suddenly hears a terrible noise and watches in horror as water and garbage spew from the disposal all over the floor. The irate customer refuses to pay the caterer and threatens to sue for the cost of replacing the garbage disposal that was ruined because of (in the customer's words) the caterer's "negligence."

- After catering a flawless party at a client's home and loading the catering truck to capacity, the caterer is shocked to learn from the client that all 15 bags of trash must be removed from the client's property because of the neighborhood's zoning ordinances.

- The caterer's rental company representative calls the caterer the morning after an event to say that the $600 rented chafing dish is missing. It was at the event site the night before, when the caterer left the client's home.

Get the picture? Oh, we could tell horror stories all day! Seasoned off-premise caterers agree that these are only a few of the thousands of obstacles that stand in the way of completing a catered event. Communication, both with clients and staff, and organizational skills will help prevent such disasters. This book addresses the various ways to professionally and successfully deal with difficult situations.

With all of these very real potential problems, why are thousands of people starting their own catering companies, risking their savings on dreams of future success? The reasons are numerous. They may love the adventure of working in new and exciting places. They look forward to—or at least, they don't fear—the peaks and valleys of the business cycle. They enjoy the feeling of satisfaction that comes from successfully pulling together all the elements for a spectacular party. They love the myriad challenges of this fascinating profession. Many are their own bosses, with no one to answer to but their clients. Many pick and choose only those parties and events they wish to cater. Many make six-figure incomes each year; others cater occasionally, just for the fun of it.

Comparing Off-Premise and On-Premise Catering

What are the differences between off-premise catering and on-premise catering? Let's examine these differences, from both the client's and the caterer's viewpoints.

From the Client's Viewpoint

Most clients assume it will be less expensive to hire a caterer to help them entertain in their homes, or at unique off-premise sites, than to host an event in a hotel or restaurant. They forget to consider the cost of the rental equipment—such as tables, chairs, linens, china, glassware, and flatware—when they engage an off-premise caterer. In fact, an off-premise catered event can be more expensive, considering not only the cost of the rental equipment, but also other costs: transportation of food and supplies to the site, any specialty labor and/or décor, tenting, air-conditioning and/or heating, and other expenses.

Clients may save some money by buying their own liquor, but this savings can be insignificant when compared with these added costs. However, for many clients, the additional expense is far outweighed by the benefits of entertaining in the privacy of their own homes, or the uniqueness of hosting an event at a special off-premise location: a museum, state-of-the-art aquarium, antique car dealership, or historical site.

From the Caterer's Viewpoint

Off-premise caterers must plan menus that can be prepared successfully at, or transported to, the client's location. They have to think, for instance, about whether there will be a space with proper ventilation on site if foods are to be fried—a small kitchen in a high-rise office building's employee break room just won't do. On-premise caterers are not as limited in this regard, and they are generally supported by built-in, on-site equipment that can accommodate a wider variety of menus.

On-premise party personnel are often more familiar with the party facilities than those who work at a variety of unfamiliar locations. Off-premise catering generally has greater seasonal and day-to-day swings in personnel needs, which can create a greater challenge in terms of recruiting and training staff; turnover is usually high because such work is on an as-needed basis.

There is definitely a greater potential for mishaps and oversights in off-premise catering. Backup supplies, food, and equipment can be miles away or even inaccessible when catering, for instance, aboard a yacht miles from shore.

In spite of the uncertainties, however, off-premise catering offers the opportunity to work in a greater variety of interesting locations. The work is more likely to be different each day, resulting in less boredom and more excitement. For those looking for unlimited challenges and rewards, off-premise catering may be the answer.

Advantages and Disadvantages of Off-Premise Catering

Specializing in off-premise catering offers several advantages for the catering professional. First, most off-premise caterers require some form of advance deposit prior to an event. This deposit provides the caterer with some security if the event is canceled and also can be used to purchase some or all of the food and supplies for the party.

There is no need for large amounts of capital to get started since most off-premise catering operations begin by using the existing kitchen facilities of a restaurant, club, hotel, church, or other licensed foodservice business. (It is common knowledge that many start their catering businesses in their home kitchens, but it is imperative to state that this is in direct violation of most local zoning, health, and food safety ordinances.) In addition, all of the necessary catering foodservice equipment, such as china, glassware, flatware, tables, chairs, and linens, can usually be rented, thus avoiding having to invest in expensive equipment inventories.

Food and supply inventories, as well as operating costs, are much more easily controlled, because clients must advise the caterer in advance as to the number of guests that are expected. Off-premise caterers need buy only the amounts necessary to serve the event, unlike a restaurant where there is a large variation from day to day regarding the number of patrons and their menu selections.

Hotels, clubs, and restaurants are not typically known for providing off-premise catering services, but for those that do, it can be a source of additional revenue. They can generate even more profit by providing other services, such as rental equipment, flowers, décor, music, entertainment, and other accessory services.

Off-premise caterers can arrange their own payment terms directly with clients, eliminating a middleman, whether it's a wedding planner or on-site food and beverage director at a venue. This form of direct payment provides for better cash control and fewer folks to share the profit.

Off-premise events generate tremendous amounts of free word-of-mouth advertising, which can produce future business without the necessity of advertising. Many off-premise caterers feel that satisfied guests at one party will either book another party or indirectly generate another booking by speaking favorably to friends and coworkers about the event and the caterer. In other words, one party can create future parties.

Off-premise caterers also have the advantage of being somewhat selective about their clients. There are no laws that require you to accept every request to cater. If the job doesn't meet your standards, politely decline. In sticky situations where you've already begun to work with a client but find that your communication styles just don't mesh—or, as sometimes happens with weddings, the client is not heeding your advice and you can't even decide who's really in charge—you can walk away, as long as you do so within the terms of your written agreement.

Off-premise catering has its disadvantages too. Catering managers, owners, and staff undergo periods of high stress during very busy periods. Deadlines must be met, and there are no excuses for missing them. Stress is compounded because the workload is not evenly spread throughout the year. For most off-premise caterers, 80 percent of the events are scheduled in 20 percent of the time. For most, weekends are generally busier than weekdays. Certain seasons, including Christmas, are normally busier than others. Of course, caterers must maintain general business hours too.

Many have left the catering field, burned out by the constant stress and high energy demands. The seasonality of the business makes it difficult to find staff at certain times. Revenues are inconsistent, making cash flow management challenging, particularly during the slower periods when expenses continue yet revenues do not.

For those caterers who operate hotels, restaurants, clubs, and other businesses, the time spent on the off-premise business—away from the main business—can be a detriment to their on-site operations. No matter how well organized you are, it is impossible to be in two places at the same time. Many hoteliers and restaurateurs find the rigors of off-premise catering too great. Some quit after realizing the difficulty of catering away from their operations. They feel that the financial benefits are insufficient compared with the effort required to cater off-premise events.

Traits of the Successful Off-Premise Caterer

What does it take to become a successful off-premise caterer? What experience is necessary, and what personality traits are desirable?

Work Experience. Prior experience in the catering profession or the foodservice industry is important. Experience in food preparation and foodservice (both back-of-the-house and front-of-the-house) helps caterers understand the procedures and problems in both areas and how the two areas interface. Those with a strong kitchen background, for example, would be wise to gain some front-of-the-house experience, and front-of-the-house personnel should learn the kitchen routine.

Many successful off-premise caterers began by working as accommodators. Accommodators are private chefs who are hired to prepare food for parties. Many assist the client with planning the menu, purchasing the food, and even arranging for kitchen and service staff. The food is prepared and served in the client's home or facility, eliminating the need for a catering commissary. Accommodators receive a fee for their services. The party staff is paid directly by the client.

Passion. Successful professionals are passionate about their work, and caterers are no exception. They love what they do. Clients and staff members will quickly detect a lack of passion, and it will cost you business and good workers. If you don't love what you do, move on and try something else.

An Entrepreneurial Nature. The drive to be an entrepreneur is a highly desirable trait for off-premise caterers. A successful entrepreneur is willing to spend extraordinary amounts of time and energy to make the business successful, possesses an inherent sense of what is right for the business, has the ability to view all aspects of the business at once rather than focusing on only one or two parts, and demonstrates a strong desire to be his or her own boss and become financially independent.

Basic Business Knowledge. The list below is only the beginning. Remember, the caterer is running a company, no matter how small, and must run it just as professionally "on paper" and online as a caterer supervising a grand event at a client site. This knowledge includes:

- *A vision for the business.* The ability to create a business plan, and one-year and five-year goals, and to communicate these thoroughly and with enthusiasm to partners, investors, bankers, and others is key.
- *Accounting and bookkeeping skills.* You don't have to do your own bookkeeping, but understanding the financial aspects of operating a catering business is necessary

to work with those you hire to do it. This includes the ability to prepare and interpret such documents as a Profit and Loss Statement, Balance Sheet, and Chart of Accounts.

- *Computer skills.* You probably didn't decide to become a caterer to spend days agonizing over the design and content of your website, but it is a critical component of any successful catering operation. You'll be amazed at how much you can accomplish by using and managing e-mail, providing a website, and actively, creatively using social media tools to keep customers' attention. In addition, there are specialized programs to assist with everything from room layout for events, to costing out recipes, ordering supplies, and planning menus.

- *Legal knowledge.* It is also important to understand the legal aspects of catering. Laws that affect caterers include regulation of licensing, health, contracts, liability, labor, and alcoholic beverage service. You might not have to quote these laws on a daily basis, but you'll need to be aware of the basics, be alert for changes, and have access to attorneys and insurance specialists who can assist you if problems arise.

- *Human resource skills.* A caterer, like any other businessperson, has to be able to recruit, train, motivate, and manage people. The seasonal swings and rather transient nature of part-time workers in the foodservice industry make this particularly challenging.

- *Sales skills.* The ability to market the business creatively is key, from developing and implementing a marketing plan, to convincing the bank that you'll use the loan money wisely, to "closing the sale" when bidding against competitors for a job.

Ability to Plan, Organize, Execute, Control, and Measure Results. These are the five basic functions of management. To plan, a caterer must visualize in advance all the aspects of a catered event, and be able to document the plans so they are readily understood by the client and easily executed by the staff. Organizing is simply breaking down the party plans into groups of functions that can be executed in an efficient manner. Execution is the implementation of the organized plans by the party staff. Controlling is the supervisory aspect of the event. All well-organized and well-executed plans require control and supervision. The adage is, "It is not what you expect, but what you inspect." The premier off-premise catering firms in the United States insist on top-notch supervision at each event.

In terms of measuring results, you will be able to do this effectively only if you take the time to set goals for your company, decide on specific activities to meet those goals, and determine how you will track your progress to know when each goal has been met. For caterers, these are not just sales goals, but goals involving employee training, lowering food costs, reducing breakage in the dishroom—a whole variety of topics. We discuss this further in the "Developing a Strategic Plan" section on page 12.

Ability to Communicate with Clients and Staff. The key to good communication with clients and prospective clients is listening, paying careful attention to determine what the client needs and asking the necessary follow-up questions for clarification. A client who calls and asks, "Are you able to cater a party next Friday?" should be dealt with differently from one who calls and asks, "How much will it cost for a wedding reception?" The first caller is ready to buy your services, whereas the second caller is only shopping around. Astute caterers must be able to respond to client requests in such a manner that the client immediately gains confidence in their ability and knowledge.

Communicating with staff is often a more complex issue. In simple terms, it can be reduced to the ability to clearly tell staff what is expected so they understand and can deliver it, and the ability to receive their feedback regarding problems, both actual and potential. The result of effective communication is an off-premise catering staff that professionally executes a well-planned party that meets or exceeds the client's expectations.

Ability to Take a Risk. Off-premise catering is a risky business; it is not for the fainthearted who are afraid of the unknown. For example, it is more risky catering a corporate fund-raiser at the local zoo under a tent than serving the same group in a hotel ballroom. Off-premise caterers must know when the risk outweighs the gain. In this particular example, catering the event at the zoo without adequate shelter in case of rain would probably be too risky. The event could be ruined by inclement weather, but the tent is a "calculation" that makes the risk acceptable.

Sound Body and Mind. Off-premise catering requires working long hours without rest or sleep, lifting and moving heavy objects, withstanding intense pressure as deadlines near, and even tolerating long periods of little or no business, which inevitably cause concern. Successful caterers should be in good physical shape, have a high energy level, and be able to mentally deal with seasonal business cycles that range from nonstop activity to slow periods.

In terms of a caterer's brainpower, a "sound mind" includes common sense and the ability to reason, as well as a genuine fondness for people and the ability to feel comfortable in crowds and under pressure. A cool head will keep both staff and clients calm as potential problems are resolved professionally and efficiently.

Creativity. This is the benchmark of all outstanding caterers. Creative caterers are able to turn a client's vision into reality by producing the appropriate look, feel, menu, service, and ambiance. They're always looking around; examining current events, culinary trends, and popular culture; and trying to figure out how to incorporate them into event and party plans. Those who don't consider themselves naturally creative certainly can learn to be, or they can employ creative people for their design team.

Open-Mindedness. This goes hand in hand with creativity, as open-minded caterers enjoy trying new recipes, seasonings, and menu pairings, and encourage staff members to do the same. They are willing to prepare unfamiliar dishes when requested by clients, after thoroughly testing and understanding the recipes. In addition, they are always seeking better ways to run every facet of their businesses. If someone else has a great idea, they embrace it rather than feeling resentful that they didn't think of it first.

Dependability. Dependability is a major cornerstone of success in off-premise catering. When a caterer fails to deliver what was promised, the negative word of mouth travels fast among clients and potential clients. Even in those situations where circumstances change, making it more difficult to perform as promised, the outstanding caterer will find a way to deliver rather than use the changed circumstances as an excuse not to deliver.

Ability to Meet Clients' Needs. The needs of the client must always come first. Success in this business comes from identifying these needs and satisfying them. Unsuccessful off-premise caterers are those who get lost in trying to satisfy their own needs for money, equipment, and greater self-esteem. They forget that the primary goal is to serve the needs of the client. When a client's needs are met, the caterer's needs for revenues, profits, and positive feedback will automatically be met.

Ability to Project a Favorable Image. Prospective clients hire caterers based on their perceived image of the caterer and what the caterer will provide. In some sense, then, caterers are selling themselves more than their food. Off-premise caterers must be able to project a favorable image to the client, one that is in accord with the client's expectations. For example, a caterer whose image is sophisticated and upscale will be hard-pressed to sell a Little League banquet with a low budget. Successful caterers understand their projected images and target their marketing efforts at those clients who desire that image.

Sense of Humor. In this pressure-packed, deadline-oriented, and often stressful business, it is easy to get carried away with the magnitude of the undertakings and become so tense and uptight that work ceases to be fun. Laughter at the right time can relieve that tension and stress, putting a renewed sense of fun into the work at hand.

Managing an Off-Premise Catering Operation

Even those who possess the qualities necessary for off-premise catering success must know how to put these talents to use effectively. Off-premise caterers should be hands-on managers who are constantly customer focused. They must be able to lead staff and clients alike, while conducting business in a professional manner. They must be able to make timely, ethical decisions, while understanding what makes for a successful event. They must also avoid those situations that cause a business to fail.

Developing a Strategic Plan

A strategic plan is a roadmap to help you determine the direction you wish your business to go, and the specific goals you must accomplish to get there. It begins with a statement of core values, which may include factors like client satisfaction; ethical business practices; staff satisfaction, training, and motivation; community service; and operation of an environmentally conscious business.

From these core values, a caterer can develop a *Mission Statement*—a succinct sentence that sums up the company's mission. Here's an example:

> Our company will meet the catering needs of the corporate community by providing high levels of service and food quality, which will result in repeat business and vital growth.

After the Mission Statement comes the *Vision Statement*—a concise summary of where you want to be in the future. Again, an example:

> Within five years, our company will be the top-ranked catering firm in our area, with continuing sales and profit growth, while giving back to our community.

It isn't enough to brainstorm about these statements. Writing them down is the first step to making them a reality. Only after they are put in writing can you develop more specific objectives to increase sales and profits, measure customer satisfaction, size up your competitors, and plan the ways in which you will give back to the community.

Your Mission and Vision Statements lead naturally to the next step: to establish goals for the operation. You may have heard time management experts use the term "SMART" when describing goals. The acronym stands for:

Specific. The goals to be accomplished must be easily understood, concise, and unambiguous.

Measurable. There should be no question about whether one attains, or falls short of, a goal. It may be measured in terms of quality, cost, quantity, or time.

Attainable. The goals may be just out of reach, but they should not be out of sight. The best goal challenges and motivates you and your team. If it's practically impossible, it may be too frustrating.

Relevant. The goals must fit well with your long-term mission and vision, your objectives, and the results you expect.

Time-Bound. There must be a specific deadline for completion of each goal.

An example of a SMART goal might be to increase sales and profits by 20 percent each year for the next five years.

While goals are important, remember not to set too many, too quickly. It will scatter your energy and make progress more difficult. Typically, every goal requires certain trade-offs. To increase sales, for instance, you may need to drop prices, hire more staff to be able to cater more events, or spend money on advertising. The major goals can be broken into smaller, intermediate steps, with a time line to keep the company, and individual managers or department heads, on track.

Goals are not just for the owner of a company. The staff and other professionals employed by the company—accountant, banker, attorney, and all vendors—should also be well aware of the goals. You will need their help to achieve them, and you want them on your side, committed to your goals. Too often, caterers believe they can do everything themselves. They fail to ask for or accept advice from outside consultants and colleagues. It is far more intelligent to ask for assistance when you need it. Someone familiar with your plans and your passion for them is far more likely to be helpful.

Finally, as soon as a goal is set, take some action on it.

The last part of a strategic management process is to reevaluate your mission, vision, and goals periodically. Times change, trends change, and you become aware of new information. Let's say a caterer's sales year showed a 50 percent increase, when he or she had set a 20 percent annual goal. In this case, the next year's goal might be more realistically revised to a 30 percent increase.

Hands-On Management, Attention to Detail

Have you ever heard the old saying, "The devil is in the details"? Another way to put it is that we've all been bitten by a mosquito or stung by a bee, but none of us has ever been bitten by an elephant. It's always the little things that get us.

In catering, the details are almost endless, a stream of tiny elements, any of which might go wrong and result in a catastrophe. One thing forgotten, misheard, or misplaced can ruin an event. So it's important to check and recheck and to be prepared for last-minute emergencies.

It is simply not possible to run this kind of business from behind a desk, reading computer printouts and delegating all tasks. Off-premise catering companies must be managed from the center of the action, whether that is serving the guests or preparing food in the kitchen. Success comes from checking and rechecking every detail to ensure that it meets the highest of standards. It comes from inspecting for the best and expecting the best. Some call this management style "management by walking around." In one sense that is true, but there is more to it than walking around. Astute off-premise caterers must:

- Obtain feedback from clients and guests regarding the food and service.

- Oversee the catering staff to ensure they are performing as directed and as expected.

- Help out when a table needs to be cleared or when the bar suddenly becomes very busy. Help in the kitchen during critical times, such as hot food dish-up, and even help scrape, stack, and wash dirty dishes if that is what's necessary.

It's a roll-up-your-sleeves kind of profession, and you should never be totally satisfied with the way things are. Always look for new ways to present food and make it more flavorful, and for better and more efficient ways to do things.

Customer-Focused Management

An off-premise caterer's full-time mission must be to satisfy the needs of clients. Unlike a restaurant, in which the owners often have the advantage of market research to determine who their target customers will be in a particular location, a caterer must be comfortable serving multiple demographic groups, at all sorts of locations and a variety of price points. At its simplest, what this means is maintaining flexibility, while keeping prices fair and controlling costs.

Managerial Decision Making

Off-premise catering managers must make decisions that keep their operations running smoothly. They realize that some decisions will be better than others, that there is no perfect solution to every problem, and that the goal in almost any situation is to find the best possible solution with the least number of drawbacks.

Although hundreds of books have been written about effective decision making, the following tips from management consultant and author Connie Sitterly should be helpful. They're paraphrased from an article she wrote back in 1990 in *The Meeting Manager*, but they are still up-to-the-minute when it comes to making tough decisions successfully.

- Remember that there's seldom only one acceptable solution to the problem. Choose the best alternative.
- Make decisions that help achieve the company objectives.
- Consider feelings whenever people are involved. Even if you must make an unpopular decision, you can minimize repercussions if workers know you have taken their feelings into account.
- Allow quality time for planning and decision making. Pick a time when you are energetic and your mind is fresh.
- Realize that you will never please everyone. Few decisions meet with unanimous approval. The appointed authority, not the majority, rules.
- Make time for making decisions. In business, delaying a decision can cost thousands of dollars.

- Put decision making in perspective. Every executive feels overwhelmed at times by either the enormity or the number of the decisions that must be made during a business day. For peace of mind, accept that you are doing the best job you can with the time, talent, and resources you have.

- Don't wait for a popular vote. Rallying your colleagues around your decision before you take action or waiting for their vote of confidence before deciding anything may cost too much in terms of time. There are times when you just have to do something.

Leadership

There are major differences between those who lead and those who manage. Catering companies need both types of executives, and some who can do both. If a catering company is earning seven- and eight-figure annual revenues, you can be certain its owners and managers are people with leadership skills.

Leaders are able to get people to do things they don't necessarily like to do—and even enjoy them. You might say:

A manager . . .	A leader . . .
Maintains	Develops
Administers	Innovates
Relies on systems	Relies on people
Counts on controls	Counts on trust
Does things right	Does the right things
Works within the system	Works on the system
Manages things	Leads people

A leader is more like a thermostat than a thermometer. A thermostat sets the standard temperature for the space in which it is located. A thermometer simply records the temperature; it can't change anything. And one more important trait: Leaders take a little more than their share of the blame, and a little less than their share of the credit.

Professionalism and Common Business Courtesy

Off-premise caterers who are not professional in their business practices will never reach the pinnacle of success in the field. Before we address the technical aspects of catering in the succeeding chapters, it is of utmost importance that we define professionalism.

The following guidelines are adapted from an article by Carol McKibben in *Special Events* magazine:

- Become known for doing what you say you will do.
- Give price quotes and commitments only when you know everything about the event.
- Treat clients and staff members with respect.
- Build relationships with clients. Do not look at them as accounts or projects.
- Be on time, or a bit early, for appointments. Be prepared for an appointment.
- Be honest; don't play games.
- Stand behind your work. If it is wrong, make it right.
- In the face of abuse from others, don't respond by becoming abusive. Try to detach yourself from it emotionally and handle it logically. Of course, do not use your position of power to abuse others.
- Dress professionally.
- Enjoy your work as an off-premise caterer. When work ceases to be enjoyable, it is time to quit and find a new career.

It might surprise you to learn that these tips were written more than 20 years ago. They are proof that professionalism truly never goes out of style.

Ethics in Management

In today's business world, lack of ethics is among the most widely discussed topics. We read and hear of illegal payoffs, scandals, and other forms of questionable behavior bringing down some of the nation's largest corporations and politicians. Off-premise caterers are in no way exempt from ethical concerns. Even the smallest caterers deal with issues of fairness, legal requirements, and honesty on a daily basis. Examples include truth in menu disclosures, product substitutions, advertising claims, dealing with unexpected or unjustified last-minute add-ons to an event price, and even underbidding a competitor when the client has inadvertently disclosed the competitor's price.

The ethical caterer will assume responsibility for the host to ensure that the host plans an event that is in the best interests of the guests, in every respect. For instance, a host who wishes to serve alcohol to underage guests is out of line and must be advised that this is not acceptable. An ethical caterer will refuse to cater an event that is clearly not being planned in the best interest of the host or guests.

There are times when a caterer is given a free hand in planning a menu. Perhaps a grieving client calls for food after the funeral of a loved one, saying, "Please send over food for 50 guests tomorrow night. You know what we like." The ethical caterer will not take advantage of this situation by either providing too much food or overcharging the client.

Another temptation arises when the caterer is pressed to schedule more events on a certain day or evening than the company can reasonably accommodate. The extra money certainly is tempting. Unethical caterers will rationalize that they can juggle all the events, even if an inexperienced supervisor or staff must oversee these events, or the kitchen staff will not be able to prepare their usual high-quality food because of lack of time and personnel. Caterers who take on more work than they can reasonably accommodate are greedy and are considered by many observers to be unethical.

In the foregoing situation, the caterer should decline the work and perhaps recommend another catering company. Some caterers refuse to do this; they worry that if the client is not pleased with the other firm, the caterer who initially turned down the business will be blamed for the recommendation. Other caterers freely recommend one or more companies when unable to cater events.

There are times when it is very hard not to bad-mouth a competitor, but this is considered unethical, as well as rude. Those who are ethical would rather point out their own strengths than downgrade the competition.

It can be very tempting for self-employed caterers to underreport income or overstate expenses. They rationalize that no one will know if they accept cash for a party, and then fail to report it as income and pay the associated tax, or that no one will know if they happen to charge personal expenses now and then to the business. Some caterers who are licensed to sell liquor by the drink or by the bottle are tempted to bill clients for beverages that were not consumed. These practices are not only unethical—they are illegal.

Other ethical violations occur when caterers receive under-the-table cash kickbacks from suppliers, misrepresent their services to potential clients, or bid on party plans or ideas stolen from other caterers.

Caterers also soon learn that some clients are unethical. A few are masterful at finding fault with a wedding or other important event, and then demanding a "discount" based on whatever flaw they feel they have uncovered. Some will refuse to pay for linens that were damaged by candles they lit on them. You'll find people who, midparty, will ask you to stay "a couple hours of overtime, just to wrap things up"—and then not show up to pay you for the extra time the next day, as agreed. Others will haggle over the tiniest details on an invoice or try to engage more than one caterer in a bidding war to lower prices. Caterers who deal with "middleman" organizations, like destination management firms or production companies, may find that a client of one of these companies will come back later to try to deal directly with them, thus cutting out the middleman who recommended them.

As a catering professional, you need to expect a certain amount of this behavior and must protect yourself if you suspect an ethical question may arise. Insisting on security deposits, having a valid and authorized credit card number on file for unforeseen charges, refusing to look at other caterers' written bids, and standing firm on your own invoice prices are just a few ways ethical problems can be avoided. And rather than cut out a legitimate middleman-type vendor, you can either refuse to deal directly with a client who tries such a maneuver or suggest a commission be paid to the middleman.

You will also be put in some uncomfortable situations, as—during tough times and even good times—certain clients will make unrealistic requests. They've often been good, regular clients too. But they'll promise you future business if you'll cater their party "at cost" or defer payment for them, or they'll ask for some other special favor "just this once."

These requests are unfair, and you are right to be squeamish about them. Off-premise caterers should be extremely wary when approached in this fashion. As a general rule, clients who do not pay their bills in a professional manner, or who are not willing to pay a fair price for catering services, are not worth the headaches they cause.

The Jefferson Center of Character Education has set forth a list of ten "universal values": honesty, integrity, promise keeping, fidelity, fairness, caring for others, respect for others, responsible citizenship, pursuit of excellence, and accountability. These values should provide some solid guidance for any businessperson who considers himself or herself a true professional.

Separating Yourself from the Competition

Great caterers do more than imitate—they innovate. They may build and improve on someone else's concept, but they strive to take the idea to the next level. Rather than mimicking another's success, they imprint their own signature on their menus. As with any career, staying ahead of competitors requires catering professionals to reexamine their business strategies from time to time.

Look at the caterers in your own community and you will note the distinct advantages of those who offer unique menus and services, perhaps even in unique locations. Then again, some simply do what they do best—they have a niche, a particular client base or type of event for which they are well known, and never vary their formulas. Their clients love them and get exactly what they expect.

Other caterers seem to copy everyone else. They ricochet from one concept or recipe to the other, and you sense that they probably never bother to gauge clients' reactions or see if their services really meet their clients' needs. If they read about a trendy dish in a magazine, they feel they have to serve it, whether they do a good job of it or not.

Most caterers fall somewhere between these two extremes, blending successful ideas from the past with new twists and interesting concepts.

Great caterers also separate themselves from competitors by using the resources around them to build their businesses. In South Florida, for example, one caterer specializes in event planning for doctors, through his hospital foodservice management job. Another has an exclusive off-premise contract for a sports facility; a third is the on-premise caterer for a city club, with the added benefit of extra catering business from the club members. Capitalize on the audience you have—they're (almost) already yours!

Personal Management

Off-premise caterers work an average of 59 hours a week, according to the industry group *CaterSource*. Time management, stress management, and personal organization skills must be mastered to manage your own work life, as well as your business, at peak efficiency. Time is our most precious commodity, and to waste it because of being over-stressed or disorganized will inevitably result in less-than-desirable results.

Stress Management

Stress generally comes from interaction with others and from having to meet deadlines, although it is often self-imposed. A certain amount of stress and tension is necessary to achieve the best results—and you might enjoy the adrenaline rush you feel when you're in the middle of a busy event and know there's a lot at stake. However, consistently high stress levels over prolonged time periods can cause chronic fatigue, irritability, cynicism, hostility, inflexibility, and difficulty in thinking clearly. Catering managers who are over-stressed are unable to perform at maximum capability.

Stress cannot always be eliminated, but it can often be controlled through:

- Daily exercise. This might mean a brisk walk or run, some dedicated time on a spinning bike, or other aerobic pursuits that increase the heart rate. Some folks purposefully take their minds off work when they exercise; for others, the daily walk or run is a time to reflect on the week's priorities or get organized for the coming day.

- Relaxation techniques, including meditation and yoga.
- Writing down the issues that cause stress. Identify those facets of your life that can be controlled, and decide to make the best of those that cannot. Brainstorm ways to deal with the controllable stress factors.
- Reading articles and books on stress reduction.

Furthermore, reducing stress is a natural offshoot of hiring excellent people, training them well, and trusting them enough so that you can delegate some of the event details and responsibilities to them.

Time Management

There are only 168 hours in each week, and the greatest rewards come to those who accomplish the most meaningful things during this fixed amount of time. Off-premise caterers realize that if they can accomplish more meaningful production in less time, they will have more time for pursuits other than work. They also realize that working smarter, not harder, through the effective use of time will produce greater results.

The key to effective time management is to set goals for certain time periods: a lifetime, five years, and/or for each year, month, week, and day. Without written goals, off-premise caterers will find it impossible to effectively manage their time. Time management involves choosing how to spend your time, so there's no way to make proper choices without knowing the desired outcome or goal. The captain of a ship without a destination cannot choose the proper course. He or she will cruise aimlessly at sea, never reaching his or her port of call.

It is equally important to schedule downtime for yourself—for family, friends, hobbies, and interests other than work. You are guarding against burnout when you insist on some personal time.

Off-premise caterers can choose from an array of time-saving techniques and technical advances to help them in their quest to efficiently manage time:

- Make daily, detailed lists of goals and objectives.
- Do as much online and on the computer as possible. It saves paper, produces files that are easily shared with others, and creates an electronic trail that can be useful when you have to prove when something was e-mailed or received.

- Use an up-to-the-minute mobile device to stay in touch while away from the office. Even cell phones are lifesavers at off-premise catering locations when emergency and other calls are necessary. If you have unexpected downtime, they enable you to use it efficiently by checking e-mail or returning phone calls.
- Handle incoming papers only once. Here's the rule: Do it, delegate it, discard it, or file it. (Better yet, hire someone else to file it.)
- Do your most important work at times when you happen to be most alert. Most of us know whether we are "morning people" or "night owls." Take advantage of your peak energy periods to handle your most challenging tasks.
- Sign up for a time management seminar or course to learn more techniques.

One of the biggest time wasters for a caterer is also a source of business that cannot be ignored: the prospective client who calls or e-mails with questions. This is, however, an interruption that can be controlled. Whoever answers the phone at your business should always qualify inquiries by asking:

- The date of the event
- Whether a location has been selected
- The number of guests
- The budget for the event

In addition, as you set up your website "Contact Us" section, you might want to include prompts to obtain this information. Why? First of all, time can be wasted by talking about an event before you ask the date and discover you are unable to do it in the first place because of a scheduling conflict. Perhaps the number of guests is too small or too large for your particular company, the budget is insufficient, or the proposed location is already booked for another event.

Always focus on results by asking yourself, "Will this activity help me achieve any of my goals?" Prioritize tasks in order of their importance and know when to delegate them to others. Most people waste countless hours, days, weeks, and years chitchatting on the phone, shuffling papers, running errands, and doing other things that are easy enough but offer little or no payoff. Learn to delegate these types of tasks whenever possible. Pay other people to do them, and don't tell yourself you can't afford it—you can always make more money, but you have only so much time. The true achievers, in catering and in other fields, minimize the time they spend on low-priority, low-payoff tasks and turn their attention to those things that will bring the greatest rewards.

These essential tasks are often difficult to accomplish, take a great deal of time, and involve at least some risk. For example, a caterer could spend the entire day showing prospective clients numerous suitable locations for a major event. The caterer would then spend the next three days preparing a written proposal for an event at each of the locations, with no guarantee that the event will even take place. However, if the caterer is hired, there's a five-figure profit to be made. Worth the risk? Certainly!

Another high-payoff task might be writing a new catering menu. Both this and the aforementioned task require large chunks of time and involve some risk, but more than likely will produce major rewards in increased revenues and profits.

In summary, off-premise caterers who best manage their time will be the most successful in the long run. They become the leading caterers in their communities, in their states, and in the country.

Getting and Staying Organized

When projects, tasks, catering kitchens, and offices are well organized, things run much more smoothly and efficiently. The time spent looking for things and jumping from job to job is wasted time that could be put to much better use. Many off-premise caterers have found various methods that work for them:

- Create a system that ensures that every step of every client transaction—from the first contact, to follow-up communication, contract, changes to the plan, and a post-event debrief—can be traced, and that there's someone to take responsibility for each step along the way. Once again, strive to create a trail that can be double-checked at any time.

- Take a tip from event planners, who start a separate notebook for each event they are working on. Into this three-ring binder go all notes, contracts, sketches, and color and fabric samples—anything for that particular job. No matter how much planning can be done on a computer, a binder system can be very useful for complex jobs.

- Consider hiring a professional organizer to come to your office and set up a filing and record-keeping system that works for your business.

- Keep frequently used items close by.

- Focus on one project at a time, rather than jumping from one thing to another. This can be more easily accomplished by blocking out some uninterrupted time during the day to work on major projects.

- Whenever possible, try to schedule time to return phone calls and/or e-mail messages. That way, you can handle them all at once, instead of scattering them (and your thoughts) in five-minute intervals throughout the day.

- At the end of each day, prepare a list of things to do for the following day. Some people manage to do this as the very first thing in the morning.

To summarize, off-premise caterers who can effectively deal with stress, manage their time, delegate tasks, and keep things organized will lead their peers into the future. They will set the standards for others to follow. They will accomplish more and will be in a position to receive the greatest rewards as a result.

The Seven Habits of Highly Successful Caterers

Let's examine some additional techniques, philosophies, and real-life ways to be successful in the challenging field of off-premise catering.

Habits are things we do automatically, like brushing our teeth, combing our hair, or straightening a tablecloth that's uneven as we help set up a banquet room. We hardly think about them; we just do them. Stephen R. Covey wrote *The Seven Habits of Highly Effective People*, which has been a bestseller for years—you should read it if you haven't already. But what are some habits that mark successful caterers? What separates star performers from the rest of the crowd? With a nod to Mr. Covey, here are seven key habits.

Being Willing to Take Calculated Risks

A popular saying is, "A turtle goes nowhere until it sticks its neck out." To succeed, we must be continually growing and improving, and the only way to do this is to leave our comfort zones—and stick our necks out.

If you're right-handed, you feel quite comfortable writing with your right hand. Try writing with your left hand; you're definitely out of your comfort zone. But after a while, you might find you can actually write with either hand. In the same spirit, successful caterers make things happen by taking calculated risks, whether the risk is trying new menu items, implementing new buffet display concepts, or accepting a job in a new and challenging off-premise location. Caterers who refuse to take risks fail to grow and learn—and eventually are left behind in this competitive industry.

Expressing Sincere Concern for Others

Nobody cares how much you know, until they know how much you care. Empathy and genuine concern for your clients and staff are paramount to long-term success. What are the needs, wishes, and desires of the people you work with and for? What are their concerns and their "hot buttons"? By putting ourselves in their positions, we can begin to show concern for others and understand them. When we do this, we develop meaningful relationships and, not coincidentally, loyalty. We give them what they want, and we get what we want.

Keeping Up with Current Trends

It isn't just a matter of food and presentation and theme trends, although these are critical. Caterers who are not tech-savvy, including the use of social media, are missing out on huge opportunities to create "buzz" about what they are doing.

At the very least, you and your support staff must get into the habit of regularly updating websites, responding to promptly to e-mail correspondence, and providing proposals, contracts, and other documents electronically. If you are not in the habit of working online, you're now hopelessly behind the times.

Managing Your Time and Setting Priorities

You get 20 percent of your sales and profits from 80 percent of your clients, and 80 percent of your sales and profits from 20 percent of your clients.

None of us ever goes home at night thinking all the work is done—it never is. It's simply a question of what's most important, as well as what's most urgent. Urgent things are never really an issue. There's no question that if you have a catered event today, the work will get done. But what is most urgent is not necessarily what's most important. You must understand the difference.

For example, you could spend a day catering three small parties for 25 guests each but fall behind on preparing a proposal for another job, in three months, for 500 guests—and lose it to a competitor whose proposal was submitted on time.

Successful caterers spend their time in the areas that generate the biggest paybacks in terms of money, quality, and other rewards. They make a habit of planning their days, leaving time for the most important, as well as the most urgent. At the start of each day, they prepare an agenda that details both short-term objectives and long-term goals. If you're a student, you should already be using this technique to accomplish as much as you can in school.

Putting Quality Before Quantity

The previous example aside, bigger is not necessarily better. Still, many of us get caught up in that way of thinking. If our sales are $1 million, let's go for $2 million. If they're $2 million, what's wrong with $4 million? And if $4 million is good . . .

There's nothing wrong with building sales if quality does not suffer. However, when the quality of your products and services suffers, so does the quality of your daily life. More business means more hours at work, and doctors will tell you they've never met a man or woman who, on a deathbed, expressed a wish that he or she had spent more time working.

As long as the business we have is both enjoyable and profitable, we need to make a habit of continually asking ourselves whether we might be better off with a little less business, to leave more time for ourselves and our families. We need to continually examine the overall quality of our work to ensure that it isn't slipping because we've allowed ourselves to take on too much.

Being Detail-Oriented

A baseball player who bats .250 gets three hits for every 12 times at bat. One who bats .333 gets four hits for every 12 times at bat. The difference—one more hit for every 12 times at bat—means the difference between an average major league ball player and a Hall of Fame inductee.

Do you make it a habit to continually look for the little things? A good caterer isn't nitpicky but is forever finding something that needs to be tweaked, adjusted, redone, or improved—little things that most customers won't notice but that greatly affect the overall professionalism of an event. An awareness of the details of flavor, appearance, aroma, and tidiness separates the average caterers from the superstars. And, by all means, check the spelling, grammar, and punctuation in all your written materials, from brochures to contracts—or hire someone to do it. Again, the goal is to present a professional image. Remember, the devil is in the details.

Setting High Standards

If you refuse to accept anything but the very best, you very often get the best. Successful caterers set their standards high and expect excellence from themselves and their staff members. They are rarely happy with the status quo, always striving to make each party, wedding, or event better than the last. They debrief after an event, asking staff for input and improvements. They know that if they fail to improve, they're leaving the door open for their competitors to capture a good customer or a larger share of the market.

Successful caterers also make a habit of lifelong learning. They're forever reading, attending trade shows, and exploring areas that will help them improve their own businesses with new ideas. They challenge and reward their staff members for having the same attitude.

Vince Lombardi, the late NFL coach, who during his career coached the first team to ever win the Super Bowl, put it this way: "The quality of a person's life is in direct proportion to their commitment to excellence, regardless of their chosen field of endeavor."

How Does an Off-Premise Caterer Gauge Success?

There are a number of signs to look for when evaluating an existing off-premise catering business. Healthy companies rate highly in all these areas. Those that are unhealthy, perhaps even on the brink of failure, will not rate nearly as well.

- Management thoroughly plans, organizes, executes, and controls each catered event.
- Proper controls are in place for costs, accounts receivable and payable, and liquid assets, such as cash and inventories. Theft prevention is also a priority.
- Food and service quality is well controlled and meets or exceeds clients' approval.
- Pricing for food and services is fair and competitive with that of other firms in the marketplace. There is a spirit of healthy competition.
- The catering firm enjoys good working relationships with both clients and suppliers.
- Time and attention are given to food safety in storage, preparation, and display. Employees know the local health codes and follow them.
- There is sufficient working capital to operate the business. The firm can make loan payments as they become due. Excessive credit is not extended to clients.
- Budgets are prepared and followed. Business records, insurance coverage, and licenses are kept up to date. The information derived from these records is used to provide data to help manage the business.
- Sales growth is controlled. There are sufficient financial and personnel resources to operate as business steadily grows.

- Market trends are anticipated and regularly discussed.

- Management and staff have a good working knowledge of the off-premise catering field.

- There are solid, trusting relationships between management and staff. Staff members are well trained and feel truly appreciated—because they are.

- Management works closely with a qualified accountant to plan for payment of taxes.

- And, finally, management is willing to seek qualified professional assistance if problems arise.

Looking Ahead—Catering in the Future

What does the future hold for caterers—and who will survive in the roller-coaster economy? When the Institute of Food Technologists listed its Top Ten Food Trends in *Food Technology* magazine (April 2011), the economic downturn known as the Great Recession was named as the reason for some of them. Americans told pollsters that the majority (71 percent) now bring their own snacks from home to ballgames and movie theaters to save a few dollars. In 2010, more than half (58 percent) of full-time workers told the Food Marketing Institute they packed their lunches instead of eating out on their lunch breaks, up from 27 percent just three years earlier.

Other factors, however, look more promising as trends for off-premise caterers to watch closely. Consumers that say they prefer fresh, locally grown and produced foods, rather than processed products from faraway factories. They are interested in trying more whole-grain, high-fiber, low-sodium, and no-trans-fat foods. This gives the savvy caterer an excellent reason to seek out and nurture relationships with the best local purveyors, as well as to update recipes with the goal of better nutrition. (If anybody can make something delicious and beautiful out of so-called healthy ingredients, it would be a good caterer!)

The U.S. Department of Agriculture replaced its food pyramid with a new symbol, a dinner plate, in 2011. The change (explained at www.choosemyplate.gov) is supposed to be an easier visual cue to help consumers understand how to balance their meals based on the five food groups. You can bet that savvy caterers are studying it too.

As health-conscious as Americans have become, the market research also shows they still love their treats. The popularity of baking is surging, although most home cooks admitted in a 2009 survey that they're not very skilled at it. This could mean a niche for elegant desserts, artisan breads, and/or homestyle pastries. The American Culinary Federation says mini and bite-sized desserts are among its member chefs' most popular menu additions—another perfect trend for the catering business.

On supermarket shelves, some of the fastest-growing product categories are specialty chocolates, cookies, and wines, and 63 percent of adults said that they purchased "gourmet foods" in 2010, an increase of 17 percentage points over the previous year.

Perhaps one way to interpret the trends is that most people know they should eat healthier, but they also want (and believe that they deserve) to stray from those restrictions once in a while. Catering is all about making special occasions special, so there will continue to be a market for it.

Staffing woes will continue to be monumental, as hiring, training, and retraining get tougher. Foodservice has always been a somewhat transient industry. Astute caterers will use preemployment aptitude and personality testing, master online staff scheduling systems, and develop their own training programs. They will also realize, if they haven't already, that they must treat their employees at least as well as they treat their clients. Along the same lines, in a top-tier catering operation, caterers will understand that their employees must treat each other with the same courtesy and respect that they show their clients.

Caterers of the future will come to realize that bigger is not necessarily better. Having a large volume of business is admirable—but only when the quality of your work rises to the same level. A company can grow to the point where quality slips, gross profit margins lag, more equipment is needed, overhead costs expand, and the bottom line shrinks proportionately. Intelligent caterer will downsize and watch margins and profits grow—and overall stress levels diminish—as they become more selective about the clientele they service.

Caterers are realizing that "high tech" will never replace personalized service, or "high touch," but that without high tech, they'll limit their potential for high touch. In an industry where, amazingly, some caterers still don't accept credit cards, savvy businesspeople are learning to embrace new technology, launching interactive websites and e-mail marketing campaigns. Caterers can now generate proposals, rental orders, packing lists, staffing schedules, and instant financial statements digitally. And they're realizing that computer-savvy business owners have more time to do what they love—which is run their business.

Competition will continue to increase. Sales will grow, but not without some dips, because economic woes and news headlines—from terrorist attacks to wild weather—and the resulting fears cannot help but affect the catering profession. An increased use of security staff and cameras at high-profile events (and in some cases, to thwart theft) are the results of this heightened awareness.

Mega-event catering is acknowledged as an excellent way to grow business—at golf and tennis tournaments, NASCAR races, political conventions, air shows or boat shows, and more. In addition to being profitable, mega-events expose the caterer to a wider range of potential clients. Then again, one caterer from Augusta, Georgia, generates enough revenue from serving sandwiches and beverages at the Masters Golf Tournament that he need not cater at all the rest of the year. The pressure experienced in servicing huge, multiday events is as big as the events themselves, but the rewards can be significant.

The Off-Premise Catering Model

Exhibit 1.1 is a diagram of interrelated factors in off-premise catering. It is included to prompt discussion about how management philosophies and current laws trigger multiple planning efforts in every aspect of the caterer's business, from how the company

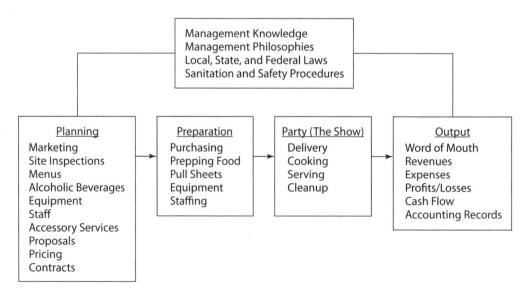

Exhibit 1.1 Off-Premise Catering Model

will go about obtaining business, to the types of food and beverages to be served, to the add-on services (florals, event design, and music, etc.) that will be offered and what the prices will be.

Together, these details form the basis for what the caterer can offer a client—first, in the form of a proposal (which is then agreed on or modified), leading to a contract being prepared and signed.

As the party or event date approaches, certain operational elements are addressed, such as:

- Hiring and scheduling staff
- Informing key staff about event details
- Purchasing and pre-preparation of menu items
- Ordering equipment as needed from rental companies
- Booking contractors who will provide add-on services
- Obtaining necessary licenses and permits for use of the site, serving alcohol, and so on
- Preparing a pull sheet, or packing sheet, that includes all items to be supplied by the commissary to produce the party
- Coordinating all beverage and accessory services with the client and the vendors

All the preplanning elements culminate on the day or night of "the show." This is the point at which the staff, equipment, food, and other vendors arrive at the site, and the event takes place. Of course, for large events, the setup process may take as long as a week.

After the event, there are also certain necessary outcomes; on the diagram they are referred to as *output*. These include:

- Invoicing
- Getting feedback from clients and guests about the successes (and/or problems) associated with the event
- Getting feedback from key staff members about the event, from praise for servers to any concerns that may have arisen
- Determining revenues and expenses
- Updating accounting records and paying employees and contractors

By reading and studying this book, you will gain a thorough understanding of how all these elements combine to produce a successful off-premise event for a professional caterer.

☐ Summary

This chapter provides a wide-ranging look at what is necessary to start an off-premise catering company or develop an off-premise catering division of an existing foodservice operation.

Much of the focus of this chapter is on the individual who plans to start the company—his or her personality traits, temperament, and sense of ethics. This is because catering is both a very personal and intensely social, hands-on type of business. Organizational skills, time management, financial acumen, and an eye for culinary and entertainment trends are just a few of the important skills mentioned in the chapter. Some of these skills can be learned or honed; others are more instinctive.

The chapter also summarizes some trends in consumer behavior that will affect caterers, for better or worse. These include Americans' continued health consciousness, growing preference for locally produced foods, and concerns about the economy after the Great Recession. The latter has prompted many people to cut corners in their food decisions but also has created a customer base that believes it's okay to splurge once in a while on high-quality items, whether the treat is a decadent dessert or a loaf of artisan bread. Caterers can use their knowledge of such trends to market to prospective customers.

☐ Study Questions

1. Choose any three catering "crises" from those listed on pages 3–4 and write a short explanation of how you would handle the crisis if you were the caterer living the nightmare, and why.

2. Why can it be more expensive for clients to host a catered event at their home than at a hotel or restaurant?

3. What questions should a catering company's receptionist learn to ask incoming callers, and why?

4. This chapter includes "The Seven Habits of Highly Successful Caterers" (page 24). Write a paragraph about what the eighth "habit" would be, in your view, based on what you have read in this book so far.

5. Are there ever instances in which it is acceptable to turn down potential business as a caterer? Explain your answer.

Getting Started: Laws, Locations, and Contracts

You might have decided to become a caterer because you've been told you are a terrific cook or because you know you're an excellent event planner. The goal of this chapter is to introduce all the other elements of running a catering business that you might not be familiar with, any one of which can trip you up in creating your new business if you don't get them right. It is an important first glimpse of the following topics:

- The licenses and laws caterers must typically have and follow
- Forming a corporation and finding a facility
- Writing a business plan
- Funding sources for your catering company
- Developing a catering contract that protects both the company and its customers
- Developing policies about deposits, cancellations, and refunds

The first two points on the list—understanding the legal ramifications of operating a business and finding a suitable location—seem to be ignored regularly by would-be caterers. Many operate illegally from their homes, with neither proper licenses nor insurance. It is imperative that readers understand that this is a clear violation of local and state statutes, and violators risk being prosecuted and fined. Professional off-premise caterers follow the laws of the municipality, state, and federal government. Illegal caterers not only damage the reputation of our profession, they also make it more difficult for licensed and insured caterers to compete with those who do not have the expenses of licenses and insurance.

The purpose of this chapter is to inform readers about the legal steps necessary to establish an off-premise catering business to help elevate the standards for our fast-growing profession.

The following discussion is somewhat general because each city, county, and state has its own regulations regarding the operation and licensing of businesses. It is impossible in this text to address specific laws for specific locations. It's up to you to contact your local and state authorities and do your homework about the rules and laws in your area before selecting a location or starting your business.

Local and State Requirements

Zoning. Most municipalities require zoning permits to ensure that businesses conform to local laws. For example, zoning laws prohibit off-premise caterers from building catering commissaries in residential neighborhoods. Many require a certificate of use and occupancy before business may be conducted.

Businesses located in an existing structure previously used for similar purposes will usually have few zoning problems. Off-premise caterers who construct a new facility, convert an existing building used previously for other purposes, or extensively remodel an existing facility will need to carefully check zoning regulations. A zoning variance or conditional-use permit is required to operate a business on land not zoned for that purpose. Filing fees can exceed $1,200, and it can take 90 days or longer for a decision. To change zoning can take six months or longer and require extensive legal work.

Occupational License. After receiving a zoning permit, an off-premise caterer must apply for the appropriate occupational licenses required by the city, county, and state. In South Florida, for example, an off-premise caterer located in the City of Miami needs two occupational licenses, one for the City of Miami and one for Dade County.

License to Sell Food to the Public. Many states require this license, which normally is obtained through the state's Department of Business or Commerce.

Health Permit. A business dealing with food must have a health department permit. Prior to issuing a permit, the health department will inspect the off-premise caterer's facilities. Readers should refer to Chapter 12, "Sanitation and Safety," to gain an understanding of health department requirements.

Fictitious Name Registration. This is also commonly known as a *dba*, short for *doing business as* . . . A "fictitious" business name doesn't mean the business is not real, or that the people running it are trying to mask their identities. It means the company name that has been chosen either does not include the surname of the individual owner or partners, or the nature of the business is not clearly evident in the name. For example, doing business under a name like "Smith & Brown Associates" or "Young, Old, and Sons" would require a fictitious business name to be registered even though the surnames of the owners are stated. The words following the surnames suggest that there are other owners who are not specifically named. However, doing business under a name like "Teresa Harrington Catering" would not require registering a fictitious business name because the owner (Teresa Harrington) is conducting business under her legal name and the nature of the business is described. In the case of a corporation, a fictitious business name is "any name other than the exact corporate name as stated in the articles of incorporation."

Each state has rules about filing for a dba. It usually involves filling out a short application and paying a registration fee to the County Clerk. Sometimes you have to give the clerk a copy of your Articles of Incorporation, if you are incorporated. Other states require the placement of a fictitious name ad in the local newspaper. Generally, the newspaper that prints the ad will file the necessary papers with the county for a fee. The easiest way to determine the procedure is to call a local bank and ask if it requires a fictitious name registry or certificate for you to open a business account.

State and Local Sales Tax. Off-premise caterers should contact the Department of Revenue and Taxation for their state and city for requirements. Sales taxes are further discussed in Chapter 10 of this book.

Worker's Compensation. This type of insurance is a state requirement for those who employ staff, including part-timers and corporate officers. This topic is discussed in Chapter 7, "Human Resources."

Other State and Local Permits and Taxes. Numerous other permits may be required—fire department permits, signage permits, and so forth. To avoid costly mistakes regarding signs, it is imperative to check local ordinances and to obtain written approval from the landlord before installing signage of any type. Many states have corporate income taxes, intangible asset taxes, personal property taxes, and unemployment taxes. There are a number of places where you can ask for state-specific details: your County Clerk's office, your Secretary of State's office, your state's Department of Commerce or Economic Development. It's also smart to talk with an attorney.

Federal Requirements

Employer Identification Number. Off-premise caterers who employ staff must obtain an Employer Identification Number (EIN) using IRS Form SS-4. Employers are responsible for four types of federal payroll collections and payments:

1. Income taxes withheld from employee wages
2. Employer/employee Social Security tax (FICA)
3. Employer/employee Medicare tax (MICA)
4. Federal unemployment tax (FUTA)

Employment Taxes. Off-premise catering firms, as well as other businesses, are required by law to withhold federal income and Social Security taxes from wages paid to employees, and to file a quarterly return, Internal Revenue Service (IRS) Form 941. Self-employed persons also pay more Social Security tax—the full 15 percent—because they are responsible for both the employer's and employee's shares of the tax (normally 7.5 percent each).

Monies withheld from employees must be paid when due to the federal government. New businesses with insufficient cash to pay all creditors may try deferring or underpaying their taxes so they can keep their suppliers paid, but penalties are severe. A $10,000 tax liability can increase to $14,050 in six months. Many businesspeople have found out the hard way that it is easier to take out a loan to pay the IRS than to deal with the consequences of paying late or not paying at all. Off-premise caterers should also be aware of federal reporting requirements for employees receiving tips. This subject is discussed in Chapter 7.

Unemployment Taxes. Off-premise caterers are also required to pay federal unemployment tax. IRS Form 940 is used for this purpose. In those states that require state unemployment taxes, the amount of federal unemployment tax required can be reduced.

If a worker's job is terminated (through no fault of his or her own), unemployment benefits provide a small amount of income for a given time period or until the person finds a new job. The system is funded by a tax levied on employers. Federal unemployment taxes are paid using IRS Form 940.

States normally require employers to pay unemployment taxes based on the amount of wages they pay, the amount they have already contributed to the state unemployment fund, and whether any of their discharged employees have been compensated from the fund. State taxes paid are credited against the federal tax.

Established caterers, with minimal unemployment claims, will pay at a lower rate than new caterers or those who have had more unemployment claims against their businesses.

Income Taxes. All off-premise catering firms are required to pay federal income tax, in addition to state and city taxes.

Immigration Requirements. All employers are required to verify the immigration status of all new hires on Form I-9. See Chapter 7 for more information.

Antidiscrimination Law Compliance. The Americans with Disabilities Act (ADA) of 1990 is a federal law that says companies with 15 or more employees cannot fire, or refuse to hire, persons with disabilities unless the impairment prevents a person from performing a particular job. Most citizens know the ADA as the law that requires companies to provide "handicapped" parking spaces, wheelchair-accessible entrances and restrooms, and the like. Refer to Chapter 7 for more information.

Legal Forms of Operation

The four main legal forms of doing businesses are sole proprietorship, partnership, limited partnership, and corporation. Each of them has advantages and disadvantages.

Most businesses in the United States are sole proprietorships, owned and managed by one individual. A sole proprietorship requires no legal incorporation papers to be filed, although the business owner may need a city or state license for some types of businesses, and a dba or fictitious name filing. The major advantage of sole proprietorship is its simplicity. The disadvantage is that creditors can force the sale of personal property and liquidate bank accounts when the sole proprietor is unable to fulfill financial obligations—in other words, the company's debts are the owner's sole responsibility.

In a partnership (or General Partnership), two or more people are co-owners in a business. Again, no state filing of incorporation papers is necessary, but a dba may be required. Assets contributed by all partners become equity in the partnership, and both income and expenses are allocated to the partners. Each partner is legally responsible for the actions of the other partners. In a legal action, each partner will be sued personally. Each partner's share of the profits must be reported on that partner's individual tax return.

Limited partnerships are commonly used for real estate syndications and are used very infrequently for off-premise catering firms. The legal costs for starting a limited partnership can be quite high because they are complex and involve a number of investors.

In a Limited Liability Company (LLC), the liability of each partner (or "member") is limited to the amount of his or her investment, and each partner is personally liable for his or her own negligent acts.

Most off-premise caterers choose incorporation as a realistic form of operation because the corporation is a separate legal entity from the caterer. The corporation alone is generally responsible for its own actions and debts. In a corporation, off-premise caterers are protected in most situations because, technically, they are employees of the corporation. A corporation must be operated in a correct legal manner, though, or this protection may be forfeited. There are two basic types of corporate structures, C Corporations and S Corporations (named after the IRS Code sections that govern them). The S (or "Subchapter S") form is recommended for most caterers because only the corporation pays tax on its profits. In a C Corporation, the corporation pays tax on its profits, and the owners also pay individual taxes on their income.

There are other, hybrid forms of incorporation, including Single Member Limited Liability Companies (SMLLCs) and Personal Service Corporations (PSCs). Each has its own unique tax laws, reporting requirements, and loopholes. It is advisable to consult with a tax attorney or accountant when making the decision to create a business, but ambitious off-premise caterers can complete the necessary paperwork and file for incorporation on their own, thereby saving the attorney fees for that portion of the work. Your Secretary of State's office will have all the required forms and instructions.

Writing a Business Plan

Putting your business plan together is one of the most valuable exercises you will undertake as a new off-premise caterer because it forces you to decide on and describe exactly what you are planning—from the vision for your company, to what will make it unique and where it fits into the market, to the sales projections and expense estimates you will share with investors. It makes your dream tangible—and achievable.

Do not write the plan by yourself, although your own notes will be useful. Rather, you will need to assemble a team of your closest advisors, including people with financial, legal, and business backgrounds, as well as family members (if it's a family business), and the top staff members for the company. Together, you will create a plan that describes:

- What makes your business unique in your region
- The strengths that you and key staff members contribute
- Where your business is now: its mission, vision, and financial situation
- Where you want it to be one year from now in terms of products and profits
- Where you want it to be several years from now
- Your plans to meet these goals

At first, it might seem frustrating to you that you are spending a lot more time looking at other catering companies than focusing on your own business. However, market research is where you will discover your niche, and we discuss it further in Chapter 9. In your research, you are looking for two things: as much information about your competitors as possible, and as much information about your potential customers as possible.

From competitors, you want to determine if there is an area of expertise that no one else has laid claim to, or an advantage that you can bring to the marketplace that will be attractive to customers. From demographic research about your area, you will find out where your potential customers live and work, and who is likely to shop for and purchase your services. You may also uncover a need for a service your company will be able to provide that you hadn't thought of before.

Business plans follow a specific format, although there is a great deal of room for creativity in terms of the information you share in the plan. The basic format includes the following:

- A cover sheet—"A Business Plan for XYZ Catering, Inc."—gives the document a polished, professional look. (Decide on your name before you finish the plan.

It doesn't look good to list multiple choices and say you're still thinking about it.) The names of the business owners and their contact information are also on the cover sheet.

- An executive summary is a high-level overview of the plan's content for those who want to do a quick scan of the business idea before they commit to reading the whole document. You can write the longer, individual sections, and then create this summary from those contents.

- A table of contents, like the executive summary, is a courtesy for the reader.

- The business concept section includes a description of the idea and/or company, along with its mission and vision statements; information about the owners and their background and ability; and the types of services the company will offer. Operational details include the type of corporation you've decided to be, the location you have chosen, and details about how the business will be operated and staffed.

- The marketing section is the place where you position your business in the market-place. Show that you've done your homework about competitors, and describe how your business will stand out from the field. Convince the reader that you also know about your prospective customers, and explain how you intend to reach them and why you know they'll be receptive. Some people include a marketing calendar, out-lining the promotions and advertising they plan to offer for the first year. If you have a catchy slogan, signage, or website design, this is the place to show it off. Some people split this into two sections: the competitive analysis and the marketing strategy.

- Extensive financial data is required, as you will use this plan to attract private investors and/or get bank loans. If you are asking for money, the loan application document should be part of this section of the business plan. Investors will want to know about the types of equipment and supplies you will need, including cost estimates. They also want to see how the business will work, financially. This includes a Balance Sheet, a Profit-and-Loss Statement, a break-even analysis (explained in Chapter 14), and a *cash flow projection* (sometimes called a *pro forma*). Projections must be more detailed for the first year, providing monthly information, but you can forecast by quarter for the second and third years. Include the assumptions on which these projections are based. You will most likely need some help from an accountant to pull these together.

- Supporting documentation for the potential lenders will include résumés of every principal of the company (some people include key managers' resumes, particularly if they have important skills for the business), plus three years' worth of income tax returns from all partners in the business, and personal financial statements. (Banks have personal financial statement forms.) If there are leases or purchase agreements for commissary space, include them, along with licenses, letters of intent from suppliers, and any other legal documents.

If you are saying, "How in the world can I project sales three years out if I haven't even opened my doors?" then you aren't ready to open them yet. Think of the business plan as a chance to test your concept and your financial ability to make it work, on paper. If this is going to be your livelihood, you had better be able to plan for growth and figure out how you'll pay the bills month to month. Would *you* invest money in a company that couldn't tell you that? Further, a solid business plan will serve as a roadmap for you in the coming years. You can refer to it again and again as you set priorities and carry out the plans you are putting on paper.

In most communities, there are resources for small businesses to help them write and fine-tune the information, to make it as professional and complete a picture of the business as possible. One such organization is the Small Business Administration (www.sba.gov), mentioned numerous times in this book. You will also find plenty of online advice about drafting this important document.

The Family-Owned Business

Many catering businesses are family owned and operated, which can be both good and bad. When family members perform their jobs well, there are few problems, but when they don't perform up to standards, huge problems can arise.

According to Walter Sasiadek of Business Development Strategies, a former chef and now a management consultant to foodservice businesses, these practical tips can help maintain harmony in the family-owned workplace:

- *Have written contracts.* Handshakes and verbal agreements are fine at a family dinner, but not in business. Hire an attorney to draw up an acceptable contract for everyone involved to sign.
- *Define job roles.* If a family member does not want to accept the responsibilities and adhere to the professional standards that are expected in the industry, the individual shouldn't draw a paycheck, period.

- *Business is business.* Don't allow favoritism to affect sound business judgment. Make sure that incompetence doesn't affect employee morale. Don't lie to employees about their advancement opportunities if the position is being saved for someone in the family.

- *Conduct weekly meetings.* Meetings should be structured the same way each and every time. Always begin with the same topic and progress according to plan. The structure will help keep everyone focused on the mission. Example: Start with profitability. Go over the Profit and Loss Statement item by item. Address every concern, and then move on. Call for a ten-minute break if tempers flare.

Denny Thurman, owner of Biz-Align Strategies and Consulting in Salt Lake City, Utah, is a big fan of the SMART goals mentioned in Chapter 1. He says every business runs better when its management team sets the company's goals, decides together on the critical success factors required to meet those goals, and also agrees on the methods to be used for measuring progress. When family members work together, this becomes even more important.

"Families get adjusted to keeping the peace, which often means avoiding talking about problems," explains Thurman. "So there needs to be a method for doing this, to continually steer the conversation at meetings to focus on what's important for the business, on a regular basis."

He also notes that in family businesses, family should come first.

"Any decision has to take the impact on the family into account," he says. "You don't want to put family relationships at risk. That's another critical reason for putting a method and a process in place—nobody has to be the 'bad guy,' and people aren't always second-guessing each other. Everyone knows what they're supposed to be working toward and since you've determined how to measure progress, everyone can recognize when something needs improvement."

Finding a Facility

There are three basic options for off-premise caterers when considering facilities:

1. Operate the business from an existing foodservice operation where the caterer already works—a hotel, restaurant, club, or similar facility. This option is excellent because it minimizes start-up expenses.

In fact, aspiring off-premise caterers may wish to look to the corporate world for start-up assistance. Since the tax deductibility of business meals has been whittled to only 50 percent, many companies have found it convenient and economical to hire their own chefs, upgrade their corporate foodservice, or bring in caterers for on-site meetings.

Start-up caterers may wish to affiliate with a corporation and, with its permission, use its facilities as a commissary for off-premise events. The added benefit to this arrangement is that the corporate in-house diners will likely become off-premise catering clients as well.

2. Operate from a commissary already used exclusively for off-premise catering. This can be an expensive option and should be reserved for off-premise caterers who have a well-established business.

3. Find an existing facility that has an underutilized kitchen, and arrange to use it in exchange for a rental fee and/or providing the facility with needed foodservice. For example, a church kitchen that is used only occasionally would be an excellent option. The off-premise caterer would pay the church for the use of the kitchen on a monthly or "as-needed" basis. Part or all of the rent could be paid for in services rendered. The off-premise caterer may cater some of the church functions at a reduced fee in exchange for rent credit.

In summary, the best and most cost-efficient facilities are those that require no initial investment and may even offer a built-in client base. A South Florida caterer developed a $2 million catering business with a small investment by offering catering services to a downtown business executives' club. The caterer served lunch to the members at a reduced fee and, in exchange, was able to cater functions for club members, both at the club and off-premise, using the club's facilities. The caterer retained the profit.

Selecting a Catering Commissary

This section is not for the off-premise caterer who is operating from a restaurant, hotel, club, or other regular foodservice operation, nor is it for the caterer who has set up operation in a church or other facility. This discussion is directed at those off-premise caterers who are evaluating whether to rent their own commissary locations.

Ability to Pay

The best values are found in industrial areas located near expressways or major thoroughfares. Rents in these areas are fairly inexpensive, and access to major highways facilitates deliveries. The site should be clean and safe, but it need not have a prestigious storefront or be located in the center of town since few (if any) clients will visit the commissary. Most off-premise catering sales are made with the client at the event site or in the client's home or office.

A good rule is that the total annual rent should not exceed 10 percent of projected annual sales. For example, a new off-premise caterer who expects to generate $100,000 in sales during the first year of operation should keep rent for the year at $10,000 or less.

Most small-to-medium off-premise caterers can operate well in facilities ranging in size from 1,000 to 2,000 square feet.

Key Points to Negotiate

The ideal leases are short-term contracts with renewal options. For example, a lease for one to two years with two five-year renewal options would be ideal for most off-premise caterers.

When inspecting a proposed site, look for:

Leaks in the roof or elsewhere

Sufficient staff parking arrangements

Sufficient restroom facilities

A grease trap

A delivery door for receiving and shipping foods

Adequate lighting

Adequate electrical and gas service

Sufficient exhaust venting over the hot line

Adequate storage

Adequate and accessible dumpster space

Good ventilation and air-conditioning

Insurance—what will the building owner pay for, and what are you responsible for as the tenant?

Overall security—good locks, night watchman, regular police patrols, and so on

Manageable traffic during rush hours

Repairs that are—and are not—included as Common Area Maintenance (CAM)

Other issues to discuss and/or negotiate are provisions for repairs to your specific space—if something must be fixed, who pays? If you want to make some significant changes to the space, such as remodels or upgrades, who pays? Sometimes a caterer can agree to make improvements in lieu of rent payment for a few months, but if that is your arrangement, be absolutely certain to get it in writing. Normally, leases include a requirement that you have the landlord's written permission to erect signage, do land-scaping, paint, add exterior lighting, or change the structure in any noticeable way. If improvements involve modifications to the roof, the original roofer should be hired to make them; otherwise, any warranty will be void.

It seems as if it should go without saying, but you should also ask specifically about what additional kind(s) of permission you'll have to get to operate a catering company in this space. If the owner rents to you, and you then discover upon move-in that the busi-ness park where the building sits has insurance limitations or covenants that restrict you in some way, you'll have a problem. And if there are problems, whom do you call? Is there a management company? Does the owner want to know about and hire every handyman to fix every leaky faucet, or is it okay for you to get it done and pass along the bill?

The lease should protect you as the tenant, not just the building owner. To that end, it should include some "outs" in case of trouble. For instance, the lease should be:

- Conditional, meaning you'll move in only if and when you obtain all the necessary licenses and permits to cater there. (And that if, for some reason, you are denied one of the licenses or permits, you can void the lease.)

- Assignable, meaning if you want to move or close the business before the lease has expired, you can allow another party to move in and assume the lease.

- Flexible in case of emergency. This means if you die, for example, your spouse or partner can terminate the lease without penalty. If the city condemns the building for some reason unrelated to your business, you can move without penalty. If you are moving in your own equipment, you also have the right to remove it as long as you restore the building to its original shape (less "normal wear and tear"—a very important clause.)

One more important note: Talk with the owners of some of the neighboring busi-nesses, without the owner of the rental site present. Ask questions: How responsive is the management company? What do you know about the owner? Who were the last tenants? How long did they stay, and why did they move? Meeting the neighbors can be a real eye-opener! You may not even like them, which might ultimately be a factor in your decision about whether to sign the lease.

Using an Attorney

You must always have an attorney review the lease to ensure compliance with all legal requirements such as zoning, signage, and other matters. Above all, never commit to a lease agreement until all aspects of the lease have been thoroughly reviewed. This is one area in which haste can result in huge financial obligations.

It's best to interview lawyers (and accountants too) before you ever need them. It is critical to find people who have experience with hospitality industry clients and are somewhat familiar with the industry. You also want someone who is dependable and will be available on short notice in case a problem arises. There are a number of online legal resources that you may wish to explore, such as the Hospitality Lawyer website.

Funding Alternatives

Many caterers have started their firms with little cash and plenty of "sweat equity." They have used clients' advance deposits to essentially fund their start-up costs. Others have invested considerable amounts in facilities and equipment. For most brand-new caterers, it is best to keep the initial investment conservative, although experts suggest a cushion of at least six months' worth of operating expenses for a start-up business.

Some people opt to become caterers instead of opening a restaurant, and little wonder. One only needs to look at the thousands of restaurants that fail each year because of the huge investments required to open their doors to the public. Caterers, on the other hand, can start with substantially fewer up-front costs. Funding can come from a variety of sources, including:

Personal savings

Family members

Investors

Credit cards

SBA loan products

Bank loans and lines of credit

Equipment financing

Each of these sources has advantages and disadvantages. The ideal situation is, of course, to use your own funds to get started, as long as this does not put your personal or family financial situation at risk. Bringing in outside investors or family members is an alternative, but with them come almost certain problems and disputes about how funds are being spent. Outside investors expect a return on their investment, which is a realistic outcome, and therefore feel they have some say in how their funds are being used. Most caterers prefer to cater rather than spend hours explaining their business decisions to disgruntled investors or family members.

Caterers should avoid using credit cards to finance their business—or use them only if they are able to pay off the balance in full each month. A new business need not be saddled with extra interest charges.

Banks run hot and cold when it comes to financing catering businesses, mostly because of their lack of knowledge about the industry. Bank loans are generally short-term loans. Banks require personal guarantees and more equity than other funding sources, but their interest rates are generally the lowest of the available options. At a bank, sole proprietors can often use the value of their homes as collateral for a business *Line of Credit*, which also carries lower interest than most credit cards and requires monthly repayment. Lines of Credit are excellent tools for borrowing short-term amounts. You borrow only what you need and pay back some or all of it as funds become available. You pay interest only on funds that you use. A Line of Credit can be unsecured, or secured by assets like your accounts receivable, marketable securities, or real estate equity. A Line of Credit is usually extended for a year at a time and renewed after the lender reviews updated financial records each year.

The U.S. Small Business Administration (SBA) offers loans to small businesses, including an *Express Loan*—an expedited review process for loans of up to $250,000. SBA-guaranteed loans provide opportunities for those who may not otherwise qualify, although some feel their terms are very restrictive. Still, caterers are excellent candidates.

The SBA offers a variety of loan guarantee programs, which include:

- *7(a) Loan Guarantee:* Larger loans of up to $2 million
- *Low Doc and SBA Express*: Limited to loans of up to $150,000
- *Microloans:* Very small loans (up to $35,000) for start-up businesses

For more information, visit www.sba.gov. In addition to extensive information about borrowing money, the site also has advice about writing business plans, finding mentors, and more.

Home equity is another source of funds. A new, larger first mortgage or a second mortgage can provide a lump sum of cash that can be used to launch a catering business. The housing downturn in recent years has greatly eroded property values, making this a less attractive option, but for longtime homeowners who have significant equity in their property, it might still be valid. Other forms of collateral, such as stocks, bonds, or mutual fund shares, can also be pledged as collateral for a business loan.

Catering equipment can be financed through companies that specialize in loans of this type. Local restaurant equipment dealers have relationships with firms that provide such loans. Their interest rates are generally higher than those of most bank loans but lower than credit card interest rates. And you have the advantage of dealing with someone who is familiar with the equipment, its uses, and its problems, if any arise while you're paying it off.

Developing a Catering Contract

Off-premise caterers should develop a standard catering contract prior to accepting off-premise business, and an attorney should review the contract to ensure it meets basic requirements.

Before delving into the specific elements of this type of contract, note that there are some elements that are critical to an off-premise caterer's understanding of—and involvement with—contracts, according to attorney Donald A. Blackwell, a partner in the Miami firm Seipp & Flick, LLP.

1. **Have a working knowledge of what constitutes a binding contract and how a court is likely to construe its terms.** A contract is a definite agreement between two or more competent people or parties to do, or refrain from doing, some lawful thing. The difference between a contract and pure negotiation is that there must be a meeting of the minds on all essential terms and obligations. For example, a caterer's proposal to perform service becomes a contract only when signed and agreed to by the client.

2. **Be specific**. Each contract should be clear and unambiguous. No one should ever sign a contract that contains blanks. The failure to be specific about what an off-premise caterer plans to do could certainly be embarrassing the night of the event

if the client expects something different. A roast beef dinner might mean "top round" to the caterer and "beef tenderloin" to the client. The caterer should be as specific as possible regarding quantity, quality, and method of preparation.

3. **Know the three general theories upon which caterers can be held liable.** These are:

   - *Breach of contract:* The caterer agrees to perform a service and does not perform the service.

   - *Third-party liability:* The caterers must use reasonable care or they can be charged with negligence. (In a dispute between the guest and host of an event, the caterer and other vendors are considered third parties.)

   - *Statutory violations:* The caterer fails to follow laws, from adherence to fire codes, to service of alcoholic beverages.

Off-premise caterers may be involved in assisting clients with site selections, as well as subcontracting for certain accessory services for the party, such as music, entertainment, flowers, décor, and valet parking. As a general rule, off-premise caterers have a legal duty to exercise "reasonable care" for the safety and well-being of the guests attending an event. Although courts have not yet clearly defined the parameters of that duty, it can be safely assumed that it encompasses:

- Investigating prospective party sites to determine that they are reasonably safe
- Investigating the service and safety records of prospective subcontractors of accessory services
- Warning clients and guests of known or reasonably foreseeable dangers

Off-premise caterers who fail to make a thorough safety inspection of a proposed party site before recommending its use—or who make the recommendation despite knowledge of potentially hazardous conditions—do so at their own risk. Similarly, caterers who fail to investigate the safety and service records of subcontracted suppliers substantially increase their risk of liability.

Proposal or Contract?

A catering contract is a blueprint for performance of a catered event. It creates an obligation on the part of the caterer to perform certain services, and an obligation on the part of the client to pay for these services. A contract requires a degree of trust, but it also provides for legal recourse in case either party violates (or is accused of violating) that trust. Signed contracts may even be used as loan collateral in some situations.

It is common sense to draft a written catering proposal that spells out in detail all the services the caterer will provide at an event, and to use this information to "fill in the blanks" on the contract. Some caterers use separate forms for proposals and contracts, but this is not necessary.

Proposals are discussed in greater detail in Chapter 9. For this discussion, let's assume that a proposal, agreed to and signed by both client and off-premise caterer, is—for all practical and legal purposes—a contract. In most catering firms, it is the salesperson who reviews the contract with a client and answers questions about it, although it is the owner of the catering company who signs the contract.

Components of an Off-Premise Catering Contract

The terms of off-premise catering contracts vary according to what is appropriate for the events, but they should include most of the following information:

1. **Caterer's name, street address, phone number(s), and e-mail address.**

2. **Client's name, street address, e-mail address, and pertinent phone numbers.**

3. **Date the contract was signed.**

4. **Date and day of the catered event.**

5. **Starting and ending times for the event,** as well as other important times, such as the time a meal will be served, or the specific times the band will start and finish.

6. **Minimum number of guests.** This is the lowest number of guests to which this contract price will apply. When a caterer quotes a price per person for a minimum of 100 guests, this means that the per-person price will apply for 100 guests. If there are fewer than 100 guests, this "minimum guarantee clause" gives the off-premise caterer the right to raise the price per person. An extreme example of this is a situation in which a client and caterer agree to a price per person for a group of 100, but one week prior to the event, the client advises the caterer that there will be only 25 guests in attendance. Reasonably, the caterer cannot be expected to cater this party for the same price per person. This clause gives the caterer the right to charge more per person.

    Of course, the number of guests attending an event is always an estimate. There are always last-minute changes that affect the attendance. Approximate attendance figures may be determined by asking the following questions:

- How many attended the same event last year?
- Is it a business-related event where attendance is mandatory or a purely social event?
- Will there be celebrities or prominent guest speakers?
- Are competing events being held at the same time or within 48 hours of this event?
- Is there a charge for attending?
- What types of food and beverages are to be served?
- What time of day is the event to be held—morning, afternoon, or evening?
- How long is the event expected to last?

7. **Date for final "head count" guarantee.** Four to seven days prior to the party date is the standard time by which clients are required to give the off-premise caterer a guarantee of the number of guests to be paid for. Many caterers require that their clients provide this guarantee in writing, and the client is required to pay for at least that number, even if fewer guests attend. This clause is essential protection for the caterer, who should not have to suffer financially when the client overestimates guest counts.

8. **Location of the event.** This should include as much detail as possible—street address, building name, floor number, and any other information that will clarify the event's location. This may be the place to spell out who will make weather-related decisions for outdoor events (and how soon before the actual event) in case of inclement weather, and what the contingency plans are, such as an alternate site or a rented tent.

   This section of the contract should specify the exact times the space will be available (for setup, event, and cleanup) and how long the space will be held without a deposit for this event.

9. **Menu specifics.** This section should include all menu details discussed with the client. Nothing should be left out or assumed. Major changes in menu or other elements should necessitate a new contract, and the existing contract should say so. Some caterers add a sentence stating that the menu must be finalized by a certain date and cannot be changed after that date; another option is a substitution clause, which states that if a certain item that was contracted for is not available, a suitable replacement may be substituted with the customer's approval. When a

menu is e-mailed to a client, make sure that it is a PDF document or a screen shot—formats that cannot be changed.

Once in a while, you will have clients who insist on providing their own special "family favorite dish" to commemorate an occasion. It is a nice idea, but fraught with potential problems—health, food safety, and liability issues, to name a few. So be sure to include a disclaimer in the contract that you are not responsible for either the contents or preparation of food brought by anyone not employed by you. Some caterers charge a "service fee" for handling food that they do not provide.

10. **Beverage arrangements.** This section should include a complete listing of the nonalcoholic beverages to be provided by the caterers, as well as verification of the types and amounts of alcoholic beverages to be supplied by the client. In states where off-premise caterers may sell alcoholic beverages, this section would be modified appropriately.

11. **Equipment.** From candelabras to chafing dishes, this section contains a list of all equipment to be supplied by the caterer—tables, silver, chairs, linens, china, glassware, flatware, dance floors, stages, portable bars, and tenting. This section should also address who is responsible for loss or damage of items, as well as any rules about use of equipment to be provided by other sources (rental companies, the party site, etc.).

    If there is anything specifically not allowed, this should also be mentioned. Whether it's rice or birdseed, lit candles, fireworks, flower petals, or certain types of streamers or confetti (which many hotels and churches consider to be too messy), if the event site has a rule, it should be stated here.

12. **Staffing.** In this section, most off-premise caterers include the number of staff to be provided, the hours they will work, how they will be attired, and the applicable charges for their services. If other types of workers are needed (electricians, for instance), the contract should specify whether they are union workers and, if so, agree to pay prevailing union labor rates.

13. **Floor plan and seating chart.** Some events—weddings, business seminars with head tables, and the like—are complex enough that such items are necessary. The client should have final say about who is seated where, within the reasonable bounds of etiquette. There are computer programs available to assist in providing professional-looking layouts.

14. **Vendors and accessory services.** This area of the contract spells out important ancillary items and the vendors or contractors who will provide them: flowers and

other decoration, music, audiovisual equipment, valet parking, and other details that may be arranged for by either the off-premise caterer or the client. The contract should state that any vendor hired by either the caterer or the client must cooperate fully with the caterer or event manager on-site, must provide proof of liability insurance, and must deliver and set up its wares or equipment at specified times.

15. **Method for determining head count.** Exactly how do you gauge the number of people at an event? For billing purposes, you must be specific about how this is determined. There are a number of ways to do this—taking tickets, counting plates or napkin-rolled flatware, or keeping track at the door with a handheld counter or, at some larger events, with the use of a turnstile. For larger special events where this could be a sensitive issue, the method of determining the number of guests should be included in the contract.

16. **Charges for additional guests above the guarantee.** This is generally a per-person charge, which in some instances may be less per person than for those included in the base price. The rationale here is that the cost of serving these additional guests is generally less since certain expenses (like rental equipment and number of kitchen staff) may be fixed whether there are 100 or 150 guests.

    The real problems arise when a caterer suspects the client is underestimating the number of guests, only to raise the guarantee substantially on the day of, or day before, the event. This sends the caterer scurrying for more food, more staff, and so forth, which is technically unfair after an agreement has been reached. Professional caterers deal with this situation in two ways in the contract—they spell out a higher per-person charge for extra guests added within 48 hours (or 72 hours, or other specified time period) of the actual event, or they plan for a certain percentage over the guarantee, and again, they spell this out in the contract. In either case, the point is not so much to generate additional income as to discourage clients from making last-minute additions.

17. **Deposit policy.** This is one of the most important parts of any catering agreement. Normally, off-premise caterers require an advance deposit upon signing the contract. The deposit amount, along with due dates and amounts of future payments, must be listed in the contract. Specifics may be found in the "Deposits, Cancellations, and Refunds" section of this chapter.

18. **Charges for extra hours.** Normally, the labor charges for extra hours are at a premium rate since in many parts of the country, catering staff is paid at a

higher overtime rate when parties go longer than planned. The astute off-premise caterer will always approach the client or person in charge of the event before this becomes a problem—a polite reminder that things should be wrapping up or the staff will be going into extra hours. Entertainers should be instructed by the client and/or caterer not to go past the specific times agreed to without first checking with one or the other.

However, a caterer who is slow in serving a meal through no fault of the client certainly cannot charge overtime. Common factors that affect overtime include the following:

- Certain locations, like museums and historical sites, have curfews that may eliminate the problem of overtime.
- Clients holding events in high-rise office buildings should be advised that overtime charges will apply if the off-premise caterer is significantly detained from leaving after the event when elevators are not available (usually cleaning or moving people use them exclusively in the evenings).

19. **Special instructions.** There is always something else that must be considered. This section can incorporate details, such as:

- "It's a surprise party—use caution when calling the client!"
- Specific instructions for the day of the event. "Give special attention to Uncle Joe," "Serve Aunt Mabel light drinks," and so forth.
- Specifications about whether the caterer will provide meals for the band and other persons working the event.

20. **Security.** Who will ensure that alcohol is not served to minors or to anyone who already appears to be intoxicated? If it's a charitable event, such as an auction or dinner gala, there may be quite a bit of cash at the registration tables. Who keeps an eye on it? As a caterer, you are not responsible for the personal property of clients or guests. One of the ancillary services you may provide (through the building or site where the event will be held) is a certain number of paid security personnel, whose salaries are specified in the contract. It should be stated in the contract whether any security person will be carrying a firearm and, if so, that this person is licensed to do so.

In addition, there are timing concerns that will affect security at some venues. There may be elevator lockdown times, automatic "lights off" functions in some buildings, and parking garage closing times. The security staff will have to deal with these issues—so they'd best be aware of them.

21. **Setup and cleanup.** Exactly who is responsible for decorating and for tearing down afterward? List them. Musicians will want to set up their own equipment, but otherwise some hotels, country clubs, and other facilities will have rules about using their personnel to do setup and cleanup. Find out what these rules are, and include them in the contract.

22. **Disposition of leftover food.** Leftovers at an event can sometimes create problems for caterers—whose food is it, anyway? Does it belong to the caterer, as "emergency extras," just in case they were needed? Or does it belong to the client? A number of good alternatives are discussed in Chapter 3. Generally, raw ingredients are yours, but prepared foods are negotiable. However, consider your potential liability if someone takes home leftovers and becomes ill. This is a quality-control issue, not a matter of being miserly! So determine an overall policy on this issue, and spell it out in the contract. A plan for any unopened beverages should also be included. Caterers can sometimes return them and credit the client.

23. **Adherence to laws and ordinances.** This is a broad statement indicating that you will abide by all the pertinent laws and ordinances of your area, and that you expect the clients and guests to do the same. When it comes to alcohol service, this section include certain specific statements: that bartenders will check IDs, that the client will also be vigilant about any liquor law violations and will assist the caterer in handling these situations tactfully, and that the caterer has the right to close the bar if there is a problem. The fire department also has concerns about too many persons in a space that is too small, so compare the guest list with the room capacity. Also check—and include in the contract—whether or not smoking is permitted in the space.

24. **The service fee.** A service fee covers the catering company's general costs—from the time it takes to plan and shop for the menu, to overhead expenses like transportation, commissary rent, and dishwashers. It's what clients pay for having a caterer handle their event instead of doing it themselves. The service fee is charged at the discretion of the catering company and ranges from 18 percent to 20 percent. It is not a gratuity and should be dealt with separately from gratuities.

25. **Taxes and gratuities.** List the applicable taxes and who is responsible for paying them. If catering for a tax-exempt organization, add a line stating that you must be given a copy of its tax-exempt certificate or number prior to the event (which

should be kept on file in case of a later audit). Even service charges are subject to your state's sales tax.

If the servers are going to be tipped (or not), this fact—and the amount—should be mentioned in the contract. If the only tips are for bartenders, who keep an empty bowl or jar at the bar for this purpose, it should still be stated in writing.

26. **Insurance requirements.** This clause should state that you, the caterer, have liability and worker's compensation insurance and that you require proof that your subcontractors, and any hired by the client, also have liability coverage.

    On the topic of insurance, although it is certainly not a requirement, intelligent caterers suggest that clients obtain cancellation insurance, especially for weddings. In the sometimes stormy weeks and months before the nuptials, they're simply ensuring that in case the whole thing is called off, the caterer and vendors will be paid.

27. **Legal statements.** These are phrases that add some "teeth" to the contract. They establish binding authority—that the person signing this agreement is the one authorized to do so: "The client has read and fully understands the contract and is aware of its financial implications." You might also include an assignment clause. This restricts the client's ability to hand over his or her contract obligations to someone else without your knowledge and agreement and/or a whole new contract. In short, neither party should be able to make a change to the contract without the other's knowledge and written consent.

    An indemnification clause states that the client agrees to hold the catering company, its employees, and its subcontractors "harmless" for losses, damages, and expenses related to the misconduct or negligence of the client, its subcontractors, or its guests. A severability clause states that even if a court finds part of the contract unenforceable, the rest remains valid.

    Many companies specify a bad check charge in their contracts, as well as a clause that allows the caterer to tack on the additional cost of hiring a collection agency if it becomes necessary to do so.

28. **Cancellation and refund policies.** This topic is discussed in detail in the "Deposits, Cancellations, and Refunds" section of this chapter. Suffice it to say that the cancellation and refund policy should be clearly spelled out in the contract.

    On the advice of your attorney, you might add a contract clause about liquidated damages. It means that both parties agree to a specific dollar amount to settle an obligation if it is impossible to assign a monetary value to the amount of financial harm the claimant (caterer) will suffer when an event is canceled. The amount of liquidated damages increases as the date of the event approaches. The rationale is that a caterer could have booked something else in that time slot, worked many hours on the planning, and lost business as a result of the client's decision to cancel. However, if the date is rebooked, the clause should also include a predetermined cancellation fee to be refunded to the client.

29. **Detailed list of charges.** This part of the contract is a summary, usually on a separate page, of all charges pertinent to the agreement: food, beverages, equipment, staff, accessory services, other charges, service charges, gratuities, sales taxes, and totals.

30. **Dated signatures of both caterer and client(s).** In the case of weddings where brides, grooms, and their families are involved, according to Elio Belluchi, professor of law at Florida International University, "It is advisable for off-premise caterers to obtain as many signatures as possible on the contract—from both sides of the family—in case it is necessary to proceed with legal collection procedures. Collections are much easier when contracts are in writing and when there are signatures."

   Belluchi also advises that all changes in menu, other arrangements, and guaranteed head counts be made in writing. As he puts it, "If it is not in writing, it never happened. Oral agreements are not enforceable if they are over certain amounts, which are determined by state statutes."

In summary, an off-premise catering contract should contain all the details necessary to execute a catered event. Not every contract will require all 30 of the categories spelled out, and you should take care to use as much language as you need without making your agreement into an intimidating legalese mess. A good contract should be reassuring, not off-putting, to the clients, who understand that, between the lines, catering an event does involve a high degree of mutual trust. However, it also involves a high degree of organization and the ability to thoroughly document plans. Maxine Turner, who founded Cuisine Unlimited in Salt Lake City, Utah, more than 20 years ago, gives her clients the following information in writing:

> The majority of errors in catering occur not from initially placing the order, but from changes that occur after the order has been placed. To help us reduce the chance of an error, please have all information when placing your order. We ask that any changes to your order be made by 10:00 a.m. the day before your event. Changes made after that time will incur a 10 percent service charge to the changed portion, pre-tax. We will not accept cancellations after 3:00 p.m. for an event scheduled for the following day.

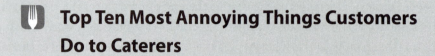

Top Ten Most Annoying Things Customers Do to Caterers

1. Think they can postpone, or even cancel, an event without consequences.

2. Fail to return phone calls, e-mails, or letters.

3. Fail to make promised or agreed-upon payments on time.

4. Not agree to pay the minimum, predetermined cost figure for their event.

5. Allow significantly more guests to attend an event and expect the caterer to produce, with no notice and at no extra charge, the additional food and service to accommodate them.

6. Tell the caterer they won't be able to pay "all" the money—on the date that it is due.

7. Have completely unrealistic expectations.

8. Expect the caterer to deal with issues that are beyond the scope of the written agreement.

9. Claim they were "promised" something that is not in the contract, on any menu, or in any notes from their conversations with the caterer.

10. Decide that they "own" all the surplus food that the caterer brought to the event just in case it was needed.

Deposits, Cancellations, and Refunds

As money changes hands and expectations come into play, these topics can become the focus of some of the most troublesome situations in the catering industry.

Deposits

First, do not be shy about asking for a deposit! It is an accepted practice in the social and corporate marketplace. A deposit assists cash flow and is especially helpful during the slower seasons when parties are minimal. Deposit policies vary from caterer to caterer, but a typical and workable arrangement is to ask for 50 percent of the estimated cost of the event at the time the contract is signed. An additional deposit might be required if the caterer is responsible for purchasing alcoholic beverages for the event.

A general rule is that the larger and more expensive the event, the larger the deposit. Moreover, a contract signed many months or years prior to the date of the event will require a smaller deposit than a contract signed only a few weeks or months in advance of the event.

Clients are expected to make their deposits and payments on time. When they do not, without making other arrangements, they should be sent a letter or e-mail message stating that they are "in default under the terms of the agreement." This letter should include a deadline for the payment, stating that if it is not met, the contract will be canceled. Most clients pay immediately after receiving such a notice. For those who do not, the event is canceled.

Cancellations and Refunds

A cancellation, for whatever reason and by any signatory, is a breach of the contract. Cancellation policies should be spelled out very carefully and reviewed by an attorney. In some states there are laws about cancellations and deposit refunds. A cancellation should be handled like any other contract modification—it must be made in writing and agreed to by both parties before it is valid.

At the time of a cancellation, most off-premise caterers will have already received at least one of a client's deposits or payments. Should all, some, or none of the deposit be refunded? There are no clear answers, but there are some questions that can be asked on a case-by-case basis to lead to a reasonable solution:

- What is the reason for the cancellation?
- When is the cancellation occurring—how soon before the actual event date?
- What are the actual losses to the caterer in terms of food, other costs, and turned-away business?
- How much is the caterer's time worth for having planned the event?

The main objective should be to maintain future goodwill with the client. Most clients are understanding as long as they feel the caterer is fair and is not trying to take advantage of a situation. A good idea is to allow the client five to seven days after the contract is initially signed to cancel without consequence. It's a good-faith gesture that allows the client to really read the agreement and think it over. (And, when you think about it, do you really want this person as a client if he or she is hesitant about the details from the beginning?)

In circumstances when the cancellation happens a year or more prior to the event, a good policy may be to refund the deposit as soon as the date is rebooked. In fact, a New York court ruled that unless the caterer could substantiate damages, the catering firm was obligated to return the advance deposit for an event more than three years away. The judge felt this was plenty of time for the caterer to rebook the date.

When bad weather threatens the event, the off-premise caterer should call the client two or three days beforehand, just to advise them that it is necessary to procure and begin preparing the food now. At this point, the caterer can give the client the option of canceling, changing the venue, or going ahead with the event—with the understanding that if it is canceled after the food has been purchased, the client will be charged the caterer's expenses for the food and related costs, with no markup. (Under no circumstances should the caterer charge more than his or her own costs in this situation.)

Occasionally, an event must be canceled at the last minute because of a tragedy involving one of the principals. In these cases, it is best to be gracious and wait a period of time before discussing refunds.

Finally, off-premise caterers should also allow for their own right to cancel or postpone in extreme circumstances—labor strikes, acts of God (natural disasters), personal tragedies—anything beyond their control that would prevent them from performing their duties under the contract. Again, spell out a refund policy to cover this situation.

Honest Mistakes, Unhappy Clients

It is inevitable that a caterer will sooner or later fail to live up to a client's expectations, creating a need for some form of refund or credit. When a mistake is made, it is always good policy for the caterer to proactively bring it to the client's attention rather than wait for the client to bring it to the caterer's attention. We know a caterer who, during a busy holiday season, forgot to bring one of the eight hors d'oeuvres to be served at a Christmas party. In such a case, assuming there is no time to correct the situation, it is best to simply advise the client of the problem before the guests arrive, offer some type of refund or credit, and make arrangements to augment the menu with another item that can be easily obtained, perhaps from a local supermarket. The worst course of action is to say nothing and hope the client does not notice—you will almost surely lose future business with that client, and perhaps receive less money for the event than you would by simply offering a credit in advance.

When faced with an irate customer, you should:

- Let the customer vent his or her anger and displeasure without interrupting or offering excuses.
- Take notes and ask pertinent follow-up questions.
- Acknowledge that you have heard the customer and summarize his or her points to reinforce the fact that you understand.
- Let the customer know you empathize with his or her situation.
- Follow up on the complaint quickly and get back to the customer, preferably face-to-face and perhaps with a "peace offering," such as a bottle of wine or freshly baked cookies.
- Avoid the temptation to berate staff members who have been involved in such a situation. Recognize that this is an opportunity to improve staff performance, and remember to discuss the things that were done right too.

When a real disaster strikes that is clearly the caterer's fault, it might be worthwhile to mail or deliver a box of gourmet chocolates or a few of your best cookies, beautifully wrapped, to everyone who attended the event, along with a bright note that exonerates the host.

Of course, caterers should also be wary of those people who complain about everything. Many grouse solely because they suspect it will get them price concessions, even with bogus or trivial complaints. When something does go wrong, regardless of whose fault it is, most caterers feel terrible. However, catering contracts should be designed to limit liability to the actual value of the product or service for which the customer has contracted. For example, if the client paid for a display of crudités and the caterer did not provide it, the caterer should be required to refund only the actual value of the display, without exorbitant additional amounts for embarrassment, pain, and suffering.

In fact, savvy caterers know how to make the most of customer complaints—by turning them into positives. In addition to providing a refund, many caterers provide the customers with a discount for a future event that will ensure that they return. Obviously, it is also important to give these customers very special attention when they do return, so that they will, in turn, spread your goodwill to others.

Contractual Nightmares

Whenever there is a contract for an event, there is at least some chance that fate and circumstances will combine to either delay or cancel it. Postponement and cancellation are two different things, but they each involve a major commitment of time and resources, and the additional hassle of getting things changed or cancelled. The caterer's policy should depend largely on how much notice has been given.

Then again, we have heard of nightmare situations in which, for example, a fiftieth anniversary party was cancelled due to the husband's death. The banquet facility's policy—which is the norm—was that if the room is rebooked for that date, the deposit money is refunded; otherwise, no refund is given. And yes, most catering contracts do state that deposits are nonrefundable. So yes, it is a contractual issue, but in this case, what about compassion?

An additional, critical piece of advice gleaned from wedding consulting is to determine very early in the planning process exactly who the real decision makers are. If there's a pre-event crisis—from a hurricane to a change of heart—who will have the last word? The catering company may be "hired" by the bride-to-be, but if her parents are paying the bill, they should be signing the contracts jointly with their daughter and should be given the same information about postponement and cancellation policies.

Communications experts say that most of us know up to 50 other people we share information with regularly by word of mouth. When customers have had an unpleasant experience, they'll tell 9 or 10 other people; 13 percent will tell more than 20! Is keeping the deposit money worth that risk?

Common sense, courtesy, and compassion are all necessary in unusual situations. No matter how long or how technical the contract, the bottom line should always be to treat each client with honor and respect when unfortunate things happen, as they sometimes will.

How to Survive a Lawsuit

Type the words "catering lawsuit" into any Internet search engine and you might be astonished at the numbers and types of entries available for your perusal. Today, as we do the research for this chapter, here are a few of the highlights from our own online search:

- A wedding guest has filed a food poisoning lawsuit against a "banquet and catering service," claiming she fell seriously ill after eating the food at a relative's wedding held at the caterer's banquet facility.

- A group of servers for a prominent catering company has filed a $200 million lawsuit. These servers are black and allege they have been discriminated against; they say that they were passed over for work at certain high-profile events and subjected to racial slurs by supervisors.
- Several sexual harassment cases are pending against caterers, by both male and female employees.

It seems that in today's litigious business climate, even top caterers who pay their insurance premiums, mind their operations, and train their staffs can end up in court. Lawsuits brought by members of your own workforce are another topic entirely, but when it comes to customer complaints, a smart caterer will handle these immediately, doing their best to give the clients what they want. Even if the caterer is not to blame, it is usually best to go overboard to avoid legal action on the part of an irate customer.

To determine your course of action in the face of a client lawsuit, take these important first steps:

- Quickly locate employees who may have been involved, and ask for their cooperation.
- Contact an attorney.
- Contact your insurance company.
- Determine whether this is a "nuisance" suit or one with real potential for damages. The longer you wait, the higher the risks and the larger the legal fees.

We have seen lawsuits filed years after an incident, making it virtually impossible to locate former employees to testify. However, you can often track down former employees through their Social Security numbers.

It is critical to keep good notes about adverse incidents. You might ask your attorney to draft an *Incident Report*, a simple sheet that you can print out and have on hand for the captain or supervisor at every event along with the rest of the paperwork, just in case. In a serious situation, such as a crime or natural disaster, it is also important to caution staff members to politely decline questions from news reporters and/or guests and to inform you immediately. In cases in which a supplier could be involved, contact that person or firm too.

Before rushing into court, it is advisable to consider types of Alternative Dispute Resolution (ADR). These include mediation and arbitration.

Mediation involves retaining an objective individual as a go-between, essentially a facilitator who attempts to resolve the issue. This process requires time, patience, and the ability to compromise. Mediation is a voluntary procedure, however, and discussions made during mediation are not admissible in court.

Arbitration takes place before a single person, or a panel of three persons, who listens to both sides and makes a decision on the case. For more information on arbitration, visit the website of the American Arbitration Association (www.adr.org).

 Summary

For would-be caterers, this chapter is not intended to replace professional legal advice, and there is no way a single book can cover the intricacies of the federal, state, city, and county laws that affect caterers. However, our goal is to make you aware of the basic requirements for going into business. Registering a business name, deciding which legal form of business yours will be, looking into the various types of licenses, and preparing to pay taxes are some of these requirements.

Families often go into business as catering companies, and the chapter contains advice for a family-owned business. Setting goals and measuring progress are key for any catering company, but they also keep families focused on the business, rather than on personal squabbles.

You will also need a place to do business. In the case of off-premise catering, this means a kitchen facility where you can store and prepare the food you will be serving. The chapter contains a brief discussion of options, from sharing space at existing kitchen sites to negotiating a lease for your own commissary and office space.

Raising money to start a new business is always a challenge, and catering is no exception. The chapter contains a very basic discussion of potential funding sources. It also goes into great detail about exactly what needs to be covered in a standard catering contract.

The chapter ends with a discussion of what happens when things go wrong, as they sometimes do in a business where Mother Nature, human error, and differing expectations can occasionally combine to create misunderstandings. From refunds and cancellations, to preparation when threatened with a lawsuit, caterers who communicate clearly and carefully document each event as it is planned along with the changes and correspondence related to the event, are the best prepared to make things right—and perhaps even satisfy the pickiest client.

Study Questions

1. A new caterer is going to do all her own cooking and hire occasional, part-time servers on an hourly basis, without benefits. Why would this caterer choose to incorporate instead of doing business as a sole proprietor?

2. What is an assignable lease? Is it a desirable quality for the person or company leasing the space, or not?

3. Why is it important to include a minimum guarantee clause in an off-premise catering contract?

4. What is an indemnification clause in an off-premise catering contract? Do you think it should be required or optional?

5. Briefly state the main objective in drafting a refund and cancellation policy for catering services.

Menu Planning 3

You've established your catering business and have clients willing to hire you. Now you have to decide what to offer them. So what's on the menu? For an individual event, menu planning can range from clients who tell the caterer, "You know what I like. Just send me a menu!" to those who already know exactly what they want to serve and are simply asking the caterer to provide a price to prepare it.

Most menu planning falls between these two extremes, with clients who have some general ideas about what they'd like to serve but are interested in their caterer's opinions, additions, and suggestions. This is where keeping up with trends and being a trusted source of information can really pay off.

In this chapter, you will learn the techniques and principles of menu planning, including the following:

- What caterers should ask their clients to plan an event
- What clients should ask of caterers to ensure they get the type of event they want
- The types of meals and foodservice that off-premise caterers provide
- Truth-in-Menu guidelines, and how to write menus that are both accurate and inviting
- How to determine food quantities and yields

- How to calculate food costs
- Options for dealing with leftover food

A properly planned menu is a major part of the success of an event. A badly planned menu can ruin an event.

It is important to note that this is not a cookbook. There are thousands of wonderful cookbooks and online resources for recipes that can be adapted for use in off-premise catering. What this chapter can do is teach you what to look for when selecting such recipes for use at off-premise events.

Planning Principles

Before you begin asking menu-related questions, as we have already mentioned, it is important to qualify the client in terms of the date of the event, the number of guests, the location, and the budget. By asking these questions first, the astute off-premise caterer will avoid wasting time discussing a menu for an event that is not feasible in the first place. Your time is better spent planning menus for those who are realistic business prospects.

The event location is critical because, of course, it determines the type of kitchen—if any—and other facilities and services available for use by the catering staff. An off-premise menu can be planned only when you know whether you will have refrigeration, water, electricity, adequate cover, ventilation, and so on. All of this determines what type of cooking can be done on-site. For example, frying food to order in a high-rise office building, in an empty office without ventilation, will fill the whole floor with the smell of grease.

Successful caterers are one step ahead in this process. They develop and maintain relationships with the popular event venues in their area, keeping all the pertinent information on file—and not just back-of-the-house details like kitchen facilities. They also know how big the rooms are, and how many people they accommodate; the rental options for tables, chairs, glassware, and more; the availability of audiovisual equipment and whether there is someone to set it up. When a client suggests a particular site as a possibility, the caterer should already be able to answer almost as many questions about that site as the venue manager! The caterer's sales representative should suggest a walk-through meeting at the event site, with the client and the venue manager.

After prequalification and selection of the event site, the menu planning process begins. The menu and service style will determine all of the following:

- Foods to be purchased
- Staffing requirements
- Equipment requirements
- Transportation needs (for food, equipment, and even guests)
- Off-premise facility layout and space utilization
- Décor for buffets and food stations
- Food production and preparation requirements
- Beverages, both alcoholic and nonalcoholic

What Caterers Should Ask Clients

Menu planning involves asking the clients a lot of questions to determine what they perceive and want. Suggested questions include:

- What is the overall purpose of the event?
- Do you have a theme in mind, and what kind of mood do you hope to achieve?
- What is the budget for this event?
- Do you plan to serve liquor, beer, or wine, or no alcoholic beverages?
- How many guests are you expecting?
- Is there a kitchen or other area for cooking?
- Questions about the "group dynamics" for the event: Who are the guests? Are they male or female? Singles or couples? What is the age range? Are they fairly sophisticated partygoers?
- Do you want guests to be seated at tables and served, or would you prefer a buffet or food stations?
- Are there any foods that you particularly want (or do not want) on the menu? Are there any special dietary needs? Any socioeconomic, ethnic, or religious factors that might affect the menu?
- What will your guests be doing before and after this event? Where will they be when the caterer arrives for the setup? Do we need to arrange transportation for them to or from the event?

- Have you hosted or attended this type of event in the past? If so, what did you like (and dislike) about the menu and the food?

- Are there any particular affiliations in this group that might affect the menu? (You would not serve chicken, for instance, to a Cattlemen's Association, or pour Pepsi products at a meeting of Coca-Cola bottlers.)

- What would you like your guests to say about the menu and food after the event?

- Who is the responsible party for billing?

By asking these and other related questions, the off-premise caterer should be able to spark a dialogue that begins the menu-planning process. The end result is a menu for the event that combines the client's wishes with the caterer's food knowledge.

What Clients Should Ask Caterers

At Cuisine Unlimited Catering and Special Events in Salt Lake City, Utah, caterer Maxine Turner has found that clients don't always understand what is expected of them in the event-planning process. To minimize confusion and potential miscommunication, she gives them a sheet of questions to ask her or her sales staff. It not only prompts clients to really think about what they want, but also gives the caterer a lot more information that can be used to plan a successful event. The list includes the following questions:

- What types of foods do you recommend for my budget, number of guests, and type of event? Are there recommendations for foods based on the season?

- What type of service (buffet, stand-up, sit-down) do you think would be best?

- What is a reasonable cost per person for this type of event, and what types of food can you provide at that cost?

- If this is a delivery, setup, and pick-up event, when will you return to pick up, and will you also handle the site cleanup?

- How much time will you need to set up? To break down and clean up?

- Do you provide linens? Is there an additional fee? Is there a color selection?

- Do you supply glasses, plates, and silverware? Is there an additional charge?

- Can disposable, recyclable materials be used? How does the cost compare to traditional rental of glasses, plates, and silverware?

- Who is responsible for renting tables, chairs, and decorations? Who delivers and returns these items?

- Can you handle other services, such as floral arrangements, photography, music, or other entertainment?
- Can I review the event layout with you—table locations and seating arrangements—in advance?
- Do you supply liquor for the bar setups? If so, is there an additional charge?
- If I provide my own wine or Champagne, do you charge a corkage fee per bottle?
- Who will personally handle and attend my event from your company?
- Do you require a guaranteed number of guests?
- What is the last date before the event that I can give you a final guest count?
- When will you provide a final, per-person cost for the event?
- Are gratuities (tips) already figured into the total price? If so, what percentage is being charged?
- Are any special licenses or permits needed for this event? Can you handle that or do I need to do it?
- Who arranges for security at this venue, if it is needed?
- Do you have a contract?
- What is your payment policy? Do you accept credit cards?
- Is a deposit required?
- What is your refund or cancellation policy?
- Explain your service fees and/or equipment usage fees.
- When can I expect a written proposal from you?

Between these two extensive lists of questions, you can see that both caterer and client will emerge from their initial meeting(s) with a much clearer idea of their expectations and responsibilities. That's the start of a great event!

Types of Service and Menu Categories

Catered foods can be served at any hour of the day or night. Off-premise caterers are asked to serve sunrise breakfasts, midday lunches and brunches, evening dinners, post-theater desserts, box lunches, and everything in between. Menus vary just as widely depending on the caterers and the types of clients they serve. Menus also vary depending on the style of service: buffet, stand-up, or seated. Think about events you have attended. If you're at a cocktail party with nowhere to sit and no utensils, how will you juggle a dinner plate and a wineglass? Service style is influenced by the purpose of the event, the allotted time for dining, and the location of the event, to name a few factors.

Here are some basic types of special event service:

- Seated, served meals
- Buffets
- Food stations (sometimes called *action stations*)
- *Stand-up* dining, such as at cocktail parties, where food is *butler-passed*
- Barbecues and picnics
- Combinations of any of these

Seated, Served Meals

In planning menus for seated, served meals, caterers must serve foods that are suitable for serving at a table, either individually plated or from platters. Served meals may be preceded by cocktail receptions, which may or may not include various hors d'oeuvres passed by servers, or appetizers presented at food stations and buffets.

The basic courses for a seated, served meal include:

- Appetizer or soup
- Salad
- Sorbet (*intermezzo*)
- Main course: entrée, starch (optional), vegetables, and garnish
- Cheeses (with or without fruit, nuts)
- Dessert
- Coffee (regular and decaffeinated) and tea

There are endless variations to this format. In European-style menus, the salad is served after the main course but prior to the cheese course. The appetizer course may be eliminated if the premeal hors d'oeuvres are plentiful. Some menus include a fish course instead of an appetizer or salad. A sorbet course should be served only if there are two or more courses served prior to it. Many main course menus eliminate the starch and include two or more vegetables. *Dual entrées* (also called *duets*) feature two main courses, such as sliced tenderloin of beef with a fish or chicken dish. Portion sizes of each are roughly half a full-size portion. This works very well, as it satisfies the tastes of most people, and if a guest asks for a plate of all fish or all beef, the request can easily be accommodated.

Many Americans are unfamiliar with the cheese course unless they have spent time in Europe. It is a profitable addition to an upscale dinner menu and can also be fun to put together. (Learn more about cheese courses on page 90.)

Some clients prefer a combination of served and buffet-style courses. For example, a chilled soup appetizer could be served or preset at the tables; the guests then make their main course selections from a buffet. Another interesting variation is to serve all courses except the dessert and coffee at the table, allowing guests to get up for dessert and coffee and mingle with guests from other tables. In this situation, dessert selections should be bite-sized and/or easy to eat while standing, and coffee should be served in an attractive mug to eliminate the need for a saucer.

Buffets

In buffet service, the guests are directed to the buffet table(s) where a variety of foods may be selected. Guests either help themselves or are served by attendants. The advantages of offering a variety of foods, plus the need for fewer service staff, make a buffet a very popular choice for off-premise events. When the client wants variety, this service system is more practical and cost-effective than providing a served meal that guests order à la carte from a menu.

One of the most frequently asked questions by clients is, "Which is more expensive, a buffet or a served meal?" The answer varies from caterer to caterer. Generally, buffets require less labor to serve the food, but greater food quantities. A buffet table should be continuously replenished during service so as not to be (or look) empty after the last guest eats. There is no simple answer, but you can truthfully tell clients that the cost will depend on the menu choices, the level of service required, and other factors. A buffet table filled with expensive seafood and beef tenderloins will cost more than a simple three-course chicken dinner served by a waitstaff. A seven-course served meal that includes caviar, lobster tails, and desserts flamed at tableside will cost more than a buffet consisting of simple salads, a chicken dish, rice, and a vegetable.

Buffets may or may not be preceded by hors d'oeuvres. If the client does not want to include hors d'oeuvres, it is wise for the caterer to be prepared for guests to eat more heartily from the buffet.

At a minimum, a buffet selection should include one salad, one or two entrée choices, one starch (rice, potato, or pasta), one vegetable or a vegetable medley, bread or rolls, and butter. Desserts and coffee may be placed on the same table, although we think a separate table is preferable. These may also be served directly at the dining tables.

Food Stations

Food stations work well when food needs to be offered on different floors within a large venue, or when such different types of foods are offered that they wouldn't "go together" well on a single buffet—for instance, international foods from a variety of countries.

For large groups or small, food stations also encourage guests to mingle. They can also help with organizing flow patterns of foot traffic, as the stations can be set up to keep people moving and prevent overcrowding of any one area of a room. Vinwood Caterers in Ipswich, Massachusetts, offers entire meals that consist of stations, with one server per 15 guests to handle cook-to-order, carving, and other duties. One of their station ideas, "From the Atlantic," capitalizes on the fabulous fresh seafood available in their area.

Some popular food station concepts include:

- *Stir-fry:* Raw and blanched vegetables and several types of marinated meats and sauces are cooked to order in a wok by a chef.

- *Mexican food:* Fajitas, quesadillas, tacos, and enchiladas are served with accompaniments of salsa, sour cream, jalapeños, and other condiments.

- *Pasta:* Various types and shapes of cooked pasta are heated on tabletop stoves and topped with a variety of sauces, such as marinara, pesto, and cream. Crusty Italian bread and Caesar salad go well with pasta.

- *Crepes:* These are quick to make, and people seem to love to watch the process of making them, whether it is a savory crepe stuffed with grilled veggies, chicken, and seafood, or a dessert crepe filled with fresh fruit and whipped cream.

- *Gourmet pizza:* Pizzas with a variety of toppings are cooked to order in a small oven or pizza oven.

- *Raw bar:* Freshly shucked oysters, sushi rolled to order, smoked salmon, and crab or shrimp cocktail are as colorful as they are delicious.

- *Meat carving:* One or more meats are carved to order. Beef tenderloin, turkey breast, loin of pork, and rack of lamb are popular choices. Many caterers serve them on rolls or breads as sandwiches with appropriate sauces.

- *Wine and cheese:* Instead of just having bartenders pour the wines, station a server at a beautifully garnished table of gourmet cheeses and artisan breads.

- *Children's station:* If there will be lots of little ones at an event, indulge them with a station all their own: macaroni and cheese, mini pizzas, chicken fingers, and fruit. Chilled juice boxes—or for fancy occasions, a "bartender" to "mix" Shirley Temples and Roy Rogers—will satisfy the kids and charm their parents.

- *Dessert, coffee, and cordials:* Assortments of pastries, fresh fruits, tarts, éclairs, cookies, and chocolate desserts are served with a variety of coffees. Quality and flavor are more important here than size. Crème brûlée and chocolate are the most popular dessert items, and caterers can never go wrong serving high-quality ice creams and sorbets. Cordials and cognacs may also be served in accordance with state liquor laws. Make sure the coffees are excellent, with accompaniments like whipped cream and cinnamon, and that decaf is offered as well as caffeinated.

These are only a few of so many fun food station possibilities. It is always an option to use a limited number of food stations, in lieu of (or in addition to) passed hors d'oeuvres, prior to a served meal. Some clients prefer to offer food at stations throughout the evening, which keeps a party less formal. Seating for all guests at a food station party is optional. Some clients prefer to have no seating, or seating for only a portion of the guests, which encourages them to mingle. Others prefer that each guest have an assigned seat, with each place setting prepared with all the necessary flatware and glassware.

Stand-Up Dining

In the United States, hors d'oeuvres are customarily served at cocktail parties, which may or may not precede lunch or dinner. But in recent years, a younger generation has embraced this less formal dining style as the new norm for entertaining. They'd prefer to share plates and stay mobile, rather than be seated and served at a banquet table.

Food servers can walk around serving the hors d'oeuvres on trays—a practice known as *butler-passing*, whether or not there's a butler in sight—or the hors d'oeuvres can be arranged, garnished, and placed on buffets.

Hors d'oeuvres should be bite-sized and easy to eat. The location of the party will influence the hors d'oeuvre selection; for example, where cooking space is limited, cold selections are more practical. Honey-coconut shrimp, which is a fried item, cannot be cooked to order in a building without sufficient ventilation. (Although a client once insisted on conch fritters for a cocktail party on an office building's sixteenth floor.

The fritters were cooked to order on the loading dock, transported on the passenger elevators, and served within minutes!) Please note that it is important to serve fried foods quickly because they soon become dry, cold, and relatively flavorless.

Barbecues and Picnics

Webster's New World Dictionary defines a picnic as "a pleasure outing at which a meal is eaten outdoors." Many off-premise caterers make an excellent living catering outdoor events in public parks and other open-air locations. Menus can range from simple (or gourmet versions of) burgers and hot dogs to chicken and ribs to steaks and seafood kebabs. They can also include Maryland crab fests, New England clambakes, Caribbean barbecue, Southern fries, pork barbecues, oyster roasts, grilled pizza, and Louisiana shrimp boils, each with its own flavors, accompaniments, and décor.

A caterer's ability to barbecue at any venue depends on the availability of sufficient numbers and sizes of barbecue grills. One consideration in making equipment decisions is whether you'll be doing enough of this type of catering to justify purchasing your own grills and hauling them to event sites, or renting them as needed.

For cutting-edge barbecues and picnics, try:

- Ancho chili–braised barbecued lamb shanks with black beans and red tomato
- Grilled elk loin with bourbon sauce
- Grilled ostrich with chipotle cream sauce
- Grilled Texas quail with Parmesan cheese grits and Smithfield ham sherry-maple glaze
- Wood-grilled wild Alaskan salmon with wild-rice pilaf and Zinfandel-cranberry sauce

In some situations, it is necessary to provide pre-prepared, boxed meals for picnics. In these cases, the ability to keep food at the correct temperature until it is served is absolutely critical.

Catering Menu Guidelines

Federal Truth-in-Menu laws require that caterers and other menu planners correctly describe and represent every item on their menus. According to the National Restaurant Association, the major points to observe include the following:

- *Brand names:* A copyrighted or registered trademark must be used "as is" and may not be used to represent a generic product.

- *Means of preservation:* You can't call something "fresh" if it has been previously frozen—ever! This includes items like shrimp and salmon.

- *Merchandising terms:* Don't say anything served commercially is "homemade." It wasn't actually made in someone's home, and thank heavens! That would be an unlicensed facility! Use words like "home-style" or "traditional" instead.

- *Point of origin:* This refers to the original spot where the product was grown or harvested, such as Maine lobster or Florida stone crabs.

- *Price:* Cover charges, service charges, and gratuities must all be contained in a contract or communicated by letter. They should never be hidden or go unmentioned in negotiations.

- *Product identification:* Sometimes a product must be substituted at the last minute because what was ordered was not available, not delivered, too expensive, or otherwise impossible to use. Be certain to state the correct products being used, but reserve the right to substitute, with the customer's permission, under extraordinary circumstances.

- *Quality:* Grades of meat and poultry products should refer strictly to USDA-recognized terminology (Prime, Choice, Select, Standard, and Commercial) or accepted variants thereof (Grade A, Good, Number One, Fancy, Grade AA, and Extra Standard).

- *Quantity (and/or portion size):* Steaks are often sold by weight, and *weight before cooking* is the generally accepted term.

- *Type of preparation:* Use the proper terms for the cooking methods you are actually using on the particular food item: baked, broiled, fried, sautéed, smoked, roasted, and so on.

- *Verbal and visual presentation:* Have you noticed that, on most product packaging in supermarkets, the gorgeous food photo has a little caption? It says, "Serving Suggestion." This legally covers the food processor in case the end result does not look quite as perfect as the food in that professional photo. Take a hint from that part of the industry and be certain that what is described by the waitstaff—or on the menu, or photographed for reproduction on menus or table tents—actually represents what the customer receives.

Dietary and Nutritional Claims

Dietary terms, such as *fat-free* and *low-sodium*, must be accurate and not misleading. Frequently, guests who are allergic to certain foods will ask a server about the ingredients in a particular dish, so it is extremely important that servers have the proper information about foods and ingredients. They should be instructed to ask the kitchen staff or management prior to answering questions about a food's ingredients because people may become ill, or even die, from eating certain ingredients. The most common food allergens, responsible for about 90 percent of all allergic reactions, are commonly known as the *Big 8*:

- Eggs (including some egg substitutes, which contain egg whites, and some foaming products used to top specialty coffee drinks)
- Milk (from cows or goats, and in butter, yogurt, cheeses, and lunchmeats containing casein or whey)
- Peanuts (or mandelonas, peanuts soaked in almond flavoring)
- Tree nuts (almonds, Brazil nuts, cashews, hazelnuts, filberts, pecans, macadamia nuts, pine nuts, pistachios, walnuts, etc.)
- Fish (crab, crayfish, lobster, shrimp, etc.)
- Shellfish (clams, mussels, oysters, scallops, etc.)
- Soy
- Gluten (A type of protein found in some grains, including wheat, rye, and barley. When used as an additive for thickening or stabilizing foods, it is sometimes called *dextrin*. Even some types of imitation crabmeat contain gluten.)

In addition, sesame seeds and sulfites (a food preservative used in many types of cooked and processed foods, as well as a natural by-product of beer and wine making) also cause allergic reactions in some people. For more information about food allergies and the Big 8, check the website of the Food Allergy and Anaphylaxis Network (www.foodallergy.org) and the U.S. Food and Drug Administration (FDA) (www.fda.gov).

It is good to have nutrition content information available for clients who want to see it, although caterers who choose to offer it must be able to support the data in accordance with FDA guidelines. For example, if a caterer claims that a particular menu item is "light," the caterer should be able to prove that this particular menu item contains at least one-third fewer calories than the regular item. To support this claim, the caterer may need an expensive laboratory nutrient analysis. The lesson: Before making a claim, be aware of the costs that may be involved to support it.

Birds of a Feather: Understanding Chicken Labels

One area in which you must be careful of the claims you make is the labeling of various chicken products. From *Santé* magazine, here is a handy explanation of commonly used terms that will help you correctly describe your chicken offerings:

- *Free-range* means chickens have free access to the outdoors for a significant portion of their lives. This is just a marketing tool, and anyone with a door on his or her chicken coop meets the technical definition of raising "free-range" birds. There are no criteria for what the chickens eat, what antibiotics they receive, or the amount of free-range space.

- *Free-roaming chickens* is a marketing label that means only that the chickens are allowed access to the outdoors. Most are kept in barns and are allowed outside occasionally.

- *Natural* implies that chickens are fed antibiotic- and hormone-free grain, but currently there is no strict legal definition of "natural" chicken.

- *Organic* means that the chickens were raised on land certified as "organic" by the U.S. Department of Agriculture (USDA). This means the land has been free of chemicals, pesticides, and herbicides for at least three years, and extensive bookkeeping records and inspections are required. Organic chickens are not fed antibiotics, as are some conventionally raised chickens. A USDA-approved third-party private or state certification program must certify organic foods. Caterers and restaurants do not have to be certified to serve organic foods; however, organic and nonorganic foods cannot be stored together and must be properly identified on the menu. Caterers also need to prove organic claims by keeping records that document the certification of whatever organic foods they serve.

Sharing Menu Ideas and Prices

Most off-premise caterers prepare some form of printed menu to share with customers, and today's computer programs make it easier than ever to keep these on file, alter them as necessary, and make them look their best when they are printed out or e-mailed to clients. These menus may or may not include prices, depending on the caterer's clientele. Usually, those caterers who market to a more budget-conscious client in lower-priced markets will include prices on their menus. Upscale caterers who prepare food at event locations and custom menus for each client will generally not preprice their menus but will provide price quotations for specific menus on request.

Giving menus to clients so they can make their own food choices offers some advantages:

- The client can respond quickly by reading the menu and making selections without long consultations with the catering sales staff. Providing menus automatically gives clients menu ideas and might even minimize the number of required sales staff.

- These menus help "control" clients by giving them specific choices, rather than allowing them the freedom to come up with items that you may not be familiar with or that won't fit their budget or the off-premise preparation constraints.

- The kitchen staff will be familiar with the menu, thereby enabling them to work more efficiently.

One disadvantage is that because a caterer's menu is generally quite extensive, it could confuse or frustrate clients, giving them too many choices and too much to think about, and possibly causing delays as they round up other people's opinions. That's why many caterers also create sample menus for different event types and in different price ranges—dishes that already complement each other, often with wine recommendations.

Depending on how you feel about "showing your cards" to competitors, you can also put menu (and price) information on your website, along with high-quality, profes-sional photos of your beautifully styled food. Our feeling is that listing specific prices can be problematic, as food costs fluctuate so often. On a website, it can be better to offer a price range per guest for certain types of events. Search online under the term "off-premise catering prices," and you'll find plenty of examples of each theory in practice.

Whether a menu is in print or on a website, it should reflect the image the caterer wishes to project. A menu should be attractive and easy to read and not appear too "busy." As much as 50 percent of the page can be white space, with wide borders and space between listings. Menus should reflect a good balance of marketing and ingredi-ent information. We've all had restaurant experiences in which we were disappointed when the food arrived at the table and didn't come close to matching the waiter's glow-ing description of it. It is also a good idea to include short descriptions of any items that may be unfamiliar to the reader.

Terms to Enliven a Menu

One way to make your menu more compelling is to use adjectives and adverbs the way you use garnishes—just enough to make the food look better without overdoing it. Terms you can use to describe specific dishes include:

Artisan, bouquet, caramelized, chilled, choice, creamy, crisp, crunchy, delicate, early-harvest, earthy, extra-large, fluffy, fresh, freshly baked, freshly prepared, garnished, half-pound, hand-battered, handmade, heirloom, home-style, hot, house-made, icy, juicy, jumbo, light, luscious, mellow, natural, one-pound, original, oven-fresh, plump, prime, saucy, savory, silky, sizzling, smooth, soft, tender, USDA Grade, velvety, warm, whole, wood-fired, zesty

Descriptive phrases that can work for a general menu, or individual dishes, include:

Created exclusively for . . .

A delightful (array, blend, combination . . .)

Infused with a hint of . . .

Balanced with a hint of . . .

Newly harvested

Locally (grown, produced, sourced . . .)

Winter, spring, summer, fall, farm-to-table, new, seasonal, chef's, harvest, rainbow, signature, special

Words that might help you sell your offerings include:

Affordable, alluring, aromatic, colorful, enticing, exclusive, exotic, exquisite, fabulous, fascinating, flavorful, flawless, genuine, glistening, impeccable, irresistible, lavish, melt-in-your-mouth, memorable, mouthwatering, one-of-a-kind, radiant, solid, spectacular, striking, substantial, succulent, sumptuous, tantalizing, tempting, unforgettable, unique, unsurpassed, upscale, vivid

See Chapter 9 for more information on using menus as a marketing tool.

An excellent resource for menu writing is the *Prentice Hall Essentials Dictionary of Culinary Arts* by Steven and Sarah R. Labensky and Gaye G. Ingram (Upper Saddle River, New Jersey: Prentice Hall, 2007). Another extensive dictionary of culinary terms is part of the What's Cooking America website. We would also recommend the Official Food and Beverage Spell-Checker, a software program that takes the guesswork out of spelling more than 17,000 culinary and beverage terms.

Nothing says "unprofessional" like misspelled words or grammatical errors on a menu, brochure, website, contract, or proposal. The fact is, however, that you are a caterer, not a writer. If you are not confident of your ability to draft appealing, thorough, and catchy menu copy, hire a food writer to do it for you. A good relationship with a local freelancer at a reasonable hourly cost will ensure you have someone to take one last critical look at written materials before you send them out or post them on the Internet.

Basic Menu-Planning Guidelines

There are no strict, do-or-die rules for planning off-premise catering menus. Exceptions arise from regional preferences, a client's desire for something innovative, and the capabilities of the caterer and staff. For example, most caterers would not advise serving chocolate soufflés to a group of 500 dignitaries at an off-premise location with no on-site kitchen, although there are caterers who have perfected their techniques and organizational skills well enough to serve 500 soufflés at the peak of perfection. Toques (chef's hats) off to them!

As a rule, it is always better to keep off-premise catering menus as simple as possible. With client input, the off-premise caterer should strive to create menus with the following characteristics:

- They have worked well for past events.
- The staff has prepared them before, for groups of the same approximate size.
- They feature signature dishes for which the caterer is known.
- They feature locally grown and raised foods. In California, this might mean abalone and artichokes, or stone crabs and Key lime pie in Florida.

Some clients request that their guests be offered a choice of entrées at a seated, served meal. For example, they will ask that a caterer offer the guest a choice of fish, beef, or chicken and that an order be taken from each guest at the function. It is also smart to offer a vegetarian alternative as well. Offering such choices may seem impractical because it requires the caterer to have extra portions of each entrée, as well as the extra staff to take and serve the special orders. However, if the client's budget allows for the extra cost, the caterer should comply with the request. If the budget does not allow for the extra expense, it is far better to persuade the client to offer a buffet meal that allows guests to choose from a variety of entrées.

Another option is to offer a dual entrée: smaller portions of two or more entrées on each plate. If the client insists on the seated served meal with entrée choice, give the client the responsibility of taking entrée orders in advance (as part of the RSVP to the event), and then providing a count to the caterer a few days prior to the event, along with the seat assignments for each guest.

Well-planned menus take food flavors, colors, textures, and shapes into account and seek to balance these. Too much of any one component is not good. Flavors should be interesting, with some highlights, but not too tart or pungent. Natural colors—red, reddish orange, peach, pink, tan, brown, butter yellow, light and dark green—are good. Contrasting textures, as simple as crispy croutons in a salad, add interest and excitement to the course. Interesting shapes are always welcome, as long as they are not all the same. For example, a plate with round tomato slices, round sliced beef tenderloin, and round scoops of potato salad and coleslaw would not be as visually appealing as one with the items presented differently: Layer the tenderloin slices on a bed of radicchio, cut the tomatoes into wedges, and serve the salads in bright hollowed-out vegetables.

Here are some additional guidelines for menu planning:

- Serve foods that are popular. For example, pork tenderloin will be better received by more guests than fillet of shark. Well-liked and trendy restaurant menu items can be varied and adapted to meet off-premise catering needs.

- Butler-passed hors d'oeuvres should be one or two bites in size, and not messy to eat. Passing hors d'oeuvres makes it much easier to control consumption, rather than holding them in chafing dishes where a few guests may overindulge and leave only scraps for the rest of the group. The quality of cooked-to-order, hot, butler-passed hors d'oeuvres is usually superior to that of those that are cooked in advance and held in chafing dishes.

- Be careful not to duplicate items on the menu, such as serving stuffed pea pods as an appetizer and again as the vegetable, or lobster bisque as the first course and lobster tails as the entrée.

- Develop menus that mesh with the capabilities of your kitchen staff. A caterer who wants to specialize in home-style cooking, such as chicken and ribs, does not need a five-star chef. Conversely, a caterer who wants to market gourmet dinners to an upscale clientele will not be successful with a short-order cook as head chef.

- Astute caterers consult with their chefs when planning menus with clients. They also need to know when to turn down unusual client demands. (For instance—and yes, this was an actual request, declined by the caterer—a bathtub full of multicolored, fruit-flavored gelatin for what promised to be a rather rowdy party.) There are two sides to this situation: If caterers say no, they may lose the client, or at least appear uncooperative—but if they say yes, their kitchen staff may have difficulty producing the food. Unusual requests can be honored when possible, particularly during slower seasons and for smaller-size groups. The busy holiday season, however, is not a time to experiment.

- There are no hard-and-fast rules for the number of items on a buffet, or the number of courses in a seated, served meal. These can and should vary based on the client's needs. Smart caterers always remember the big picture when planning courses. What is the purpose of the event, and what will satisfy the majority of the guests?

- No menu is complete without including the appropriate beverages for the meal. This may mean a selection of wines to accompany particular courses, coffee with dessert, or perhaps imported vodka with caviar.

- Garnishing food is an art that is frequently overlooked. When you plan menus, presentation should always be considered. Many caterers garnish plates with herbs or other ingredients used in preparing the dish; others use items that add color and/or enhance the appearance of the plate.

- Concentrate on what is good and fresh. Local, seasonal ingredients will be at their peak, so take advantage of them to create your own versions of regional culinary traditions. Buying in season is also smart for the budget, as your produce should cost less.

- Be sure to always include vegetarian selections. People who don't eat meat deserve a good meal at your events, and meatless dishes can also be more profitable.

Other thoughts on developing your menu include just keeping your eyes open and your own palate alive and curious. Ask your clients where they like to go when they dine out. Eat there too, and see what you think. Plan an occasional visit to a city known for its great food. Scan the latest cookbooks and food magazines. Attend a few of your competitors' events, not as a "spy" but as a legitimate guest when you are invited.

Special Diets

According to *Vegetarian Times* magazine in 2010, more than 3 percent of Americans are vegetarians, but another 10 percent say they "largely follow a vegetarian-inclined diet." In total, that's more than 30 million people! It is probably accurate to say that few are familiar with the strictest definition of the term: a person whose diet consists of vegetables, fruits, grains, and nuts. Many who use the term do not eat red meat but will occasionally eat fish or chicken. As the U.S. population ages and becomes more health conscious, many families simply choose to have a couple of "meatless meals" every week. Here are a few important subcategories:

- *Vegans* are the strictest vegetarians. They do not eat anything from an animal source, including honey because it is produced by bees.
- *Lacto-vegetarians* eat no animal products except milk and dairy products.
- *Ovo-lacto-vegetarians* eat no animal products, with the exception of eggs and milk products.

There are other types of special diets to be aware of, as they may be mentioned in meal planning:

- *Low-cholesterol:* These diets are low in fats derived from animal sources. No trans fats, and minimal use of eggs and full-fat dairy products.
- *Low-fat:* These diets are low in fats derived from any source.
- *Gluten-free:* These diets contain no barley, rye, or wheat. (Some doctors recommend minimizing the use of oats, as well.) No prepared foods containing dextrin. No soy sauce (many soy sauces contain wheat). No licorice, and no candy containing wheat (many candy bars contain wheat products). Can eat rice, potatoes, and quinoa. Can eat flour made from rice, beans, potatoes, peas, or coconut.
- *Anti-allergen:* These diets focus on foods prepared with no gluten, eggs, seafood, or nuts.
- *Diabetic.* Minimize sugar or use alternative sweeteners in these diets. Focus on low-carbohydrate foods, nonstarchy vegetables, and whole grains.

(Continued)

- *Kosher:* This diet contains foods that have been selected and prepared in accordance with Jewish dietary laws.
- *Low-salt:* For people with high blood pressure or heart problems, intake of less than 1 teaspoon of salt per day is advised. This diet requires that foods be seasoned with fresh herbs or use unsalted products; avoid most processed meats and sauces, which are high in sodium.
- *No MSG:* This diet contains no monosodium glutamate, a flavor enhancer often used in Asian cooking.

You may occasionally get a request for a dish that is prepared without garlic, onions, nuts, or a particular spice. This usually indicates a guest's allergy or digestion problems, which should always be taken seriously. The same goes for coffee service; you should always have alternatives to caffeinated coffee since caffeine intake can be a problem for some people.

Food Presentation and Display

Consider all five senses in menu planning: sight, hearing, touch, smell, and taste. Texture, aroma, temperature, color, and spiciness are parts of the overall flavors of the foods you serve. Bright colors may indicate freshness or proper doneness. Steaming foods implies heat. You can "hear" the flavor in a sizzling fajita platter, the crunch of an apple, the fizz of Champagne being poured into an elegant flute.

Eating is a sensuous pastime, and the way the food is presented is as important as the way it tastes. Buffet and food station presentation can also make or break your reputation as a caterer. Everything matters—from the height of the buffet table to the quality of the linens that drape it; from the way the foods are grouped to the lighting that shows them off. It is important to remember that although the guests may never focus on these individual elements, they definitely notice and appreciate the overall presentation.

Let's remove the imaginary food from our mental buffet tables now, and look at the architecture beneath the food—how it is held, and how it is kept at safe temperatures.

Serving and Holding Options

One key to an interesting food display is to vary the heights at which the foods are placed on the table. Try elevating heat-resistant sturdy platters on glass blocks with canned heat (such as Sterno) underneath. This works best when all guests go through the line at once, but it is not recommended for buffets that last for long periods of time.

Use polished aluminum platters elevated on wrought iron stands. The cost of nice-looking platters is quite modest, their uses are endless, and you will receive many compliments on the results.

The latest chafing dish innovation is a butane-fueled chafing dish that actually cooks. These state-of-the-art chafers burn for four hours on one can of butane. You can bring your food cold to an off-premise event and quickly reheat it.

Some caterers use large granite slabs raised on glass blocks with canned heat underneath. At chef stations, your crew can prepare foods to order in front of guests, to be served from woks, skillets, griddles, and sauté pans.

A simple and cost-effective way to display cold foods, such as bite-sized desserts, is to elevate two or more pieces of Plexiglas. Support them with Martini glasses or those old-fashioned, wide-rimmed Champagne glasses, adding loose floral buds for a final touch of color. This type of display works well with chocolate-dipped strawberries or mini fruit tarts.

Chilled ice displays are fun and dramatic. They can range from small pieces that chill and display fruit or seafood to complete buffet tables carved out of ice. Molds are available that allow a caterer to create fairly simple ice displays; for custom or more complex designs (company logos, etc.), you should have a good vendor relationship with an ice sculptor.

In Vancouver, British Columbia, caterer Debra Lykkemark of Culinary Capers came up with her own tiered table, using three or four round tables of successively smaller sizes. The bottom table is a 60-inch round, placed on the floor with legs extended. A large box is then placed on the table, and a 48-inch round table is placed on top of the box without the legs extended. On top of that, another box is placed, and then a 30-inch round. Linens are draped over the top, and the entire table looks like a gigantic wedding cake.

Visit stores like Home Depot, Target, and Pier 1 Imports for design inspiration. We have been told that some Pier 1 Imports locations actually allow caterers to use their pieces and return them (undamaged, of course) for 20 percent of their purchase cost. It's great publicity for the store, particularly if you can include (small, tasteful) signage letting guests know where they can get that colorful stoneware bowl or elegant wooden platter.

Don't forget your local thrift stores for truly inspirational bargains and unique period pieces. When designing buffets for ethnic meals, be sure to visit local stores that carry the particular cuisine's ingredients, where you will often find indigenous (and often inexpensive) props.

The International Caterers Association suggests using small boxes or Styrofoam slabs to elevate foods. Or save Styrofoam packing peanuts, place them in plastic bags, tie them shut, and use them as "beanbags" to prop up salad bowls and platters at attractive angles. The Internet is an incredible resource for buffet design ideas. Type "buffet and food station presentations" in a search engine, and you'll find thousands of matches.

Garnishing

Garnishes should accent and enhance rather than upstage the food, although those garnishes that are produced with an obvious degree of difficulty do improve the overall presentation. The point of a garnish is to provide a color or flavor complement to the food, and the garnish should also be edible. It dresses up the food and makes the dish look just a little bit tastier and more professional. There are so many interesting garnishes:

- Balsamic and red wine glazes
- Miniature vegetables: cucumbers, and bell peppers
- Lemon, lime, and orange slices
- Champagne grapes
- Fruit or vegetable "caviar"
- Crisply fried leeks, basil, or other herbs
- Chocolate shavings
- Cocoa powder and powdered sugar
- Rice paper and flowers
- Shiso sprouts and micro-greens
- Seeds and nuts: toasted pumpkin, pine nuts, and sesame
- Mai fun noodles
- Sun-dried lemon, orange, and fennel

- Caramelized nuts, herbs, and seeds
- Edible flowers
- Lemongrass
- Lavender sprigs
- Dried-bean mosaics
- Enoki mushrooms
- Baby corn
- Fresh bamboo shoots
- Ginger: roots or pickled
- Cinnamon sticks
- Hearts of palm
- Exotic fruits: kumquat, mango, and star fruit

Then again, be sure not to lose the food amid all the props, lights, linens, and greenery! In the words of the late, great caterer John Mossman, "The best advertisement is on the end of the fork." We all hear stories about events where the buffets looked beautiful, but the food wasn't hot enough or simply lacked flavor, or the caterer didn't bring enough to satisfy the crowd.

Culinary Trends

Off-premise catering is an industry most definitely affected by food trends. Some caterers simply refuse to acknowledge them and continue to operate by serving the tried-and-true classics they have served for decades. Others seem to want to be on the cutting edge of trendiness. There is room for both types of caterer, as well as those who would rather offer a mix of trends and traditions.

As time passes, it is evident that some things change and others stay the same. Yesterday's comfort foods, like mashed potatoes and meatloaf, reemerge as today's trends. Budget is still a constant concern when it comes to planning menus. There is a strong demand for value, as well as quality. We see a continuing emphasis on diet and nutrition, yet most folks throw their dietary concerns to the wind when planning a once-in-a-lifetime celebration like a wedding. They will include special meals for kosher or vegan guests, but for everyone else, it's prime beef, fresh seafood, and rich, beautiful desserts.

A number of notable foodservice trends have emerged in recent years.

Local and Sustainable. By far, the most striking trend we're seeing is a sincere desire to support local agriculture, organic and microproducers, and "green" products, and to advertise their use by including the brand names on menus: Niman Ranch beef, Rockhill Creamery cheeses, and so on. This trend applies not only to the foods themselves, but to the use of eco-friendly products, such as disposable plateware and flatware that is recyclable. We predict this is not just a trend, but a true shift in dining priorities.

Make It Yourself. Can your kitchen staff make their own cheeses? Cure meats? Churn their own ice cream—with milk from a local dairy, of course—and hand-make the cones? If so, you're in luck, as the signature dish has become intensely personal.

Small-City. We've also noticed the focus is on, for example, not "Paris," but "French country village." Anything that brings the guest closer to the source of the ingredients is considered a plus. *Restaurant Hospitality* magazine has called this trend "Basic, Only Better." This idea also can make for some unique event themes.

Cheese Courses. Popular in Europe, a cheese course is served after the main course but before dessert (or sometimes in lieu of dessert). Limit the selection to no more than five types of cheese, and choose a variety of flavors, intensities, and textures. Again, local artisan cheeses and breads are preferable. Take the cheeses out of refrigeration in time to reach room temperature by serving time.

Gourmet Burgers. In 2011, burger restaurants were the fastest-growing fast-casual type of chain in the United States, and caterers should take note. Of course, they're not just any burgers! Purveyors seem to be trying to outdo themselves and each other with gourmet touches and artisan buns for these premium patties. Even the Cheesecake Factory has a "Glamburger" topped with wild mushrooms, arugula, and herbed goat cheese. Fries are also getting a makeover, fried in healthier olive or peanut oil and dusted with herbs, spritzed with malt vinegar, and served with upscale dipping sauces.

Street Foods. This category includes anything traditionally served from carts or informal food stands—kebabs, fish and chips, and "walk-around" items like beignets and churros. (A catering truck could be an interesting way to grow your business.) Korean foods have become especially popular in this setting, from noodles and dumplings to kimchi and traditional Korean-style barbecued meats.

Desserts, Downsized. The only thing cuter than a perfect cupcake is a miniature version of a perfect cupcake—and you can eat three of them! Two-bite desserts enable caterers (and their bakers) to maximize variety and have a lot of fun with presentation. They also allow health-conscious guests to indulge just a bit without feeling they've blown their diets.

Computing Food Quantities

After the planning of a proposed menu with a client, the next step for the off-premise caterer is to determine the quantities and portion sizes for each menu item. This is necessary not only to be able to calculate the cost of the menu, but also to determine food quantities necessary for purchasing, preparation, and production purposes.

Computing how much people will eat is guesswork to some degree, but with experience a caterer begins to develop certain standards for consumption. Astute caterers keep records of the food production and consumption of prior events, and by combining this information with current requirements, can better determine food quantities for future off-premise events.

Too much food is always better than too little. Caterers should never run out. Extra food is necessary for a number of sensible reasons:

- Staff can make mistakes: spills, overcooking, miscounting food items.
- A few extra guests always manage to show up.
- Guests may be unusually hungry.
- There may be special, unforeseen requests. It may be necessary, for instance, to feed the musicians or other people, at the last minute and at the client's request. In addition, most off-premise caterers, at their own expense, feed the catering staff.
- There are few worse feelings than worrying during an event about whether there will be enough food to feed the guests. Every caterer at one time or another has had to reduce portion sizes during the dish-up period to ensure that there would be enough for everyone. For your own comfort, be sure there's enough.
- And finally, heed the main rule for computing food quantities: Don't guess who's coming to dinner. *Know* who's coming to dinner!

There are many true stories about caterers who were expecting one type or size of group, only to be completely unprepared when another type arrived. The off-premise caterer who says to a client, "Don't worry! I know what your group will like!" may be asking for trouble, particularly if the result is a decadent, high-cholesterol meal—for a group whose members happen to be on a low-cholesterol diet.

Some particulars to determine when planning food quantities take us back to the questions to ask clients listed earlier in this chapter:

- What is the average age range of guests?
- Are they male or female?
- Where were they before the event, and where are they going after the event?
- Are they from out of town on holiday or local?
- Are they sophisticated partygoers or occasional partygoers?

Why ask about these particulars? Well, the local or more sophisticated guest generally will eat less than the person from out of town or who goes out infrequently. Guests who are active and have eaten little all day will be much hungrier in the evening than those who have been sitting in a meeting room all afternoon after a heavy lunch. Guests will eat more if food is served buffet-style. They will eat less if the room is crowded because it will be more difficult for them to reach the food tables. And, usually, men eat more than women. Another factor: People eat more during cold weather.

Record keeping after each catered event will assist the off-premise caterer in determining future food quantities. A post-event report that includes the following information should be part of every client's file:

- Number of guests guaranteed and number who attended
- Quantity of each menu item prepared
- Leftover amount of each menu item
- Any unusual factors that may have affected consumption
- Recommended future changes to food quantities

By keeping accurate records and information about the group on file, with each successive event you should be closer to correct planning and budgeting.

So how much is "enough"? Experienced caterers generally provide between 5 and 20 percent extra for each menu item. The percentage varies based on the group's guaranteed head count, plus the potential for extra guests. The smaller the group, the larger the percentage overage; the larger the group, the smaller the percentage overage. Here are some examples:

Number of Guests Guaranteed	Percent Overage	Order Food for . . .
20	20.0	24
50	15.0	58
100	10.0	110
200	7.5	215
400	5.0	420

Note that these are general guidelines. The amounts may vary by caterer or by region.

Who pays for this extra food? The client does, because it is important that the caterer include this extra food in the cost calculation for the particular event. Specific techniques for costing are discussed in Chapter 10.

The following are general guidelines regarding suggested food quantities per person for various food items. Please be advised that these are only guidelines. Once again, food portions can vary from region to region, and from caterer to caterer.

Item	Portion Per Person
Assorted hors d'oeuvres	4–8 pieces if before dinner
	8–12 pieces if served at food stations
	18–24 if served in lieu of dinner
Large shrimp	1–2 if passed as hors d'oeuvres
	4–12 if on a buffet
Soup (first course)	6–8 ounces
Salads	1–4 ounces
Main course	4–8 edible ounces
Starches, vegetables, side dishes	2–4 ounces
Dessert	Varies (the richer the item, the smaller the portion)

For the uninitiated, determining food quantities can be stressful and difficult. Inevitably, novice caterers will, at least once, err on the side of too little food, and they can only hope that there is a nearby store or a backup plan to fill the void before the guests notice.

Determining How Much Food to Order

After you determine desired portion sizes, the next step is to determine how much food to order. Most recipes are not written for the exact number of guests at an off-premise event. Luckily, all it takes is some basic math to convert the recipe to serve the group size. Here is a simple example.

An off-premise caterer has booked a party for 100 guests. Allowing for a 10 percent overage, it will be necessary to prepare food for 110 guests. The caterer plans to serve four items, and the recipe for each of these items is written to serve 8, 12, 25, and 50 guests, respectively. The off-premise caterer needs to convert each of these to feed 110. The conversion formula is to divide the number of required servings by the number of servings in the recipe to determine a factor as follows:

$$\frac{110}{8} = 13.75 \qquad \frac{110}{12} = 9.2 \qquad \frac{110}{25} = 4.4 \qquad \frac{110}{50} = 2.2$$

The next step is to multiply the factor by the various items in the recipe to determine the quantities of each recipe ingredient. If the recipe for 50 calls for 2 gallons of milk, for 110 guests the caterer must multiply 2 gallons of milk by 2.2 to get 4.4 gallons of milk.

For some ingredients, such as baking powder, baking soda, yeast, and some seasonings, the factor method will not always work. So caterers need some overall knowledge of quantity food preparation techniques. Otherwise, experimentation before the event occurs is mandatory.

Determining Yields

Determining food quantities becomes more complicated when dealing with foods that need to be trimmed, cut, and processed before preparing. An example is freshly cut fruit. How many strawberries, grapes, melons, and kiwis will it take to produce 10 pounds of fruit?

An excellent tool to help caterers determine yields, not only for fruits, but for all types of foods, is *The Book of Yields: Accuracy in Food Costing and Purchasing*, 7th Edition, by Francis T. Lynch (Hoboken, NJ: John Wiley & Sons, 2007; available in paperback or on a CD).

Here are some specific yields for a few popular vegetables:

Vegetable	Percentage of Loss After Trimming
Asparagus	45
Broccoli	20
Carrots	30
Onions, peeled	15
Potatoes, peeled	20
String beans	15
Tomatoes	5

A basic, reliable fomula for computing an amount to order is:

$$\frac{\text{Serving Size}}{\text{Yield}} = \text{Raw Portion Size}$$

For example, suppose a caterer wishes to serve 8-ounce sirloin steaks, which will be cut by the chef from top sirloin butts. The caterer knows that 50 percent of the top sirloin butt can be used for steaks after the fat is trimmed off. So how much top sirloin butt is needed to prepare 110 steaks?

$$\frac{\text{Serving Size (8 oz.)}}{\text{Yield (50\%)}} = 16 \text{ oz. per steak before trimming}$$

$$\text{For 110 steaks, 16 oz. each} = \frac{1,760 \text{ oz.}}{16 \text{ oz./lb.}} = 110 \text{ pounds of top sirloin butt}$$

Sirloin butts average 15 pounds each, so if the caterer is ordering them only for this event, the total number of pieces needed can be calculated by dividing 110 (total pounds needed) by 15 (pounds each), which equals 7.33 sirloin butts. You should always round up, so this order would require 8 sirloin butts, for a total of about 120 pounds.

Calculating Food Cost

The food cost for each menu item can be determined by multiplying the amount of each ingredient by the cost per unit for the ingredient. In the preceding example, if the top sirloin butt costs $2.50 per pound, the total cost for the top sirloin butt is:

$$120 \text{ lb.} \times \$2.50 = \$300.00$$

To determine the cost per steak, simply divide $300 by 110 steaks, to get $2.73 per steak.

The cost of the meal can be determined by simply adding the costs of all menu items to be served, including:

- Hors d'oeuvres
- Appetizer(s)
- Soup(s)
- Salad(s)
- Intermezzo course
- Entrée(s)

- Starch(es)
- Vegetable(s)
- Garnish(es)
- Rolls/bread/butter
- Dessert(s)
- Coffee/decaf/tea/cream/sugar/low-calorie sweetener
- Any other food costs (spices, frying oil for cooking, etc.)

Later chapters in this book deal with the ramifications of food cost, as well as various methods for pricing menus.

Leftovers

Obviously, there are no leftover foods if the caterer runs out of food, but good caterers do not run out of food! There may be an exceptional situation in which extra guests are fed, but normally there are leftovers. Buffets and food stations usually generate more leftovers than seated, served events because the buffet and food stations need to look full even as the last guests are served. So occasionally leftovers are the result of extra food that the caterer brings to serve extra guests over the guaranteed amount. In most cases, however, leftover food results from guests not showing up.

The disposition of leftovers can be a major problem for off-premise caterers. Do they leave the leftovers with the client? Do they throw the food out, or perhaps donate it to a charity? Can any of the food be reused? Most off-premise caterers have established policies for disposition of leftovers, and we recommend that these be included in the catering contract. When determining these policies, you have several options to consider.

Discard. "When in doubt, throw it out." This rule should apply to any foods that have not been stored at temperatures below 40 degrees Fahrenheit or above 135 degrees Fahrenheit. There is no need to risk food poisoning. Foods that have been left out on buffets and foods that do not clearly appear fresh should be discarded.

Foods that have been exposed to contamination should never be used again. Individual unwrapped portions of food that have been served to customers may not be used again.

It is important to note that it is not always possible to identify food spoilage by appearance, smell, or taste. Food may appear to be safe even when it contains toxins or large numbers of harmful microorganisms. To repeat: When in doubt, throw it out.

Give to Client. Normally, clients who have an in-home or small business party ask for the leftovers, and this is understandable. The clients paid for them! Some caterers comply with these requests, and others refuse. Those who refuse to leave leftovers take the position that they have no control over how the food will be handled after they leave. Perhaps the client may leave potato salad out for hours before refrigerating it, only to eat it the next day and become violently ill—and the caterer gets the blame. Some caterers advise the client that the local health department prohibits them from leaving food behind. This makes the health department the villain, not the caterer.

Many caterers bring foods, such as large cheeses, that are used for display purposes and will be used at a number of events over a short time span. These are not the client's property since the cost is not normally charged in full to a particular client, but prorated over a number of events.

Many off-premise caterers who cater wedding receptions will prepare a "goody basket" of foods for the bride and groom to take to their hotel. Corporate clients for upscale events are usually not interested in keeping the leftovers; however, an exception may be company picnics, where most clients ask that their employees be able to take home the extra food. (Bring plenty of aluminum foil and carryout containers to these events, but use caution and never package food for take-home if there is any doubt as to its freshness or how it will be handled.) There are caterers who ask that their clients sign disclaimers in case anyone becomes ill from leftover food. An attorney should be consulted prior to preparing such a disclaimer form.

Donate to Homeless Shelters or a Local Charity. The Good Samaritan Food Donation Act of 1996 encourages food donations to nonprofit organizations by protecting the food donors from civil and criminal liability. This legislation makes it much easier for caterers and their clients to put leftover foods to good use in charitable feeding programs. Food donors still must comply with any state or local regulations. In addition, a food donor is liable only when acting with the knowledge that the donated food might harm another person.

Many agencies will pick up food, either from an event site or at the caterer's commissary the day after the event. For large events, some caterers schedule a food pickup at the event site, knowing that more than likely there will be leftovers. This can reduce the extra work of taking the food back to the commissary for storage until disposition. Contact the food bank in your community, or check the website of Feeding America (formerly Second Harvest), a national nonprofit organization that has long championed the cause of using food overages for charitable purposes (www.feedingamerica.org).

Some caterers erroneously think that food given to a nonprofit organization can be written off as a charitable contribution. This is not the case because the food originally was charged to the caterer's operation as an expense when it was purchased. Deducting it again would be a violation of federal tax law. The same holds true for corporate clients who deduct the caterer's bill as a business expense. They cannot "double-deduct" it, claiming it again as a contribution.

Those clients who are not deducting the cost of the party may perhaps receive some tax credit if the food is donated to a charity, but an accountant should be consulted regarding questions of this nature.

Use for Staff Meals. Many caterers allow their staff members to eat leftovers before they leave an event site, but only after it is absolutely clear to the hosts of the event that the staff isn't eating food that the hosts have legitimately paid for. The caterer very often brings extra on purpose, just to be safe, and has no intention of charging the client for it if it goes unused.

To avoid that dilemma altogether, some caterers pack box lunches specifically for their employees, particularly if it will be a lengthy event and the staff members get a break and/or are expected to eat between setup time and event start time.

Most off-premise caterers do not permit their staff to take home extra food, feeling that it may prompt them to also take home things other than leftovers.

Use at Other Facilities. Some off-premise caterers operate other facilities where left-overs may be reused. For example, a caterer who operates a restaurant may be able to resell leftover roast beef as a "barbecued beef sandwich special" the next day. Extreme caution must be used when doing this to ensure that the food has been properly handled. One way a caterer may do this is to keep any extra food packed under refrigeration or in coolers. This food is usually the *extra*—sometimes referred to as *insurance*—that was brought for unusual situations. It is kept out of the client's view, because often the cost of this food has not been added into the overall costs of the party and the food is only there for emergencies, such as the arrival of extra guests. Because this food is truly the caterer's property, it can be reused as long as it is properly stored in the meantime.

Reward Helpful People. Those who are behind the scenes at the event site and who assist the caterer are good candidates to receive food. The helpful security guard, the loading dock attendant who assists the caterer while entering and leaving the building, or the building engineer who helps out when a fuse blows should be rewarded. Food is always a welcome reward, and giving it away is less expensive to the caterer than tipping these helpful individuals.

Return to Vendor. Under certain conditions, if prearranged with a supplier, unused food can be returned if it has been held at proper temperatures and remains unopened. For example, a caterer who is serving expensive beluga caviar might arrange with the supplier to return any unopened containers that have been kept on ice. Some wine suppliers will also allow returns of unopened bottles, but only if state law permits this.

As you see, there are plenty of options for leftover food other than letting it go to waste. It is extremely important that, as an off-premise caterer, you establish a leftovers policy in advance of events, and that you inform clients of this policy as part of your contract negotiations to prevent misunderstandings after an event. There have been plenty of perfectly catered parties with unhappy clients who blamed their caterers the next day for "taking off with" leftover food "that I paid good money for!" Don't let it happen to you.

 # Summary

Menu planning involves more "planning" than it does "menu," as you have discovered in this chapter. Organizing an event involves getting as much information as possible, as early in the process as possible—from the time of day the event is to be held, to the purpose of the event and the types of people who will attend.

It is just as critical to ask the clients enough questions to feel you truly understand what they want and expect for the budget they have established. This chapter includes extensive lists of questions to be answered by clients and caterers to fine-tune their event and menu plans. The service style and the location of the event are key in determining what types of foods can be served.

When preparing the menu to share with the client, describing foods in writing can be fun, but also problematic. If you're going to make any nutritional claims about menu items, they must be accurate and you must be able to prove them if challenged. Food needs to look as good as it sounds in its descriptions, and for that, this chapter contains a basic discussion of how to round up unique serving and holding pieces, "props" for tables, and garnishing options to catch the eye.

After a brief rundown of culinary trends, the chapter explains the methods and simple formulas for determining how much food to order, along with the reasons to err on the side of too much rather than too little, and a first look at food cost calculations. The chapter ends by describing options for use of leftover food—including "when in doubt, throw it out."

Study Questions

1. Think of one additional question you believe that a caterer should ask a client, and one that a client should ask a caterer, to augment the lists in this chapter on pages 69 and 70.

2. Plan an entire food station, from the design and color scheme to the foods that will be on it and how they will be displayed. Make a sketch of the station, and include recipe ideas.

3. Use the food portion and ordering information in this chapter to create a food order for the food station you have just designed, for an event with 50 guests.

4. Come up with a descriptive food word that is not on the list on pages 81–82 and explain what kinds of foods you would use it for.

5. Can a caterer use leftover foods donated to a charity as a charitable tax deduction? Why or why not?

Beverage Service 4

Beer, wine, and liquor are expected at most catered events today. In one respect, this is great news for the off-premise caterer because beverage service can be one of the most profitable aspects of an event. Even in states that do not allow caterers to make money on the alcoholic beverages themselves, caterers can charge for all the components of beverage service—ice, mixers, juices, and so on—and for providing the bartenders who pour them. However, selling alcohol is perhaps also the riskiest part of off-premise catering. It requires extensive knowledge of licensing and legal responsibilities, extra precautions against theft, and familiarity with a whole world of beverage brands and products.

Clients frequently ask off-premise caterers the quantity and the types of alcoholic beverages to serve. The caterer who is uninformed in this area certainly won't inspire much confidence in the client, particularly when other caterers' proposals include beverage recommendations. Gaining such expertise can mean the difference between being hired or not.

In this chapter, you will learn about:

- Some of the typical liquor laws with which caterers must comply
- Responsible alcohol service and how to provide it
- How to choose liquor, wine, and beer to purchase for events

- How to determine beverage quantities
- Guidelines for serving water and soft drinks
- How to set up a beverage station at an off-premise event

State and Local Liquor Laws

Each state, county, and city has its own laws for the sale of alcoholic beverages. These laws do not always make sense to folks in the foodservice industry, but they must be followed nonetheless. A standard that applies in every state is that if an alcoholic beverage is sold, the vendor must have a license to sell it. The definition of the word *sold* is that money must change hands as a required condition of accessibility to the alcohol.

The process of obtaining a liquor license can range from very easy to extremely difficult. The application process often involves a background check of the catering company owners, including disclosure of the company's financial records. It may take anywhere from 30 to 120 days from application to approval. The process may be complicated by the location of the business—many cities have ordinances about alcohol service within a certain distance from schools or churches, although off-premise caterers can typically work around this restriction because their service sites vary. In some states, a caterer must buy the license from someone else, rather than directly from the state. In addition to licenses, cities or counties often require special alcohol permits for single events.

The details vary by state, but depending on your area, there are five basic possibilities for the sale and dispensing of alcoholic beverages:

1. Off-premise caterers are permitted to serve, but not sell, alcoholic beverages. They cannot charge the client for the alcohol itself, but they may charge for mixers, ice, glassware, and other items needed to serve it. In this case, the caterer may pick up the beverages from a liquor vendor, but the caterer may not "front" the money for the alcohol. Instead, payment must be made with the client's check or credit card, payable to the liquor vendor and for the exact amount of the purchase.

2. Off-premise caterers or their clients may obtain a special or temporary permit that allows them to sell liquor at a specific event, at a specific time, in a specific place. This type of permit is almost always sold for charitable events, not regular corporate or social functions.

3. In a limited number of states, the off-premise caterer can obtain a license to sell and serve alcoholic beverages off-premise on a regular basis. The off-premise caterer must already possess a license to sell alcohol at an on-premise location. For example, a restaurant owner, licensed to sell alcohol at the restaurant, may apply for a license to sell it at off-premise events that the restaurant caters.

4. In a growing number of states (including Florida), off-premise caterers may purchase a license to sell alcoholic beverages at off-premise events, but they must purchase the alcohol from a retail liquor outlet and cannot buy directly from a wholesale distributor.

5. Many states have different licensing requirements for selling liquor versus selling only beer and wine.

As you can see, not knowing the legal licensing and permitting requirements in an area can get you in trouble. The first step is to contact the department in your state that controls the sale of alcoholic beverages.

Liquor Laws and Legal Liability

There is an additional challenge in today's litigious society, and that is the question of liability. Who is responsible for damage, injury, or death that results from someone's drinking too much and acting irresponsibly?

In states that follow so-called common law, the responsibility for intoxication rests with the consumer of the alcohol, rather than the person who tended bar or sold the drinks to the consumer. However, the increasing social concern over alcohol abuse (and its impact on innocent victims) has prompted most states to pass some sort of *dramshop law*. The word is a combination of *dram*, originally meaning a small drink of liquor, and *shop*, meaning the place where it is sold. The term comes from England, where in the 1800s laws penalized pub owners who continued to serve "habitual drunkards" after being warned of their intoxication by their families or employers.

Today, even where common law is in force, courts often use the dramshop law concept, holding that those who serve alcohol must take some responsibility for its downside; that it is unacceptable for a business to provide drinks to a person who is, for instance, underage, already intoxicated, or has a known drinking problem. They say servers must use *reasonable care*, doing whatever is normal and prudent to foresee possible harm and protect others from it. (This idea, in legal terms, is called *foreseeability*.) This situation has prompted any number of responsible alcohol service training programs and certifications for servers and bartenders, which is a good thing regardless of legal wrangling over liability. You'll learn more about such programs later in this chapter.

Interestingly, dramshop laws may not apply to a catering staff serving alcohol that was purchased by a client, rather than by the catering company. However, there are plenty of other laws that do apply. There are several types of legal liability when it comes to alcohol service.

Third-Party Liability. An overall concept that the server or seller of the alcohol is just as much a part of the incident as the person who was harmed, or the person who did the harm. A "third party" can be a bar, restaurant or caterer, or individual server or bartender, among others.

Administrative Liability. This applies to the holder of the liquor license. This is the penalty for breaking an alcohol-related law. It may result in a fine, a temporary suspension of a license, or even its complete revocation. The penalty is always levied against the third party.

Social-Host Liability. This term is used in some states. It means that when an off-premise catering staff person serves a party guest, and that guest then injures or kills himself or herself or someone else, if the guest is deemed intoxicated under state law, the staff member, catering company, and party host could be named in lawsuits and be liable for a portion of the damages.

Criminal Liability. This means the alcohol server has broken the law by being negligent or selling alcohol irresponsibly. Criminal charges can be filed against a licensed business, the individuals it employs, or even the host of a social gathering at which alcohol was served. Being found guilty of criminal liability usually means serving jail time in addition to paying fines.

Sometimes both civil and criminal cases are filed in the same incident. If so, they are decided independently. One court, or both, may convict.

It is the responsibility of off-premise caterers in each state to know the laws and follow them. Off-premise caterers should remember that there are legal costs even to prove noninvolvement and even when there is no liability on the part of the off-premise caterer or staff. Before you ever need it, it is wise to have a discussion with an attorney about these issues. He or she may also suggest additions (or a separate addendum) to your catering contracts to alert clients about your responsibilities—and theirs—when alcohol is served at functions that you cater. You should include a clause stating that your workers will refuse to serve minors or guests who are either intoxicated or clearly at risk of becoming intoxicated.

You can also purchase liquor liability insurance. Your insurance provider should have some valuable insight about your business risks and should explain exactly what is covered by your insurance policies.

Legal Definitions of Intoxication

As with liability laws, states also vary in their definitions of intoxication and how allegedly intoxicated persons are tested and charged. In any state, a person is considered "drunk" when the percentage of alcohol in a person's blood exceeds that permitted by law. This percentage is known as *blood alcohol content*, or BAC, at the time the person's blood is tested. A BAC level of .10 means one-tenth of one percent (.1%) of the person's blood content is alcohol.

While that doesn't sound like a lot, it shows what a powerful effect alcohol can have. The chart on page 106 is from Loyola Marymount University's HeadsUP! program in Los Angeles, California. Its goal is to improve life and wellness through interventions and programming aimed at promoting mindful alcohol use and reducing risky drinking among students.

The debate about acceptable BAC levels has been long and heated because so many factors determine how any particular human body will absorb alcohol. Sex, age, overall health and mental state, weight, medications, the type of alcohol, and whether it is ingested with food all have an impact on how quickly it is absorbed into the bloodstream.

BAC levels are used to determine convictions for drunken driving, usually known as *DUI* (driving under the influence) or *DWI* (driving while intoxicated/impaired). About half the states also have *per se laws* (from the Latin *per se*, meaning "by itself"). A per se law says that a blood alcohol test is the only evidence needed to convict a person of a charge like drunken driving or public intoxication. An administrative per se law goes a little further, giving a law enforcement officer the power to immediately arrest

BAC Levels and Their Effects on Behavior

.020	Light to moderate drinkers begin to feel some effects.
.040	Most people begin to feel relaxed.
.060	Judgment is somewhat impaired.
.080	Muscle coordination and driving skills are definitely impaired. This is the legal intoxication level in most states.
.100	Reaction time and control are clearly deteriorated. This is legally drunk in all states.
.120	Vomiting usually occurs (unless this level is reached slowly or a person has developed a tolerance to alcohol).
.150	Balance and movement are impaired. At this BAC level, an equivalent of a half-pint of whiskey is circulating in the bloodstream.
.150–.250	Most people begin to experience blackouts.
.300	Many people lose consciousness.
.400	Most people lose consciousness, and some die.
.450	Breathing stops. For most people, this is a fatal dose of alcohol.

(Used with permission of HeadsUP!, Loyola Marymount University, Los Angeles, California.)

or revoke the driver's license of anyone who refuses to take, or fails to pass, an alcohol breath test. In some states there are presumptive laws, which allow arresting officers to make their own decision about a person's sobriety after they have administered a test at the scene. (You've seen these tests in movies, no doubt: An officer makes a person walk a straight line, touch a finger to the nose, answer questions, etc.) Drunken driving penalties vary widely among states, but one thing is certain: in the last 20 years, they've gotten a lot tougher.

The other two types of laws that concern caterers and their staff members are drinking age laws and so-called open container laws. Every state's legal drinking age is 21, and there are severe penalties for serving alcohol to minors, even when they have evaded the law with fake identification. Most states also have a law that prohibits drinking while driving, or having open containers of alcohol in a vehicle. Remember this when someone wants to cork a partial bottle of wine and take it home from a party you are catering.

Responsible Alcohol Service

The food and hospitality industries have been very active in promoting responsible service and consumption of alcohol. To be able to serve alcohol, your staff members are required in most states to take a course and pass a responsible beverage service test. Even if it is not a requirement, it's certainly a good idea, and this type of training is readily available. Liquor distributors, insurance companies, law enforcement agencies, and state restaurant associations may offer courses or can recommend a video version. Encourage all people who work for you, part-time or full-time, to take such a course and to sign a statement that they have completed it.

Many of the solutions offered in these courses are common sense:

- Encourage shorter cocktail hours. Rather than a one-hour cocktail time, serve drinks for half an hour, and then immediately serve the meal.

- Be sure to serve plenty of attractive hors d'oeuvres at cocktail receptions. Cheeses, fried foods, and other hors d'oeuvres that are high in fat content are excellent choices because they help reduce the amount of alcohol that is absorbed into the system.

- Have plenty of delicious, attractive nonalcoholic beverages available, such as soft drinks, fresh juices, still and sparkling waters, a tropical punch, and/or nonalcoholic wines, beers, and champagnes. Make them look just as refreshing as the alcoholic drinks.

- Have servers pour wines for the guests, rather than placing the bottles on the table, and have servers tap beer kegs and do the pouring. This helps control the rate of consumption.

- Close the bars well before an event is over; schedule last call up to an hour before the official ending time of the party. This is already an accepted practice at most sporting events and concerts, and it's easier on your staff too.

- Serve plenty of coffee and pastries toward the end of an event. Coffee will not "sober up" a person who is already tipsy, but it will help slow the absorption of alcohol and is an alternative to drinking more.

- Instruct staff members never to allow guests to pour their own drinks, no matter how busy the bar area gets.

- Never pour double shots, and do not serve mixed drinks that contain two or more spirits (Cosmopolitan, Long Island Iced Tea, Manhattan, Martini) at last call. A person's BAC level can continue to rise even after he or she has stopped drinking because the body processes the alcohol the person has already consumed.

Everyone socializes differently, but there are a few common signs of intoxication:

- Alcohol almost always impairs motor skills. People who've had too much to drink may stagger, bump into things, fumble with objects, and just seem awkward. This inability to control balance and coordination is known as *ataxia*.

- A related effect is that the drinker's reaction time is slower. Words are slurred, sentences go unfinished, or the person can't remember what he or she was trying to say. At times a person can look and act sleepy.

- Alcohol causes most people to relax their inhibitions. They may become louder, more animated, boisterous, or affectionate; they may swear more or become argumentative. For many people, drinking brings emotions to the forefront, causing them to laugh or cry more easily and without embarrassment.

- Judgment is impaired when a person drinks too much. At this point, people are less cautious and may, for example, buy drinks for strangers, switch to a stronger drink, guzzle drinks instead of savoring them, and so forth. A typical lapse in judgment is evident when they argue with anyone who tries to take their car keys from them: "I'm fine! Of course I can drive!"

As you can see, responsible service also means being vigilant and recognizing when someone appears to have been overserved. In a traditional bar or restaurant setting, a good server will chat briefly with people when they order their drinks, at least partly to assess their sobriety. A bartender will keep an eye on how many drinks a person has ordered and how those drinks appear to have affected the drinker's personality. Together, the bar staff and the waitstaff can agree to slow the speed of service to a table where the shots are being slugged quickly or the mood is getting a little rowdy.

In catering situations, this is not always so easy. However, the event captain should be notified immediately if intoxication appears to be a problem with any guest, or if an adult is sharing alcohol with minors at a party. It is the captain's responsibility to take the issue up promptly with the client or event host and, if necessary, make the security staff at the event aware of it as well. The advice in the following section should help.

Management Responsibilities

As a caterer, do not forget that it is not just the guests you are watching, but your staff members as well. Part of their work agreement with your company should include a signed statement that they will abide by the alcohol sales and service laws of your area, that they will not show up for work after drinking alcoholic beverages themselves, and that if caught drinking on the job or pilfering extra liquor meant for client functions, they will be terminated immediately.

In addition to overseeing the servers, there is plenty that a caterer/company owner can do to limit his or her liability on a job site. Simply being visible, or having a manager in the area where guests are being served, exhibits a sense of responsibility and gives clients confidence that things are being taken care of. Understaffing big events is a serious mistake when alcohol is being served. It is far better to hire more workers than needed, so that identification can be checked and there are more eyes to watch for potential problems related to drinking.

At functions like weddings and family reunions, enlist the help of the hosts in a discreet way. Ask in advance (politely, of course) whether there is anyone about whom the host or family has a particular concern, and they will probably tell you, candidly, that a little extra vigilance would be a good idea for Aunt Mabel or Uncle John. In such cases, assign a staff member to do this.

The other part of being a manager is being available to staff members who have a problem drinker on their hands and may need your assistance in dealing with the person directly or asking the host to assist in this role with an invited guest. The off-premise catering owner, manager, or supervisor should generally handle the actual "cut-off" procedure, with the support of the party host if possible. According to the Learn2Serve program created by HotelTraining.com (www.hoteltraining.com), when refusing to serve someone, caterers should be diplomatic, avoid an audience, make direct eye contact, and be sure to have the support of security or other staff members in case of an altercation. It is also important to use nonjudgmental statements:

"I am sorry. I have served you as much as I am allowed."

"I am sorry. I'm not allowed to serve people under age 21."

"I am sorry, but if I serve you another drink, we might lose our license" (or, "I might lose my job)."

Do not permit the guest to bargain, intimidate, or argue with you. You have made a decision to refuse further service for good reasons, and you must stick with it. It is best to leave the table or immediate area after you have made your statement, which prevents being drawn into prolonged explanations or arguments. You must also inform coworkers when a guest has been cut off to prevent the person from simply ordering more alcohol from an unsuspecting staff member.

In rare cases, an unruly guest must be asked to leave. It may be advisable to make the necessary transportation arrangements, such as calling a taxi or arranging for the person to ride with another party guest. (Note that a guest cannot legally be detained.) In the event that an intoxicated guest drives away, notify the police of the make and model of the car, its license number, and the direction in which it was traveling. Just because the guest has left the party does not excuse you, or the party host, from liability if something terrible happens.

Each situation is different, and your presence as an owner or manager lends automatic authority in getting a problem solved. Trust your staff members. If they are challenged by a belligerent guest who wants more to drink when he or she is clearly overserved, back them up.

A caterer should always maintain a diary or log of alcohol-related incidents that includes significant details: date and time of the occurrence, action taken by management, witnesses to the occurrence, and any other significant details that may be supportive if the caterer is required to appear in court at a later time. This can be part of the captain's report turned in after any event.

Beverages for Off-Premise Events

Off-premise caterers frequently provide alcoholic beverage service as part of their events. It is not necessary for off-premise caterers to be as knowledgeable about beverages as, for instance, a hotel bar manager, but some knowledge is necessary—the ingredients in a Martini, a few basic drink recipes, and how to stock a typical off-premise catering bar. This section offers basic knowledge in regard to beverage types and ingredients.

Stocking the Off-Premise Bar

The challenge for off-premise caterers is that, most often, you must bring everything with you—from the portable bar, to all the liquor, mixers, garnishes, glassware, and accessories necessary to mix and serve drinks. As a result, you won't be able to stock every brand of alcohol or every type of liqueur to please every discerning guest. Then again, you won't be expected to. As long as your bartenders can produce most of the basic, popular cocktails, you'll be fine.

For that, your bar setup will require the following types of alcohol. For each, we have included a short definition of what it is and some widely known brand names.

- *Blended whiskey:* A blend must contain at least 20 percent straight whiskey, plus neutral spirits. The blend may be made of two whiskies and a neutral spirit. Blended whiskies do not have to be aged. Example: Seagram's 7 Crown.

- *Canadian whisky:* Imported from Canada, it is usually a blended whisky that has aged at least three years. It has a reputation for being smooth and light-bodied. Examples: Canadian Club and Seagram's VO. (Note that *whiskey* with an *e* is usually a product of the United States or Ireland; Canada and Scotland spell it without the *e*. A few American brands with Scottish heritage also remove the *e*.)

- *Bourbon:* Whiskey distilled at not more than 160 proof, from a fermented mash of at least 51 percent corn (and usually other grains as well). It must be aged at least two years in new charred-oak barrels. Examples: Jack Daniel's, Jim Beam, Knob Creek, Maker's Mark, and Wild Turkey.

- *Gin:* A neutral spirit flavored with juniper berries for a strong, aromatic taste. Examples: Beefeater, Bombay, Gordon's, and Tanqueray.

- *Rum:* Liquor distilled from the fermented juice of sugarcane, sugarcane syrup, sugarcane molasses, or other sugarcane product. Examples: Bacardi, Captain Morgan, Mount Gay, and Ronrico.

- *Scotch:* Whiskey that is imported from Scotland. It is usually blended, and very distinctively flavored because the grains from which it is made are dried over peat fires, giving them a unique, smoky taste. Examples: Ballantine's, Chivas Regal, Cutty Sark, Dewar's White Label, and Johnnie Walker.

- *Tequila:* A distinctively flavored, relatively low-proof spirit made in Mexico from the fermented juices of the blue agave plant. The tequila made from 100 percent blue agave is known as *tequila puro*; there is also *mixto* (at least 51 percent blue agave, with sugars and spices added) and *mescal* (made from other types of agave, or not made in one of the five government-sanctioned growing regions for tequila). Examples: Jose Cuervo, and Sauza.

- *Vodka:* A neutral spirit, which is not aged, has no color, and has been filtered (usually through activated carbon) to remove any aroma or taste. Examples: Absolut, Aquavit, Grey Goose, Smirnoff, and Stolichnaya.

Off-premise caterers are frequently asked to recommend to clients those items that should be provided at bars. Preferences vary, depending on locale and the trendiness of particular drinks—for example, bourbon is more popular in Kentucky than in the northern United States; wines are more popular in California than in West Virginia. Therefore, our suggestions are intended to be general guidelines. Regional differences (and clients' budgets, of course) will play a major role in any caterer's final recommendations.

Basic liquors for any bar in the United States are the building blocks for most mixed drinks. Within each of these types, there are three general categories of items:

- A relatively inexpensive "well brand"
- A medium-priced "call brand" with a good reputation
- A more exclusive "top shelf" or premium brand

Any liquor retailer or wholesaler will be glad to share information about which brand belongs in which category, but an experienced bartender should certainly know that much already. An interesting trend in recent years is that people tend to drink less but drink better-quality liquors. This means growth for the "super-premium brands" and the rarer "boutique" Scotches, gins, and so forth. Always ask about the preferences of the host and his or her intended guests before stocking the bar. The sophistication of the clientele will also alert you to the need for stocking specialty items like cordials, brandies and Cognacs, and liqueurs.

A more complete bar, which will enable bartenders to produce a wider variety of drinks, can include the following:

- *Amaretto:* Generic name for an almond-flavored liqueur.
- *B&B:* A blend of Benedictine (a famous French herbal liqueur) and Cognac.
- *Baileys Irish Cream:* A popular liqueur made from Irish whiskey, cream, and a proprietary blend of honey, coffee, and herbs. Often used instead of cream to "spike" coffee.
- *Brandy:* A spirit that is actually a distilled wine, made from grapes and bottled at 80 proof or higher. Most American-made brandies contain added flavoring. Higher-end brands are for after-dinner sipping, but a good domestic brandy is a component of many mixed drinks (Brandy Alexander, Sidecar, and Stinger, etc.)
- *Cognac:* Upscale brandy made specifically in the Cognac region of France from only specific types of white grapes.
- *Cointreau:* The brand name of a distinctive liqueur made with bitter oranges and other types of citrus fruit.

- *Crème de cacao:* A cream-based, chocolate-flavored liqueur. Can be brown or colorless.
- *Crème de menthe:* The generic name for a mint-flavored, cream-based liqueur. Most people are familiar with its deep green color, but there is also colorless crème de menthe. That's important because some drinks (like the Stinger) require the colorless liqueur, while others (the Grasshopper) need the green specifically for its color.
- *Drambuie:* The brand name of a Scotch-based liqueur flavored with honey.
- *Frangelico:* The brand name of an Italian hazelnut-flavored liqueur.
- *Grand Marnier:* The brand name of an upscale Cognac-curaçao blend aged in oak casks before being bottled.
- *Kahlúa:* The brand name of a popular coffee-flavored liqueur. Tia Maria is another option.
- *Schnapps:* A sweet, relatively low-alcohol liqueur, either fruit- or mint-flavored. Apple Pucker schnapps is an ingredient of the popular Appletini; peach schnapps is a favorite for the cocktails Fuzzy Navel and Woo Woo.
- *Southern Comfort:* A popular, flavored whiskey-based liqueur. It is lightly sweet and contains peach juice, among other ingredients. Some bartenders use it as a substitute for bourbon.

 Just Fun to Have . . .

Cachaça: Once considered rum's poor cousin, cachaça (pronounced "ka-SHA-sah") has a tremendous following today and is the key ingredient of the Caipirinha cocktail. Instead of being distilled from molasses, cachaça is distilled from unrefined sugarcane juice. Twice as much cachaça as rum is produced in Brazil, and the government has been trying to get the name reserved only for products made there.

Chambord: Made with raspberries, vanilla, and honey, this thick, sweet liqueur is a festive addition drizzled into Champagne or sparking wine.

Goldwasser: This strong herbal liqueur made in Poland or Germany is fun and distinctive because it contains flecks of real gold in the form of paper-thin gold leaf, believed in past

(Continued)

centuries to have a beneficial medicinal effect (and today, certainly not considered harmful in such small quantities).

Limoncello: Sweet because it is made with lemon peel, not lemon juice, this bright yellow, Italian liqueur is typically served ice cold. It can be sipped by itself, or added to club soda, lemonade, or even iced tea.

Midori: The name of this melon-flavored liqueur is the Japanese word for "green." It is sometimes mixed with lemonade or used to make Sours, Margaritas, and the vodka-based drink called Swamp Water.

Ouzo: This Greek liqueur is perhaps the best known of a whole family of anise- or licorice-flavored products called *pastis* (pronounced "pos-TEESE"). They include Herbsaint from New Orleans, Pernod from France, and sambuca from Italy.

Sake: This Japanese spirit has been compared to white wine, although it is made more like beer, by fermenting rice with water, and then straining and bottling it. The result is a beverage with 14 to 16 percent alcohol that should be served lightly chilled—some restaurants heat it, which is an old-fashioned practice originally intended to mask poorer-quality sake. In a few states, adventurous American brewers are making sake.

Shochu: Many fans of this distilled Asian alcohol compare its flavor to vodka, but it has also been compared to Scotch because the flavors depend on the characteristics of local ingredients used to make it—rice, soba, buckwheat, tapioca, and even chestnuts. It is usually in the 25 percent range for alcohol content but can contain up to 45 percent. In Japan, it is served simply mixed with hot water on cold days, but it is also a cocktail ingredient.

Mixers and Condiments

There are also common drink components that vary with the drink menu you offer. Here are the most popular ones, with some notes about types, ingredients, and/or uses.

Juices. Bartenders make use of a variety of juices; the most common are orange, tomato, lemon, lime, and grapefruit, although cranberry-juice cocktail, pineapple juice, and the vegetable juice known as V8 make appearances in some drink recipes. It is in vogue in bars to tout freshly squeezed citrus juices, but for the most part, this is difficult and time-consuming for the off-premise caterer who must store and transport the juice products. Many juices are available as frozen concentrate, but purchasing cans or bottles is probably preferable for catering purposes. Some juices are available in shelf-stable containers.

Juices in cans should be transferred to glass or plastic containers after being opened, which keeps them tasting fresher, and "older" products should never be mixed with newly opened ones. Always keep juices on ice so that, when added to a drink, they won't melt the ice too quickly and dilute the cocktail.

Mixes. Many off-premise caterers realize the value of ready-made products that require no additional preparation, including drink mixes to which the bartender has to add only liquor, ice, and garnish. They are widely available for many popular cocktails: Bloody Mary, Collins, Daiquiri, Mai Tai, Margarita, and Piña Colada, to name a few. In terms of convenience and product consistency, they can't be beat. However, using ready-made mixes can be as expensive as making your own drinks from scratch, and either can affect your profitability. Mixes can also be purchased in less expensive powdered or concentrate form, to be mixed with water. Other factors for whether to purchase premade mixes are the preferences of the event host, the type of event and type of guest to be served, the skill level of the bartenders, and how busy they will be during the event.

Vermouth. You will need dry vermouth if your drink menu includes Martinis, and sweet vermouth if it includes Manhattans.

Syrups. *Grenadine* is a sweet syrup used to impart its red color to drinks like the Tequila Sunrise. It was originally made from pomegranate or cherry juice, but various brands use other types of berries (black currant and raspberry). Once in a great while, you might get a request for a Queen Mary, which is a combination of grenadine and beer.

Simple syrup really *is* simple: One part granulated sugar to one part water, heated on a stovetop until the sugar fully dissolves. Cool it, bottle it, and use it in a multitude of drink recipes. It is such a staple that it is often referred to as *bar syrup*.

Another must-have is Rose's Lime Juice—which is not really a juice, but a well-known, name-brand syrup made of lime juice and sugar. It is an ingredient of Margarita, Gimlet, and Kamikaze recipes, among many others.

Mix equal parts simple syrup and lemon or lime juice, shake vigorously with ice, and you have *sour mix*, a staple of the Whiskey Sour and Vodka Sour.

Flavorings. In a cocktail recipe, a *dash* is a measurement of about 10 drops, equal to ⅛ teaspoon. Many flavorings are packaged with a dasher right on the bottle, a dispenser at the top that allows only a drop or two at a time to emerge. Bitters are just one example. Flavored with tree bark, herbs, or fruit (but never sugar), these spirits are used in drops or dashes in some mixed drinks. Popular brands of bitters include Angostura and Campari.

Tabasco sauce is the famous liquid hot-pepper sauce; Tabasco sauce and the dark, spicy Worcestershire sauce are the nonalcoholic flavorings for the Bloody Mary.

Salt and Sugar. *Rimming* is putting salt or sugar on the rim of a glass to enhance the flavor of the cocktail within. *Coarse salt* (also called *kosher salt* or *Margarita salt*) is needed for rimming a Bloody Mary, Margarita, or Salty Dog. *Superfine sugar* (sometimes called *bar sugar*) is the choice for rimming.

Dairy Products. For cream drinks, you might need milk, half-and-half, cream, and/or for garnish, whipped cream.

Soft Drinks

After years of steady increases, soft drink consumption in the United States is now on the decline, with a couple of notable exceptions: the "flavors" categories (like orange and root beer) and the diet soft drink category. Colas and lemon-limes are still quite popular, but their sugar content and alleged contribution to America's obesity epidemic has prompted people to choose alternative beverage types.

At most catered events, however, soft drinks are absolutely necessary to meet the needs of nondrinkers and the underage crowd, as well as for mixing with liquor. In most situations, generic colas or other bargain sodas are not acceptable. A basic lineup should include:

- At least one major brand of cola
- At least one major brand of diet cola
- A noncaffeinated cola
- A couple of "non-colas" (orange, lemon-lime, ginger ale), both regular and diet
- A couple of "non-carbs" (lemonade, bottled teas)

When used in a mixed drink, a carbonated soft drink must be as cold as possible—otherwise, it loses carbonation quickly and the drink tastes flat. For large, informal events, most soft drink distributors will provide fountain-style beverage service stations using five-gallon tanks of syrup mixed with carbon dioxide and water, dispensed from spigots. This is the most economical way to serve large gatherings.

Two-liter bottles are also economical for crowds. However, for making cocktails, smaller soft drink bottle sizes or cans are preferable for a few reasons: They can be opened as needed and, if kept very cold, they ensure a fresh-tasting drink with excellent carbonation. The use of smaller bottles and cans also presents a more upscale image.

Water

For catering use, tonics, seltzers, and club sodas are important cocktail ingredients and should be part of the bar setup:

- *Club soda* is filtered and artificially carbonated water, with mineral salts added.
- *Seltzer water* is also filtered and artificially carbonated, but without the added mineral salts.
- *Tonic water* is filtered and artificially carbonated, and flavored with small amounts of citrus juice and *quinine* (a mineral salt made from the bark of the cinchona tree that gives tonic water its slightly bitter taste).

Having sufficient quantities of tonic water and club soda is especially important because guests often ask for them instead of an alcoholic beverage. On ice and nicely garnished, no one has to know the person has chosen not to imbibe.

Chilled bottled water is another staple at catered functions, and it is an excellent marketing tool for the caterer. Put your logo and company contact information on a classy label, and have a local water distributor bottle inexpensive purified water by the case for you. Offer your "branded water" thoroughly chilled at the bar, and/or on ice in receptacles around the room.

It is also true that purified bottled water generally makes a better mixed drink than tap water. However, the world has a love-hate relationship with bottled water nowadays, as a result of the serious problem of overflowing landfills and the energy and resources required to make millions and millions of throwaway plastic bottles. So ask your hosts if they have strong feelings about this topic—and/or look for some of the newer bottle styles that contain less plastic or are biodegradable. There is almost no way to get around the use of bottled water in off-premise catering.

Another way to use water is to make it part of your beverage lineup. At a wedding reception, add edible flowers to water and ice in an elegant punchbowl and it becomes a festive drink option, particularly on warm summer days. Glass or clear plastic containers of chilled water with sprigs of fresh mint and lavender are pretty, and the greens impart a light, refreshing flavor. For seated dinners, a slice of cucumber or lemon in the water glass adds a touch of class.

If you have time, making *agua fresca* can set your catering operation apart from the competition for lunches and brunches. Using any seasonal fruit that can be easily pureed (pears, berries, mango, melon), mix fresh water with an equal amount of cut-up fruit. Puree it, and then strain it to remove the pulp. Season with a bit of sugar, mint, or perhaps some lemon or lime juice—experiment to see what tastes best to you. You can offer agua fresca to guests in carafes or large, clear containers with spigots, with chunks of fresh fruit suspended in the container.

 Garnishes

Exhibits 4.2 and 4.3 in this chapter detail all the little details and must-haves for off-premise bar setup (see pages 132–133). These include the items for garnishing many of the most popular cocktails. There are lots of fun and fancy garnish options, but these are just the basics and will get you through any catered event in style. Also remember you will need cocktail picks on which to skewer some of the garnishes.

- Fresh limes (wedges)
- Fresh lemons (wedges and twists)
- Green olives (pimiento-stuffed)
- Maraschino cherries
- Celery sticks (tall enough to use for stirring)
- Cocktail onions (tiny onions pickled in brine)

Selecting Wines for Catered Events

In March 2011, a blogger named Will Richey with the Wine Guild of Charlottesville posted this general complaint online: "We all know that most catered events pour some of the worst swill one could ever conceive of as even being called wine."

That's quite an insult to a good off-premise caterer, implying that only the cheapest possible wines are poured at catered events. Caterers know this is not true in most cases—and that the host's preferences always prevail, in terms of what is served and how much they are willing to pay for it. In some cases—at charitable events, for instance—merchants have donated the wine, and the hosts simply accept what has been given and ask the caterer to pour it.

As a caterer, the best way to fight such preconceived notions about wine quality (or lack thereof) is to have enough wine knowledge to steer clients to choices that will fit their budgets, food choices, and guests' wishes. You should also be able to turn to your wine suppliers with questions and special requests. It is critical to have good working relationships with local distributors for all types of beverages.

Since many guests will rely on your recommendations for wine choices for their events, we suggest maintaining a basic list from which to pull these recommendations, which can change seasonally. In addition to the obvious advice of trying to match wines with the foods you'll be serving, some general guidelines for creating such a list include the following:

Price Points.   For every type of wine you offer when planning an event, have three selections in mind to present to the client—a lower-priced but reliable brand, a midpriced wine, and a high-end wine. Don't be shy about sharing this information with clients, so they can compare prices per bottle and make the best choice for their event and the overall wine sophistication of their guests.

Mind the Weather.   If it's a summer event, add a refreshing Vinho Verde to the list, a light Portuguese or Spanish wine with a slight spritz of bubbles, available in white or rosé. Or offer sangria with fresh fruit or a sparkling wine punch in lieu of (or in addition to) the bottled wines—easier on the budget, and a nice change of pace for the guests. For winter, how about hot spiced wine? People tend to drink more white wine in the spring and summer, and more reds in fall and winter.

Interesting Variety.   Don't just offer a Chardonnay and a Cabernet when you can get people excited about trying something just as good and a little out of the ordinary. This is where wine knowledge becomes invaluable. Offer a Sangiovese from Tuscany, a crisp Pinot Grigio from Oregon, a Carmenere from Chile, a Pinotage from South Africa. Wine knowledge enables you to recognize good deals on excellent wines from distributors, who regularly turn their inventory with special sales—and who will allow you to taste before buying in bulk.

A note of caution, however: Don't put anything on a printed wine list to offer to customers if it is not readily available in sufficient quantities from a local supplier. You might use the interesting varietals to create a seasonal "specials" list for "more discerning" clients.

Think Local. When catering events for visiting groups from out of town or for the local convention bureau, try including local wineries' products. It is a way to showcase these businesses and provide a unique welcome to out-of-towners.

Almost every state has a winemaking industry now, and it would be impractical to describe them all here. It will be to your benefit to get to know these products—and even the people who make them. Visiting a winery is fun and interesting, and your clients will benefit from your insider's knowledge.

Here are just a few websites to get you started:

- mywinetutor.com (basic info, with maps and some winery recommendations)
- vino.com (listings and links to the individual wineries of all major wine-producing countries. Invaluable!)
- winespectator.com (information from the archives of *Wine Spectator* magazine)
- wine.about.com (very readable site, written by self-taught Massachusetts-based wine expert Lisa Shea)

State or Region	Website Address
Arizona	arizonawines.com
Canada (British Columbia)	bcwine.com
Canada (Ontario)	Winesofontario.org
Idaho	Idahowines.org
Missouri	missouriwine.org
Nebraska	nebraskawines.com
New Mexico	winesofnewmexico.com, nmwine.net (New Mexico Wine Growers Association)
New York	newyorkwines.org, uncorkny.com
Pennsylvania	pennsylvaniawine.com

Rhode Island	visitrhodeisland.com/what-to-do/vineyards
Texas	texaswines.org (Texas Wine and Grape Growers Association)
Virginia	virginiawine.org
Washington	washingtonwine.org

A great overall reference book for caterers is *The Wine Bible* by Karen MacNeil (New York: Workman Publishing Company, 2001). This paperback is a reference text of more than 900 pages. It covers everything from assessing and tasting wines, to wine-making and grape varietals, and includes an in-depth analysis of all the world's great wine-growing countries and regions. This is a "must read" for any caterer who is serious about learning more about wines. Unfortunately, it is more than ten years old and therefore lacks some information about more recent trends and up-and-coming wine regions—China, for instance, or the newer American Viticultural Areas (AVAs) in the United States.

Another excellent (and more recent) choice is *Exploring Wine*, billed as the "Completely Revised 3rd Edition," by Steven Kolpan, Brian H. Smith, and Michael A. Weiss (Hoboken, NJ: John Wiley & Sons, 2010). The authors are wine educators at the Culinary Institute of America. Among its strengths are chapters on matching food and wine and explanations of how to price wines—both necessary skills for caterers.

Longtime wine writers for the *Wall Street Journal* Dorothy Gaiter and John Brecher summarize selecting wines for parties this way: "We suggest wines that simply taste good without explanation and aren't fussy." Who could argue with that?

The Classics: Grapes and Wines

Wine appreciation is one of those topics about which the more you know, the more there is to know. Of the 24,000 or so names for grape varietals, these nine are considered "classics":

White Grapes

- *Chardonnay:* The world's most popular white wine grape produces a dry, full-bodied wine with medium to high acidity and a distinctive flavor. It is often (but not always) aged in oak casks, which imparts a whole range of interesting characteristics. It is a bestseller in California and is the grape used to make French Chablis and white Burgundy wines.

- *Chenin Blanc:* These grapes are used to make both still and sparkling wines, including Vouvray in France.
- *Riesling:* This white grape is known for its combination of natural sugar and acidity. Perhaps best known as a sweet German wine or dessert wine, Rieslings are sometimes considered cloying, but some are quite sophisticated and dry, with a lovely, fruity aroma.
- *Sauvignon Blanc:* The predominant white grape of the Bordeaux region of France, this grape is also grown in New Zealand and in California, where some are known as *Fumé Blanc.* Sauvignon Blanc grapes are used to make these French wines: Graves, Pouilly-Fumé, Sancerre, and Sauternes.
- *Sémillon:* This rich, fruity but dry white grape was once used primarily for blending with Chardonnay but has now gained popularity on its own.

Red Grapes

- *Cabernet Sauvignon:* The world's most popular red grape makes some of the best reds in California, Australia, Argentina, Chile, and France, to name a few. The tannins that occur naturally in the grape's skins, stems, and seeds impart a sharpness or bitterness that is not unpleasant and also help preserve the wine, allowing it to age and mellow in the process.
- *Merlot:* This red grape produces wines that are mellow, easy to drink, and not as tannic as Cabernet, so Merlot wines can be consumed younger than many Cabernets. California, Italy, and the Bordeaux region of France are known for their Merlots.
- *Pinot Noir:* The great French Burgundy wines are made from Pinot Noir, and it is also used to make very fine Champagne. Pinot Noir is lighter than Cabernet in body and color. Oregon and California winemakers are making terrific Pinot Noirs.
- *Syrah:* This hearty red grape makes the intensely tannic, full-bodied wines that are also known as *Shiraz* in Australia. Syrah is used to make the Côte-Rotie and Hermitage wines of France.

When you taste wines, what are you looking for? The four components that make up a wine's structure are as follows:

- *Sugar:* Yes, grapes naturally contain some sugar. Sweetness is one of the first sensations you will notice at the front of your mouth, where the taste buds are most sensitive to sweetness.
- *Acidity:* This is the tartness or sharpness that you'll notice mainly on the sides of your tongue.
- *Tannins:* This is the astringency or bitterness found mostly in red wines. It might pucker your mouth.
- *Alcohol:* A wine that is high in alcohol content might prompt a sensation of warmth in the mouth. It also enhances any sweetness in the wine and imparts a feeling that some describe as fullness or richness in the mouth.

Ideally, the four components balance to create a wine in which none of the four overpowers the others. Of course, the age of the wine has a lot to do with its balance. *Glycerol*, another naturally occurring substance in the winemaking process, is a type of alcohol that contributes a small amount to the overall sweetness of the wine and some believe it helps determine whether the wine is full-bodied or light-bodied.

Color is also important. Wines get their color from the contact of the grape skin with the grape juice when the grapes are crushed. So rosé wines, for instance, are made from red grapes, but the juice is strained away from the skins after only a short contact period—hence, their lighter color. Wines that have a very dark yellow color (from white grapes) or an orange hue (from red grapes) might be past their prime. Wines don't last forever in top condition. Discoloration might indicate the bottle was stored improperly and the wine has oxidized, meaning it has come into contact with oxygen and aged too quickly.

Champagne and Sparking Wines

So many catered events are special events that Champagne and sparkling wines deserve a special mention in this chapter.

True Champagne comes only from one region, also called Champagne, about 90 miles northeast of Paris—and yes, "Champagne" is capitalized. Champagnes are blends of many still wines. They are produced by a complex process (called *méthode champenoise*) involving the addition of yeast and a bit of sugar to wine that has already been bottled, to prompt a secondary fermentation (or re-fermentation) in which natural carbon dioxide is created inside each bottle to become the bubbles in the "bubbly."

By law, wines made in the United States may also legally be labeled Champagne if they are made using méthode champenoise. The label might say "méthode champenoise," or "fermented in this bottle."

On their labels, Champagnes are categorized by sweetness. The words don't literally match the actual descriptions of the flavor, but they are traditional.

Label Term	Definition
Extra brut	Very, very dry
Brut	Dry
Extra dry	Off-dry
Sec	Slightly sweet
Demi-sec	Sweet
Doux	Very sweet

Most Champagne is clear to straw or light golden in color and is made from Chardonnay, Pinot Noir, and Pinot Meunier grapes. Blanc de blancs Champagne ("white from whites") is made entirely from Chardonnay grapes. Rosé champagnes, with their beautiful colors and luscious flavors, are considered prizes among those who know their Champagnes.

Some of the best known and most widely available Champagnes include:

Billecart-Salmon	Mumm
Bollinger	Perrier-Jouët
Dom Perignon	Piper-Heidsieck
Krug	Pol Roger
Laurent-Perrier	Pommery
Louis Roederer	Taittinger
Moët & Chandon	Veuve Clicquot

Sparkling wines are not as expensive as Champagne because they are made using methods that don't take as long as traditional Champagne making. When the label says "fermented in the bottle" (not "fermented in *this* bottle"), it means the re-fermentation took place in one bottle, but the wine was then filtered and transferred under pressure into another bottle to be sealed and sold.

In the *Charmat bulk process*, the wine is re-fermented in closed, pressurized tanks, and then bottled, also under pressure, to retain the carbonation. You might see any of these phrases on a sparkling wine label: champagne-style, champagne type, American champagne-bulk process.

Some of the most popular sparklers for off-premise catering in recent years are imports from Europe. They are more reasonably priced than the higher-end Champagnes and can add panache to a party beverage menu. These are definitely worth tasting and including on your wine list, so ask your suppliers about them. Among the choices:

- *Cava:* These Spanish sparklers are white, pink, or a lovely salmon color. They are generally of very high quality and made in the traditional Champagne method. On the label, the word *sec* or *seco* means dry, and *dulce* or *dolsec* means sweet.

- *Prosecco:* In Italy, the Charmat process is used to produce this sparkling wine that is often described as light and dry, with a hint of lemon. Some are only lightly carbonated (*frizzante*), while others are very bubbly (*spumante*). Prosecco is an ingredient in the popular Bellini cocktail. Argentina, Brazil, and Australia are now attempting to cash in on the craze by also growing Prosecco grapes.

 Wine Bottle Sizes

Some wines, especially Champagnes and sparkling wines, may be obtained in sizes other than standard 750-milliliter bottles. These can be especially festive at weddings and big events. These bottles have specific names, which you'll need to know to order them:

Name	Size	Number of Glasses
Split	187.5 mL	1.5
Half-bottle	375 mL	2.5
Bottle	750 mL	4 to 5
Magnum	2 bottles	10
Jeroboam	4 bottles	20
Methuselah	8 bottles	40
Salmanazar	12 bottles	60
Balthazar	16 bottles	80
Nebuchadnezzar	20 bottles	100

Beer

Americans spend more money on beer than on milk, juice, coffee, and wine combined! It is a multibillion-dollar market. Major brands, such as Budweiser, Coors, and Miller, as well as popular imports like Corona and Heineken, account for the major share of the market. But there are hundreds of smaller, regional microbreweries that produce beers for those with sophisticated palates, and plenty of interesting imports that may go well with certain types of foods: Tsingtao or Kirin with Asian cuisine, a good Belgian or German bock (strong, dark lager; Beck's is the top German import) with German food, and so on.

For most off-premise events, caterers can play it safe by offering the mainstream best-selling beers, such as Budweiser, Coors, and Miller, and their "light" cousins, and a couple of imports. This selection will appease most clients. However, you may be surprised at how many "beer aficionados" there are, many of them also home brewers. So it is extremely important to be familiar with the products of any local and regional microbreweries in your region—and to be able to offer them as options in party planning. In fact, the same guidelines for creating wine lists also apply to the beers you will offer. Take into account your menu, the type of event, the types of guests, the season of the year, interesting selections that are available locally, and clients' preferences and budget. At catered events, we believe it is smart to offer a nonalcoholic beer, such as O'Doul's, Buckler, Kaliber, or Haake Beck. Plenty of people wish to enjoy the flavor of beer, but without the alcohol.

If you're not lucky enough to live in the San Diego, California, area—where you can hire Craft Beer Caterers to select and serve the beer for your catered functions—good relationships with your local distributors are absolutely necessary for beer-related questions and/or special requests. There are also some terrific books and websites for boosting your beer knowledge. We recommend *The Beer Book*, edited by Tim Hampson (New York: DK Publishing, 2008), for its illustrations and organization by country; and *Tasting Beer*, by Randy Mosher (North Adams, MA: Storey Publishing, 2009), for its tasting tips that will also come in handy for wines and food. In terms of websites, Keith Olsen's website, "A Pint of Knowlege," is fun and contains wide-ranging information about craft beers and brewing, and British beer writer Jeff Evans's website, "Inside Beer," keeps up on Europe's brewpub scene, as well as industry news.

Serving beer from a keg is less expensive than cans or bottles but can be more difficult to handle because of the size, weight, and setup process. Kegs come in two sizes for foodservice use, the half-barrel (15.5 gallons) and the quarter-barrel (7.75 gallons). The beer system for use with a keg includes a cylinder of carbon dioxide (CO_2), with a pressure gauge, a faucet (called a *tap*), and hoses (called *lines*) that run from the carbon dioxide cylinder to the keg, and from the keg to the tap, using couplings. The carbon dioxide is necessary to keep the beer carbonated and to create just enough pressure to get it from the keg through the lines and into the beer glass. Optimum pressure (which you check using the gauge) is 12 to 15 pounds per square inch (psi). It would be wise to let your local beer distributor perform a little demonstration of keg setup and tapping for your bartending staff.

If keg beer isn't cold enough or has been jostled before being tapped, it may come out too foamy. In an off-premise catering situation, you might be tempted to allow customers to draw their own beer from a keg—however, we absolutely discourage this. Not only does it increase the risk of liquor liability problems, but many people do not know how to properly draw the beer. The biggest money-wasting "tradition" is promoted by folks who (mistakenly) believe you should fully open the tap for a couple of seconds and let the beer run, and then put the glass beneath it. Instead, put the glass under the spigot first, fully open the tap, and keep the glass tilted so that the beer flows down the side of the glass. This usually prevents a large, foamy head from forming on the beer.

For upscale catered events, bartenders should always pour beer from cans or bottles into the glasses for guests to avoid the unsightliness of beer containers around the room. Some brides are adamant about this, as they do not wish to look at beer bottles and cans in their wedding pictures. Another way to avoid this problem is to pour beer from quart bottles at the bar, thus eliminating the need for kegs or individual bottles and cans.

Figuring Beverage Quantities

Clients typically leave it up to the caterer to suggest the necessary amounts of liquor, wine, and beer for an event. Knowing the quantity of beverages to purchase (or to recommend that your client purchase) for a catered wedding, party, or event is one of the hallmarks of a professional caterer.

When suggesting quantities, it is always better to recommend too much, rather than too little, to be sure there is enough for the event, knowing that any excess can be returned or consumed later. Many beverage retailers and wholesalers will take back and credit you for any unopened, undamaged bottles of liquor and wine you return (another reason to have good relationships with your local vendors). Even bottled and canned beer can be returned if it has not been chilled and is still in its original packaging. Everyone is aware that it may be very difficult to go out and forage for more when you run out of something midparty. Avoid the problem by ordering plenty.

Local customs often help determine quantity. In South Florida, for example, the major alcoholic beverages served are Scotch, vodka, white wine, and beer. Bourbon, Canadian whisky, and gin are not nearly as popular. Caterers there say that rum is a favorite with younger crowds and those from out of town. You should know what the trends are in your area.

The next factors to consider are the length of the party, the type and purpose of the event, the time of day it is being held, and the temperature, especially if it is an outdoor event. Consumption will most always be greater at a Saturday-night wedding reception lasting five hours than at a one-hour corporate reception held at 5:00 P.M. on a weeknight.

It is true that most folks are drinking less alcohol, for a combination of health, religious, and safety reasons. It is no longer considered "cool" to drink a lot. As a general rule, guests will drink the following number of beverages, on average:

Length of Party	Number of Drinks
One hour	Two
Two hours	Three
Three hours	Three to four
Four hours	Four to five

It is important to note that from a 1-liter bottle of liquor (33.8 fluid ounces) you can pour about:

- 33 1-ounce portions

- 27 1¼-ounce portions

- 22 1½-ounce portions

In a standard bottle of wine (750 milliliters), there are 25.3 ounces and, depending on how generous your portions, that means four to five glasses per bottle.

Most beer is in 12-ounce bottles, and this is considered one serving.

A 1-liter soft drink bottle will provide five to seven servings, depending on the size of the glass and the amount of ice (and size of cubes) used.

Quantity Recommendations

One thing is certain when serving alcoholic beverages at an event: You don't want to run out. Caterers use a variety of simple formulas to determine how much to purchase. The ones we've heard most often are:

- *For liquor:* Number of guests × Number of hours of event = Number of drinks served.
- *For liquor:* For every ten guests, 1½ bottles per hour of event.
- *For liquor:* Two drinks per guest for the first two hours of an event; one drink per hour for additional hours.
- *For wine and Champagne:* One-half bottle for every guest.
- *For beer:* For every guest, two bottles per hour of event.
- *For beer:* Five six-packs for every ten guests.

Of course, the formulas do not anticipate that every guest will drink that much! It's all about being prepared—and that means bringing more than enough. What is not used does not have to be opened.

Exhibit 4.1 provides some very general recommendations regarding liquor, wine, beer, and mixer quantities. You will certainly modify these recommendations based on local customs, other extenuating circumstances, and your own knowledge over time. Suggested quantities are rather liberal, taking into account the facts that unopened mixers can be used at other events and unopened bottles of alcohol can be returned.

The list does not take into account wines that may be served at dinner tables for seated-dinner events. Off-premise caterers who provide wines poured at table can expect to serve another one to two glasses per person. Consumption will be greater if there is no preceding cocktail reception. Therefore, off-premise caterers can estimate an additional ¼ to ½ bottle of wine per guest. Caterers should insist that wine bottles be opened only at the direction of the host or caterer, so as to avoid having excessive amounts of opened wine left at the end of the event.

A Word About Ice

When determining the amount of ice needed for an event, off-premise caterers need to consider the length of the party; the need for chilling wines, beers, and Champagne; the need to fill water glasses; and the temperature at the party site. A five-hour outdoor wedding reception with temperatures in the 80s can require as much as five pounds of ice per person! There are wine and Champagne to chill, water glasses to keep filled, and

EXHIBIT 4.1 Liquor, Wine, Beer, and Mixer Quantities

LIQUOR-LITERS

	50 GUESTS				100 GUESTS			
	1 HR	2 HR	3 HR	4 HR	1 HR	2 HR	3 HR	4 HR
SCOTCH	2	3	3	4	4	5	5	6
VODKA	2	3	3	4	4	5	5	6
GIN	1	2	2	2	2	3	3	3
BLEND	1	2	2	2	2	3	3	3
BOURBON	1	2	2	2	2	3	3	3
RUM	1	2	2	2	3	3	4	4
BEER, CASE	½	¾	1	1	1	1½	2	2
LITE BEER, CASE	½	¾	1	1	1	1½	2	2
WHITE WINE, 5TH	6	9	12	12	12	18	24	24
RED WINE, 5TH	2	3	4	4	4	6	8	8

SOFT DRINKS-LITERS

	50 GUESTS				100 GUESTS			
	1 HR	2 HR	3 HR	4 HR	1 HR	2 HR	3 HR	4 HR
COLA	4	6	7	8	8	10	12	14
DIET COLA	4	5	6	7	8	9	10	11
DIET LEMON-LIME	2	2	3	4	4	5	6	7
LEMON-LIME	2	2	3	4	4	5	6	7
GINGER ALE	2	2	3	4	4	5	6	7
CLUB SODA	3	4	5	6	6	7	8	9
TONIC	3	4	5	6	6	7	8	9
SPARKLING WATER	3	4	5	6	6	7	8	9

FRESH JUICES (QUARTS)-ORANGE, GRAPEFRUIT, CRANBERRY

	50 GUESTS				100 GUESTS			
	1 HR	2 HR	3 HR	4 HR	1 HR	2 HR	3 HR	4 HR
	2	3	3	4	4	5	6	7

LIMES (165 COUNT)-CUT INTO 16 WEDGES

	50 GUESTS				100 GUESTS			
	1 HR	2 HR	3 HR	4 HR	1 HR	2 HR	3 HR	4 HR
	3	4	5	5	5	8	9	9

- LEMON TWISTS-ONE LEMON PER 50 GUESTS
- ONIONS AND OLIVES-FIVE SKEWERS EACH PER 50 GUESTS
- BLOODY MARY MIX-FOR DAYTIME EVENTS, SIX QUARTS PER 100 GUESTS; FOR EVENING EVENTS, TWO QUARTS PER 100 GUESTS

so on. A two-hour indoor cocktail reception, however, may require only ½ pound of ice per person. Again, it is best to err on the safe side by having too much ice. Extra ice can always be used to ice down leftover food.

The size and shape of the ice cubes are important considerations in making drinks. Rectangular cubes stack better than round ones, but round ones fill the glass better overall. Smaller cubes fit better in most glasses, but larger ones melt more slowly (a consideration in extremely hot weather). But the most important thing about ice is that it be clean and clear.

Another critical consideration for ice is keeping it fresh and clean at the event site. This means never touching the ice with anything but an ice scoop; never putting anything (glasses, wine bottles) in an ice bin to "cool it off"; never reusing ice, even if it is washed first; and always having a place to store the ice and keep it frozen until it is needed.

Beverage Stations (Bars)

Off-premise caterers frequently provide "service bars" for clients, along with mixers, ice, and glasses. Portable service bars take much physical abuse as they are moved from event to event, and they also provide only a limited amount of storage space. Therefore, many caterers prefer to use skirted banquet tables for beverage service. These provide more working space, provide plenty of storage space for backup supplies underneath the tables, and, overall, generally look better than service bars.

Exhibit 4.2 is a diagram of a service bar for a single bartender, using a table that is 6 feet long and 30 inches wide.

Exhibit 4.3 is a listing of all equipment and supplies (not including the beverages, mixers, and garnishes) necessary to set up and equip this single-service bar.

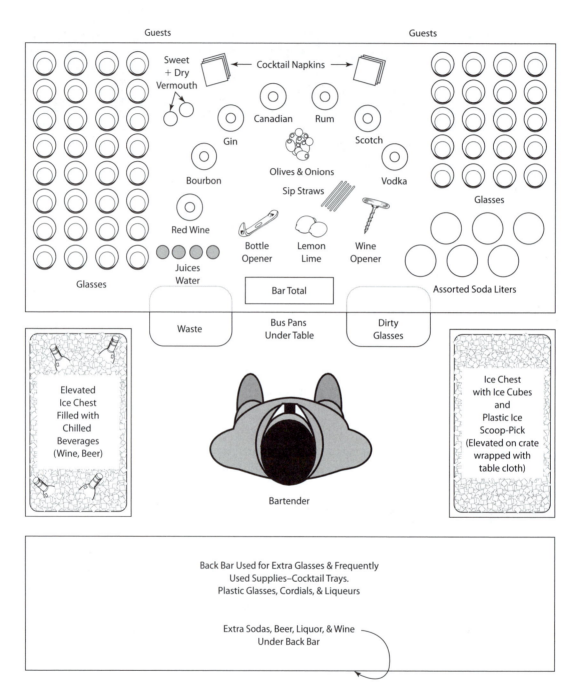

Exhibit 4.2 Beverage Station (Bar)

EXHIBIT 4.3 Beverage Station Setup: Equipment and Supplies

In addition to the liquor, mixes, juices, beer, wine and garnishes, you will need the following equipment (at a minimum) for each off-premise beverage station:

Two tables, 6 feet long by 30 inches deep

One 13-foot table skirt (can install to leave a 4-foot opening behind bar, creating an under-table storage area with easy access for bartender)

Two banquet cloths, or two 90-inch by 90-inch tablecloths (color should complement décor and other table linens)

Clips to attach table skirt to tables

Condiment trays (or bowls) for storing garnishes

Stir sticks/straws

Cocktail or "sword" picks

Wine openers

Bottle openers

Plastic pourers for liquor bottles

Ice chest (for chilled beverages)

Ice chest (for ice for use in drinks)

Plastic ice scoops

Ice pick

Bus boxes (for trash, dirty glasses)

Cocktail napkins

Cocktail trays

Plastic cups

Glassware

Plenty of clean bar towels

Empty plastic crates (on which to elevate ice chests)

Small tablecloths (to wrap around plastic crates)

Your drink recipes might necessitate other items: salt and pepper, horseradish, cranberry or grapefruit juice, orange slices, and so on. What's important is that the beverage station easy to assemble, that there's a list like this one to double-check—and that it's ready to go when you need it.

Eight-foot banquet tables may be used to set up beverage stations for two bartenders. It is best that each bartender have his or her own supply of liquor, soda, and glasses to eliminate reaching. They generally can share ice and cold beers and wines, provided the chests are strategically placed between them. For very large events, sometimes a *barback* is hired. This person assists the bartenders—opening bottles, making garnishes, replenishing supplies, and so on—allowing the bartenders to focus on filling drink orders quickly and efficiently.

There are also portable bars available on casters, some of which fold into two-foot widths for easy transport and storage. (Some facilities will already have these on-site.) It is important to choose a portable bar that it is sturdy but easy to maneuver, has a stain-resistant laminated top and storage shelves underneath, and contains enough "plumbing" to be able to drain away and store water from melting ice in the ice bins.

Bar Service Procedures

Following certain guidelines will make the bartenders' jobs easier at catered events. The caterer should always check with the client regarding whether to serve alcoholic beverages to band members, photographers, floral designers, and others engaged to work at the event. As a general rule, serving alcoholic beverages to people "working the party" is not advisable. Under no circumstances should the caterer permit any of his or her own staff members to consume alcoholic beverages while working a catered event.

Every drink should be served with a cocktail napkin, and the bartender will need about three cocktail napkins per person, per hour, because people often pick up more than one and use them for carrying hors d'oeuvres, mopping up spills, and so on.

The bartender should fill wine glasses no more than two-thirds full. This is a standard five-ounce serving, looks to be a decent size in most glasses, and keeps guests from spilling from an overly full glass.

Glasses should never be refilled—a fresh glass (with fresh ice, if it requires ice) should be provided for every beverage. And at upscale events, it is best to serve everything in glassware, with no cans or bottles for the guests to carry around.

Caterers should establish a clear policy with staff members as to how much wine and liquor to open prior to the event. Opening too little will result in wasted time during the event; opening too much will result in wine that cannot be returned for credit. A good policy is for the caterer to prohibit any staff member from opening wine and liquor without first asking the on-site event captain or supervisor.

Near the conclusion of a party during which glassware is used, it is always good policy to station a catering staff person near the exit to ensure that guests do not leave with glassware. In most states, it is illegal for persons to have open containers of alcoholic beverages in vehicles, so giving a plastic cup to those who have not yet finished their drinks is simply not proper, and probably not legal, unless the guests are leaving by motor coach, limousine, or taxi. Of course, it is permissible to provide plastic cups for nonalcoholic beverages.

Summary

Serving alcohol at events is too profitable an option for a catering company to ignore, although it comes with its own unique set of challenges and responsibilities. This chapter offers a look at them, beginning with a discussion of common liquor laws and the importance of becoming familiar with them. The various types of legal liability are defined, along with the legal concepts that guide servers of alcoholic beverages in determining when to serve—or refuse to serve—guests. The need for responsible alcohol service training is strongly emphasized, and background information is given about intoxication levels and behavior cues.

The off-premise bar presents other types of challenges. It is almost impossible to stock a "full" bar, but this chapter lists the basics that enable caterers to produce most of the popular cocktails. Information is included about mixers and juices, condiments and flavoring ingredients, and options for serving water at events.

Caterers are expected to know enough about wine and beer to make creative and useful recommendations to clients to fit their budgets, event themes, and levels of guest sophistication. The chapter contains basic guidelines that can help caterers work with local wine and beer distributors to craft those recommendations.

The chapter ends with guidelines for determining beverage quantities for events and details about bar setup.

Study Questions

1. What are the four types of legal liability an off-premise caterer should be familiar with? Briefly describe them, and their potential effects on service policies.

2. Describe the difference between Champagne and sparkling wine.

3. Create a basic wine list for a catered event with 12 wines—four wines, each at three price points—using the information in this chapter and additional Internet resources. Briefly explain your selections.

4. Create a basic beer list for a catered event, with six beers. Explain your selections.

5. Write a list of all items that will be needed, and their quantities, for a two-hour cocktail reception for 75 people.

Catering Equipment

Starting your catering business in someone else's commercial kitchen—say, a church or corporate facility—instead of your own might not seem like an ideal situation at first glance. You have to work with the space as is, instead of designing and equipping it exactly the way you want it. However, this experience can easily translate into a couple of major advantages.

First, you have no choice but to adapt to the site. That's perfect training for off-premise catering, where every event location is different, with advantages and/or limitations for caterers. Second, it gives you a chance to "test drive" equipment—to decide what works and what doesn't, what is useful and what is unnecessary—for the day you are able to set up your own commissary space.

In this chapter, let's assume that you've reached that all-important milestone and are ready to select the equipment necessary to operate an off-premise catering business. You will learn about:

- Factors that help determine equipment choices
- Guidelines for commissary space layout

- Types of equipment necessary for food preparation
- Trends and innovations in equipment design
- Food holding equipment
- Equipment and vehicles for transporting food
- Equipment for events: tables, chairs, linens, flatware
- Deciding whether to purchase or rent

An understanding of commissary equipment is essential for success in this field. This is the equipment you have in your kitchen facility for food production and is typically not portable. You need to be familiar with it, including how to buy it—and whether to buy it at all. Millions of dollars are wasted annually by inexperienced operators buying expensive equipment they just don't need. This chapter will show you how to make intelligent equipment purchases, including vehicles for transporting your wares.

Smart caterers also know that owning certain types of front-of-the-house equipment is an excellent way to generate additional profit. They figure that if they are renting similar items over and over again, at some point, purchasing them becomes more cost-effective. If the budget allows, and if there is room to store equipment and someone who can maintain it, you can then provide equipment for your own events, renting items to clients who otherwise would be paying other rental companies. It's a service for the clients, and means extra profit for you. It also gives you some negotiating room in booking events as you control the prices you charge for these items.

Determining Equipment Needs

The types of required off-premise catering equipment are determined by analyzing a number of factors.

Menu. The foods you will serve greatly influence equipment selection. For example, a caterer who plans to serve a variety of deep-fried hors d'oeuvres will require more fryolator (deep fryer) capacity than one who plans to simply offer assortments of cold canapés. The cold canapés will require rolling racks and refrigerated storage, whereas the caterer serving hot hors d'oeuvres could store them before cooking in plastic containers that could be kept cold in ice chests at the event site, in accordance with local health department regulations.

Beverage Service. Will your company offer service of alcoholic and nonalcoholic beverages? If so, glassware, bar utensils, and beverage stations (portable bars) will be necessary. The latter topic was discussed in Chapter 4.

Style of Service. How fancy will your parties be? A caterer specializing in barbecues will more than likely require only disposable plasticware and paper table coverings, whereas an upscale caterer will need plenty of silver-plated flatware, crystal stemware, fine linens, and other first-class equipment.

Existing Equipment. This category includes both the commissary equipment and whatever is available at the event site. An off-premise caterer who leases a fully equipped commissary will have little need for additional commissary equipment. If you work frequently at party sites where there are existing bars, you won't need to be concerned with purchasing or renting bars for events. In short, don't spend money when you don't really need to.

Number of Guests. What is the maximum number of guests you will most likely serve? Off-premise caterers who want to specialize in home parties for 30 or fewer guests will require substantially less equipment than those who cater mega-events with thousands of guests.

Other Factors. These could include regional influences—you might need clambake equipment for New England parties, portable meat-smokers for Southern barbecues. The specific equipment needs for each party are best determined by analyzing the party contract, and then preparing a layout of the event. Include the guest seating area, the cocktail area, the food preparation and staging preparation areas, and all buffet tables and/or food stations. Such diagrams require detailed planning, which will help you think through what is necessary for an event—and there are computer programs (such as Room Viewer, EventPro Planner, Frogware, and others) that can help with this.

Make lists pertinent to each area, including everything from tables and chairs, to the smallest details, such as toothpicks, cutting boards, and buffet spoons.

Equipping a Catering Commissary

In Chapter 2 we discussed various methods of selecting a commissary location. This section covers key factors in planning a catering commissary, including basic equipment types.

Our first suggestion may sound difficult if you're on a budget, but in the long run, it will save you money. If possible, hire a professional planner who knows how to lay out a kitchen efficiently. Almost all restaurant supply companies employ planners, and although you should take advantage of their suggestions, remember they are trained to sell as much equipment as possible, of the particular brands they happen to market. That's understandable, but it doesn't help you as much as an independent planner who will have your best interests in mind and can negotiate with multiple suppliers to get the best deals.

A professional planner will properly lay out an off-premise catering commissary, ensuring that the following major areas are arranged for maximum efficiency:

Receiving and loading

Storage

Refrigeration and freezer space

Preparation

Main cooking ("hot line")

Bakery

Pot washing and dishwashing

We've mentioned that the menu will dictate the necessary equipment, so have the menu well developed before you hire a space planner. Most commissaries will require ovens, broilers, and steamers but may not require deep-fat fryers, particularly if frying is to be done at the event site. Most fried foods, other than fried chicken, do not store well and are best cooked and served immediately. Solicit the opinions of your staff members, especially those who will be working in the commissary. These folks often have years of experience working in other operations, dealing with good and bad equipment and designs, and you can benefit from their knowledge.

Exhibit 5.1 is a generic layout for a 1,500-square-foot off-premise catering commissary, provided by Hugh Cunningham, a professional independent designer in Fort Lauderdale, Florida.

Before you start planning a catering commissary, you should also have a general idea of the projected sales volume. A caterer who's happy with sales of $250,000 per year definitely will not need a commissary capable of producing $5,000,000 per year in sales. The most important guideline: It is usually better to err on the smaller size, with the option of expanding. A facility that is overly large will require extra upkeep and maintenance and is simply not as efficient as a more compact facility in which distances between storage and work areas are shorter.

In creating the design (and you should have a hand in it, even when you do hire a professional), equipment should be placed according to these guidelines:

- Excessive walking (and carrying of heavy supplies) should be reduced.
- Electrical equipment should be close to major utility connections.
- Multipurpose equipment should be close to all staff.
- Equipment used most often should be close at hand.
- Employees shouldn't have to walk more than ten feet to a sink.

It's always advisable to order movable equipment on sturdy casters (wheels). This makes it easier to clean, allows different areas to share dual-purpose items, and allows for future flexibility if the layout changes.

Equipment mounted on walls is another big plus as far as cleaning is concerned. In addition, equipment equipped with floor grates for spillage, and stainless steel backdrops behind ovens and deep fryers, make cleaning easier and improve fire safety.

It is imperative to have separate areas for incoming ingredients and supplies and finished products that are being delivered to event sites. Another consideration is the overall appearance of the commissary. As part of your sales pitch, you may be required to show the kitchen to clients, who often want to see it, so make certain it is clean and well lit.

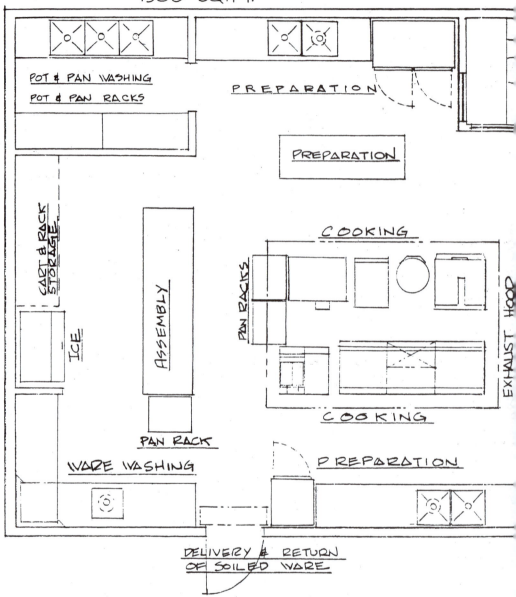

Exhibit 5.1 Generic Catering Commissary Design

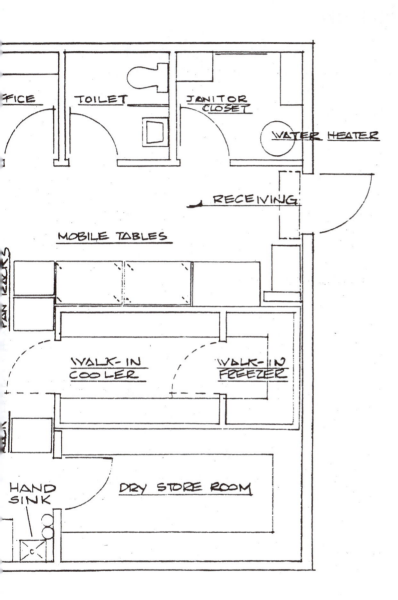

OFFICE   TOILET   JANITOR CLOSET

WATER HEATER

RECEIVING

MOBILE TABLES

PAN RACKS

WALK-IN COOLER   WALK-IN FREEZER

HAND SINK   DRY STORE ROOM

Exhibit 5.1 (*Continued*)

Commissary Equipment

A discussion of all basic commissary equipment follows, along with the criteria for purchase. Off-premise caterers should be aware that each catering operation requires a different equipment mix and perhaps a unique layout, as each will have different menu requirements and constraints. Use this discussion as a basic checklist and a guide. It is divided into cooking appliances, other types of appliances, and food holding equipment.

Cooking Appliances

We begin with a discussion of the most recent innovations, as of this writing, that could benefit off-premise caterers. The combined needs to save space, energy, and time in most foodservice businesses have prompted manufacturers to create multiuse equipment that eliminates the need for multiple, individual commercial appliances that, until now, have been the workhorses of any kitchen.

For instance, Rational has unveiled its Self-Cooking Center. The company says that it replaces "up to 50 percent of all conventional cooking appliances, such as hot air ovens, stoves, boiling pans, steamers, and deep fryers," and that it cooks food 15 percent faster than conventional combi-steamers. The unit automatically detects the optimum cooking time, temperature, and conditions (moist or dry heat, air speed) for the product, and can bake, blanch, broil, poach, roast, steam—whatever is necessary. More than one food can be cooked simultaneously.

Of course, some will see the biggest advantage as its simplicity and programmability, which means less need for kitchen workers. A machine that is easy to operate and can cook all night, unsupervised, can't help but appeal to busy caterers.

The Self-Cooking Center comes in either electric or gas models, in sizes from tabletop (which can be stacked) to 800-pound, 5-foot-tall units with output of 300 to 500 meals per day.

Another company, IRINOX, is touting its MultiFresh unit for quick-chilling, freezing, proofing, and thawing just about any item—fruits, meats, seafood, bakery items, soups, and so on. Blast-chilling or shock-freezing—both terms for quickly reducing a cooked food's temperature to get it out of the danger zone for food safety purposes—enables a catering kitchen to prepare foods in advance and preserve them at their peak until they are needed. The company says that its technology works so well that it triples the shelf life of products, increases food yield by 10 percent, and eliminates the problem of freezer-burned foods. MultiFresh is an electric unit, available in seven sizes, with yields from 23 pounds to 155 pounds per cycle.

We would suggest a visit to a restaurant equipment show or a commercial kitchen showroom to learn more about these and other exciting advances in cooking technology. In the meantime, we'll include the following discussion about the tried-and-true basics of most catering kitchens.

Range Top. The most often used piece of commercial kitchen equipment is the range top, the heated cooking surface commonly known in home use as a stove. Range tops can be ordered with different kinds of surfaces:

- Individual burners, either gas or electric—these are often known as *open top* or *grate top*, indicating the open-flame (gas) burners and metal grates over each burner on which the cookware sits.
- A smooth, single-surfaced flat top or hot top—*flat-top* ranges are best to accommodate various large pots and pans, but they take more time to heat up and cool down than open-top ranges.
- A combination of both.

There are also three basic types of ranges:

- The restaurant range, also called a *café range*, is popular for smaller foodservice businesses, or places where it is not going to be used constantly. It usually contains between six and ten open burners.
- The *heavy-duty range* is more of a workhorse, made of heavier materials, with burners that cook hotter and faster than restaurant ranges. It is designed for frequent and high-volume cooking.
- The *specialty range* is any one of several types of custom ranges outfitted for specific types of cooking—Asian, Mexican, soups and stocks, and so on.

Most chefs prefer gas ranges, and gas is usually the most readily available heat source in a commercial kitchen, but all appliances are also made in electric configurations.

Range Oven. Most caterers want to make the best use of their kitchen space, so they order ranges with single or double ovens below. An oven with more than one cavity and set of controls is called a *stack oven* because up to three of these ovens can actually be stacked, one on top of the other, to save space.

A main concern is the power source for these kitchen workhorses. Based on the specific location of the commissary, an experienced designer can determine the best power source: gas, electricity, or both. The floor of the oven is called the *deck* (that's why it's sometimes called a *deck oven*) and it's made of either stainless steel or ceramic (ceramic is best for baking bread). Most ovens also have at least one metal rack to hold pans, but you can order more. Some models have steam injection capability for crusting breads and rolls.

Convection Oven. A popular alternative to the conventional oven is the convection oven. It uses internal fans to circulate the air inside the oven cavity, which results in 25 percent less cooking time and temperatures that can be 20 percent lower. It also requires a shorter warm-up period. Convection ovens tend to dry out the food, so many caterers select a convection steam oven to introduce moisture into the cooking process. These ovens can do double duty as pressureless steamers. Many are computerized to provide different types of heat for different purposes. For example, they can first steam a duck to seal the pores, and then roast it, and, finally, at the end of the cooking cycle, circulate hot air to brown the bird before serving.

Rapid-Cook Ovens. TurboChef, a division of the Middleby Corporation, invented the first rapid-cook technology, which uses impinged, forced air to brown food, and microwave energy or infrared heat to cook food from the inside. It sounds pretty technical, but the results speak for themselves: Rack of lamb in less than five minutes, fresh pizza dough in three minutes, and more. One of their chief advantages for caterers is that these can be used without an exhaust hood.

Combination Oven/Steamer. This piece of equipment can bake and roast like a convection oven, steam and poach like a steamer, and cook or reheat food without drying it out. With three operating modes, it can perform these functions:

- Cook with pressureless steam at 212 degrees Fahrenheit
- Convection-cook at temperatures up to 500 degrees Fahrenheit
- Use a combination of steam and heat to provide typically faster cooking than dry heat alone, while browning the product and limiting shrinkage

These versatile units are available in all sizes, from small-volume countertop units, to floor-mounted rolling units with large capacities for banquets and institutional use.

Cook-and-Hold Oven. This type of oven roasts at low temperatures for many hours, resulting in greater moisture retention and better portion yields than conventional ovens. Most manufacturers claim 7 to 10 percent shrinkage, compared with 25 percent for meats cooked in traditional ovens. A 14-pound prime rib, for instance, yields 11 servings when cooked in a convection oven versus 15 servings when produced in a cook-and-hold oven.

Microwave Oven. Don't assume microwave ovens are just for home use! They also come in handy in commercial settings, to thaw and reheat small amounts of food quickly, and can also be purchased with a special attachment for browning. It is important to buy a commercial-grade microwave—the home-use models are not sturdy enough.

Fryer. Often called *deep fryers* or *deep-fat fryers*, these appliances come in countertop and freestanding floor models with capacities of anywhere from 15 to 130 pounds. A standard rule for calculating fryer size is that it takes six times as much fryer oil (the "fat") by pound as the item to be fried. For example, a 15-pound fryer will fry 2.5 pounds of food at a time (15 divided by 6). A caterer who specializes in fried chicken will need a larger-capacity fryer than one who does little frying. There are gas, electric, and infrared models. Technological improvements in this equipment category have created quick-recovery fryers, capable of reaching ideal frying temperatures very quickly, even after being loaded with food that is frozen. The quicker the optimum temperature is reached, the less oil is absorbed by the food.

Griddle. This cooking surface can be smooth, or grooved for frying hamburgers and other meats. It is typically used in commercial settings for frying or scrambling eggs, making pancakes, grilling sandwich surfaces, and sautéing. The griddle surface is called its *plate*, and most surfaces are sectioned into two or three separate plates with separate heat controls, so you don't always have to heat the whole surface.

Tilting Braising Pan. This flat-bottomed appliance looks like a griddle with raised sides, and, indeed, it can be used as a griddle, kettle, frying pan, or even a grill. It's a very handy workhorse that can reduce preparation time by as much as 25 percent simply because it tilts easily (with a hand crank or, for larger models, an electric motor) to remove the cooked foods.

Broiler. This appliance cooks food by bringing it into close proximity with intense, radiant heat, from either below or above. It browns the surface while keeping the inside of the product tender and moist—and not just meats. When the heat surface is above the food, the appliance is known as an *overhead* or *overfired broiler*, for obvious reasons. When the heat comes from below, it's called an *underfired broiler* or *charbroiler*. Broilers may be heated with gas or electricity or by burning wood.

Barbecue Grill. This appliance comes in handy if your menu includes barbecued foods. Its heat source is either charcoal or propane gas. Charcoal grills are less expensive than gas grills and produce excellent flavors, particularly with the addition of various types of wood chips. Gas grills provide a quick start, controllable heat, and a fast cool-down.

Steam-Jacketed Kettle. Kettles range in size from 20 quarts to 300 gallons and come in table-mounted and freestanding floor models. The steam-jacketed kettle is like a big bowl within a bowl; between the bowls, the empty space fills with steam, and the pressure of the steam can be adjusted higher (to cook foods quickly) or lower (to cook them slowly). Smaller models tilt to ease the removal of food. Steam-jacketed kettles are extremely versatile and excellent for preparing soups, stocks, and sauces. The latest innovation is a steam-jacketed griddle, with a flat surface. It allows for more uniform surface heat and quicker surface-heat recovery time. This means more uniform searing and browning and generally less energy use.

Compartment Steamer. Also known as a *pressure cooker*, this appliance cooks food by transferring heat from steam onto the food, in this case, building pressure inside the cavity of the appliance. High-pressure steamers will cook small quantities of food very quickly, and low-pressure steamers will cook larger amounts of food, but not as quickly. They run on either gas or electricity, but a key consideration is whether there is an existing steam source in the commissary. If there is not, acquiring steam appliances will mean ordering them with a self-contained steam generator.

A third option—and the most up-to-date—is the pressureless steamer. It has the same advantage as the others, of cooking foods with less loss of color and nutrients. However, pressureless steamers use up to 85 percent less water than pressurized steamers, and less energy as well.

Other Appliances and Needs

Coffeemaker. Most commercial coffee companies provide coffee-making equipment in exchange for using their coffee products. These units are installed in catering commissaries, where the coffee is prepared, and then the coffee is transferred to thermal containers and delivered to the party site.

The three main types of coffee-brewing apparatus are urns, satellites, and bottles. Urns are still the traditional means of brewing coffee in large batches; you've seen them in commercial businesses for years, made of stainless steel with a tap at the bottom to serve from. Satellites brew coffee directly into insulated containers for distribution to points of service. Bottles are used for producing smaller batches of coffee. Air pots are insulated containers, handy for holding and transporting coffee in small quantities. Depending on the need for setting up a full-service coffee bar with baristas making the brews, many caterers now purchase espresso-brewing equipment, and even coffee grinders to roast their own beans.

For brewing coffee at an event site, you can use standard plug-in coffeemakers or portable urns. Farberware's brewer is highly polished stainless steel, suitable for placement on most buffets. At very high-end events, however, silver-plated samovars are necessary.

Food Mixer. Technically, this item is called a *vertical mixer* or *planetary mixer*, and it is used for mixing, blending, kneading, whipping, and emulsifying. In addition to the standard beaters (or agitators), stainless steel attachments, such as whips, dough hooks, and pastry knives, can be used. They are more expensive than aluminum attachments but will last longer and not react with (and discolor) food products.

Almost every kitchen has a 5-quart mixer, and often a couple of larger ones too. Countertop mixers are called *bench model mixers* because of the stainless steel bench (table) they sit on. These come in capacities of 5 to 20 quarts; larger floor models range from 20 to 80 quarts. A 20-quart mixer can handle most mixing jobs for a small- to medium-sized caterer; the largest mixers are used by operations that make a lot of dough (no, not money!), such as commercial bakeries and pizzerias.

There are lots of nifty attachments for mixers for cutting and chopping, as well as bowl adapters (to use smaller bowls with larger mixers), bowl guards (to cover the bowl during mixing, thereby protecting the user's hands), bowl dollies (to roll big, heavy bowls instead of lifting them), and more.

Handheld Mixer. This is an absolute requirement for caterers doing small-batch cooking because of its portability. Many models are cordless and can be recharged in three hours or less. They can be fitted with agitators to blend, beat, stir, and knead dough, and their mixing shafts are detachable for easy cleaning. For even smaller jobs, we also like Cuisinart's cordless, rechargeable hand blender, which is lightweight and durable.

Food Processor. There are two standard types of food processors, used for cutting, chopping, and mincing foods quickly. The bowl-style processor has a rotating bowl and two blades (sometimes called *plates*) to do the work. Some models have different types of blades to do different cuts. The food is placed in the bowl, which is then sealed; the chopping is done; and the food is removed.

There are also continuous-feed processors; the food is placed in a chute at the top and comes out another chute, sliced, chopped, or otherwise processed. Home-use food processors just won't hold up under commercial rigors. For catering, a minimum of ½ horsepower is required, and a 5-quart capacity bowl is the minimum. Some models come with larger bowls and more horsepower. Processors are sold with a variety of options, including slicing disks for cutting vegetables and fruits, shredding disks for julienning vegetables and grating hard cheeses, and so on. A Buffalo chopper may also be used in off-premise catering operations, with a bowl that turns as the blade cuts soft foods like cooked vegetables.

Food Slicer. In addition to its ease of use for various tasks, as opposed to hand-slicing meats, cheeses, onions, and so on, a food slicer cuts more accurately than a knife. This means better portion control, a more uniform product, and cost savings. Slicers may be manual or automatic; both types involve moving the food back and forth on a carriage that slides it across a revolving blade. Slicers are usually identified by the diameter of the cutting blade, and the thickness per slice can be adjusted by setting a gauge plate on the equipment.

Refrigerator and Freezer. You'll need a number of these, and there are several basic types of refrigerated appliances:

- Walk-ins (or roll-ins) are large enough to stand in or to roll carts into. These can be either refrigerators or freezers and are used for bulk storage.

- Reach-ins are refrigerators installed near the work areas. They look the most like home refrigerators, but they must be kept colder because they're "reached into" very often, which affects the inside temperature. Some commercial reach-ins have several compartments with a separate door for each.

- Pass-through refrigerators are a type of reach-in, with doors on two sides, opposite each other, so they can be shared by two work areas. Food can be placed in one side and taken out of the other; for instance, salads made in a prep area can be taken from the other side as needed by the waitstaff.

Walk-in refrigerators and freezers should be installed flush with the floor, so it's easy to roll heavy items inside. They should have doors with handles that open from both inside and outside (to avoid shutting anyone in accidentally) and a door closer that works automatically when employees forget to shut it. Some have heavy-duty plastic strip curtains inside the big door, which can save energy by holding cold air in even when the door is open. Most commercial freezers and refrigerators have a safety light or buzzer that signals when the internal temperature is too high, and exterior-mounted thermometers so you can check the temperature without having to open the door or enter the unit.

Ice Machine. Ice-making equipment is rated by the number of pounds of ice it can produce in 24 hours. However, this rating is based on an incoming water temperature of 60 degrees Fahrenheit and an air temperature of 70 degrees Fahrenheit. A 10-degree increase in air temperature will reduce capacity by as much as 10 percent.

Your choice of ice machine will also depend on the types of cubes you need—you may wish to buy more than one machine, for cubed ice and crushed or flaked ice. Water-cooled ice machines are good for indoor use because they reduce the amount of heat generated within the kitchen.

To determine the best capacity for an ice machine, estimate the amount of ice needed for the busiest week. Multiply that amount by 1.2, and then divide by 7. This will give you an amount you can compare with the manufacturer's rating of the machine. The bin that stores the ice should normally hold twice as much ice as the machine can make in 24 hours. If your catering company has heavy weekend demands, you may wish to obtain bins with even larger capacity.

Ice machines require good drainage in addition to a water source. You should also install a water filter on the water line that feeds the machine. This will extend its life, as well as improve the taste of the ice and avoiding "off" odors. Many machines have self-cleaning capabilities and rust-free features.

Dish Machine. The type of dish-washing system you'll need depends on the volume of dishes (and pots and pans) to be washed and the amount of space you have. Commercial dish washing must be done at certain temperatures for sanitation reasons, and the heat generated makes ventilation a must in your dishroom. (The dishroom must also include space to stack and scrape dirty dishes and to dry clean ones.)

The basic machines require dishes to be placed into dish racks for washing. The racks are placed either inside the machine or on a conveyor belt that runs through the machine.

(The latter type is called a *flight machine* or *rack conveyor*.) Many dishwashers require a booster heater to bring the rinse water temperature to 180 degrees Fahrenheit for sanitation purposes, but some of the newer models are equipped with low-temperature, chemical sanitizing units. You can hire a chemical company to provide detergent for the machine, as well as parts and preventive maintenance services.

Food Waste Disposer. What is known as a garbage disposal in a home kitchen is referred to in a commercial kitchen as a *food waste disposer*. It is installed as part of the dish-washing system, usually at the "dirty end" of the dish machine. It grinds up food scraps, which end up as part of the kitchen's overall waste output. Disposers are usually rated according to their horsepower. Other points to consider are the type and volume of the food waste and its physical size, the ability to reverse the flywheel that grinds the waste (to free it up when it jams), the availability of parts and service, and local health department regulations.

Sinks. Heavy-duty kitchen sinks should be made of stainless steel, have coved (not sharp) corners (rounded, not sharp), and be wall mounted whenever possible to make them easier to clean underneath. A three-compartment sink is used for pot washing and is almost always required by local health departments. Each part of the sink should have both hot and cold water, an overflow drain, and a faucet that can swivel to reach all three compartments.

Separate hand sinks for hand washing are also required by health codes. They don't have to be very big, but they do have to be convenient to kitchen workers.

Ventilation Equipment. Local health departments require that exhaust hoods (or canopies) and grease filters be placed above all commercial cooking equipment (your "hot line") to remove the heat from the commissary, as well as filter out the grease, which becomes a fire hazard. There are building codes that will specify how well the system must work; the industry norm is that the ventilation system must exhaust a total of 4 cubic feet of air per minute per 1 foot of floor space in the room. And, of course, ventilation hoods must be cleaned regularly, and their filters changed, to reduce the chance of fire.

Fire and Security Systems. Fire-retardant systems are required in new commissaries, and security systems will help keep insurance rates lower and deter criminal activity. Local police and fire departments can provide excellent advice on these systems.

Receiving Scale. A receiving scale is a must for all off-premise caterers. Incoming supplies bought in bulk should be weighed to make sure you're not being shortchanged. There are several types of scales for this purpose, ranging from countertop scales (to measure goods of 50 to 200 pounds) to beam scales that can roll on casters (wheels) and weigh objects from 100 to 1,000 pounds. Another option is digital electronic scales, which are precise, as well as compact.

Stainless Steel Preparation Table. Prep tables should be conveniently located throughout the commissary and should include adequate storage space underneath and above them. Their edges should be rolled or coved, and the table height should be about 4 inches below the worker's elbow, for comfort.

Rolling Racks. These are aluminum-frame racks on wheels that hold sheet pans. Depending on the racks' size and purpose, some types are called *bakers' racks* or *bread racks*. They can be used to store food and supplies or may be wheeled directly into walk-in and some reach-in refrigerators, and even into high-volume ovens in commercial bakeries.

InterMetro is a company in Wilkes-Barre, Pennsylvania, whose name has become synonymous with commercial storage, so much so that the foodservice industry refers to rolling racks as *metro racks*, or simply *metros*. See the company's website for photos, dimensions, and rolling rack and cart options.

Shelving. The width of the shelves should be determined by the items to be stored in the area. For #10 cans, 18- or 24-inch shelves work well, and 21-inch shelves are good for steam table pans. The best shelving lengths are 4 and 5 feet. Shelving is often purchased in four-tier units, but an optional fifth tier can expand capacity by an additional 25 percent.

When selecting shelving material, you have several factors to consider. Vinyl-coated steel gives a nonskid surface; open-grid wire shelves allow air circulation and make it easier to see the wares; and solid stainless steel shelves contain spills the best and are easy to clean but need to be dusted occasionally.

Food Holding Equipment

In all cases, the best food transportation equipment is lightweight, rugged, and leakproof. It can be secured; it has wheels or can be easily transported on dollies.

For Hot Foods. This equipment should hold food at a desired temperature and the proper consistency, without cooking it further or drying it out. Infrared heat is best for holding food that is to be served within 15 minutes, and heats only the food, not its surroundings. For up to one hour, medium-term holding equipment, such as steam tables and insulated cabinets, works fine. For holding times of more than an hour, cook-and-hold ovens are excellent.

Numerous manufacturers offer metal warming cabinets that keep preplated foods and bulk foods hot. Some models include humidity controls. The cabinets come in various sizes and heights and are also excellent for packing items upright in transit. Sheet pans filled with food slip directly into the cabinets, which can be wheeled directly into delivery trucks. Look for models that can reach the desired temperature and humidity level as quickly as possible. Check the website of Food Warming Equipment Company, Inc., for a closer look at the options.

The past decade has seen the development of portable and insulated pizza, food, and catering bags, many of which come with adjustable shelves to fit various-sized pans, as well as handles that can be separated, allowing two people to carry them.

Hot foods can be transported to party sites in steam table pans, half- and full-size sheet pans, and food boxes. Rubbermaid and Cambro manufacture insulated food transportation carriers ranging in size from single-pan to multiple-pan carts. Visit their websites for some examples.

For seated, served dinners with guest counts in the hundreds, some caterers use banquet carts, which are often called *hot boxes* or *carters*. A banquet cart serves two primary functions: the first is to hold plated meals hot and safe while the kitchen staff is dishing up additional plates; the second is to transport the meals from commissary to the dining site. With the use of these carts, hundreds of guests can be served in a manner of minutes.

Look for a banquet cart that is capable of holding plated meals and has quick heat recovery, inasmuch as the door will be open and closed a lot. Most carts use a minimum of 1,500 watts of electricity and are very well insulated. Also look for a heavy-duty base to support the weight of the food as it is transported over various (frequently uneven) surfaces. Look for durable hinges and latches that do not protrude from the cart.

For Cold Foods. Cold foods can be held in mobile refrigeration units, freezers, or ice chests. For transporting, refrigerated trucks are excellent because baker's racks can be rolled right into the back of the truck. You can also pack the food into well-sealed plastic containers and chill it in ice chests with ice, but only if this is approved by your local health department. It is important that the food is sealed and that it never makes direct contact with either the ice or water from melted ice, for sanitation reasons. Igloo's website has some good samples of what's available for cold food storage and transport, as does the website for Food Warming Equipment, Inc., which we also recommended for hot food transport options.

When transporting cold beverages like iced tea or lemonade in bulk quantities, caterers use insulated beverage carriers. When selecting these containers, be sure that they can be stacked easily and conveniently, retain temperature for up to five hours, seal securely, are rustproof, and have dripproof spigots that are recessed or protected from being accidentally flipped open when the carriers are stacked close together.

Transporting Food and Equipment

Most caterers will need at least one vehicle for transporting food and supplies to event sites. Some smaller off-premise caterers can transport everything they need in an SUV, and larger operators may require a fleet of regular and refrigerated trucks.

Before investing in a vehicle, most caterers should rent vehicles of various sizes and try them out. Will a van be sufficient, or is it necessary to invest in a larger truck? Some caterers have installed portable, propane-powered cooking equipment in vehicles. Others have invested tens of thousands of dollars in elaborate "kitchens on wheels." Here we consider a few of the options.

Vans are very practical and quite economical for small- to medium-sized caterers who generally rent tables and chairs for events, rather than supply these items themselves. It is recommended to always use a van with a heavy-duty suspension. For example, in the Ford line of vans, the 350 model is preferable to the 150 because it carries more weight, better. Caterers who have purchased the 150 (or other lightweight models) and wish to carry heavier loads with more stability should look into upgrades like heavy-duty shock absorbers, larger tires, and additional leaves in the springs.

Refrigerated trucks are not cheap. New models cost $25,000 or more, depending on size and features. After selecting a truck chassis, you can hire a local refrigeration or fabrication company to refrigerate and customize the vehicle. The best option is a self-contained refrigeration unit with a built-in generator; another option is a refrigeration unit that can be plugged into an outside power source.

Many caterers find it more cost-effective to rent trucks, and others believe in leasing or owning to ensure guaranteed access during busy periods. Some caterers purchase their smaller vehicles that travel more miles and lease the larger vehicles that are not driven more than 12,000 miles per year.

A few caterers have invested in mobile kitchens built into tractor-trailers, converted buses, and mobile homes. A leading manufacturer of mobile kitchens is Carlin Manufacturing, whose line includes sizes from portable "special event kitchens" that can be towed by SUVs, to huge self-contained trailers. Visit Carlin's website for a closer look at some of the options. If you are interested in using a food truck, pushcarts (for hot dogs, ice cream, and so on), or kiosks in your business, All Star Carts in Bayshore, New York, is another terrific source of ideas.

Whether you buy, lease, or rent, ask yourself these questions when you're selecting a food truck:

- Is it a reliable make and model that is easy to maintain?
- Is it an appropriate size? It should normally be no longer than 22 feet for driving ease and ability to turn corners in residential neighborhoods. Will the height of the truck allow it to enter areas where overhead clearances are limited?
- Are there dual wheels in the back to offer more stability and the ability to carry a heavier load?
- Do the wheel wells cut into the cubic space available inside? Wheel wells that cut into the available space should be avoided because at times you'll need every bit of it!
- Does it have side doors? These are handy for loading and unloading items.
- Is there a lift gate? Lift gates are very desirable if you'll be transporting very heavy items, such as ovens, dollies filled with chairs, or baker's racks filled with food.
- Is there adequate lighting in the carrying compartment?
- Is the truck insulated to protect the contents from extreme heat and cold?
- Are there guardrails on the inside walls?
- Does the kitchen have plenty of counter space? Are the countertops stainless steel?
- Is there a drain for easy cleaning?
- Is there sufficient electrical capacity for your needs?
- What are the safety features of the vehicle? Consider not only the need to secure the loads, but also the safety of your drivers and other employees.
- Is there an audible backup alarm that sounds when the truck is in reverse gear?

Design your catering fleet to meet the needs of busy periods, but also to minimize the time the vehicles must sit idle during slow periods. A food truck emblazoned with your logo may look fantastic—but not if it's sitting in your parking lot most of the time, unused.

As with any other vehicle, be sure to invest in regular preventive maintenance by either a reliable in-house mechanic or a trusted nearby service station. Another sound investment is a brief safety training program for your drivers, which will help keep insurance premiums as low as possible. And finally, also designate a staff member—or rotate this duty among staffers—to keep the company vehicles fueled up and clean, inside and out. They really are rolling billboards for your company, and catering can be a messy business! You want them to look sharp whenever and wherever they are seen by the public.

You have no idea how difficult it is to get food and all related serving supplies to a party or other event site without squashing or otherwise damaging it—until you are an off-premise caterer.

Transporting food offers its own unique set of challenges. Options we like include the following:

- Cut full-size sheet pan racks in half and bolt them to the walls of the van. (The standard half-size sheet racks tend to be too tall for this purpose.) This enables you to load sheet pans directly onto the racks. When the pans are placed sideways, their contents do not fall out. Wrap the "open end" (facing the door) with plastic wrap or stack additional equipment there to prevent the contents from sliding off the racks.

- Use bakers' racks for delivery of lightweight items, such as disposable trays or box lunches. They must be secured in place in the van as they can tip over and/or contents can shift.

- Be sure that there are heavy-duty casters on all your metro carts so they will roll easily even when loaded down with heavy equipment. Load each cart and then Cryovac it (wrap it with heavy-duty plastic wrap) to keep everything in its place during transport.

- The black ice chests made by Igloo, black on the outside and metallic gray on the inside, look classy and don't show dirt, inside or out, like the white coolers. We know one caterer who has affixed plywood pieces to the bottoms of his black ice chests to prevent them from wearing out as quickly. Busy catering employees have a tendency to drag full, heavy coolers on the ground, and this helps protect them.

- Never leave the commissary without a two-wheel hand truck (or dolly) to easily transport full ice chests, cases of sodas, and other heavy items that are easily stacked. (Dollies have four wheels and are good for transporting heavy loads over level surfaces, but are impractical at sites with steps or staircases to navigate.)

Pieces of equipment like coffeemakers are best transported in custom-made plywood boxes, which offer more protection than their original cardboard box packaging. Plastic crates and containers are a must for transporting items of various sizes, and it is sometimes best to make them yourself to fit your equipment. Cuisine Unlimited has built boxes out of laminated, corrugated plastic for coffeepots and beverage servers with spouts, and cargo boxes for transporting decorations. For some party themes, the cargo boxes themselves can be used as part of the décor—for example, for jungle, wharfside, and beach scenes!

Breakable items can be wrapped in old linens or plastic bubble wrap and packed in plastic crates. Bus boxes—those plastic tubs used to clear dishes from tables—with lids are also good for packing smaller items. Take hints from your local rental companies; notice how they pack things in bulk, and adapt their techniques.

Back-of-House Equipment

Exhibit 5.2 is a listing of the miscellaneous equipment necessary for most off-premise catering operations. These items, used for mixing, measuring, and so on, are known collectively as *smallware*. The list is not meant to be all-inclusive, but may be used as a guideline or checklist for caterers who are just getting started in business.

 Kitchen Knives

The higher the percentage of carbon steel in a knife blade, the better it can hold its edge and stay sharp. The best knives are made of forged steel, shaped and ground from hot steel under pressure; lesser-quality knives are stamped from thin sheets of steel, in cookie-cutter fashion. A good chef's knife should have sufficient heft, but its weight must also be balanced between handle and blade, and it should feel comfortable in the hand.

EXHIBIT 5.2 Back-of-House Equipment and Smallwares

Worktables with folding legs (4, 6, 8, and 10 feet)
Portable propane ovens
Portable fryers
Portable grill
Propane gas tanks
Electric coffeemakers
Electric tabletop convection ovens
Heat lamps
Electric countertop grill
Tabletop cassette au feu stoves
Electric hot plates
Rolling baker's racks
Metro racks
Warming cabinets
Chafing dishes for keeping food hot
    in kitchen
Stockpots (3, 6, and 10 gallon)
Woks
Sauté pans (8, 10, 12, and 14 inch)
Sauce pans, straight and slope-sided, nonstick
    (1.5, 2.75, 3.75, 5.5, 7, and 10 quarts)
Sauce pots (14 and 26 quarts)
Steam table pans (full and half size)
Sheet pans (full and half size)
Smaller baking pans to fit in convection
    and home ovens
Roasting pans with locking lids
Baking pans for pies, cakes, cookies, muffins,
    and spring pans
Bread pans
Double boilers (8 and 12 quarts)
Brazier pots
Egg poacher
Blender
Stainless steel bowls (assorted sizes)
Cutting boards, composition plastic
    (assorted sizes)

Skimmers
Fry baskets
Ice cream scoops (assorted sizes)
Wire whips (assorted sizes)
Piping bags with assorted tips
Ladles (assorted sizes)
Tongs (assorted sizes)
Knives (French, carving, cheese, bread, paring,
    boning, cleaver, etc.)
Knife sharpener
Steels
Cook's forks
Funnels (assorted sizes)
Serving spoons (regular, slotted, and
    perforated)
Spatulas (assorted sizes)
Rubber spatulas (assorted sizes)
Spaghetti servers
Pie servers
Pie markers
Egg beater
Rolling pin
Can openers
Vegetable peelers
Melon ballers
Garnishing tools (zesters and strippers)
Pastry brushes
Garlic press
Parmesan cheese grater
Paddles (30 and 49 inches)
Juice extractor
Box grater
Broiler scraper
Fruit corers
Poultry shears
Clam and oyster knives
Colanders

(Continued)

EXHIBIT 5.2 Back-of-House Equipment and Smallwares (*Continued*)

China caps
Sieves
Food mills
Thermometers (meat, candy, and deep fat)
Bus boxes with lids
Portion scales
Plastic food containers with lids (assorted sizes)
Beverage urns for holding cold and hot beverages
Bar kits
Ice chests
Garbage cans
Dollies
Hand trucks
Mop, bucket, and wringer

Brooms
Dust pans
Floor squeegee
Carton opener
Ingredient bins
Rubber floor matting
Oven and freezer mittens
First aid kits
Fire extinguishers
Extension cords
Hoses
Large funnel and metal containers for used cooking oil
Nonslip rubber floor mats

Front-of-House Equipment

The *front of the house* means the areas that guests will see. Front-of-the-house equipment can be classified as follows:

Tables   Glassware
Chairs   Flatware
Linens   Tenting
China   Miscellaneous equipment

Tables

For off-premise catering, tables are generally classified in one of four types:

- *Banquet tables* are used for seated dining, buffets, food stations, and bars. The three most frequently used sizes are 8 feet by 30 inches (seats 8 to 10), 6 feet by 30 inches (seats 6 to 8), and 4 feet by 30 inches (seats 4 to 6). Of course, longer tables can be created by placing smaller ones end-to-end.

- *Round tables* are used for food stations and buffets, as well as for guest dining at catered events. They're considered to be more "upscale" and to foster conversation better than long banquet tables. Sizes are identified by diameter in inches, as follows: 72-inch (seats 10 to 12), 60- or 66-inch (seats 8 to 10), 48-inch (seats 6 to 8). The smaller sizes—36-inch (seats 4) and 30-, 24-, and 18-inch (all seat 2 to 4)—are used primarily for cocktail party setups.

- *Conference tables*, also known as *classroom tables*, are narrower than regular banquet tables (18 inches wide versus 30 inches) and are effectively used when space is limited. For example, when you work in a narrow hallway, a conference table may fit, whereas a banquet table will be too wide. These tables also can be set up parallel to a banquet table to create an executive (wider) table. The most common conference table lengths are 6 and 8 feet.

- *Special tables* are used primarily for buffets and food stations to create various shapes other than simply straight lines. These include arc-shaped serpentine tables, which can be placed together to make semicircles and S shapes; trapezoids that create (when two are placed together) a six-sided table; quarter-rounds (8 or 10 feet in diameter), half-rounds (5 feet in diameter), or quarter-pies (30 inches in diameter), which can be used to "round out" the corners of square or rectangular tables and create a little extra seating; and 72-inch rounds. *Highboy tables* are those that are 42 inches high and are generally 36 inches in diameter. Guests can stand next to them or sit on tall stools. There are also cake tables on wheels, which come in diameters of 36 and 48 inches.

Chairs

The type of chair used at off-premise catering events varies depending on the type of event. The most recent additions to chair choices are made of resin, which can be more durable than wood. The *ghost chair*, of clear Plexiglas, is an excellent choice for its versatility.

Simple wooden folding chairs, usually in brown, are the least expensive and are used when cost is a major concern. Folding Samsonite chairs, available in various colors, are good when a "classier" look is required. The wooden chair with a padded seat is a very popular and versatile style, and it comes in virtually any color: white, black, hunter green, natural wood, and more. The most expensive chair used at off-premise events is the *ballroom chair*, also with a padded seat.

For upscale events, the *Chiavari ballroom chair* is an excellent choice. Originally introduced in the 1980s by Regal Rents of Los Angeles, it is now an industry standard and Chiavari offers it in a range of custom colors. The mahogany Versailles chair looks similar to a wooden chair found in home dining rooms and also features a padded seat.

Regal Seating Company has modified the original Chiavari chair by painting it with duotone finishes, such as "Tuscan" (a rustic white with gold brush strokes) and copper patina with copper and green. Regal also offers a *Chameleon chair*, so named because it has four different removable backs.

Chair covers are wildly popular and can add an elegant look to a catered affair. There are covers made for most chair styles in hundreds of colors, fabrics, and sizes, along with opulent chair ties and chair jewels to adorn each seat. Some of the most innovative and contemporary chair covers are manufactured by Sculptware. This company's line of sleek, stretch-to-fit spandex covers for chairs and tables has set the pace for innovative looks in this very trendy field. For corporate clients, Sculptware can print logos on the linens.

When renting chair covers, be absolutely sure that they fit the chairs to be used at the event because many covers are made exclusively for stackable chairs used in hotels, restaurants, and banquet halls.

Linens

An integral part of most parties, linens are noticed by the guests as soon as they enter the room. The linens should blend with the atmosphere, have no wrinkles, and be placed evenly on each table so that the bottom edges are parallel to the floor (except, of course, on the corners of rectangular tables topped with rectangular cloths). For upscale events, linens should reach the floor; for others, they should fall at least 12 inches from the top of the table on all sides.

When purchasing linens, off-premise caterers should ask the following questions:

- Are stains easily removed during washing?
- Will the linens fade?
- Do they easily resist mildew damage?
- Are they fire retardant?
- Do they require pressing?

- What is the useful life span?
- Can the napkins accommodate fancy folds?
- How absorbent is the fabric?
- Will they shrink?

Most linens are either cotton, cotton and polyester (the best known brand name is Visa, by Milliken), or all polyester. Cotton linens are considered more elegant, but they do tend to fade and shrink and are labor-intensive, requiring pressing before each use. Polyester linens are more colorfast, and many do not require pressing if properly washed and dried. The main disadvantage of polyester linens is that they are nonabsorbent, which is an undesirable quality, particularly for napkins. Blends of polyester and cotton combine the advantages and disadvantages of both.

Round tablecloths, like round tables, are classified by inches in diameter. When ordering round tablecloths to cover round tables, you should add 60 inches to the diameter of the table if you wish the cloth to reach the floor. For example, a 120-inch cloth will reach the floor on a 60-inch round table. A 90-inch round cloth will cover a 60-inch round table, but it will not reach the floor; it falls about 15 inches from the table edge, all around. If you want a cloth that covers the entire table, to the floor, rent or purchase what is known as a *radial banquet linen*.

Frequently requested round tablecloth sizes are 90, 108, 120, and 132 inches. Linens for rectangular tables are available in assorted sizes, such as:

- 60 by 120 inches (covers 8-foot by 30-inch tables)
- 60 by 90 inches (covers 6-foot by 30-inch tables)
- Other sizes dictated by local preference

Linen trends change from year to year, so many caterers choose to rent linens to create a specific look for a specific event. Most linen suppliers recommend purchasing the basic solids—black, white, wine, ivory—and renting the trendy linens only as needed. Caterers should consider their client base before purchasing linens and can, of course, reuse those that have been purchased at other events, at a profit. For corporate events, under-the-sea prints and tropical motifs are fine, but for weddings, sheers, brocades, and satins are best.

One way to stay trendy on a budget is to own your own basic solids, and then rent toppers or overlays as needed. These are second table linens, most often in an accent color, laid over the base cloth. Sheer overlays are always in style. Source the major linen suppliers online and see what they have to offer this year. There are dozens; here are just a few names to start with:

> Cloth Connection
> Dove Linen, Inc.
> Christofle Hotel
> Tablecloth Designs
> Table Cloth Factory

Table skirting is available in any color imaginable. Most are made from polyester fabrics for long life and wrinkle resistance. Common sizes are 8, 13, 17, and 21 feet. Skirting should be used for all buffet tables, food stations, and head tables where guests are seated on one side. Measure the linear feet to be skirted to determine the amount of skirting needed. For example, to completely skirt a 30-inch by 8-foot table, you will need a 21-foot table skirt. This is calculated by adding the dimensions of all four sides of the table:

$$8 \text{ feet} + 8 \text{ feet} + 2\frac{1}{2} \text{ feet (30 inches)} = 21 \text{ feet}$$

Many rental companies also offer custom-made covers for banquet tables. These will fit over the table, covering to the floor, thus eliminating the use of skirting, top cloths, clips, pins, and labor. We also mentioned stretch-to-fit Sculptware in the section on chairs; the company offers table coverings of all sizes as well.

China

The best china for use at off-premise catered events is simple, durable, and lightweight. The pattern should be in keeping with the caterer's image, the menu, and the caliber of the event. Plain white china is the most popular, followed by china with silver or gold trim; black china can add an interesting and distinctive touch. Some foods, such as smoked salmon, can be very elegantly presented on black plates. Coffee cups should have sufficiently large handles to avoid burning one's fingers.

When you order china, it is imperative to consider both the menu and the type of event. Basic china items include:

Platters

Chargers (plate liners, charge plates)

Dinner plates

Salad plates

Bread and butter plates

Dessert plates

Soup and cereal bowls

Bouillon cup and underliner

Vegetable dishes ("monkey dishes")

Coffee cups and saucers

Coffee mugs

Demitasse cups and saucers (for espresso)

Sugar and cream sets

Gravy or sauce boats

Salt and pepper shakers

As with linens, trendy new styles are always being added to tabletop lines. New geometric shapes and colors continually emerge, including square and triangle-shaped dinnerware. For an up-to-date look at some of the latest trends in dinnerware, keep an eye on the websites of 10 Strawberry Street and Fortessa.

Glassware

The quality of the glassware must be in line with the overall caliber of the event. Plasticware is adequate for picnics and barbecues. For parties around swimming pools and in certain public places that simply don't allow glass to be used, the use of plastic is a necessity. Stemware is used for more upscale and elegant affairs, whereas tumblers suffice for many midscale events.

Annealed glassware is the least expensive. Tempered glassware is more durable because there is an additional step in its manufacturing process that gives it greater strength than annealed glass. Leaded glassware (also called *crystal*) is manufactured by adding lead oxide and potassium silicate to the molten glass, making a very clear glass that produces a distinctive ring when struck lightly.

When selecting glassware, remember these points:

- The thicker the glass, the more durable it is.
- A straight-sided glass has less strength than one with curves or bulges.
- Glasses with rounded edges are easiest to clean.
- A flared glass has a greater tendency to chip, crack, and break.

- Crystal carries the highest price tag and has the least durability, but also offers the finest and most delicate appearance.
- The two most common reasons that glasses break are impact (hitting something else) and thermal shock (fast temperature change).

Many caterers use a 13-ounce balloon-style wineglass as an all-purpose glass for water, wine, and most bar drinks except Champagne, brandy, and cordials served straight up. Tulip- and flute-shaped Champagne glasses are often used for upscale events. The saucer-style Champagne glass continues to be used by some caterers, although it is not recommended. The wide rim of this type of glass allows the bubbles to dissipate rapidly, so the Champagne goes flat too quickly.

To check glassware trends, contact some of the leading manufacturers:

> Arcoroc
> Cardinal International
> Christofle Hotel
> Libbey Glass
> Riedel Crystal of America

Flatware

Place settings reflect a caterer's image as much as any other detail and signal to guests the number of courses to be served. The weight of the flatware is probably its most important characteristic. The heavier the flatware, the higher the perceived value.

Flatware should be comfortable to touch, hold, and use. Balance is essential. Basic flatware is either silver plated, stainless steel, or chrome. Gold-plated flatware is also available and can be used for an elegant touch, but it is very difficult to maintain because it chips easily. Silver plate is more expensive, more formal, and harder to maintain than stainless steel because it needs to be burnished regularly. Stainless comes in a broader range of prices and is generally more casual. Chrome is the least expensive.

Silverplate means a layer of silver has been fused onto a base utensil of another metal–often copper, but sometimes an alloy. The price varies depending on the amount of silver used–the better manufacturers add a little extra at common points of wear–and the types of metals that make up the base utensil.

The most expensive silverplate is known as "18/10," which stands for 18 percent chrome and 10 percent nickel. The chrome adds corrosion-resistance; the nickel adds a warm luster to the utensil's color. There is also an 18/8 blend, 18 percent chrome and 8 percent nickel. Among the most durable flatware is 70/30, an alloy that contains copper, nickel, and zinc. It is also known as *nickel silver*, or *brass*.

The flatware might be stamped with letters to indicate the type of base. EPNS stands for electroplated nickel silver. EPBM means electroplated base metal.

Basic flatware pieces for catered events include:

Dinner fork

Hors d'oeuvre fork

Salad or dessert fork

Oyster fork

Dinner knife

Butter knife

Teaspoon

Iced tea spoon

Soup spoon

Bouillon spoon

Serving spoon

Demi teaspoon

Dessert spoon

For more information on the latest trends in flatware, visit the websites of Corby Hall and Oneida Foodservice, Inc., among others.

From Cuisine Unlimited Catering & Special Events in Salt Lake City, Utah, we learned of a terrific option for storing flatware. For every flatware pattern owned, this caterer has purchased a sturdy rolling tool chest typically used for hammers, wrenches, and so on. Each pattern is stored in its own toolbox, ready to roll onto the delivery truck to an event site.

See the "'Going Green'" section on page 170 for information on disposable, biodegradable dishes and utensils.

Tenting

The main purpose of tenting at an off-premise event is to protect the guests from rain and other elements. Other purposes include augmentation of an existing structure, as in placing a tent alongside a building to add room for the guests or simply to create a more festive mood and enliven an otherwise uninteresting space.

There are several basic types of tents and canopies on the market:

- *Rope and pole tents:* These are commercial-grade tents, supported by poles and pulled tight using guy ropes attached to stakes. These tents have center poles and range in size from 20 to 150 feet wide, with expandable lengths. They must be installed by professionals.

- *Frame-supported tents:* The fabric of these tents is strapped or buckled to an aluminum frame. Sizes range from 10 to 40 feet in width, with expandable lengths. These tents have no center poles.

- *Multistory tents:* There are now two-story and three-story tent structures available, providing virtual "temporary buildings" for large groups or functions.

- *Marquees or walkways:* These long, narrow tent structures are used mainly for sheltering walkways or defining an entry into a tent. Widths are from 6 to 10 feet, with expandable lengths.

- *Canopy tents:* These are residential-grade, pole-supported tents that are pulled tight using guy ropes attached to stakes. Sizes range from 10 by 10 feet to 30 by 40 feet.

- *Tension structures:* These are commercial grades of pole-supported tents that utilize the strength of the vinyl-laminated fabric instead of the web or rope superstructure. Sizes range from widths of 30 to 80 feet, with expandable lengths.

- *Clear-span structures:* These are aluminum I-beam structures with fabric panels between the beams. Sizes range from 30 to 100 feet in width, with expandable lengths.

- *Quick-up framed canopies:* These are accordion-like canopies with collapsible legs that can be assembled quickly. Sizes range from 8-foot squares, to 10 by 15 feet.

- *Economy canopies:* These are inexpensive frame-supported canopies, usually 10 by 10 feet.

The formulas for determining tent sizes are covered in Chapter 6. As an off-premise caterer, you should be knowledgeable about tents as you will use them often. For instance, many rental companies do not provide sides with tents unless sides are specifically requested. When you order sides, it is important to specify whether they are to be clear, opaque, or opaque with windows. For events held after dark, and whenever opaque sides are used, lighting is essential. Theatrical-style lights are popular, as are elegant chandelier lamps that hang from the tent frame.

For the tent floor, off-premise caterers can choose from Astroturf, wooden floors (for dancing or to provide for firm, even footing), or a combination of both. Frequently, flooring is installed over swimming pools to provide additional party space. Leave the floor installation to experts, and insist that they are fully insured. An installation mistake could result in disaster.

Platforms are used to elevate musicians, guest speakers, head tables, and bridal party tables. The risers to create platforms usually are available in 4- by 8-foot sections and can be installed at heights of either 12 or 24 inches. Railings and steps are excellent safety precautions, and skirting can be attached to the platforms to improve their appearance.

Tent poles are necessary in some cases, but unsightly. To disguise them, caterers may wish to place trees or shrubs next to the poles or to use canvas pole covers. For very elegant affairs, fire-retardant tent liners may be used to completely cover the interior framework and poles.

Temperature control inside a tent is critical, particularly in very warm or cold climates or whenever it is necessary for all tent sides to be closed. Overhead or floor fans create air movement for cooling, but air-conditioning is usually required for comfort in a truly hot, humid climate. Costs for air-conditioning are very high, unlike the cost of portable heaters, which are rather economical.

Finally, you must be knowledgeable about any local regulations concerning the use of a tent. For safety reasons, many cities require a special permit for tenting, which must be obtained before the tent is set up. Tent rental companies can assist in this process, but it is your responsibility as the off-premise caterer to ensure that this technicality has been taken care of before the event—and to get written proof of it. The last person you want to see at the party is an inspector who asks to see the permit—which was never obtained.

Leading tent manufacturers in the United States include:

> Academy Tent and Canvas
> DeBoer Structures USA
> Eureka! Tents & Seasonal Structures
> KD Kanopy, Inc
> Olympic Tent
> Tentnology

Exhibit 5.3 lists the major front-of-the-house items used at off-premise catered events. Exhibit 5.4 includes other types of items, often used but disposable—that is, not reusable. Both lists are meant as guidelines; your own requirements will vary.

EXHIBIT 5.3 Miscellaneous Front-of-House Equipment

Chafing dishes (stainless steel, silver plated, one and two gallon)
Serving trays and platters
Serving bowls
Serving spoons, forks, knives, ladles, and tongs
Cake and pie servers
Assorted baskets for buffet items
Assorted buffet decor items (shells, nets, blocks, and mirrors, etc.)
Water pitchers
Samovars (urns for holding hot beverages)
Coffee pots
Water pitchers
Champagne fountains
Champagne and wine buckets
Candelabras
Bread baskets
Carving boards with warming lights
Carving knives, carving forks, and sharpening steels
Cassette au feu stoves for warming and cooking
Punch bowls
Ashtrays
Votive candles (small candles in glass cups)
Glo-ice trays (used for raw bars, ice carvings, and cold food displays)
Ice chests for ice for water glasses and chilling dinner wine
Oval waiter trays
Tray stands
Cocktail trays
Bus boxes and lids
Trash cans
Staple gun
Fire extinguishers
Machines for popcorn, sno-kones, cotton candy, and hot dogs
Wedding props (please refer to wedding section of text)

"Going Green"

Of course, no current discussion of disposable products would be complete without addressing the topic of recycling. The smart off-premise caterer will not only embrace this concept, but also transform it into a selling point on his or her website and in

EXHIBIT 5.4 Catering Supplies

Disposable steam table pans
Cold cups (cold drinks, wine, and Champagne)
Hot cups
Lids for cold and hot cups
Plastic plates (assorted sizes)
Plastic knives, forks, and teaspoons
Paper dinner napkins
Paper cocktail napkins
Doilies for trays and underliner plates for soups, etc.
Beverage stir sticks
Coffee stirrers
Swordpicks and skewers for skewering foods
Drinking straws
Film wrap
Aluminum foil
Heavy-duty tape, such as duct tape
Plastic baggies
Wet-naps
Fuel for cassette au feu stoves
Sterno
Plastic gloves
Bug spray for flying insects and crawling insects (outdoor events)
Charcoal and charcoal lighter fluid
Business cards
Dish soap, silver polish, sponges, and scrubbing pads
Plastic for covering tables
Plastic table covers for kitchen worktables
Heavy-duty plastic for covering floors and carpets (like that used in homes and offices on which
    equipment is placed)
Paper liners for sheet pans
Disposable bowls, platters, and utensils
Garbage can liners
Disposable portion cups in various sizes
Disposable chef's caps
Wooden corn-on-the-cob skewers

discussions with clients. Reducing waste, reusing, and recycling can truly pay off in terms of business, in addition to their environmental benefits. In Portland, Oregon, for example, the city's Bureau of Planning and Sustainability offers an online list of "Green Caterers," with a checklist by company of which services each provides. (See it at www.portlandonline.com/bps/index.cfm?a=166123&c=44622.) The caterers on the list say they have adopted these measures:

- Offer recycling when it cannot be done at the event site
- Wash and reuse their dishware instead of using disposables
- Use compostable serviceware, including biodegradable packaging and utensils
- Serve food family-style rather than in individual servings to minimize waste
- Avoid individually packaged items (beverages, condiments)
- Offer local, seasonal, and organic food choices
- Donate edible leftovers

Technology today is making it much easier to go green, and catering is no exception. There are biodegradable bamboo plates, corn cups, and cornstarch utensils. Keeping these items in stock may cost more for the caterer, but for events for which disposable plates and utensils are needed, they really fit the bill. We've seen high-end disposables too, such as flatware by Christofle and stemware by Mikasa.

We have noted caterers who market "green" services, such as using hormone-free meats, nontoxic cleaning products, energy-efficient lightbulbs, and biodegradable produce bags that decompose within 90 days. These caterers compost leftovers for their own gardens and champion online ordering as reducing wasteful paper use. If their local government offers a "green" or sustainability certificate, they go for it.

Not every option will be practical for every off-premise catering company. Many require additional expenditures, including labor. How green can you be? Ask your staff to help you determine a workable sustainability policy, or engage the services of a "green" consultant.

Equipment Decisions: To Buy or to Rent?

Students of catering management, as well as newcomers to the business, frequently ask, "Is it better to rent or buy equipment?" The answer is, "It depends." A variety of factors influence this decision. Nearly all off-premise caterers own some and rent some equipment. Most off-premise caterers will purchase back-of-the-house equipment first, in their business-building phase. One way to make the rent-or-own decision is to ask yourself if you'll use any particular piece of equipment six or more times per year. If the answer is yes, consider buying it. Otherwise, rent it.

Another philosophy is that providing equipment—ranging from on-site food preparation appliances to salt and pepper shakers for tables—is simply part of being a service business, which is, of course, what off-premise catering is. The corollary, then, is that you're the expert. You're responsible for producing the successful wedding, party, or other event, and you deserve to make a profit for your work. Do you make more profit by renting, or by buying, particular types of items?

First, let's examine the advantages of renting equipment:

1. There is no capital investment.

2. There is no need to maintain the equipment.

3. As long as the caterer satisfies the "minimum order for delivery requirements" of the rental company, the rental company is responsible for delivering the equipment to the event site. However, it is still the caterer's responsibility to see that the rental company does deliver, on time, the correct items.

4. There is no need to store rental equipment, thereby saving space and avoiding inventory hassles.

5. Many rental companies require only that dishes and equipment be rinsed free of food when returned after an event. They wash the dishes and equipment.

6. The caterer has automatic access to a much wider variety of items because rental companies have a wide assortment and the caterer is free to rent from more than one company.

7. Rental companies have much larger inventories than an individual caterer and can even sublease from a competitor to provide very large quantities of items. It's difficult for an individual caterer to have enough of everything.

8. It is easier to pass on the costs of rental equipment than the costs of owned equipment to clients. There is no question in a client's mind that there will be a charge for the rented items since the caterer cannot be expected to pay for them from profit. Yet without an invoice in hand for an exact amount, some caterers charge less for use of their own equipment—or don't charge at all.

Now consider the advantages of owning equipment:

1. Off-premise caterers who own equipment have greater control over the time of delivery. They are not dependent on the rental company's schedule.

2. Rental companies can be short of certain items, or out of stock altogether, and unable to fill the order. Or, in the case of a rural community, there may be no rental equipment available in the area.

3. Rented equipment may not be maintained up to the caterer's standards.

4. Rental companies are not always accurate when counting returned equipment back into inventory. They have been known to miscount in their own favor, then charge the caterer to replace "missing" items.

5. When rental companies invoice clients for lost or damaged equipment, they bill at "replacement cost," which is often higher than the actual cost. Their reason for this is that it takes time to reorder, and while the item is not in service, it cannot be rented, thus resulting in lost revenue.

6. In a competitive bidding situation, you can discount the cost of your own equipment, or even not charge for it, to underbid the competition. This certainly is not a good business practice on a routine basis, but there may be particular situations in which it is appropriate.

7. You may be able to rent your own equipment to other caterers, or to clients who need only the equipment, not the food.

8. Off-premise caterers who own equipment can create a distinctive signature or identity with the style of equipment they choose.

In a case study prepared by Teri Woodard Polster for off-premise catering seminars conducted by the National Restaurant Association, certain assumptions were made equipment with to compare the cost of owning renting equipment. In this study, it was assumed that a caterer would purchase or rent sufficient equipment to serve two dinners and two cocktail receptions per week for 100 guests. In addition to the actual cost of the equipment, she computed theoretical costs for:

Renting warehouse space	Cleaning supplies
Utilities	Laundry equipment
Truck lease	Insurance

Rental warehouse manager
Truck driver
Utility person
Necessary packing containers
Repair and maintenance
Shipping containers
Replacement of broken and missing equipment

Payroll benefits
Advertising
Bad debt expense
Security
Depreciation
Any other miscellaneous expenses

In this example, the rental expense for the year was double the cost to purchase and maintain the equipment. This example will in no way directly apply to every off-premise caterer, but it does identify the indirect costs of owning, as well as the high costs of renting.

Of course, you have to determine the best solution for your own circumstances. There is no single "right way." One Washington, DC, caterer began as a rental company and now owns a huge equipment inventory that contributes greatly to the firm's bottom line. Another caterer rents all equipment for the front of the house and charges the client a price slightly higher than list. For this particular business, income from rental equipment adds at least 5 percent more profit to the bottom line.

It really does boil down to profit, and that's hard to pin down, especially for a brand new business. But over time, it's smart to examine your income statements and determine what percentage of profit you generate from (1) equipment or items that you own and rent out; and (2) equipment or items that you rent from others, passing on the charges to clients.

There are dozens of possibilities for owning your own equipment, including props to be used in creating theme parties and events. We know caterers who stock everything from "Wild West" saloon storefronts to faux pine trees and life-sized toy soldiers for Christmas parties. Again, it is all a matter of what you can afford—and how much you are able to store and maintain.

Dealing with Rental Companies

The relationships between rental equipment dealers and off-premise caterers can be win-win for both parties—or a constant source of mistrust, tension, and aggravation.

The key to working with a rental dealer is to understand dealers' terms. The following terms, obtained from a prominent South Florida firm, are typical:

1. List prices are for one day's use only, and they apply to all rented equipment even if some is not used. If equipment is returned late, there will be an additional charge; however, there are special rates for rentals in excess of one day. For example:

One day	Pay one-day rate
Two days	Pay for one and one-half days
Three days	Pay for two days
Four to seven days	Pay for three days

2. Most rental dealers provide special containers for china, glassware, flatware, and other equipment to ensure that all equipment is received sterilized, undamaged, and table-ready.

    It is imperative that all rented equipment be counted and inspected upon receipt. Shortages and any item that came in damaged should be reported to the rental company immediately. If this is not done, the caterer will more than likely be billed for replacement costs for equipment not received, or for that which was damaged upon receipt. Rental companies also charge for missing shipping containers and other items, such as hangers for table linens.

3. Rental companies generally do not set up tables and chairs, and they expect the tables and chairs to be taken down and stacked upon conclusion of the event. Some companies will do the setup and breakdown, but at an additional charge. Care should be taken not to leave equipment where it may get wet by being exposed to lawn sprinklers or rain.

4. The caterer's staff is usually responsible for rinsing all china, glassware, and flatware free of food particles and packing these items back into the shipping containers. Some companies require that all equipment be washed; others, only the china, flatware, and stemware. If equipment is not washed as required, they add a ware-washing charge to the invoice.

5. Table linens should be shaken out (no food residue is to be left on them) and dried to prevent staining and mildew. If linens are wet, it is best to spread them out to dry after the party ends.

6. Most rental companies charge additional fees for deliveries above the street level, to locations outside their normal delivery areas, and to any other unusual locations where extra labor or time is necessary.

7. The off-premise caterer takes full responsibility for rental equipment from the time of delivery to the time of return. The rental company's insurance does not cover equipment while it is out on rental. Off-premise caterers must ensure that rental equipment is secure and protected from the weather. The rented items should all be counted again at the end of an event, and an attempt should be made right then to look for missing items. Generally, a complete inspection of the party site will turn up missing items—don't wait until the next day to do this.

8. Rental companies generally do not require advance deposits from established off-premise caterers, and many extend credit and offer discounts. First-time renters can expect to pay "cash on delivery" (COD), plus a security deposit. In some cases, a rental company charges a cancellation fee to a caterer who orders equipment in advance and then cancels the order so close to the party date that the rental company is unable to rerent the equipment. Most rental companies have minimum order amounts for delivery of equipment.

Loss Prevention

Off-premise caterers can purchase insurance that covers loss of major items while at a party site. One off-premise caterer was billed $900 for the replacement cost of a 400-pound oven that was left overnight and stolen from a party site. Insurance is available to cover this type of substantial loss, but not for smaller losses like pieces of flatware or china.

Another way to limit losses is to ask that the rental firm pick up the equipment at the end of the party, instead of waiting until the next day. If the pickup occurs late at night, this usually results in an additional charge. Some off-premise caterers do not leave highly pilferable items at a party site, but take them back to their commissaries for pickup there by the rental company. These types of items include silver pieces, flatware, samovars, and linens.

Off-premise caterers should always train their staff to handle equipment properly. For example, staff should use caution when handling candles so as not to drip the hot wax on the linens. Staff should also provide plenty of ashtrays for smokers. When staff members are working in very windy conditions, stemware should be cleared into bus bins and transported to the kitchen area.

An organized and efficiently operated dish return area can greatly contribute to a reduction in losses. Everyone in the foodservice business has seen the chaotic dishroom where dishes are stacked from floor to ceiling and breakage is inevitable. It's much smarter to set up tables for the efficient return and handling of the soiled dishes. There should be sufficient space for trays and bus boxes, and soiled dishes should be immediately rinsed or washed, depending on the rental company's rules, and packed for return.

The relationship between off-premise caterers and rental dealers can be excellent, as long as there is mutual respect. Caterers should follow rental companies' rules, and they should ask their rental dealers how they can make their relationship work better. In turn, rental companies should recognize that off-premise caterers work under extreme pressure; that rental merchandise must be delivered on time, all the time; and that the equipment must be usable, with no shortages.

Effective Purchasing

After carefully considering the pros and cons of purchasing equipment, caterers who choose to buy all (or some) of it must consider various factors that affect the purchase decision. No matter what the item, the areas to be researched are:

- Purchase price
- Cost to operate
- Cost to install
- Cost to maintain
- Cost of insurance
- Depreciation
- Obsolescence (Is it already outdated, or will it soon be?)
- Safety (Underwriters Laboratory approval for electrical appliances; American Gas Association for gas appliances)
- Design (Is it easy to use? Does it do what it was designed to do?)
- Proper size for operation
- Stock or custom (Stock is often better and less expensive.)

Leasing equipment is generally very expensive, but some dealers will finance 40 or 50 percent of the purchase price.

As a general rule, it is best to buy what is needed to meet the current business demands, rather than buying more equipment than necessary to meet projected demands in future years. All one has to do is survey the large restaurants that have gone bankrupt, in comparison to the small ones (40 or so seats) that continue to thrive. The same concept should apply to off-premise caterers: Less equipment in a smaller space is most often better than more equipment in a larger space.

When purchasing china, flatware, glassware, and other tabletop items, off-premise caterers should be able to negotiate with the seller to arrive at a price somewhere between 50 and 100 percent of the list price. Remember that 50 percent of "list" is generally the dealer's cost before shipping. You can also get some good deals by purchasing slightly damaged linens. On a buffet table, it's easy to hide the flaws by using these linens as accent cloths. When considering quantities, off-premise caterers should plan on having a sufficient supply to handle most events, but should have the flexibility to buy additional items that are available on short notice for a particular event, or rent a similar pattern or style from a rental dealer.

Used equipment is readily available in most areas for significantly less money than new equipment. When shopping for used equipment, review the local newspaper's classified advertisements, visit the used equipment districts in larger cities, and even contact new equipment dealers who may have used equipment taken in as trade-ins.

Larry Levy, owner of Biddle Street Catering and Events in Baltimore, Maryland, suggests that before you spend time driving somewhere to check out used equipment, call first to obtain the following information:

- Name of the equipment, model, voltage, amps, and energy source
- Length of ownership, and whether the equipment was purchased new or used
- The reason the equipment is for sale
- Repair history, including who made repairs and when
- The seller's flexibility on the price

Levy also advises that when considering equipment for sale at an auction, you should obtain a list of the items to be sold, then preinspect the equipment and narrow the list to only those items that may be worthy of a bid. Conduct further research by checking service labels, learning the original cost when purchased new, and determining the installation cost. Finally, decide what your own maximum bid will be, and then *do not exceed it.* For equipment that is sold in lots, you could organize a group of buyers to purchase the complete lot or you could buy the desired item(s) from the successful bidder for the complete lot.

 # Summary

The brand-new off-premise caterer does not have to feel bad about being unable to move into a building and equip the kitchen exactly as he or she would like. Renting equipment, including delivery vehicles, or using someone else's facility at first can provide an opportunity to "try before you buy."

Equipment is an enormous investment for a catering company. This chapter began with a brief discussion of the factors that will determine which purchases are necessary, from menu to service style. Equipment is referred to as "front-of-the-house" if it is used in view of guests (tables and chairs, dishes, etc.), and "back-of-the-house" if it is used for food preparation and storage (appliances, smallware, etc.)

Before making any purchase, you must determine where you're going to install and/ or store the equipment. This chapter recommends hiring a professional foodservice planner to help create an efficient layout for your commissary. Ultimately, however, it will be up to you to make the appliance choices. Because you'll be working off-premise at most events, a critical part of your inventory should be food holding equipment to keep prepared foods at their optimal, safe temperatures.

There are hundreds of items to consider. This chapter divides them into basic categories: cooking appliances, other appliances, food holding equipment, and transportation (both the vehicles and storage options for transporting food and supplies). The discussion of front-of-the-house equipment includes information and some vendors' websites to help readers check out trends for tables, chairs, linens, flatware, glassware, china, and tents.

In many cases, items can be rented as needed. The advantages and disadvantages to renting and owning them are covered, along with tips for developing relationships with rental suppliers. Caterers' up-front expenditures will be considerable if they set out to buy all their own supplies. It is smarter to buy some, rent some, and add more to permanent inventory later as the budget allows.

▐) Study Questions

1. Look online or visit a local foodservice equipment dealer to find a piece of cooking equipment you wouldn't want to live without as an off-premise caterer. Share the sales information (including its price) and the reasons for your recommendation.

2. Would you include a food truck in your catering operation—or perhaps even make the food truck your "home base?" Why or why not?

3. Do some online research; select and determine the approximate costs for renting front-of-the-house basics (tables, chairs, china, glassware, and flatware) for a formal wedding reception and dinner for 100 people.

4. Look at the menu for an off-premise caterer in your area, and determine from that menu which types of equipment the caterer probably has in his or her commissary.

5. Source "green" products for a dozen of the items listed in Exhibit 5.4.

Logistics for Off-Premise Catering

A few months ago, one of us was helping an off-premise caterer friend set up for a large corporate cocktails-and-dinner event. The busy catering staff was scurrying to cover what was a huge "dead space"—a recessed stairwell to a floor below that would not be used at this event—with giant Plexiglas cubes. We lit them from within, plugging the lights in downstairs in the unused space, positioned them on a lightweight but sturdy frame over the stairwell opening to completely cover it, and shrouded the cubes with sheer linens to transform this otherwise unsightly spot into a gorgeous, supermodern dessert display table.

This part of the setup took about 90 minutes. No problem, right? Now, imagine the effort involved in precisely measuring that stairwell, and then custom-building and transporting the frame and the cubes, packing plenty of heavy-duty extension cords, selecting safe lights (in colors that, incidentally, were changed at the client's request during a walk-through the previous day) and sufficient quantities of just the right linens, and so on.

Ask any off-premise caterer and you will be regaled with stories of the many challenges of planning and executing events. The minute you leave the commissary, anything can happen! That's why such thorough planning is necessary, along with a good dose of flexibility. This chapter covers the often-complex arrangements that are necessary when caterers work on location and includes advice that will help you accomplish the following tasks:

- Discover unique, exciting party locations and event sites
- Become a preferred vendor for these sites
- Plan and design off-site events
- Create a packing list for an event
- Pull, pack, and load the food, supplies, and equipment for transport
- Transport and unload all items, and set up the event site
- Reload and return all items, and review the event

For an off-premise event, logistics entails everything from knowing what types of utilities are available at a site, to keeping food at safe temperatures—with or without those utilities—to transporting food and equipment so that it remains in perfect condition. First, however, let's take a look at some of the event sites.

Scouting Event Locations

A good caterer is as much a location scout as a filmmaker, going beyond the obvious spots—museums, hotel ballrooms, business conference rooms—to uncover and negotiate for the use of more unusual spots. Don't think of this kind of sleuthing as wasted time. Often, you will get a booking simply by suggesting the most interesting venue for a particular event.

Go online and see what you can find in your area. Look for theaters, museums, historical sites, and movie houses. Contact your local convention and visitors' bureau, as well as area chambers of commerce. Read local magazines and social event columns. Speak to real estate agents about private estates and homes that might be available for parties. Network with other caterers, rental firms, and suppliers. Local colleges and high schools often have facilities available; state and city film commissions know of numerous interesting spots that may be suitable for catered parties, wedding, or other events.

Clearly, many of these venues will offer unusual challenges, which must be addressed prior to your event. A thorough site inspection is mandatory weeks ahead of time, with these critical details in mind:

- Any cost(s) associated with use of the facility
- Weather, and alternate plans in case it doesn't cooperate
- Parking and valet availability, if needed
- Utilities: water, power, waste removal, and backup power in case of emergency
- Rules about deliveries
- Existing kitchen facilities or equipment that may be used
- Ability to obtain a permit for the particular use or event. Does the use meet the basic requirements, such as fire and safety codes, for the number of people expected?
- Rules about (or a prohibition of) alcohol service on the premises
- Neighbors and noise ordinances
- Sufficient space for the planned activities (seating, risers, and portable dance floor, etc.)
- Insects and pest control options (if outdoors)
- Security and emergency requirements
- Restroom facilities
- Sufficient lighting, interior and exterior (parking lot, etc.)
- Insurance and other contingencies

In fact, if a client comes to you with a site already in mind that you aren't familiar with (or more likely, a site that is not normally used for events of this type), don't promise that you can "make it happen" until you discuss each of the items on the checklist with the property owner or manager, as well as the city or county department(s) that may be involved in issuing permits.

Each venue poses unique challenges regarding layout and design. Probably the most frequent problem you'll run across is a lack of adequate area for guest seating. Will a tent be required, or can you provide additional seating areas by covering a swimming pool with a portable floor? Make sure to consider door sizes too. Every caterer at one time or another has had the unhappy experience of trying to wedge a much-needed rented oven through a door or gate that was too small.

Site Inspections

All the reasons just mentioned make it mandatory for the caterer to visit the site personally, rather than rely on a client's enthusiastic description of the location. A dose of realism is necessary, and a firsthand look is the only way to get it. In addition to permitting you to assess the items on our checklist, a visit enables you to meet the key people at the site who may be able to assist you. Most off-premise caterers bring all or some of these things to a site inspection:

- Sample menus, brochures, and business cards
- Notes or contracts from prior discussions with clients
- Paper, pen or pencil, and clipboard
- A small camera to photograph the event site and its features (if your cell phone doesn't take photos)
- An oven thermometer (if using an existing oven on-site)
- A tape measure
- Your preprinted site inspection checklist

There are two types of site visits—the one you perform on your own to get information about the site in general and to meet its event staff or manager, and the one you perform with a client before a particular event, to ensure that the client is comfortable with the site and discuss the party plans. (See "A Day in the Life of an Off-Premise Caterer: The Site Preview" on pages 200–201 for a real-life example of such a walk-through. It is proof of the flexibility that is needed as an off-premise caterer.)

Your goal is to become a preferred vendor at as many event sites as possible. This means not only can you bring business to them, but they can bring business to you, by recommending you to people who want to have events at their site. Just remember that many venues require caterers working on-site to share a percentage of their food and/or beverage profits. You must be willing to do this, and it might change the way you determine what to charge the client.

The best way to become a preferred vendor is to do what you do exceedingly well—cater events there that go smoothly, keep the site managers informed and feeling valuable during the planning process, prove yourself easy to work with, and leave the site in good shape.

Many caterers put vendor information on their websites, allowing potential clients to peruse party locations and link to their websites. If possible, and if you can keep this part of the site sufficiently updated, it's a smart move. As an example, we like the venue list compiled by Black Diamond Caterers in Saratoga Springs, New York. This feature of its website surely endears Black Diamond to the site managers of these venues, as well as to clients. Other caterers feature venue sites in their newsletters to customers.

In a site visit, what exactly are you looking for, other than the perfect ambiance for the upcoming event? A detailed discussion of each element of a site inspection follows.

Electricity

It would be unusual to find an off-premise caterer who has not blown a fuse with a basic electric coffeemaker. Every caterer quickly learns that two coffeemakers cannot be plugged into the same 20-amp circuit because each appliance requires about 16 amps. Because fire marshals are becoming more concerned with the safe use of propane, butane, and Sterno, off-premise caterers should understand some of the technical aspects of the electricity they'll be using. There are a few basic measurements of electricity with which you should be familiar:

- An *ampere* (or *amp*) is a term used to indicate how much electric current flows through a circuit. The larger the diameter of an electrical wire, the more amperes it can safely carry.

- A *volt* is the driving force that sends the ampere through the electrical wire. (One volt is the force it takes to push 1 amp of electricity for 1 second.) Common voltage needs for appliances are 110 to 120 and 208 to 240.

- A *watt* represents the actual consumption of the electric energy. (One watt equals the flow of 1 amp of electricity, at a pressure of 1 volt.) Electrical appliances are often rated in terms of both watts and volts.

To determine the total amount of electricity needed, it is necessary to compute how many watts will be needed to run all the electric appliances—everything from the lighting and musical amplifiers, to the kitchen equipment, plug-in video gear, and anything else. To determine the watts required, multiply the number of volts needed by the number of amperes needed (volts $\times$ amps = watts).

Here are some examples of power needs in off-premise catering situations:

- Kitchen lighting = 1 watt per square foot
- Tent lighting (where guests will be) = 2.5 watts per square foot (not counting "extra" stage lighting or electricity for musicians)

Luckily, wattage requirements aren't too tough to determine. On most commercial equipment, the watts are listed on the UL (Underwriters Laboratory) or other safety approval label; you can ask musicians, lighting personnel, and others for their needs.

Once the total wattage is determined, divide it by 100 to determine the total amps required. (Technically, the voltage is actually 120, but multiplying by 100 provides an extra safety factor.) For example, if 28,000 watts are needed, when this amount is divided by 100, it will reveal that 280 amps are needed—which means fourteen 20-amp circuits. To provide the necessary power, be sure to order a generator with a minimum capacity of 280 amps. And don't forget the "little details"—you can't plug too much into a single circuit. Only one coffeemaker at a time, or you'll blow a fuse!

Most buildings actually use a little more than half of their available electrical power, and there is a way to access the rest when you need it. A licensed electrician can use what is called a *gray box*, a circuit panel board, to tap directly into the power surplus for a particular event. If the event is in (or even near) an existing building, this may be less expensive and more efficient than renting an electric generator. In the event of a power outage, you do need to be prepared with a backup power source. The smallest generators usually produce 50 amps of electricity.

Water

We've already discussed the idea of bringing bottled water to party sites for mixing drinks. However, much more of this vital substance is needed for cooking and cleaning, as well as filling ice water glasses at tables. During the site inspection, identify the water sources, check the potability of the water, and note whether a hose or carrying containers are required. Obviously, if there is no water available—at a building newly under construction, for instance—then it will be necessary to bring enough water. Many caterers fill their own five-gallon containers of bottled water and haul them to the site.

Trash

When the event ends and everyone goes away smiling, who cleans up and what happens to the trash? In some areas, where there is no scheduled trash pickup, off-premise caterers must take all garbage with them. At other locations, there are trash receptacles available, and even staff to remove them. In our experience, there never seem to be enough trashcans, and they overflow all too soon. You might as well assign someone to keep an eye on them and change out the full receptacles for empty ones as needed.

It can be a "clean, green" selling point to offer additional receptacles for recycling. People are accustomed to tossing empty cans and bottles into different receptacles from those used for food waste, and they will happily do so if given the option. Other recycling tips were noted in Chapter 5.

If there will be deep-frying at the party site, you must check to see if there is a container for used cooking oil. Otherwise, it will be necessary to bring your own. You must never dispose of oil or food on the ground, or down a drain, at a party site.

Insurance

Insurance coverage is such a big part of the off-premise catering industry that we are including it in two chapters—here, and in Chapter 12's discussion of possible problems (from falls and food poisoning, to food spoilage and theft) that can occur in business. As a business owner, you should have the following types of insurance coverage:

- *General Liability* protects your business in cases of personal injury, bodily injury, or property damage. A minimum coverage amount of $1 million is suggested.
- *Professional Liability* protects your business from claims that you did not render the professional services usually associated with your business. It is sometimes called *Errors and Omissions* insurance.
- *Liquor Liability,* as its name implies, protects your business against claims that you, or your staff members, served liquor illegally or irresponsibly.
- *Workers' Compensation* is required by your state. It covers employees' on-the-job injury claims.

Why is this important as part of a site inspection? Many off-premise venues now require proof of insurance (and minimum amounts of coverage) for General Liability and Liquor Liability, as well as proof of Workers' Compensation. Many sites require that the location be named as an "additional insured." Some sites also require that the client (your customer) provide proof of insurance.

Some insurers offer a Wedding Insurance package that covers everything from wedding photos to nonrefundable deposits to damage on rented property. It is smart to know about the coverage, or to have a couple of insurance agents' names, to share with brides and grooms or their parents.

More specific policies for individual catered events include Event Assurance insurance (sometimes called *Adverse Weather Coverage*), which is highly recommended. This type of insurance policy is very specific, detailing the date, hours of coverage, locations, and weather conditions (amount of precipitation, wind speed, and temperature, etc.) under which an event will be canceled. Movie and television studios routinely get this type of insurance when they are filming outdoors—why not caterers for outdoor events? Key the term into an online search engine, and you can compare several companies' offerings.

There are other types of insurance that may cover cancellation of events due to incidents beyond your control. There is *Cancellation or Abandonment* insurance, which covers vendors' advance deposit fees in case an event (from a wedding to a rock concert) is canceled. Sometimes *Non-Appearance* is combined with *Cancellation/Abandonment* in one policy, which provides indemnity for the planners or promoters of an event if specific persons (named in the contract) don't show up as a result of accident, illness, or death. There's even a clause for *Disgrace*, meaning that if a celebrity does something that is publicly offensive before an event, his or her presence may no longer be desired there—again, leaving planners and contractors in the lurch, having already paid deposits, rented equipment, and made arrangements. The type of coverage, and who should pay for it, depends on the type of event and your role in it.

Rain Plan

A "must do" at any site inspection is an agreement between caterer and client on a plan of action in case of inclement weather. Mother Nature can smile on, or ruin, a fabulous outdoor event. Sometimes tents will provide the solution; at other times, it may be necessary to move the party indoors. The important thing is that this solution should be agreed upon in advance of the event, and the client and caterer should also agree upon the time the decision will be made. The time may be the morning of the event, so that there is enough time to call for a prearranged, last-minute tent installation or to move the party to another location. We catered one outdoor wedding at which a group of the bride's friends had a copy of the guest list, complete with phone numbers. Each member of the group was given a portion of the list, enabling them to call and confirm a location change with all the guests when it began to pour that morning.

Off-Premise Kitchen and Staging Areas

The kitchen and staging areas are where the caterer will complete on-site preparation and arrange everything for event service. Some locations—churches, synagogues, community centers, and the like—are equipped with commercial kitchens. This generally makes the job much easier; however, during the site inspection it is still necessary to check the facility's exhaust systems, trash containers, drainage, hot and cold running water, doorway size leading into and out of the kitchen, refrigeration, freezers, ice machines, and fire extinguishers.

All too often, you'll be setting up in a place where there is no commercial kitchen, making it necessary to evaluate various locations in (and around) the party site for a suitable kitchen/staging area. Think about whether the area is:

- Covered, in case of inclement weather
- Out of the guests' view
- Well lit
- Close to where the guests will be
- Close to the loading or receiving area
- Easy and safe for service staff to enter and exit

Most of all, determine whether the menu you have in mind can realistically be finished and served at this venue, even if most of the prep work is done at your commissary. Let's examine some typical locations used by off-premise caterers for cooking and staging catered events, to check out their possible advantages and disadvantages.

Home Kitchens. These are fine for small parties, but for larger events they pose many obstacles—ovens that are too small for full sheet pans and steam table pans, insufficient storage space, inadequate refrigeration, and poor layout. When a home kitchen is the only alternative, caterers must remember to bring smaller baking pans, check the oven for accurate temperature controls, store as much as possible in a back room or garage during the party to avoid cluttering the kitchen, bring adequate cold food holding equipment, and be sure there is adequate ventilation to remove cooking odors and heat from the home.

Garages and Carports. These are excellent in warmer climates because the off-premise caterer has more open space and is able to lay out the kitchen based on the needs for the specific party. Six- and eight-foot banquet tables can be placed strategically around the area for use as worktables. In most areas it is fine to cook inside garages with butane, electricity, or Sterno, but if propane gas is to be used for cooking, both the propane and the cooking equipment must not be located inside the garage. It can be placed close to the garage, but always outside, for safety reasons.

Cook Tents.   In areas where there is no suitable covered space for a kitchen, off-premise caterers will frequently rent or provide cook tents. They are available in various sizes, the smallest being 10-feet square. They frequently are used in parking lots or outside commercial or public buildings with no interior cooking facilities. Cook tents may or may not need side panels and lighting, depending on the weather and the time of day they'll be used. If all sides are closed, ventilation is limited, so it is best to close only the sides that may be affected by inclement weather.

Food Trucks.   Mobile kitchens used to have to be custom conversions of buses, vans, or motor homes. But today, you can order a fully equipped catering truck that enables you to add street fairs, corporate lunch stops, and more to your repertoire. Film industry caterers, for instance, are fully equipped to prepare a gourmet meal in custom-designed kitchens, no matter where the film crew is working. These units require a major investment of time and money, but if you'll really use them, you should investigate the options and talk with caterers who use such mobile facilities. You can learn more about mobile kitchens in Chapter 5.

Other Cooking and Staging Areas.   The options are endless, but most experienced off-premise caterers have at one time or another worked on loading docks, in alleyways covered by overhangs, in empty rooms or offices, or in vacant storefronts. Again, adaptability is key. Where there is a will to have a party, the ingenious off-premise caterer will find a place to prepare the food under safe conditions.

Additional Considerations

Existing Equipment.   Many locations already have some features necessary for the catered event—perhaps a bar, some tables and chairs, an outdoor barbecue grill. As long as you are allowed to use them and they're in good working order, they can reduce the amount of equipment you'll need to bring along. Experienced caterers note these features and discuss them with clients to decide whether they can be used at the event. Part of the agreement should include who is responsible if something is broken or damaged during the event.

Delivery and Pickup Logistics. Where will you, and any rental equipment companies, unload food, equipment, and supplies at the site? This can be very complicated, particularly in high-rise buildings where there are crowded loading docks and a couple of different sets of elevators to reach the party site. While inspecting the site, caterers should decide where to unload, and where the rental companies should do the same, because it often happens that a rental company makes its delivery long before the off-premise caterer arrives on-site. There must be a place for secure storage of this equipment, as well as someone to receive and sign for it, and a place to store it after the event until is retrieved by the rental company. If there is no secure place, then the rental company may need to pick up at a specific time (and usually at an extra cost), immediately upon conclusion of the event, or the caterer may need to keep an eye on the rental equipment or pack it up and take it.

Proposed Event Layout. At this time, the off-premise caterer (usually with the client) will begin to discuss where everything will take place during the event. Some public locations have floor plans drawn to scale; most private residences do not. Techniques for laying out and designing catered events are discussed later in this chapter. But during the site inspection, you should at least prepare a rough diagram of the event, noting the significant features that will affect the layout.

Permit Requirements. Zoning, fire, and other permits can be surprisingly problematic. Rental companies can often help in this arena. Some caterers insist it is less expensive to hire off-duty firefighters than to meet the flame-retardant codes for tenting. If guests are traveling by motor coach to a private mansion in a private neighborhood, neighbors may complain about the noise from the motor coaches. Noise restrictions in some neighborhoods can ruin a perfectly outstanding party when the police arrive to shut down the event. Ask about every possible type of permit, and its availability at this location for this type of event, before you or your clients commit to a site.

Meeting the "VIPs." You will soon learn that at many public event sites, there are people who work behind the scenes who can be invaluable to you because they are familiar with the venue and know how to get things done. They are not just the site managers, but such helpful folks as loading dock personnel (who can make deliveries and pickups more efficient), building maintenance people and/or engineers (who know the locations of utilities, circuit breakers, etc.), audiovisual technicians (who can handle the microphones, screens, sound systems, etc.), and the security staff (who can assist with securing equipment, parking rules, etc.). For home parties, many clients employ cleaning and maintenance workers, who will know where things are and can help solve minor problems before and during the event. Ask about these people during the site inspection or seek them out during the setup period, and enlist their help if necessary.

Other Site Inspection Details. There are a number of miscellaneous, but important, details to be considered: rental fees for the space (and cleaning fees afterward); rules and regulations; and policies regarding liquor service, security, and parking for guests. All of these must be confirmed at the site inspection. Many off-premise caterers have been surprised by rule changes at a facility they thought they were familiar with. For example, a caterer prepares to set up a bar in a particular spot and is informed that this cannot be done because the rules were just changed—but no one told the caterer. Some off-premise caterers require that someone from the facility sign a written copy of the rules to avoid these last-minute hassles or frustrations.

Site inspections should include a check of restroom facilities, as well as accessibility for persons with disabilities. Problems in these areas should be resolved well in advance, not during the event.

Timing. The timing for event setup and teardown is critical. Many museums and historic sites are open until late in the day, leaving off-premise caterers a limited amount of time to set up for private after-hours functions; others book back-to-back functions and let the caterers and rental companies figure out how to juggle them. At the end of an evening, most of these facilities require removal of all party equipment. Some have special fees for loading in and out, some require use of union labor, and many have restrictions on rolling tables over expensive flooring.

If there are elevators, know how they work and where they go. Be sure that the clients have arranged for their use. Off-premise caterers should allow additional time for setting up and tearing down parties that are not on a ground floor. We've discovered a major problem in high-rise office buildings the hard way—cleaning personnel often have exclusive use of some or all of the elevators, making it impossible for caterers to enter and exit. If this is the case, it is imperative that the clients or building management make the necessary arrangements.

Alerting Your Staff. Advance planning for the staff members who will work the party should include providing them with an exact address and directions to the party site, finding out where the staff will park, and determining where the staff will change into their uniforms after setup but prior to the event. There should also be an emergency phone number at the site that will be answered after hours. This can be a problem in an office, where the receptionist goes home as the party begins. It is imperative to know the name and cell phone numbers of the event captain, caterer, and fellow workers at the event.

Particularly for large and/or formal or tightly formatted events, it is helpful to give all staff members who will be attending the event a printed summary. This should include the schedule, details about the menu, and a brief outline of their table assignments and specific duties for the event. An example is shown in Exhibit 6.1.

EXHIBIT 6.1 Event Briefing and Staff Schedule

Staff Time Schedule

Time	Task	Staff
12:00 P.M.	Load In	Bruce, Jeff Marv Max, Rachel, Vicki N. Mike M. Candace,
1:00–1:30	Depart for Site; On Site staff arrives	Vicki T. Debbie, Chris, Jory, Scooter, Fernando, Scott, Jay
1:30 P.M.	Unload	
2:00 P.M.	Set up tables	VIP ATRIUM/WASATCH
2:00 P.M.	Set up kitchen	Maxine
2:00 P.M.	Set up VIP Reception	Chris/Mike
2:30 P.M.		Matt on site
2:30 P.M.	Set up Atrium	Bruce/Vicki T./Jory
2:30 P.M.	Set up Buffets	Bruce/Rachel/Candace/Scott
2:30 P.M.	Bar #1—South	Marv/Fernando
2:30 P.M.	Bar #2—North	Jay
4:00 P.M.	Bar #3—Wasatch Linens & Centerpieces Chefs on Site	Matt
4:45 P.M.	Final Staff on Site	Debbie/Scooter

(Continued)

EXHIBIT 6.1 Event Briefing and Staff Schedule (*Continued*)

5:00 P.M.	Break	
5:15 P.M.	Staff Meeting	
5:30–6:30 P.M.	All VIP Staff at Post	Pompawit/Karla
	VIP Reception	
6:30–7:30 P.M.	Butler Hors d'oeuvres/Champagne	
7:30 P.M.	Open Bar #3—Wasatch Room Open Buffets	
7:45 P.M.	Reset Desserts in Atrium	
9:00 P.M.	Dessert/Choc. Fountain Coffee Atrium	
10:00 P.M.	Breakdown	

Instruction to Staff
Read through handout
No bottled water given at bars — pour into glassware
Save all clean linen by folding on creases — especially tray stands
Keep tables clean
Quiet Service
No Tip Jars
At end of evening return jackets if not your own

Astro VIP Reception—5:30–6:30 P.M.

Private VIP Reception—Conference Room
Butler served hors d'oeuvres will include…
Pear & Bleu Cheese Filo Bundles
Stuffed Mushrooms with Fresh Herbs & Kalamata Olive
Petite Chicken Filo Bundles
Skewers of Grilled Lamb with Fried Artichokes
Beef Tenderloin Roulade
Cheese Table—Sonoma Artisan Cheese
Flatbread Crackers & Toasted Crostini

Wine & Beer Service
Iced Soft Drinks & Bottled Water

Main Reception 6:30–7:15 P.M.

Guests will descend the dramatic staircase from the 24th floor to the atrium
We butler serve:
Sparkling Champagne Flutes
California Champagne with Slice of Fresh Strawberry
Double Cheese Station will be set within the atrium

Gourmet Cheese Station

Fruit & Nut Brie Wheels—Gourmet Cheese Display
Served with Baskets of Petite French Bread Rounds, flatbreads & savory crackers, all served on hammered silver platters

Hors D'oeuvre Station

Salmon Horns with Capers & Fresh Dill
Petite Artichoke Caper Lavosh
Chicken Wontons with Plum Dipping Sauce

Full Bar Service

Two full bars will be available in the atrium. We will move one bar into the East Room at 7:30 P.M.

For the convenience of your guests, cocktail tables with black leather chairs and tallboy tables will be available in the atrium

Layout
Atrium & Turnover to Dessert Station

Smile & Enjoy!!
Thank you for being here.

At 7:15 P.M., guests will be invited for dinner in the Wasatch Room where they will enjoy a full dinner buffet, from double-sided buffets at south end of room

Chef-Carved Peppered Sirloin, served to order with a trio of sauces
 Coffee-Scented BBQ Sauce—Horseradish Sauce—Au Jus

Grilled Chicken Breasts with Lemon Thyme Sauce
 Stuffed with Fresh Asparagus, Roma Tomatoes & Zucchini

Mesquite-Grilled Salmon with Pineapple Papaya Salsa

Spinach & Cheese Manicotti
 Traditional Meatless Marinara, Asiago & Romano Cheeses

Field Greens with Grilled Peppered Pear Slices
 Goat Cheese Galettes, Champagne Vinaigrette

Grilled Harvest Vegetables
 An abundance of fresh vegetables, to include Carrots, Squash, Zucchini, Fennel, Potatoes, Pumpkin,
 Celeriac & Baby Beets

"Old Country" Panzanella Salad

Breads & Spreads
 An assortment of rolls & bread sticks with a trio of butters:
 Herb Butter—Basil Butter—Sundried Tomato Butter

(Continued)

EXHIBIT 6.1 Event Briefing and Staff Schedule (*Continued*)

The Finale Station

Dessert will be set in the atrium . . .

We offer our incredible
Almond Pound Cake
Surrounded by Fresh Fruit & drizzled with Zabaglione Cream, set on tiered Plexiglass

We will also offer an assortment of
Petite Sweets

Miniature Cheesecake with Fresh Berries

Raspberry Rugelach

Greek Pecan Crescents

Lemon Cheese Tarts topped with Raspberry

Mint Brownies

Chocolate Truffles

Bailey's Irish Cream-Filled Chocolate Cups

Served with Regular & Decaf Coffee

Espresso Martinis available from the bar

Layout

Wasatch Room — Buffets & Seating

Staff Assignment

Bruce	Captain
Jeff	Production
Marv	Bar #1 to Buffet #1
Max	Kitchen
Rachel	Buffet #1
Vicki N.	VIP Buffet #2
Vicki T.	Atrium Hors D'oeuvre station to Dessert station
Chris	Champagne to Floor Mgr.
Jory	Atrium Hors D'oeuvre station to Dessert station
Candace	Buffet #2

Scooter	Porter
Debbie	Floor
Scott	Floor
Mike M.	VIP to Bar #1 to Bar #3
Fernando	Bar #1 to Floor
Jay	Bar #2 all night
Matt	Champagne then to Bar #3
Karla	Bar #2 to Bar #3
Pompawit	Pass Champagne/Floor

Floor Staff Notes

Chris gives area assignments

Staff to work these areas all evening, but assist each other as needed

Serve on left, clear from right

Be sure person is finished before removing plates or clearing glassware

Remove linen napkin once dessert is served

Do not stack dishes on top of each other

Use tray jacks to remove silverware and food. Don't scrape dishes

Cover dirty dishes on tray stands w/linen

Folded linen on arm at all times

Stack stemware in middle dishes/flatware on outside to prevent glass breakage

Smile & Be Professionally Friendly!

Source: Courtesy of Cuisine Unlimited Catering and Special Events, Salt Lake City, Utah.

Caterers should be aware that some restrictive rules are actually subject to negotiation, particularly if they will prohibit a party from being held at a facility. Such things as early setup can be discussed with the facility manager and can sometimes be resolved by paying an additional fee. Off-premise caterers who frequently work at unique, public off-premise locations have learned to advise the client that there may be additional costs involved in catering the event due to unforeseen circumstances, and a contingency clause should be included in the catering contract. For example, when a site is not made available to the caterer on time and the caterer needs to hire extra last-minute staffers to have the party set up on time, the caterer can charge for the extra staff if the contract includes a contingency clause.

A Day in the Life of an Off-Premise Caterer: The Site Preview

The catering salesperson for every event does a walk-through with the client(s) and staff from the venue where the event will take place. This is typically done a few weeks before the event, but today it's being done in May for an event that is scheduled in September—because one of the clients, who lives in another part of the country, happens to be in town.

In preparation for this walk-through, the caterer reviews all documents related to the event so far: the initial order, the contract, and so on. She brings hard copies of the documents in case they need to refer to them during the meeting.

This event is a buffet dinner for 150 people, affiliates of a national nonprofit group coming from around the country. It's the final get-together that tops off three days of meetings. The site is the visitor center for a nature preserve in a mountain resort community, chosen to reflect the group's environmental stewardship values. It contains wildlife-related exhibits and, in the middle, a climbing wall. It also has an observation tower overlooking the preserve acreage.

The walk-through is a tour, led by a representative of the venue, where the clients discuss the layout and logistics for the event and ask questions of the site manager.

Perusing the site, the caterer thinks immediately that the indoor space is too small to comfortably hold 150 people, but if some of the exhibits are moved, it might be possible. However, the first information shared is that several of the largest displays cannot be moved from their spots. A couple of them are large and flat enough to be covered and used as buffet tables or a dessert bar without harming the exhibits, and the manager says that this is permissible. However, they're not in very good positions for crowd flow.

The caterer suggests putting the bar outdoors on the large, partially covered deck and all agree that is a good idea. It will also require a contingency plan in case of bad weather—not typical in that area in September, but not out of the question. The clients, in high-heeled shoes, note that their heels are getting caught fairly often between boards as they walk around on the deck. They make a note to tell everyone to wear flat shoes for this event, so that no one trips or falls.

The clients say that they have hired a band and want a dance floor too. This is the first the caterer has heard of this, and it further squeezes the already limited space. Four different spots near walls and corners are debated for the band. The possibility is raised that some people might have to eat, and then briefly vacate one area of the room so that a few tables can be moved to open up some space for dancing—this is somewhat awkward, but not impossible.

Lighting is turned on and off; automated window treatments are raised and lowered. The site rep says that one wall is movable, which will help. The climbing wall is not and, unfortunately, it cuts right through the middle of the room. The caterer notices some classroom-style banquet tables and asks if they can be used. The answer is yes, saving the clients that rental cost.

The clients ask the caterer how much liquor to buy. With their conference just finishing up, they say that the crowd will definitely be "in a party mood." The caterer says that she'll give them a basic list and they can change it as needed. They are on an extremely tight budget and want to know if it would be cheaper for them to purchase the alcohol themselves; the caterer explains that in this state, it is illegal for a caterer to make a profit on the alcohol. The only component of bar service that a caterer can "sell" for profit is the setups for drinks—mixes, garnishes, and so on. The clients also want to know if they can bring in volunteers with liquor service licenses to do the bartending. The caterer informs them about liquor liability, explaining that the catering company has all the necessary insurance for alcohol service and must name the venue as a coinsured party on the policy for that event. In short—nix the volunteer bartenders.

A highlight of this venue is an observation tower, several stories tall, where people can go up and view the nature preserve. The scenery is very pretty, but the tower itself is not. If guests don't take the elevator, they will climb several flights of concrete stairs with absolutely no décor, anywhere. The caterer knows the clients don't have the budget to really decorate the additional space, but she suggests adding a little bit of greenery and barrels full of ice and bottled water on the landings. They agree.

The walk-through takes a little more than an hour. The clients leave happy and excited about the upcoming event—and the caterer gets busy planning it, based on what she has learned in this all-important site visit.

Creating a Venue Database

No matter how often you cater there, you should keep an extensive and detailed database of every potential event site in your area. The database can be in table form, should be updated regularly, and should include the following information:

- Name, address, and website of venue
- Name of site manager or contact
- Site manager or contact's phone and fax numbers
- Site manager or contact's e-mail address
- Maximum number of guests for (1) a reception and (2) a formal, seated meal
- Fees charged for use of the site (or portions thereof)
- Whether beer, wine, and/or liquor can be served
- Numbers, types, and sizes of tables available on-site
- Numbers and types of chairs available on-site
- Other miscellaneous equipment (podium, dance floor, microphone, coatroom, and coatracks)
- Kitchen facilities on-site (full kitchen, prep area, warming area, staging area, etc.)
- Whether security is available and, if so, whether the caterer is charged extra for it

Planning and Designing the Catered Event

The results of the site inspection, coupled with the menu and other information, are the input for the party layout. For simple parties, the layout can be roughly sketched during the site inspection, but for most events, the rough diagrams and notes from the site inspection can easily be incorporated into an event layout on your computer—a professional-looking scale diagram you can show to clients. This diagram should include locations of all the following:

- Registration tables and check-in areas
- For weddings: gift, cake, and place card tables

- Bars, buffets, and food stations
- Seating for guests during cocktails and dinner
- Service stations for staff
- Dance floors, stages, and space for entertainers
- Off-premise catering kitchen and staging area

The diagram should be to scale to ensure that things will fit where planned. Disasters have occurred when off-premise caterers assumed after eyeing a room that a certain number of tables would surely fit—and they did not.

Caterers used to make such diagrams with a sharp pencil and graph paper, but today event design software takes the guesswork out of design and saves a great deal of time. Among caterers, one of the most popular of these programs is Vivien, the "virtual event designer," from CAST Software, a company known since the 1990s for its theater and film design production software. Vivien even enables you to simulate the time of day and appropriate lighting conditions in your computerized renderings.

Layout and Design Criteria

Front of the House (Guest Spaces). Unlike hotel ballrooms and catering halls, off-premise locations used for catering have specific primary uses unrelated to food-service, thus creating unique challenges. The size, shape, and flow of the location influence the layout and design. Questions to ask while determining an overall layout include:

- How many guests will attend?
- Where will they arrive?
- What are the menu and beverage arrangements?
- Are there other planned activities, such as dancing or speeches?
- Are there existing features to work with (or around), such as bars and seating?
- Where is the kitchen in relation to where guests will be?
- What is the theme of the party or event?

Prior to you considering each element of the layout, it is important that you understand some generally accepted square footage requirements.

Type of Event or Requirement	Square Feet Per Person
Stand-up cocktail party	5 to 6
Cocktail party, with some seating	8
Dinner, rectangular tables	8
Dinner, 60-inch rounds, set for 10	10
Dinner, 48-inch rounds, set for 6	12
60-inch rounds for 8	12
72-inch rounds for 10	12
Theater-style seating (weddings)	6
Dance floor	2 to 4
Speaker's platform	10

For bands, allow 10 square feet per musician, 20 square feet for the drummer, 30 square feet for a spinet piano or keyboard, and 100 square feet for a grand piano. If the musicians are on risers or platforms, steps and railings should be provided for safety.

For theater-style seating, allow 3 feet from the front of one chair to the back of the next one. Suggested spacing is 5 feet between guest tables at seated events. For large events with hundreds of guests, the seating area should be divided into "groups" of tables, with 6-foot-wide main aisles between sections. For example, a party with 40 tables could be divided into four groups of 10 tables each, with a 6-foot aisle in between. Head tables at which guests are seated on only one side are usually impractical at off-premise events where space is at a premium because they require twice as much space as regular guest seating at round tables.

Coat checks and registration tables should be placed near the entrance for security and the convenience of the guests. Off-premise caterers should advise clients to provide adequate registration personnel to prevent long lines, which may extend outside the event site. Bars, buffets, and food stations should be strategically placed around the room—never clustered all in one area. Bars should be set up so guests may see them upon arrival, but not so close to the entrance as to block the flow of guests into the party. Bars generally require 100 to 150 square feet of space. One bar with one or two bartenders is generally adequate for efficient guest service, depending on the type of drinks offered and the skill of the bartenders.

Displaying Food. Dramatic buffets and food stations create excitement, interest, and intrigue. They should act as magnets, drawing guests into the room and reflecting the theme (and sometimes, even the budget) of the event. A buffet is simply a style of service that permits the guests to portion and plate their own food. Buffets save on labor costs, but they can actually increase your profit margin because not everyone "loads up" at a buffet. Ironically, the more attractive the display, the less people eat, because they do not want to ruin its appearance!

Straight, long tables are boring for these types of displays; Exhibit 6.2 depicts more creative ways to fit standard-sized tables together.

There are some basic rules for buffet setup:

- Never place a buffet (or a bar) adjacent to the dance floor or music.
- Allow plenty of space between stations for guests to circulate.
- Allow adequate surfaces on which empty drink glasses may be placed.
- Attempt to locate the food as close as possible to the kitchen, to minimize the distance traveled for initial setup and replenishment.
- Place lowest-cost items first on the line.
- Expensive items (caviar, beef tenderloin) should be portioned by servers and carvers.
- Pre-portion appropriate items into smaller portions because people may prefer small amounts of certain things.
- Remember that guests tend to take less food from small containers.

If all guests are eating at the same time, 50 to 75 people can be served promptly on each line. Because two-sided self-service lines take less space, 100 to 150 guests can be served from one double-line table instead of two singles. A carver or server can stand at the end of each line, portioning or carving one or two expensive items. Exhibit 6.3 diagrams a simple buffet with food servers and one carver.

Buffets longer than 16 feet should be the width of two tables, or 60 inches. A wider buffet seems in better proportion, more like a lovely, generous display and less like a cafeteria line.

The "props" you will use to decorate the buffet lines must be organized and transported to the event site like everything else. Centerpieces and even some buffet dishes can be elevated for visual effect with the use of sturdy, empty crates or boxes made of natural wood, brushed steel, or covered with fabric. (You can purchase damaged linens from rental companies for this purpose.) Head to the hardware store or even the local

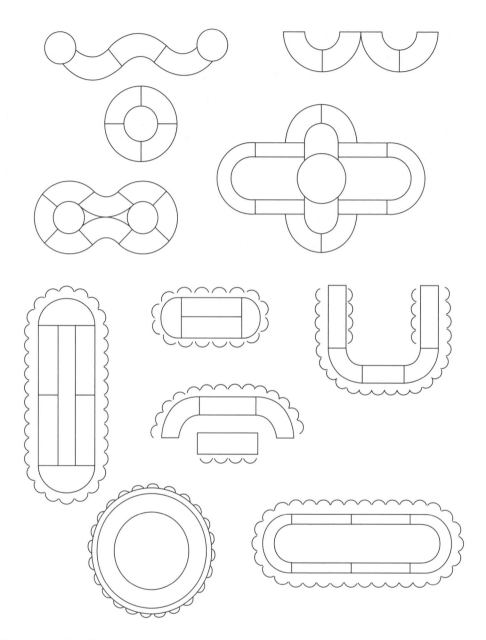

Exhibit 6.2 Buffet Table Layouts

(Courtesy of the American Rental Association, Moline, Illinois.)

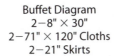

Buffet Diagram
2−8" × 30"
2−71" × 120" Cloths
2−21" Skirts

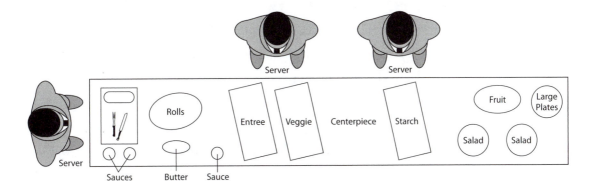

Carving Board
Carving Knife (Sharp)
Carving Fork
Napkin
Sauce Bowls + Spoons
Rolls Basket + Liner
Butter Dish
2 Tongs

3–2 Gl. Chafers
12 Sterno (6 Backup)
Serving Utensils
Matches
Teaspoon for Removing Sterno Lids
Tongs for Replacing Sterno
Appropriate Condiment Bowls + Utensils
1–Fire Extinguisher Beneath Table

Mirror/Bowls for Salads
Tongs/Spoons–Salads
Large Plates for Guests

Exhibit 6.3 Buffet Diagram

garden store or art supply retailer for ideas: Metal shelving grids are handy, sturdy, and attractive. Cargo boxes, river rocks, picture frames, and painter's palettes all can double as display elements.

Decorative mirrors can be used beneath cold foods or flower arrangements; marble slabs, acrylic trays, and tiered cake stands add interesting looks and dimensions to the display. Portable spotlights, floodlights, and lamp stands will also come in handy, as a little extra lighting will showcase a beautiful buffet. But you have to remember to bring all of these items along when you leave the commissary!

Back of the House (Kitchen and Staging Areas). For smaller events in homes and offices, off-premise caterers generally use the existing facilities, making the best of some very difficult situations. Of course, the menu must be compatible with the facility.

The answers to the following questions will help an inexperienced caterer organize an off-premise kitchen within the confines of an existing one.

- Where can backup supplies be stored?
- Where will items be cooked and kept warm?
- Where can cold foods be prepared and kept cold?
- Where will the hot and cold food plating and garnishing take place?
- Where will the food servers pick up food and return dirty dishes?
- Where can coffee be brewed?

For larger events where hundreds are to be served, cooking tents are generally erected if there is no existing (or adequate) kitchen facility. Exhibit 6.4 depicts one way to design a large, off-premise catering kitchen. The following design criteria should be considered:

- Design the kitchen so that servers can easily pick up food (and return soiled dishes) without going through the kitchen. It is good overall safety policy to keep everyone who is not part of the kitchen staff out of the cooking area.
- The busing area for dirty dishes should contain trash receptacles, water for rinsing dishes, and room for empty dish and glass crates. Ideally, this area is at a distance from the cooking area, especially at larger events.
- Four-, six-, and eight-foot banquet tables are excellent for use as kitchen work-tables. Caterers should be sure to allow enough worktables for the type of food-service to be provided.
- The coffee and dessert should be kept at the rear of the tent until ready to be served, and adequate space must be determined for all items pertaining to coffee and dessert service.
- For each course, the necessary equipment and supplies should be gathered together and kept in a common spot, to be used and then set aside as attention shifts to the next course.
- There should always be arrangements made to warm plates for hot food courses.
- Tables are necessary next to the ovens to provide space for the cooks to set down hot foods from the oven.
- The same area used to assemble ("plate up") salads can be used to plate up desserts.

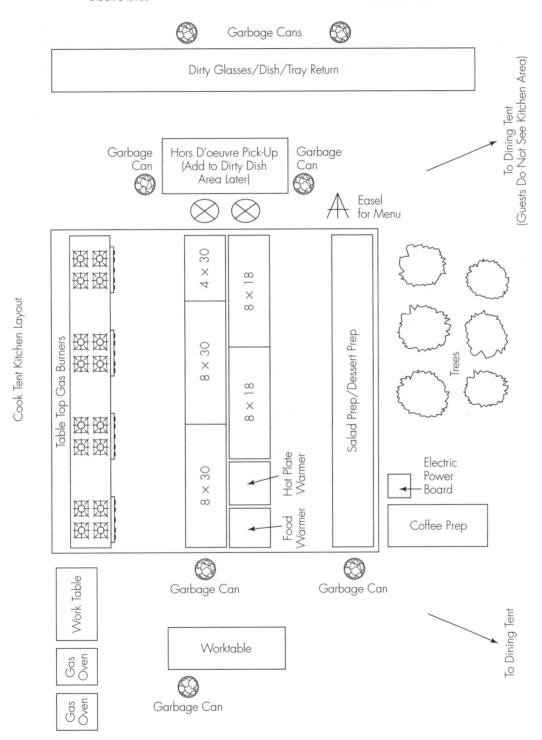

Exhibit 6.4 Cook Tent Kitchen Layout

- Place portable, liquid-fuel warming ovens at the edge of the tent for ventilation. A large sign on an easel for the event's menu, which also lists the ingredients of each item, should be placed near the food pick-up area.

- Proper placement of grill equipment is essential for safety. Barbecues fueled by gas or charcoal require good ventilation and should be placed where smoke doesn't drift over staff members or guests.

Experience is probably the best teacher in learning to utilize space for catered events. The guidelines presented here are only suggestions. Readers should remember that a well-designed party will go a long way toward satisfying the client's needs and can make everyone's job more efficient—and more enjoyable—during the event.

Rental Order Forms and Event Packing Lists

Once the layout and design are complete for the catered event, the event packing list (also called a *pull sheet*) and the final rental equipment order form can be prepared. Most off-premise caterers have forms that make these tasks easier and reduce the likelihood of errors. This section of the chapter includes samples of each list and form.

The idea behind these lists and forms is to ensure that all food, supplies, and equipment necessary for the event are delivered on time, and to the correct location. Items that are provided from the off-premise catering commissary are included on the pull sheet; items to be rented are included on the rental equipment order form. An exception to this rule occurs when an off-premise caterer obtains a small equipment order directly from a rental company. In this case, the rental equipment should be included on the packing list, which reminds the caterer's staff to bring it to the event.

Some caterers just use copies of the rental equipment order form supplied by the rental equipment company, but this may cause confusion if you deal with more than one rental company because each form will be different. It's probably easier for everyone on your staff to develop and use your own form, such as the one in Exhibit 6.5. A rental equipment order form can be developed by listing these major categories:

Chairs

Tables

Tenting and accessories

EXHIBIT 6.5 Rental Equipment Order Form

NAME OF CLIENT _____

DELIVERY ADDRESS _____

DELIVERY DATE _____   TIME TO DELIVER _____

DATE TO PICK UP _____   ORDER PLACED WITH _____ (NAME)

DATE ORDER PLACED _____

QTY ORD	QTY REC'D	QTY REC'D	ITEM AND DESCRIPTION	PRICE
			CHAIRS	____
____	____	____	SAMSONITE	____
____	____	____	WHITE WOOD WITH PADDED SEAT	____
____	____	____	BALLROOM	____
____	____	____	OTHER_____	____
____	____	____	TABLES	____
____	____	____	8 FOOT BY 30″ BANQUET TABLES	
____	____	____	8 FOOT BY 18″ BANQUET TABLES	
____	____	____	6 FOOT BY 30″ BANQUET TABLES	
____	____	____	6 FOOT BY 18″ BANQUET TABLES	
____	____	____	4 FOOT BY 30″ BANQUET TABLES	
____	____	____	72″ ROUND TABLES	
____	____	____	60″ ROUND TABLES	
____	____	____	48″ ROUND TABLES	
____	____	____	36″ ROUND TABLES	
____	____	____	30″ ROUND TABLES	
____	____	____	QUARTER ROUND TABLES	
____	____	____	QUARTER ROUND PIE TABLES	
____	____	____	HALF ROUND TABLES	
____	____	____	OTHER SPECIAL TABLES	
____	____	____	UMBRELLA TABLES AND CHAIR SETS	____
____	____	____	TENTING AND ACCESSORIES	
____	____	____	DINING TENT SIZE _____ WITH SIDES? _____	
____	____	____	COOKS TENT SIZE _____ WITH SIDES? _____	
____	____	____	CEILING FANS	____
____	____	____	TENT LINER	
____	____	____	POLE COVERS	____
____	____	____	ASTROTURF	
____	____	____	FLOORING	

(Continued)

EXHIBIT 6.5 Rental Equipment Order Form (*Continued*)

			OVENS, RANGES, AND FOOD-WARMING CABINETS	
___	___	___	SIX-BURNER RANGE WITH OVEN	___
___	___	___	FOUR-BURNER RANGE WITH OVEN	___
___	___	___	SIX-BURNER RANGE ONLY	___
___	___	___	OVEN ONLY	___
___	___	___	FOOD-WARMING CABINETS	___

LINENS, CHAIR COVERS, AND TABLE SKIRTING

- 132" ROUND CLOTH COLOR
- 120" ROUND CLOTH COLOR
- 108" ROUND CLOTH COLOR
- 90" ROUND CLOTH COLOR
- NAPKINS TYPE _____ COLOR
- 60" BY 120" BANQUET CLOTH COLOR
- 90" BY 90" BANQUET CLOTH COLOR
- 62" BY 62" CLOTH COLOR
- CHAIR COVERS COLOR
- CHAIR COVER SASHES COLOR
- SKIRTING COLOR _____ SIZE _____
- SKIRTING COLOR_____ SIZE _____

CHINA—SELECT PATTERN AND COLOR

- SERVICE PLATE (SHOW PLATE)
- DINNER PLATE
- DESSERT/SALAD PLATE
- BREAD AND BUTTER PLATE
- SOUP CUP UNDERLINER
- SOUP CUP
- COFFEE CUP AND SAUCER
- DEMITASSE CUP AND SAUCER
- CREAMERS
- SUGARS
- GRAVY BOATS
- SALT AND PEPPER SETS
- OTHER

FLATWARE—SELECT TYPE

- DINNER KNIFE
- BUTTER SPREADER

____	____	____	FISH KNIFE	____
____	____	____	TEA KNIFE	____
____	____	____	DINNER FORK	____
____	____	____	SALAD/CAKE FORK	____
____	____	____	COCKTAIL FORK	____
____	____	____	TEASPOON	____
____	____	____	SOUP SPOON	____
____	____	____	DESSERT SPOON	____
____	____	____	ICED TEASPOON	____
____	____	____	DEMITASSE SPOON	____
____	____	____	PASTA SPOON	____

SERVING PIECES AND EQUIPMENT

- LARGE SERVING SPOON
- SMALL SERVING SPOON
- SERVING FORK
- LADLE
- CAKE/PIE SERVER
- CAKE KNIFE
- ONE GALLON ROUND CHAFER
- TWO GALLON OBLONG CHAFER
- EXTRA PANS HALF _____ FULL_____
- 50 CUP SAMOVAR
- 100 CUP SAMOVAR
- COFFEE POURER
- WATER PITCHERS
- OVAL TRAYS
- ROUND TRAYS
- GLOW ICE DISPLAY

GLASSWARE

- TULIP CHAMPAGNE
- BUBBLE WINE GLASS 12 OZ
- BUBBLE WINE GLASS 9 OZ
- IRISH COFFEE MUGS
- CRYSTAL CHAMPAGNE FLUTE
- CRYSTAL WINE GOBLET
- CRYSTAL WATER GOBLET
- BRANDY SNIFTER
- CORDIAL GLASS

(Continued)

EXHIBIT 6.5 Rental Equipment Order Form (*Continued*)

____	____	____	OTHER RENTAL EQUIPMENT
____	____	____	GENERATOR
____	____	____	PLATFORMS FOR MUSIC AND SPEAKERS SIZE_____
____	____	____	STEPS FOR PLATFORMS
____	____	____	RAILING FOR PLATFORMS
____	____	____	SKIRTING FOR PLATFORM COLOR _____ SIZE _____
____	____	____	DANCE FLOOR SIZE ____ TYPE ____
____	____	____	CHAMPAGNE FOUNTAIN
____	____	____	BRIDAL KNEELING BENCH
____	____	____	BRIDAL ARCH
____	____	____	GUEST BOOK STAND
____	____	____	FLOWER BASKET STAND
____	____	____	WHITE LATTICE GAZEBO
____	____	____	WHITE LATTICE CHUPPAH
____	____	____	OTHER MISCELLANEOUS EQUIPMENT
____	____	____	_____
____	____	____	_____
____	____	____	_____
____	____	____	SUBTOTAL OF ORDER
____	____	____	EXTRA FEE FOR NIGHT PICK-UP
____	____	____	ABOVE-GROUND DELIVERY FEE
____	____	____	TOTAL PRICE OF ORDER
____	____	____	NOTES FROM RENTAL CHECK-IN, I.E., DAMAGED
____	____	____	OR MISSING EQUIPMENT, OTHER PROBLEMS
____	____	____	CREDIT DUE FOR THE ABOVE
____	____	____	BALANCE DUE RENTAL COMPANY

Kitchen equipment

Linens

China

Flatware

Serving pieces and equipment

Glassware

Other (generators, gazebos, and one-time items not commonly rented)

The rental equipment order form should include space for the size, type, and color of each item. It is a good idea to leave space on the form for caterer's or salesperson's notes. For instance, there may be four 8-foot by 30-inch tables needed for the buffets, eight 8-by-30 tables needed for the kitchen staff, one 8-by-30 table for the gifts, and two 8-by-30 tables for bar service. So a total of fifteen 8-by-30 tables must be rented, and it helps when completing this order form to have room to jot thoughts and instructions, which can save time in the long run.

The top of the form or a cover page should indicate:

- Name of client
- Date of event
- Delivery address
- Delivery date and time
- Pick-up date and time
- Rental company name
- Name of salesperson who took order
- Date the order is placed

The objective of developing a rental equipment order form is to list everything needed for the event that is not being provided by you, the off-premise caterer. The caterer's current equipment inventory and the proposal or contract will determine which items must be rented. When completing this form, check the menu, necessary kitchen equipment, and other services that will be provided. Ask questions like:

- Is there another event taking place at the same time for which your own equipment will already be needed—grills, trays, china, glassware, and so on?
- How will each menu item be presented? Think about the plate sizes and necessary utensils and whether you have enough of them on hand. Include serving pieces, not just flatware needed by the guests.
- Does the contract specify providing platforms, dance floors, audiovisual equipment, special lighting, or other items?

- Table size affects the numbers of service items needed. Will 60-inch or 72-inch rounds be used for dining? If using 72s at an upscale event, three creamers and three sets of salt and pepper shakers per table are necessary.

- What other services are being contracted? The minister may need a sound system. The bride and groom may request kneeling benches. The harpist may ask for a small platform. The musicians may need chairs.

The list is long and detailed. When developing a printed rental equipment order form, consider making it a multipart form so the same information can be used to check the order before the event and to perform an inventory after the event. Anything that arrives damaged on delivery should be noted on the form and replaced right away if possible. An inventory after the event will verify to the caterer any losses charged by the rental company.

It is important to read the contract thoroughly and to know your own inventory very well, so you'll be able to order what you need in advance—and of course, so you can avoid ordering those items you can provide from your own inventory. A Sunday afternoon, hours away from the big bridal reception, is not the time to contact a rental company because something wasn't ordered. And remember, a few additional chairs, napkins, and place settings never hurt, in the event unexpected party guests arrive.

A party packing list can be developed by listing these main categories of event supplies:

- All foods, both uncooked and prepared
- China, glassware, and flatware
- Tables and chairs
- Ovens and other types of cooking equipment
- Pots, pans, and kitchen utensils
- Coffeemakers and samovars
- Sodas, juices, ice, and bar supplies
- Coolers (with ice)
- Buffet and food station equipment and décor

There are also other essentials used at every event; you might as well count on bringing them along:

Aluminum foil and plastic wrap

Napkins

Tool kit

Broom, dustpan, and mop

Fire extinguishers

First aid kit

No two caterers will have the same event packing list, although they will include the same basic items. There are two characteristics that all lists should share. First, the lists should be very specific, including everything the caterer may bring to the event. For example, "pots or pans" is not specific enough. The details are mandatory: What size? How many of each type?

Second, the order of the list should coincide with the various storage areas within the caterer's operation and, if possible, be arranged in the same order as the shelving. If, for instance, an off-premise caterer has a front storeroom and a back storeroom, items for the front storeroom should be listed together on one section of the packing list, and those for the back storeroom listed in a separate section.

These pull sheets (indicating what to "pull" from inventory and take along) should include a front page, or cover page, that states the following:

- Name, day, and date of the event
- Client's name and contact information
- Exact address of the event, including directions
- Deadline for having catering vehicle(s) fully loaded
- Specific vehicle(s) to be loaded
- Departure time for your crew to leave for the event site
- Names of those responsible for packing and loading

The objective of developing an event packing list (like the one in Exhibit 6.6) is to detail everything that you, as the caterer, need to provide for the event. And, to save time in the process, you must know that the items you have promised to provide are, indeed, in your inventory and available for use that day, at that event.

Filling out a packing list can be daunting when you're a beginner. The best way to start is to refer to the party contract, which lists all foods, beverages, equipment, and services to be provided by the caterer, and compare that list to what's on the completed rental order form. Break things down to their individual ingredients or components.

EXHIBIT 6.6 Party Packing List

NAME OF PARTY _____

DATE OF PARTY _____

LOADED BY _____

VEHICLE TO BE LOADED _____

DEPART BY _____

NAME AND PHONE NUMBER OF CLIENT _____

LIST ALL FOOD TO BE LOADED FOR THE PARTY:

_____   _____
_____   _____
_____   _____
_____   _____
_____   _____
_____   _____
_____   _____
_____   _____
_____   _____
_____   _____
_____   _____
_____   _____
_____   _____
_____   _____
_____   _____
_____   _____
_____   _____
_____   _____
_____   _____
_____   _____

Display Fruit

_____

Display Vegetables

_____

Cheese:
    Parmesan
    Cheddar
    Swiss
    Brie
    Bleu
    Saga Blue
    Gruyere

_____

Half & Half
Whipped Cream
Indiv. Creamers

_____

_____

Butter Solids—Unsalted
Butter Solids—Salted
Butter Molds

_____

_____

_____

_____

_____

_____

_____

_____

_____

_____

Leaf Lettuce
Romaine
Watercress
Hydroponic
Bibb Lettuce
Radicchio

_____

_____

Fresh Basil
Fresh Dill
Fresh Tarragon

_____

Lemons
Limes

_____

Hearts of Palm
Hearts of Artichoke

_____

French Bread
Italian Bread
Specialty Bread
Hot Dog Buns
Hamburger Buns
Crackers
Nuts
Croutons

_____

_____

_____

_____

_____

_____

_____

(Continued)

EXHIBIT 6.6 Party Packing List (*Continued*)

Indicate quantities for all nonfood items and equipment:

Pantry Items

_____ Salt
_____ Pepper
_____ Spices
_____ Sugar packets
_____ No-cal sweetener
_____ Individual packets
_____ Salt
_____ Pepper
_____ Mayo
_____ Ketchup
_____ Relish
_____ Mustard
_____ Pam
_____ Frying oil
_____ Vegetable oil
_____ Bread crumbs
_____ Flour
_____ Olives
_____ Onions
_____ Cherries
_____ Coffee
_____ Decaf
_____ Iced tea bags
_____ Regular tea bags
_____ Pastry shells
_____ Sherry
_____ Cooking wine
_____ Cola
_____ Diet cola
_____ Ginger ale
_____ Lemon-lime
_____ Tonic
_____ Club soda
_____ Flavored waters
_____ Bloody Mary mix
_____ Orange juice

_____ Cranberry juice
_____ Grapefruit juice

Linens

_____ Napkins (Color)
_____ 62" by 62" (Color)
_____   (Color)
_____   (Color)
_____ Banquets (Color)
_____   (Color)
_____   (Color)
_____ 132" Round (Color)
_____   (Color)
_____   (Color)
_____ 120" Round (Color)
_____   (Color)
_____   (Color)
_____ 108" Round (Color)
_____   (Color)
_____   (Color)
_____ 90" Round (Color)
_____   (Color)
_____   (Color)
_____ Towel mop
_____ Bib aprons
_____ 13-foot skirt
_____ Black waiter jackets
_____ White chef coats
_____ Logo T-shirts
_____ Theme uniforms
_____ _____
_____ _____
_____ _____
_____ _____

Pots and Pans

_____ Bus pans
_____ Bus pan lids
_____ Full sheet pans
_____ Half sheet pans
_____ Full food pans
_____ Half food pans
_____ Full deep pans
_____ Medium sauté pans
_____ Large sauté pans
_____ Omelette pans
_____ Fry pans
_____ Medium sauce pans
_____ Small sauce pans
_____ Large cast iron fry pan
_____ 32-quart stock pot
_____ 15-quart stock pot
_____ Braziers
_____ Fry baskets
_____ Large colanders
_____ Medium colanders
_____ Skimmers
_____ Strainers
_____ Large steel funnel
_____ Extra large stainless steel bowls
_____ Medium stainless steel bowls
_____ Utility bowls
_____ 2-quart measuring container
_____ 1-quart plastic containers
_____ 2-gallon chafing dishes

Plate covers

_____ Full shallow aluminum food pans
_____ Full deep aluminum food pans
_____ Half shallow aluminum food pans
_____ Half deep aluminum food pans
_____ Oval waiter trays
_____ Round cocktail trays

_____ _____
_____ _____

_____ _____
_____ _____

China, Glassware, Flatware, and Tabletop Items

_____ Dinner knives
_____ Dinner forks
_____ Salad forks
_____ Teaspoons
_____ Bouillon spoons
_____ Cocktail forks
_____ Salt and pepper shakers
_____ Ashtrays
_____ Water pitchers
_____ Coffee pourers
_____ Large rectangular silver trays
_____ Medium round silver trays
_____ Small oval silver trays
_____ Silver bread baskets
_____ 12-inch silver bowls
_____ 7-inch silver bowls
_____ 5-inch silver bowls
_____ Large rectangular aluminum trays
_____ Medium round aluminum trays
_____ 4-inch Acoroc bowls
_____ 5-inch Acoroc bowls
_____ 7-inch Acoroc bowls
_____ 12-inch glass bowls
_____ Special bowls _____

_____ _____
_____ _____

_____ Black lacquer trays
_____ Oval mirrors
_____ Round mirrors
_____ Glass carafes
_____ Large punch bowls
_____ 12-ounce bubble wine glasses
_____ Tulip Champagne glasses
_____ Brandy snifters
_____ Cordial glasses
_____ Martini glasses

(Continued)

EXHIBIT 6.6 Party Packing List (*Continued*)

_____ Coffee mugs
_____ 9½-inch plates
_____ 7½-inch plates
_____ 6-inch plates
_____ Coffee cups
_____ Saucers
_____ Creamers
_____ Sugars
_____ Votive candle holders

Plasticware and Paper Goods

_____ 8-ounce styrofoam cups
_____ 6-ounce styrofoam cups
_____ 10-ounce hard plastic glasses
_____ Plastic forks
_____ Plastic spoons
_____ 10-inch plastic divided plates
_____ 10-inch plastic plates
_____ 7-inch plastic plates
_____ 6-inch plastic plates
_____ Plastic Champagne flutes
_____ 7-inch plastic bowls
_____ 12-inch plastic bowls
_____ Plastic gloves
_____ Cocktail napkins
_____ Dinner napkins
_____ Large doilies
_____ Small doilies
_____ Mini baking cups
_____ Swordpicks
_____ Wet-naps
_____ Wood stir sticks
_____ Sip straws
_____ Toothpicks
_____ Plastic storage bags
_____ Duct tape
_____ Film wrap
_____ Aluminum foil

_____ Bar kits
_____ Pourer spouts

Buffet and Food Station Décor

_____ Shells
_____ Glass pebbles
_____ Vases: type _____
_____ Hurricane lamps
_____ Glass blocks
_____ Fans
_____ Stapler gun and staples
_____ Ribbon: colors _____
_____ Scissors
_____ Floral wire
_____ Floral tape
_____ Large carving boards
_____ Oval carving boards
_____ Small baskets: color _____ For _____
_____ Medium baskets: color _____ For _____
_____ Large baskets: color _____ For _____
_____ Extra large baskets: color _____ For _____
_____ Stick candles
_____ Votive candles
_____ Candelabras
_____ Wooden crates
_____ Plastic crates
_____ Fresh flowers and ferns

_____
_____
_____
_____
_____

Heavy and Bulky Equipment

_____ Convection ovens
_____ Gas grill

_____ Hibachi
_____ Tabletop gas burners
_____ Empty coolers
_____ Coolers with ice
_____ Charcoal
_____ Garden hose and nozzle
_____ 5-gallon insulating containers
_____ Plastic tarp
_____ 100-cup coffee makers
_____ 50-cup coffee makers
_____ Garbage cans
_____ 6-foot tables
_____ Hand trucks
_____ Dollies
_____ Tall warming cabinets
_____ Short warming cabinets
_____ Rolling racks with covers
_____ Wireframe chafers
_____ Dust pan
_____ Broom
_____ Butane fuel
_____ Propane fuel
_____ Large Sterno
_____ Small Sterno
_____ Fire extinguishers
_____ Matches (place with utensils)
_____ Liquid smoke
_____ Lighter fluid
_____ Ant spray
_____ Insect repellant
_____ Extension cords
_____ Spotlights
_____ First aid kits (check supplies inside)
_____ Tray stands
_____ Table cassette au feu stoves
_____ Lava rock
_____ Rented equipment delivered to
          commissary

Utensils

_____ Plain cook's spoons
_____ Slotted cook's spoons
_____ 2-ounce ladles
_____ 4-ounce ladles
_____ 6-ounce ladles
_____ 8-ounce ladles
_____ Extra-large ladles
_____ Wire whips
_____ Piping bags and tips
_____ Pastry brushes
_____ Plastic ice scoops
_____ Can openers
_____ Bottle openers
_____ Plastic funnels
_____ 9½-inch utility tongs
_____ 6-inch tongs
_____ Silver serving tongs
_____ BBQ tongs
_____ BBQ knives
_____ BBQ forks
_____ Ice cream dishers
_____   Size_____
_____   Size _____
_____ Wooden spoons
_____ Aluminum serving spoons
_____ Sauce spoons
_____ Carving knives
_____ Carving forks
_____ Kitchen forks
_____ Cook's spatula
_____ Rubber spatula
_____ Hamburger spatula
_____ Pie server
_____ Pie cutter
_____ Cake knife
_____ Cake server
_____ Sharpening steel

Raw Ingredients. Exactly what will you need to produce the food item at the party site? A Caesar salad, for example, will require romaine lettuce, croutons, Parmesan cheese, anchovies, and a Caesar dressing (if prepared in advance) or the components to toss one at tableside.

Preparation Techniques. How will this item be prepared? For the Caesar salad, the caterer will need a large mixing bowl, a grater for the Parmesan, a ladle for the dressing, and plastic gloves for those who will be tossing and plating.

Service Style. How will this item be served? On a buffet, the Caesar salad may be served from a variety of bowls. If it's a seated meal, salad plates will be necessary. And do not forget salad forks or tongs, trays, and tray stands.

Preparation Area Requirements. Where in the kitchen will the salad be tossed and plated? Plan for sufficient worktables. Fancier salads that are assembled on-site require more worktable space than those that are tossed, stored in big containers, and simply kept chilled until plating.

Decorative Requirements. This category includes whatever it takes to make the food presentation stunning: buffet décor pieces, tables and linens, garnishes, and boxes or baskets used to display the foods at different levels on the table.

Other Services. Have other services been promised by contract? For instance, before a company picnic, if some of the guests are having a softball game, you may be bringing extra sodas, bottled water, and ice to be served separately from the meal. The term *other services* truly covers it all.

The larger the catered event, the more involved and complex the pull-and-pack process. Again, experience is the best teacher, and almost everyone has a memorable tale to tell about the time they forgot an important item and had to improvise, sometimes with hilarious results.

It requires a lot of time and total concentration to prepare pull sheets and rental equipment order forms, so it is best to do this when and where you can work uninterrupted. For some, this is early in the morning; for others, later in the evening. The lists should be prepared long before the event date so you can determine whether you and/ or your rental suppliers will have the necessary items available at that time. If not, this builds in ample time to order additional equipment and supplies.

Change Forms

No matter when you organize the food and supplies to be delivered for an event, it is critical to consult any change forms that might have been generated. As its name indicates, this simple one-page form alerts all pertinent staff members of a change in, or addition to, the event that almost surely will affect what you pull and pack. It might be a new guest count (higher or lower), a different menu item or linen color, or some other modification. A change form should include:

- The name of the event

- The date of the event

- The service order number (Caterers have their own systems to assign numbers to each job.)

- A description or explanation of the change

- The date of the change

- Authorization or approval of the change by a staff member who is permitted to do so

Party plans change all the time. Creating and using a change form is an easy, effective system an off-premise caterer can put in place to ensure that everyone on the staff who needs to be aware of changes gets the word and can adapt accordingly.

Food Production Sheets

Yes, more lists! Food production sheets are detailed lists of all the food items necessary for a particular party, wedding, or event. In the Caesar salad example mentioned on page 224, the production list would indicate the following:

- Wash and trim 24 heads of romaine lettuce.
- Prepare one gallon of Caesar dressing.
- Cut, season, and toast two loaves of Italian bread for croutons.

Production sheets also assist with ordering ingredients because they include the quantities of food required, and they help the catering team decide the order of preparation.

For example, some hors d'oeuvres can be prepared in advance and frozen. Cold sauces and salsas can be prepared a few days in advance. Meats can be marinated the day before the party. Some vegetables can be cut late in the day before the party.

As each item is completed, a check is marked on the sheet next to the name of the item, indicating that it has been completed. Another check mark is made when it is loaded.

Packing, Loading, and Delivery

Packing, loading, and delivery are critical steps in the execution of the event. A sufficient amount of time should be allocated so that everything arrives on time at the party site. For smaller events that are close to the commissary, these steps take little time, but for larger, more complex events, "pulling," assembling, packing, and loading can be accomplished one or more days in advance.

Pulling and Packing

Before "pulling the party," review the packing list and ensure that all goods on the list are actually in stock. In most off-premise catering facilities, party items are not all in one location but spread throughout the commissary or in storage. Carts, dollies, hand trucks, and even supermarket-style shopping carts will help move the items to the vehicle, or to a central assembly location, prior to loading. Teamwork by your staff makes for a much smoother operation.

As the items are located, the larger, bulkier ones should be taken to the delivery vehicle. Smaller, loose items should be assembled in a particular area and packed in containers, like plastic packing crates with handles for carrying. Fragile items should be wrapped in bubble wrap, linens, or wadded-up paper to prevent breakage. Bowls will not stick together if paper or bubble wrap is placed between them. Remember, all equipment should be checked again when pulled to see that it is in working order and/or is not broken, cracked, or chipped. A few packing tips follow:

- Old briefcases can be used for carrying knives and serving utensils.
- Plastic crates can be used for plates (plates should be wrapped in film after drying).
- Use wrapped racks for cups, glasses, creamers, and sugar bowls.
- Custom-made plywood boxes can be used for coffeemakers, samovars, and chafing dishes.

- Flatware, film-wrapped in groups, can be packed in plastic crates.
- As an alternative, see Chapter 5 for the use of rolling tool chests to store flatware.
- Most discount and larger drug stores carry an assortment of plastic packing crates.
- Empty ice chests (to be used later at the party site for beverages) can be loaded with small unbreakable equipment or utensils.
- Whenever possible, pack food in the same container in which it will be cooked at the party site; for example, stuffed mushroom caps can be placed on half sheet pans, covered with film wrap, and placed atop packed ice chests.
- Used plastic containers (like five-pound honey drums) are handy for packing such bar utensils as pourers, stir sticks, wine and bottle openers, sword picks, and ice picks.
- Plywood boxes with sliding tops can be custom made to store doilies and linens.
- "Slim Jim"–type garbage cans are excellent for packing tray stands.
- Empty bus boxes with lids can be used for packing small utensils.
- Cold foods can be stored in assorted sizes of plasticware (with lids) and should be delivered in a refrigerated truck or on ice in ice chests, depending on local health department regulations.
- Hot foods are best shipped in insulated plastic containers, warming cabinets, or insulated thermal bags.

This list is not intended to include all packing techniques but should at least stimulate creativity when it comes to the myriad ways to pack for off-premise catering events. Readers should note that parties that are packed neatly and carefully will not only be delivered intact, but will also make a positive impression on clients, who will compare this well-organized operation with the performance of caterers who arrive at a party site with food and equipment virtually spilling out of their vans in beat-up, old cardboard boxes, rattling loose with no packing at all.

Equipment and supplies designated for certain areas at the party site should be packed together and labeled for a smoother unloading and distribution process at the site. In fact, this procedure is critical for larger parties, where food stations, buffets, bars, and off-premise kitchens are spread out over a large area, or on a number of floors, as in an office building or department store. Some caterers even color-code items so their staffers know exactly where to take them as they are unloaded.

Loading the Vehicle

The loading process should not be taken lightly. It is physically demanding, and improperly packed items may break, spill, crack, or chip. Rare is the off-premise caterer who has never arrived at a party site with food spilled inside a vehicle. In addition to the tips found in Chapter 5 in the "Transporting Food and Equipment" section (page 155), here are more suggestions to minimize this risk:

- Everything should be packed together tightly. Whenever possible, crates and racks should be nestled together to prevent them from shifting in transit.

- Metro racks can be loaded by event and, when full, the entire rack can be wrapped in clear plastic wrap to keep contents on their specific shelves. The full, wrapped racks are then easily rolled into the delivery vehicles.

- Large, heavy square or rectangular items should be loaded first and kept in the bottom portion of the load. This category includes such items as ice chests, glass and china racks, soft drinks in cases, and square or rectangular plastic or plywood containers.

- Lightweight and unusually shaped items should be loaded last and inserted in areas where they will fit snugly, to help keep the load from shifting in transit.

- Cold foods should be transported in accordance with local health department regulations, which may require a refrigerated truck, or sealed and packed in ice chests.

- Hot foods should be kept at a safe temperature (above 140 degrees Fahrenheit) in insulated carrying containers, thermal bags, or hot food holding cabinets.

- Loading staff must be trained in proper lifting techniques to avoid injury. This subject is addressed in Chapter 12.

- Hooks, eyelets, and bungee cords can help secure items in the truck. Items can also be kept from slipping by placing them on nonslip surfaces, old rugs, towels, linens, cardboard, or crumpled paper.

As each item is packed in the vehicle, it should be checked off on the pull sheet. Once the pull sheet is complete, it is advisable to double-check that all items are loaded—having a two-person team responsible for this chore ensures a second set of eyes and twice as much brainpower. The checking process should be thorough for all parties, but for those that will take place far from the commissary, you cannot afford to forget even one item because there is no time to return to the commissary. (On busy days, some caterers leave a staff member at the commissary for the specific purpose of rounding up and bringing forgotten items to any of multiple event sites.)

Delivery

The delivery process involves physically moving the food, supplies, and equipment from the catering commissary to the party site. The types of delivery vehicles are discussed in Chapter 5. In this section, we discuss delivery procedures and standards.

Catering vehicles should always be free from dents and scrapes, as well as immaculately clean, inside and out. The delivery vehicle is an important marketing tool and should reflect the caterer's business image. United Parcel Service (UPS) is known throughout the world for its clean and well-maintained vehicles; the company sets the standard in this arena.

Most caterers display the company name, address, and phone number on their vehicles. This also is good marketing because it boosts name recognition to have your vans seen all over town, and you will no doubt receive some business from people who have simply seen a truck and jotted down the phone number.

The drivers of these "rolling billboards" should also be immaculately attired, uniformed, impeccably groomed, and courteous. Drivers represent your company image and are often the client's first impression when they arrive at an event site.

When it comes to improving the quality and timing of deliveries, learn from experience:

- Allow enough time to reach the destination. Many caterers allow twice the amount of time necessary or even make practice runs when traveling to unfamiliar areas. Pay attention to weather reports, check road conditions, and allow extra time if bad weather or heavy traffic is expected. It is always better to arrive early than late.

- Institute a preventive maintenance program for all vehicles. Pinpoint potential problems before they occur, rather than repairing when something breaks. (Things always seem to break when you're swamped!) Drivers should not be permitted to make their own repairs but should make daily "pre-trip" inspections, just like a professional truck driver, checking brakes, tires, lights, horns, wipers, steering, unusual noises, batteries, and oil and wiper fluid levels. Trucks with propane ovens should also be routinely checked for gas leaks.

- Drivers should be provided with petty cash, a road map, written directions, a highway emergency kit, a first aid kit, rain gear, an umbrella, and a cell phone.

- On hot, sunny days, catering vehicles must always be parked in the shade.

- For large events, many suppliers will deliver certain prepared products—such as desserts or specialty ethnic items—directly to the party site. For mega-events with thousands of attendees, your suppliers will often provide their own trucks, filled with their products, at the event site. Moreover, when circumstances dictate, caterers should consider alternative methods of delivery: taxis, UPS, or a courier service. Building relationships with these folks, just as with any other vendor, can serve you well.

Unloading at the Event Site

Off-premise caterers should have policies for unloading catering vehicles at event sites—and we don't mean simply instructions about dropping off platters, but written procedures for larger, more complex events.

The most critical unloading rule is to separate items based on where they will be used. In some instances, things can be taken directly to their final destination: the buffet, bar, food station, or kitchen. In other instances, where access is restricted, items may be stored together and moved later. This procedure does not work well, however, when delivering quantities for large parties to high-rise buildings. In these instances, sorting cannot occur until the goods reach the proper floor.

Unloading is best accomplished with only a few staff members, not the complete party crew. It is easier to keep things organized when fewer workers are present and their job is specifically to unload. Under ideal conditions, everything for each food station, buffet, bar, and off-premise kitchen should be delivered to the spot where it will be needed, so that the setup crew arrives to find everything positioned correctly. Off-premise caterers simply provide a diagram with an item list of the setup to the people responsible for the setup. This procedure alone will prevent major confusion, frustration, and wasted time by eliminating staffers' frantic searches for supplies and equipment.

Hand trucks, dollies, and carts save time and energy and should be on every delivery vehicle. People should never lift items weighing more than 50 pounds. You should also strive to minimize the number of times things are moved, creating a flow pattern to send materials along the shortest and straightest routes possible to their final destinations. Equipment, food, and supplies to be used on buffets, food stations, and bars should be stored as close as possible to their eventual points of use. This means that at a pasta station, the extra pasta, sauces, and ingredients are kept as close as possible to the station to minimize the steps required for replenishment.

Further, some tools, utensils, and equipment should be stored at every event in the same area, so staff members will always know where to go in a hurry. For example, scissors are always kept in a crate, under a worktable in the off-premise kitchen; backup soft drinks are always kept outside the cooks' tent, and so forth. Setting up systems gives your employees more confidence about successfully handling their parts of the event.

Once the necessary equipment is on-site, the setup begins. This subject is discussed in detail in Chapter 8, "The Show." For now, however, let's just assume the party is over, and it's time to reload the vehicle and return to the commissary.

Reloading and Returning

Most caterers can complete cleaning, packing, and reloading within one hour of the conclusion of their responsibilities, as long as some of the cleaning and repacking was accomplished as the party progressed. Once the catering responsibilities are complete, the caterer can leave the party site. It is best to wait to reload the vehicle until most things are packed and ready for loading, rather than load things randomly. It is just as important to pack and load the vehicle wisely on the trip home as it was when you first packed it, once again reducing the chances of spills and breakage.

Back at the commissary, most off-premise caterers require that vehicles be completely unloaded and cleaned and everything returned to its original place. This often makes for a long day—but a productive one. And it's better to clean up at that moment than to have to face these chores the next day.

Post-Party Review

A *debriefing*, or *post-event review*, should be conducted after every catered event to pinpoint specific problems that might require attention and to discuss better ways to do things in the future. The largest room in the world is the room for improvement. Try to look at the event from this perspective: If you were given an opportunity to cater it again, what would you do differently? Some caterers sit down with staff members immediately after the event; others wait until the next day or the next staff meeting to assess it. Some require their staffers to complete a report, and others request written comments from clients. Whatever the procedures, it is smart to get the comments in writing, and things requiring improvement should be acted upon immediately. Topics such as the following should be addressed:

- Time allowed for setup
- Quality and quantity of staff
- Quality and quantity of food and service

- Quality and quantity of equipment and supplies
- Adequacy and appropriateness of music, flowers, décor, parking, security, and so on
- Any particular problems to be addressed or suggestions from staffers

In addition to the post-party review, procedures should be in place for:

- Submitting payroll hours to bookkeeping
- Reporting discrepancies to the rental equipment company
- Ensuring that all invoices for the party are submitted to bookkeeping
- Invoicing client for any remaining balances
- Writing and mailing a thank-you note or letter to the client
- Establishing a follow-up date for contacting the client about future events

Exhibit 6.7 shows one event designer's (and former off-premise caterer's) system for keeping track of the logistical details discussed in this chapter. Ginger Kramer, who now heads Coast Coordinators in San Jose, California, created this Event File Routing Schedule. It could easily be adapted on a computer, with spaces for dates and identities of the staff members who perform each task.

EXHIBIT 6.7 Event File Routing Schedule

EVENT FILE ROUTING SCHEDULE

	By:	Date:
Sales & Front Office:		
Verbal Quote Only	___	___
Written Proposal Faxed & Mailed	___	___
Event File:		
File Label & Folder	___	___
Return to Sales (Tentative Status)	___	___
Acceptance Sheet Received from Client	___	___
Post to Board (Definite Status) & Master Book	___	___
Deposit Received from Client	___	___
Coordinating:		
Event Report Initiated	___	___
Pre-Schedule Staff	___	___
Send Event File to Purchasing	___	___

Purchasing:

    Food Sheet to: Chef/Kitchen Production/Inventory Control

    Beverage Order (Copy to Inventory Control) (Order Placed)   _____   _____

    Regular Linen Order   _____   _____

    Custom Linen Order   _____   _____

    Floral Order   (_____)   _____   _____

    Decor Order   _____   _____

    Guest Equipment Order   (_____)   _____   _____

    Site Rental Agreement   (_____)   _____   _____

    Ice Delivery   _____   _____

    Entertainment Order   (_____)   _____   _____

    Serviceware Order   (_____)   _____   _____

    Special: _____   (_____)

    All Check Requests Issued   _____

Coordinating:

    Complete Event Report: _____   _____

        Load Sheet   _____   _____

        Attach Map to Location   _____   _____

        Make Copies for Event File   _____   _____

        Reconfirm Staff   _____   _____

    Buffet Design Completed: _____   _____

    Final Guest Count: (#pp   ____ by ____)   _____   _____

File Completion: (Sales & Front Office)

    Client Contacted for Verbal Review

    Invoice: Copies to Acct./Event File/Invoice File   _____   _____

    Verbal Review Forwarded to General Manager   _____   _____

    Critique Letter   _____   _____

    Thank-You Card   _____   _____

    Lost Business Report forwarded to General Manager   _____   _____

    Add to Mail List   _____   _____

(Reprinted with permission of the author, Ginger Kramer, and the *CommuniCater*, official publication of the International Caterers Association.)

Summary

The clients and guests at an off-premise catered event will not be aware of even a fraction of what goes on behind the scenes to ensure its success—and that's exactly as it should be. This chapter is a discussion of the myriad systems that must be in place to assemble the food, supplies, and equipment; transport them to the event site safely; and return them safely afterward. To pull it off, event after event, will require just as much creativity as the culinary and design aspects of the event itself.

The chapter begins with a look at how to assemble a list of interesting event locations and what to look for when you visit them, so you can determine their suitability for off-premise catering. Then there is extensive information about how to design an event layout to fit a particular site, from square footage required for various event types to how to arrange buffets and kitchen areas. Advice is given on how to pull together the ingredients, even for a single dish, to be served at a party. (Indeed, you may never think of a Caesar salad in quite the same way again!) The chapter provides guidelines for packing, delivery, unloading, and reloading, culminating with tips on how to conduct a post-event review to determine if there's anything the team could have done better.

Readers may think this chapter is heavy on mundane details, from how to maintain a vendor list for party sites, to the pages and pages of pull sheets and rental forms. However, it is exactly this kind of detail that is necessary to create a system—a system that guarantees nothing is left behind when the catering vans pull out, fully loaded, to deliver all the components of an event at a remote location.

Conscientious staff members who are clear on their responsibilities are additional keys to your success in making logistics plans that work beautifully for every event you will cater.

Study Questions

1. Is it ever permissible to book an event before you have visited the venue?

2. Sketch your own salad buffet design (on two 8-foot by 30-inch tables), complete with visual display elements. Describe the reasons for your selections.

3. Why is the traditional head table, with guests seated on only one side, out of fashion today?

4. What is the most critical rule for unloading items at an event site?

5. Why would you bring an oven thermometer and a tape measure to a site walk-through?

Human Resources

Your employees—"human resources"—whether full- or part-time, are among the most important aspects of your business. They may sell the off-premise catering services, order the ingredients, cook the food, serve it with a smile, and/or clean up afterward. In many cases, they are the voices and faces of your company to prospective customers. And they cannot play their roles effectively if they don't meet your company's standards, adhere to your rules, and exhibit a positive attitude, especially in front of clients.

There are countless aspects to managing off-premise catering personnel, and we'll touch on many in this chapter, including:

- Employer-related federal and state laws
- Recruiting
- Hiring
- Training
- Compensation
- Evaluating performance
- Discipline and termination

235

In addition, we'll provide guidelines for such topics as managing turnover, selecting staff uniforms, preparing an employee handbook, and maintaining personnel records.

Excellent personnel management begins with selecting people with whom the caterer will enjoy working—and those who enjoy working in off-premise catering. This means creating job requirements and finding people who meet them, and then training these people to meet your company standards and setting rules for what happens when they don't. It also means providing a healthy working environment where managers:

- Listen to and involve staff members in operations
- Deal with employees fairly and consistently
- Discipline fairly and promptly
- Are well organized and decisive
- "Catch" the staff doing things right and tell them
- Create an enthusiastic, upbeat, and positive environment
- Are on the floor, actively managing the staff, rather than "hiding in the office"

Off-premise caterers know that happy workers are productive workers. They realize that work is not the most important aspect of many Americans' lives, and that a good employee can find employment elsewhere rather than putting up with an uncomfortable work situation.

Federal Laws

Many off-premise catering companies are small businesses, with no budget for in-house legal counsel or a separate human resources department. However, they are still expected to follow the same complex federal laws regarding hiring and paying workers, so it is important to have at least some familiarity with these laws. We will summarize the major regulations in this section of the chapter. These are:

Enforced by the U.S. Department of Labor
- Fair Labor Standards Act, Amended (FLSA)
- Immigration Reform and Control Act (IRCA)
- Family and Medical Leave Act (FMLA)
- National Labor Relations Act (Wagner Act; Taft-Hartley Act)

- Employee Polygraph Protection Act (EPPA)
- Occupational Safety and Health Act (OSHA)

Enforced by the Equal Employment Opportunity Commission (EEOC)

- Americans with Disabilities Act (ADA)
- Civil Rights Act, Title VII
- Age Discrimination in Employment Act
- Equal Pay Act of 1963 and Lilly Ledbetter Fair Pay Act

Enforced by Individual States

- Workers' Compensation insurance laws

It is important to understand the basic requirements of each law to determine its applicability. For example, the Fair Labor Standards Act affects all off-premise caterers, whereas the Family and Medical Leave Act generally exempts businesses with fewer than 50 employees. Here we review the major aspects of each of these laws; off-premise caterers should consult legal counsel with specific questions.

Department of Labor–Enforced Laws

Fair Labor Standards Act

The basics of the Fair Labor Standards Act (FLSA) are presented below; however, full details about this law are available at the U.S. Department of Labor website (www.dol.gov).

Minimum Wage. This law created the minimum wage, and it applies to most businesses that gross $500,000 or more a year. There are exceptions to the $500,000 test, which can be found on the U.S. Department of Labor website identified above. Effective July 24, 2009, the minimum wage is $7.25 per hour. It is important to remember that some states have set their minimum wage higher than the FLSA requirement, so you must also be aware of any state-specific guidelines.

Tipped employees, those who regularly receive more than $30 per month in tips, may be paid as little as $2.13 per hour, as long as the wages paid by their employer and their tips equal at least the minimum wage amount. Employees must report tips earned to their employers so appropriate amounts for federal income tax and Social Security tax can be withheld from their pay. Employers must also pay their portion of Social Security tax on the tips reported by their employees.

For workers under 20 years of age, there's an alternative minimum wage, called the Youth Minimum Wage. Currently, it is $4.25 an hour, but applies only to the first 90 consecutive calendar days—not workdays—on the job. After 90 consecutive calendar days or when the teen turns 20 (whichever comes first), the pay must be raised to the standard hourly minimum wage. A higher state or local minimum wage would also apply to workers less than 20 years old.

Overtime Pay. Pay at the rate of no less than one-and-one-half (1.5) times the regular hourly rate must be paid for working more than 40 hours within the workweek. Each workweek stands alone, and the averaging of hours from a series of weeks is not permitted. In addition, the workweek itself must be established in advance and must not be changed from week to week to avoid paying overtime. For example, a workweek can begin at 12:01 A.M. on Monday and end Sunday at midnight.

In the catering industry, where weekend work is the norm, the company can opt to begin its workweek on Friday and end the following Thursday night. This helps the caterer minimize overtime expenses during the weekends, often the busiest days of the week.

Overtime Exemptions. This section of the law establishes criteria for those employees—executives, administrative staff, certain professional employees, and salespeople—who do not receive overtime pay. This is a very technical area—a person's job title does not automatically make him or her an "exempt" employee—so this is a topic for your attorney to clarify before excluding someone from overtime payment. For example, for executives to be exempt from overtime, they must meet all the following criteria:

- They must be compensated on a salary basis at a rate not less than $455 per week.
- Their primary duty must be management of the enterprise, or managing a customarily recognized department or subdivision of the enterprise.
- They must customarily and regularly direct the work of at least two or more other full-time employees or their equivalent.
- They must have the authority to hire and fire, or make hiring, termination, advancement, or promotion recommendations.
- They must customarily and regularly exercise discretionary powers.

- They must devote no more than 20 percent (40 percent in retail or service establishments) of their hours worked to activities not directly and closely related to managerial duties. (These percentage tests for nonexempt work would not apply to an employee who is in sole charge of an independent establishment, or a physically separated branch of an establishment, or who owns at least a 20 percent interest in the enterprise.)

There are also exemption rules for those employed in outside sales, which may apply to catering companies large enough to have their own salespeople. The criteria include:

- Persons employed for the purpose of selling, who customarily and regularly work away from the employer's place of business

- Persons whose primary duty is making sales of "tangible and intangible items," meaning goods or services

- Persons whose hours worked in activities other than selling are less than 20 percent of their total weekly hours worked

The regulations include many more details regarding overtime exemptions, so it's important to get legal advice to help you make decisions about the specifics for your company.

Child Labor Laws. These laws affect those who employ young people to bus and wash dishes, set tables, and perform other tasks. Here are some highlights of employment restrictions on 14- and 15-year-olds:

- They may not work more than 3 hours on school days including Fridays, and may not work more than 18 hours during school weeks.

- They may not work more than 8 hours on nonschool days, and may not work more than 40 hours during nonschool weeks.

- They cannot work hours prior to 7:00 A.M. and after 7:00 P.M., except between June 1 and Labor Day, when they can work until 9:00 P.M.

- They cannot maintain or repair machines or equipment, cook (except in an area not separated by a partition and in customers' view), bake, or operate power-driven food slicers, grinders, processors, choppers, cutters, and bakery-type mixers.

- They cannot work in freezers or meat coolers or perform any tasks in preparation of meals for sale, except wrapping, sealing, labeling, weighing, pricing, and stocking.

- They cannot load or unload trucks or engage in occupations in warehouses, except clerical or office work.

There are also restrictions for older teens (ages 16 and 17), but these are a little less stringent. There are no hours or time restrictions on these workers, but they still can't operate, clean, or repair power-driven meat-processing machines, including slicers; nor can they operate, clean, or repair most power-driven bakery equipment, including dough mixers, roll dividers, and rounders. Pizza dough rollers with a number of safety features are an exception.

Periodically, fast-food chains come under close scrutiny regarding the hours worked by 14- and 15-year-olds. Many are now reluctant to hire these workers because of the penalties that can be incurred for violations. For example, a 14-year-old scheduled to work until 7:00 P.M. during the school year can't be asked to stay an extra half hour, even if the place is extremely busy and the teen wants to stay. It's still a violation, punishable by law.

How severe is the punishment? Penalties are assessed based on the violation, and the initial assessment amounts increased, significantly in some cases, for violations on or after January 20, 2010. Fines can range from $575 for that 14- or 15-year-old who works extra hours or during prohibited times to $50,000 for a violation that causes the death of or serious injury to a minor.

In 2010, an exception was added to Child Labor Regulation No. 3 to create a work-study program (WSP) for academically oriented youth, to allow affected youth to work during school hours, with sufficient safeguards to ensure that their employment doesn't interfere with their health, well-being, or education.

Some off-premise caterers reduce their payroll expenses by employing young people to perform simple tasks like setting tables, which can save money, and using more experienced and better-paid personnel elsewhere. Just be aware of the federal laws whenever you hire minors.

Record Keeping. The law requires that all payroll records—including time worked, schedules, and individual earnings—be kept for a minimum of three years and that they be made available for inspection by authorized individuals when requested. With today's technology, payroll information is much easier to track, as records are all computerized.

Off-premise caterers must maintain accurate records. Some employers allow workers to arrive for work early or stay late, but because this is the workers' idea, not the employers', they do not pay overtime. These employers ask the workers to clock in for an eight-hour day. Such falsification of records can cost a caterer hundreds of thousands of dollars in overtime, back pay, and penalties.

Immigration Reform and Control Act

The Immigration and Control Act of 1986 (IRCA) was passed to control unauthorized immigration to the United States and has been controversial ever since its passage by Congress. To discourage employers from hiring illegal entrants, employer sanctions and penalties are assessed. This law requires employers to obtain a completed Form I-9 from each employee by close of business on the first day of work. Employers are required to obtain written proof of a worker's identity and employment eligibility and to record the information on the I-9 form within three days of the worker's first day on the job. Acceptable proof of identity and employment eligibility documents change periodically, but they are listed on the I-9 form. (The I-9 form itself changes periodically; see the current version online at www.uscis.gov/files/form/i-9.pdf.)

According to attorney Andre Michniak of Philadelphia and Reading, Pennsylvania, who specializes in immigration law:

Many employers mistakenly believe that there exists a blanket "work permit." No such document exists. Other employers incorrectly assume that a Social Security card is sufficient proof of employment eligibility. A Social Security card is one of the documents that may be an indicator of the right to work but by itself is insufficient. The most common forms of work authorization documents are as follows:

1. Form I-94 is a white card issued by the INS at a port of entry to nonimmigrants and people who are here temporarily.

2. Form I-551, the Alien Registration Card (often referred to as a *green card*), is given to people who have become permanent residents.

3. The Employment Authorization Document (EAD) is a card containing the person's photograph, and is issued to individuals who are awaiting their green cards or to those who are eligible to work under certain conditions. This card establishes both employment authorization and identity.

In addition, Michniak points out that the worker has the responsibility for filling out Form I-9 correctly. He says an employer is only required to show "good faith" compliance with document verification.

Under federal law, there are criminal penalties for those who engage in a "pattern or practice of knowingly hiring or continuing to employ unauthorized aliens" or "engage in frauds or false statements, or otherwise misuse visas, immigration permits, and identity documents."

Do not confuse Form I-9 with Form W-9, which new workers must also sometimes complete. W-9s are for obtaining the Social Security or Taxpayer Identification numbers of part-time workers, such as freelancers or contractors—those you will be paying, but not withholding any taxes from their paychecks because they pay their own.

The IRCA applies to any company with four or more employees. Employers must retain an I-9 form for as long as an individual works for them. Once a worker's employment ends, the I-9 form must be retained for either three years from the date of hire or one year after the date employment ends, whichever is later. Employers may be fined if they do not meet I-9 retention guidelines. In addition, when an employee's employment eligibility document expires, employers must verify the new document for the person's employment file.

 Immigration Reform and the Foodservice Industry

There is currently almost no federal employment topic more controversial than immigration law. In recent years, the advent of the Electronic Employment Verification System (EEVS), commonly known as *E-Verify*, has complicated the issue even further. An employer can check a job applicant's identity and employment eligibility in the EEVS federal database, operated by the Department of Homeland Security. These checks are currently optional in all but five states. (At this writing, late in 2011, the mandatory E-Verify states are Alabama, Arizona, Georgia, Mississippi, and Utah.)

Legislation in Congress has sought to make E-Verify a requirement nationwide. Critics of that idea say such a database is so massive that even a small percentage of errors will leave millions of unemployed workers with inaccurate files and no job prospects until they convince the federal government to find and correct the error.

Further, organizations like the National Restaurant Association (NRA) (www.restaurant .org/advocacy/issues/) have expressed concerns that small businesses are unprepared to determine whether identity documents are legitimate, and that a clear process should be in place for contesting inaccurate findings. The NRA supports what it calls "sensible, comprehensive immigration reform," and says, "Employers who act in good faith deserve fair enforcement."

The Migration Policy Institute (MPI) (www.migrationpolicy.org) also has recommended that changes be made to E-Verify that could allow the system to function more successfully on a national scale. As a result of E-Verify's inability to authenticate a worker's identity, MPI also advocates pilot testing of several possible alternatives to the existing system, including secure documents, PIN precertification, and biometric scanning.

According to MPI, "The current E-Verify model places employers at the center of the identity authentication process, which has resulted in difficulties for employers and workers alike. The proposed pilot programs would move from an employer-centric to a more employer-neutral model, streamlining the steps employers are required to take to confirm work authorization for new hires; reducing incentives and potential for identity fraud; and removing the guesswork in authenticating the identities of new hires."

This is a debate that will not be resolved any time soon. In our view, it is an issue every off-premise caterer should be following.

Family and Medical Leave Act

The purpose of the Family and Medical Leave Act (FMLA) is to protect the jobs of those who must take off work for specified family or medical reasons. Effective since August 1993, this law permits employees to take up to 12 weeks of unpaid leave in a 12-month period for the following reasons:

- Birth of an employee's child, and to care for the newborn within one year of birth
- Placement of a child with the employee for purposes of adoption or foster care, and to care for the newly placed child within one year of placement
- Care of a spouse, child, or parent who is seriously ill
- An employee's own serious health condition that makes him or her unable to perform the functions of his or her job

In 2008 and 2009, the FMLA was amended to add provisions for those who provide care to family members in the military due to any qualifying need or emergency arising from the fact that the employee's spouse, son, daughter, or parent is a covered military member on "covered active duty." Circumstances could provide for 26 workweeks of leave during a single 12-month period to care for a covered service member with a serious injury or illness who is the spouse, son, daughter, parent, or next of kin to the employee ("military care giver leave").

The act does not require the company to pay the worker's salary during the leave, but the company must hold the worker's job for that worker and maintain his or her health coverage while that person is on leave. There are also some important exemptions to this act:

- An employee who has less than one year of employment
- A part-time employee who worked less than 1,250 hours over the previous 12 months
- Companies with fewer than 50 employees within 75 miles

The 50-employee requirement, along with the exemption of part-time staff, means this law affects only larger off-premise caterers.

National Labor Relations Act

The National Labor Relations Act is union-related and prohibits an employer from restraining employees in any way as they exercise their collective bargaining rights. This means a company can't discriminate against a worker for joining a labor union, can't interfere with the operation of a union, can't donate to the union to sway its members or officers, can't refuse to participate in collective bargaining on behalf of union members, and so forth. The law also prohibits unions from engaging in the same types of behavior, including not discriminating against a worker who chooses not to join a union. A division of the U.S. Department of Labor, the National Labor Relations Board (NLRB), enforces this act.

In 2011, the NLRB proposed some rule changes to make it easier for workers to form unions, changes with which some employers and business lobby groups strongly disagree. The rule changes require votes on forming a union to be taken more quickly after the initial filing, with employers' objections heard after the vote; and for employers to share more of workers' contact information (such as e-mail addresses) with union organizers.

Employee Polygraph Protection Act

A federal labor law, the Employee Polygraph Protection Act of 1988, restricts the use of polygraph (lie detector) tests, except in certain specific cases. For instance, it is acceptable to test an employee when a company is investigating a theft or economic loss, or to test prospective security guards or job applicants who would have access to controlled substances. In most cases, the catering business does not include these types of situations.

Occupational Safety and Health Act

The Occupational Safety and Health Act is enforced by its own special branch of the U.S. Department of Labor, the Occupational Safety and Health Administration (OSHA). This act on ensuring workplace safety and requires employers to keep accurate records of, and make periodic reports about, on-the-job safety, injuries, illnesses, and deaths. It also specifies criteria for "minor injuries," which do not need to be reported.

In addition, the act prevents companies from retaliating against workers who make health- or safety-related claims against them. Violation of the requirements of this act may result in penalties. Because OSHA is concerned primarily with companies that "engage in interstate commerce," its rules may or may not apply to off-premise caterers, depending on their business area. OSHA is also mentioned in Chapter 12, in regard to safety inspections.

EEOC-Enforced Laws

Americans with Disabilities Act

The ADA turned 21 in 2011. This federal law prohibits discrimination on the basis of disability against a qualified person who, with or without reasonable accommodation, can perform essential functions of a job. Discrimination applies to hiring, firing, paying, promoting, and other terms and conditions of employment. This act is enforced by the Department of Justice.

Employers must "reasonably accommodate" the disabilities of qualified applicants or employees unless doing so would result in an undue hardship. An accommodation poses an "undue hardship" if it requires significant difficulty or expense or would fundamentally alter the nature or operation of the business, accounting for such factors as company size, cost, and type of operation.

According to a study by the Job Accommodation Network (JAN), a service of the U.S. Department of Labor's Office of Disability Employment Policy, "Workplace accommodations not only are low cost, but also positively impact the workplace in many ways. The employers in the study reported that a high percentage (56%) of accommodations cost absolutely nothing to make, while the rest typically cost only $500." To minimize associated costs, think about how to accommodate workers by restructuring jobs, modifying work schedules, and allowing for part-time positions.

In recent years, the Department of Justice has made some updates and clarifications to the ADA rules for "public accommodations and commercial facilities," and released 2010 Standards for Accessible Design. These are available online, and your architect or space planner should refer to them in case you intend to build or remodel your commissary or office.

In terms of hiring, employers may not use employment tests or other selection criteria that screen out people with disabilities unless they can show the tests are job-related and consistent with business necessity. Employers also have the right to reject applicants or fire employees who pose a "direct threat" to the health or safety of other individuals in the workplace.

The ADA states that employers may not discriminate against employees who are infected with the HIV virus, whether or not it has manifested itself as AIDS, as well as those who "are perceived to have" this disability. An important note: Caterers cannot make an HIV test a requirement for hiring or continued employment unless they can justify or prove the test is a "bona fide" occupational qualification for a particular job and that it is administered to all employees entering this job category. Persons with AIDS can certainly perform catering functions because the virus can be contracted only by intimate sexual contact, exchange of blood products, or mother-to-infant contact during pregnancy or delivery.

All employers with 15 or more employees must comply with this law; employers with 15 or fewer employees are exempt.

For handling ADA issues, the best practices for off-premise caterers are reflected in the following guidelines from the Florida Restaurant Association:

- Compile accurate written job descriptions before advertising or interviewing. Carefully list the essential functions of each job.

- Limit questions on the application form to those that concern the applicant's ability to do the job.

- Don't ask job interview questions about disabilities, past health problems, use of prescription drugs, hospitalization history, or Workers' Compensation claims.

- Review the way you conduct interviews to be certain you focus on an applicant's ability to do a specific job.

- Conduct all job interviews at locations that are accessible to people with physical disabilities.

Civil Rights Act, Title VII

Title VII of the Civil Rights Act of 1964 prohibits discrimination on the basis of a person's sex, national origin, skin color, or race. It also forbids sexual harassment in the workplace. The act has been amended over the years, so be sure that you are working with the current version of the law. Workers who successfully prove they've been harassed or discriminated against on the job can recover back and future wages, lost employment benefits, attorneys' fees, and court costs, as well as compensatory damages—for the pain, suffering, and embarrassment caused by the harassment—and punitive damages to punish the company for its actions (or lack thereof). The law applies not only to managers, but also to employees. Supervisors can also be held accountable if employees they manage are participating in discriminatory or harassing behaviors and nothing is done to stop them.

Interestingly, in bar or restaurant businesses, sexual harassment can also be claimed when servers are hassled by guests. Anything that is considered "intimidating, hostile, or offensive" can be cause for a harassment claim. You can protect your workers by taking these steps:

- Issue a strong policy against sexual harassment, including a clear definition using examples of inappropriate behavior and procedures to report sexual harassment.

- Distribute and communicate the policy to all employees and encourage them to ask questions.

- Provide periodic employee training about the policy and types of behavior that are unacceptable.

- Ensure that reported incidents are taken seriously and investigated promptly.

- Take appropriate corrective action immediately.

Before investigating this type of claim, a caterer must get the claimant's permission in writing. Then, using discretion, the caterer should perform a thorough, well-documented investigation. When it is complete, the employer must take immediate corrective action (as warranted) that effectively ends the harassment without penalizing the claimant. Look online or ask your attorney to help you draft a standard form to use for documenting and following up on these claims.

It is also illegal to fire, demote, harass, or otherwise retaliate against people because they filed a charge of discrimination, complained to their employer about discrimination on the job, or participated in an employment discrimination proceeding, such as an investigation or lawsuit.

Age Discrimination in Employment Act

We've discussed younger workers, but what about older ones? The Age Discrimination in Employment Act states that companies that employ more than 20 persons cannot discriminate against job applicants or workers who are over age 40. Discrimination applies to hiring, firing, paying, promoting, training, and any other term and condition of employment.

Equal Pay Laws

The Equal Pay Act of 1963 requires equal wages to be paid for jobs that are "substantially equal in skill, effort and responsibility, and which are performed under similar working conditions." In short, it prohibits sex-based wage discrimination by paying men and women differently for performing the same tasks. It applies to all employers, both private and government.

In 2009, the Lilly Ledbetter Fair Pay Act was signed into law. This act amends other antidiscrimination laws, such as the Civil Rights Act of 1964, the Age Discrimination in Employment Act of 1967, and Americans with Disabilities Act of 1990. It changes the rules for calculating the 180-day statute of limitations for an employee who files a pay-related discrimination complaint. The time line now resets with each new "discriminatory" paycheck, not just after the initial instance of pay discrimination. The act also clarifies the point at which an unlawful employment practice occurs with respect to violating equal compensation guidelines.

State-Enforced Laws

Workers' Compensation

Each state has its own insurance fund that covers bodily injury, work-related illness, and death while a person is on the job. Employers pay into the fund based on the number of employees and type of business they have (the cost depends on the amount of risk or exposure to injury that workers in this field generally have). Penalties can be assessed if an employer does not pay into the fund on a timely basis or under-states the number of workers to try to save money. Any employee who is injured on the job or becomes ill as a result of his or her work has the right to file a Workers' Compensation claim.

Workers' Compensation is administered at the state level, and benefits vary from state to state. These laws must be followed to avoid serious penalties, which may even be severe enough to contribute to business failure. Therefore, it is strongly recommended that off-premise caterers work with an attorney to ensure a complete understanding of the laws and requirements of each state in which they operate.

Determining Staffing Needs

Start-up caterers usually find themselves performing most job functions themselves—sales and marketing, food preparation, and staff scheduling. As the business grows, staff members should be added to your operation based on two key factors: business volume, and your own business strengths and weaknesses. Some caterers prefer to cook, so they hire other people to handle sales and administration; others prefer to do their own sales and marketing, so they hire a chef. As the business grows, additional kitchen staff is hired, as well as off-site event managers and an operations manager—and so it goes. Some of America's largest catering firms employ sales staffs of 20 or more, with scores of chefs, prep cooks, and off-site event captains, and lists of on-call service personnel well into the hundreds.

Another key to staffing for off-premise caterers is to have the proper balance between regular staff members who handle the day-to-day operations, and part-timers who are on call as needed to staff off-premise events.

As a general rule, payroll cost as a percentage of sales should be between 30 and 33 percent. Smaller caterers may employ only one or two regular staff members and schedule the remaining staff as needed for events. When you compute payroll costs, it is very important to consider, in addition to the hourly wages paid, the cost for benefits such as:

- Employer's share of Social Security benefits
- Federal and state unemployment insurance
- Workers' Compensation insurance
- Health insurance paid by the employer
- Personal time off (for vacation, illness, holidays)
- Employee meals
- Bonuses and other compensation

These costs can add 20 to 28 percent or more to payroll cost, over and above the regular hourly wages paid. It's important to understand that for every $1,000 a caterer pays in wages, the true cost is actually $1,200 or more.

Off-premise caterers are continually perfecting the art and science of properly staffing individual events. It helps to create staffing charts, such as the one in Exhibit 7.1, for different types of events. You will find yourself referring to them often. Many tangible and intangible elements go into deciding how many people should staff an event. These include:

- Number of guests expected
- Level of service expected by the client
- Price charged for staff
- Type of menu (sit-down dinner, self-serve buffet, etc.)
- Competency of the staff
- Arrival of guests (all at once or staggered)
- Use of china and glassware or plastic disposables

When determining the size of the caterer's regular staff, it is always better to err on the low side. For most caterers, it is easier and more cost-effective to bring in additional staff during busier times than to keep a larger staff in anticipation of busy periods, paying them when business does not always warrant their presence.

EXHIBIT 7.1 This chart outlines the staff breakdown for a full, sit-down dinner using nondisposable dishes and glassware, based on event size

Full-Glass, Seated Meal

# of Guests	Type of Staff	# of Staff	Regular Price	Discount Price
1-200	Event Captain	1	25.00	20.00
201-400	Floor Captain	2	25.00	20.00
401-600	Floor Captain	3	25.00	20.00
601-800	Floor Captain	4	25.00	20.00
801-1000	Floor Captain	5	25.00	20.00
10-20	Server/Bartender	1	20.00	18.95
30	Server/Bartender	2	20.00	18.95
45	Server/Bartender	3	20.00	18.95
60	Server/Bartender	4	20.00	18.95
75	Server/Bartender	5	20.00	18.95
90	Server/Bartender	6	20.00	18.95
100	Server/Bartender	7	20.00	18.95
120	Server/Bartender	8	20.00	18.95
135	Server/Bartender	9	20.00	18.95
150	Server/Bartender	10	20.00	18.95
165	Server/Bartender	12	20.00	18.95
180	Server/Bartender	12	20.00	18.95
195	Server/Bartender	13	20.00	18.95
210	Server/Bartender	14	20.00	18.95

(Continued)

EXHIBIT 7.1 This chart outlines the staff breakdown for a full, sit-down dinner using nondisposable dishes and glassware, based on event size (*Continued*)

Full-Glass, Seated Meal

# of Guests	Type of Staff	# of Staff	Regular Price	Discount Price
300	Server/Bartender	20	20.00	18.95
400	Server/Bartender	28	20.00	18.95
500	Server/Bartender	33	20.00	18.95
600	Server/Bartender	40	20.00	18.95
200	Chef	1	35.00	25.00
400	Chef	2	35.00	25.00
600	Chef	3	35.00	25.00
800	Chef	4	35.00	25.00
1000	Chef	5	35.00	25.00
200	Kitchen	5	20.00	18.95
400	Kitchen	10	20.00	18.95
600	Kitchen	15	20.00	18.95
800	Kitchen	20	20.00	18.95
1000	Kitchen	25	20.00	18.95
100	Scullery	1	20.00	18.95
200	Scullery	2	20.00	18.95
300	Scullery	3	20.00	18.95
400	Scullery	3	20.00	18.95
600	Scullery	4	20.00	18.95
800	Scullery	8	20.00	18.95
1000	Scullery	10	20.00	18.95

Buffet Service with Disposables

# of Guests	Type of Staff	# of Staff	Regular Price	Discount Price
1-400	Captain	1	25.00	20.00
401-800	Captain	2	25.00	20.00
801-1000	Captain	3	25.00	20.00
1101-1500	Captain	4	25.00	20.00
25	Server/Bartender	2	20.00	18.95
50	Server/Bartender	2	20.00	18.95
75	Server/Bartender	3	20.00	18.95
100	Server/Bartender	4	20.00	18.95
125	Server/Bartender	4-5	20.00	18.95
150	Server/Bartender	5	20.00	18.95
175	Server/Bartender	6	20.00	18.95
200	Server/Bartender	6	20.00	18.95
250	Server/Bartender	7-8	20.00	18.95
300	Server/Bartender	8-10	20.00	18.95
350	Server/Bartender	8-10	20.00	18.95
400	Server/Bartender	10-12	20.00	18.95
500	Server/Bartender	12-15	20.00	18.95
600	Server/Bartender	18-20	20.00	18.95
700	Server/Bartender	18-20	20.00	18.95
800	Server/Bartender	20-25	20.00	18.95
1000	Server/Bartender	23-25	20.00	18.95
100	Kitchen/Carver	1	20.00	18.95

(Continued)

EXHIBIT 7.1 This chart outlines the staff breakdown for a full, sit-down dinner using nondisposable dishes and glassware, based on event size (*Continued*)

Buffet Service with Disposables

# of Guests	Type of Staff	# of Staff	Regular Price	Discount Price
200	Kitchen/Carver	2	20.00	18.95
300	Kitchen/Carver	4	20.00	18.95
400	Kitchen/Carver	4	20.00	18.95
500	Kitchen/Carver	6	20.00	18.95
600	Kitchen/Carver	6	20.00	18.95
700	Kitchen/Carver	6	20.00	18.95

Source: Courtesy of Cuisine Unlimited Catering and Special Events, Salt Lake City, Utah.

Recruiting Workers

How do off-premise caterers build a staff of qualified and highly motivated people, both full-timers and part-timers? This process begins with recruitment through a variety of sources. There are thousands of people who would love off-premise catering work. The hours are flexible, the work is interesting and can be exciting, and the pay is pretty good.

One of the best recruitment sources is referrals from existing employees. Most will recommend only those people they believe will succeed. Employees who recommend others tend to feel that their own reputations are on the line, and they also want to work with people with whom they are compatible. However, use caution in hiring too many staff members who are close to one another, friendly away from work, or even related to each other. A problem with one of them could result in a problem with both, or all. It is always best to recruit a variety of people with different backgrounds and interests. Some suggestions for finding them:

- When you are hiring, update your website to reflect your needs. "We're busy! We need dependable sous chefs, call-in servers, delivery staff, and night shift dishwashers." Include information about how and where to apply.

- Let your suppliers know when you need more staff. They can put out the word on your behalf.

- When you are dining out, take some business cards. If you get excellent service, compliment the servers, and give them a card. Tell them if they're interested in some additional part-time work, you'd like to talk with them.

- If your area has a university with a culinary department, make contact with the department chair or instructors. Ask them to steer their best students in your direction.

If you place employment ads, either on online job-posting sites or in newspapers, they can simply state the need for part-time staff members who are energetic and hardworking. Applicants need not be experienced, but they must be willing to learn. And why call it a "job"? Refer to it as a "position" or an "opportunity." "Come be part of the team!" is the attitude to have. Say your business is expanding, which reflects your success and offers a positive impression.

Ads should reflect no bias against individuals because of their race, color, religion, sex, national origin, or disabilities. Smaller companies are not immune from charges of hiring discrimination, even if they consist of only a few employees. In fact, it's smart to ask an attorney to review employment ads before you use them.

What are the qualities necessary for success as an off-premise catering staff member?

- Shows initiative (looks for things to do, is a self-starter)
- Is personable and enthusiastic
- Has a high energy level
- Is well organized and detail oriented
- Is assertive, yet tactful
- Is a team player
- Is flexible (can do or learn different jobs)
- Is an extrovert
- Is good under pressure and can think and react quickly on his or her feet
- Enjoys serving others
- Is well groomed

Some of these traits can be determined in advance through interviewing and checking references, but the best way to see if people will be successful in off-premise catering is to watch them work. That said, it is important to note that all too often, busy caterers put new servers on event crews without sufficient training. The remedy for this is to first require that any new staff member attend your company's training session. Then assign this person to an event captain to "shadow" at an event. (The client is not charged for this person's time, and the person is not given a job assignment—her or she is simply there to accompany and observe the trainer.) The trainer's input will be critical in determining whether the new hire has the necessary traits to become a regular part of the team.

Interviewing and Hiring Staff

For many off-premise caterers, hiring is like a guessing game. They have little or no idea what to look for, or they are so desperate for staff during busy times that they will hire almost anyone who indicates an interest in the work. All too often, they hire people they like instead of those who may be a better fit for the job.

Caterers who understand the hiring process realize the interview is the key factor in making the hiring decision, particularly with servers and salespeople who will have extensive dealings with the public on behalf of the catering company.

Prior to the interview, you will have screened out those who do not seem to possess the necessary experience—now, it's time to talk with applicants, one-on-one.

The Employment Interview

Employment interviews can be tough to squeeze into an off-premise caterer's busy day. However, our advice is to give them the same degree of preparation and effort you would give a client consultation. After all, if you hire this person, you will be seeing him or her a lot more often than any client of your catering business!

Before you meet with applicants, be sure to review their résumé and/or online application and jot some questions. Today, there are many guidelines about what a prospective employer can and cannot ask. While they may seem restrictive, the goal is to prevent discrimination on the basis of age, race, skin color, national origin, religion, sex, and disability. You might want to prepare a standard list of questions, with the help of an attorney, that you can use for every interview.

Please note that this section of the chapter is not intended to serve as legal advice; and that the attorneys and law firms referenced herein are not responsible for any claims or actions that may result from the use of this information. Employment law is a fast-changing field, and we would suggest hiring your own attorney for specific situations and/or advice.

Based on guidelines issued by the EEOC, and with the assistance of Christopher Tinari, a partner in the Employment Practices Liability Department at the law firm Margolis Edelstein in Philadelphia, Pennsylvania, here's a brief list of topics that are to be avoided during a preemployment interview:

- *Age:* You cannot ask for people's age (or age range), date of birth (unless it is to show that they are of legal age to serve alcohol), or graduation date. You also cannot ask to see proof of age, such as a birth certificate.

- *Race or national origin:* You cannot ask about people's country of origin or birthplace. (You can mention that, if they are hired, they will need to submit proof of citizenship and/or their legal right to work in the United States.) You cannot ask about their parents' origin, their or their family's primary language, or whether or when they were "naturalized." No questions can be asked about skin, hair, or eye color.

- *Religion:* You cannot ask if people have any religious affiliations, or whether they attend church. You cannot ask about religious customs, about holidays they observe, or if they have references from clergy members.

- *Sex:* You cannot ask about people's height, weight, or strength.

- *Disability:* You cannot ask about people's medical conditions—diseases and illnesses—or if they have a disability. You cannot ask if they have ever applied for or received disability benefits or Workers' Compensation for an on-the-job injury.

- *Family:* You cannot ask about relatives' names (unless the applicant is a minor), spouse's name or earnings, or a woman's maiden name. You cannot ask about marital status, pregnancy, or future childbearing plans. Number and ages of children, or child care arrangements, cannot be discussed.

- *Other off-limits topics:* You cannot ask about people's credit rating, about arrests that did not result in convictions, or whether they own or rent their home. If a person lives with roommates, you cannot ask their names. You cannot ask if people are a member of a club, political party, or any other organization except a professional one. If a person is a veteran, you cannot ask what type of military discharge was received.

So what can you ask? Questions related to religion and sex are off the table altogether, but the following are allowable topics and questions:

- *Age:* Are you of legal age to perform this job (such as bartending or serving alcohol), and can you provide proof of this? For minors, a parent's name may be asked.

- *Race or national origin:* Are you a U.S. citizen, or can you provide proof that you are legally allowed to work in the United States?

- *Disability:* Are you aware of any physical or mental conditions that may affect your work performance? Can you perform all the necessary functions of this job in a safe manner?

- *Family:* Can you meet specified work schedules? Do you have other activities, commitments, or responsibilities that could hinder your availability? What is the name and contact information for a person who can be notified in case of an emergency? Is anyone else in your family already employed by this company—and if so, whom?

Here are some other questions/topics that are permitted:

- Employers may ask about a person's education and/or military service experience but only as it relates to a particular job: What kinds of training have you had that would be helpful as our sour chef?

- Do you belong to any professional organizations and if so, which ones?

- Who referred you for this position?

- Whom may we contact for professional and/or personal references?

- What do you like most about off-premise catering?

- What did you like most about your last job?

- Where would you like to be in five years?

- If you could do anything in the world, what would it be?

- What do you feel are your strengths and weaknesses?

- If you could change anything about yourself, what would it be?

You may also want to ask candidates how they would respond to a specific real-life catering challenge. Their answer can provide an indication of their resourcefulness and creativity in solving problems.

State laws may be even more stringent concerning preemployment questions, so it is also important to be aware of the state-specific guidelines.

For some jobs, your company may require health exams and/or drug tests. If so, this is the time to let the applicant know about this requirement. Employers cannot ask that these be performed until the person is actually hired. They also may not photograph an applicant until a job offer is made and the person is hired.

Always take notes during the interview. It is unfortunate, but you could be challenged with a discrimination claim, and should retain your notes as documentation in that unlikely event. It is also a good idea to send a letter, either printed and mailed or via e-mail, to applicants who are not chosen, stating something like, "We have examined your qualifications, and there were other applicants who were better qualified for the job."

Background Checks

The laws vary by state about how thoroughly a prospective employer is allowed to probe an applicant's background without intruding on his or her privacy. It would be best to check with an attorney and, based on what your state permits, create a standard policy for conducting background checks if you are allowed to do them at all. The following paragraphs detail what might be part of such a policy but are by no means exhaustive.

Personal and Business References. Many employers ask for references, but is it necessary to check all of them, for every prospective staff member? The answer to this question lies in the type of position to be filled. As a general rule, the more responsibility associated with the position, the more thorough the reference-checking process should be. It would be irresponsible not to thoroughly check the references of someone applying for a general manager position, but this probably would not be necessary for applicants hired to fill a last-minute request to add two more experienced servers to a large catered event.

Previous Employers. Given the potential liability associated with any negative comments that could be made by a previous employer, many employers now only verify dates of employment. Some employers will also confirm the salary range for a former employee and a reason for leaving the position. According to attorney Christopher Tinari, if an employer provides a reference, it must be limited to the topic of inquiry, be communicated to a person with a need to know, provide information that is related to the job requirement, be true, and be communicated without malice or ill intent.

Criminal Records. More than 90 percent of the nation's counties will release criminal records by telephone or mail. However, a number of states will not release records of arrests that did not result in convictions.

Attorney Tim Owens, who specializes in employment and labor law for the firm Land, Alton, and Horst, LLC, in Columbus, Ohio, says, "Employers are on thin ice when they ask about criminal records. If you're going to ask, it's better to ask about convictions than about arrests. There must be some logical business justification in order for you to exclude an applicant based solely on conviction records. Consider, at the very least, the nature and gravity of the offense, the time that's passed, and the nature of the job being filled.

"If you are going to hire someone as a controller and discover that ten years ago, he or she was convicted of embezzlement, that is a clear job relatedness you can act upon," Owens continues. "This is a challenging area because catering employers also have a duty to screen out individuals who may harm other employees or customers. Lawsuits for 'negligent hiring' often result when an employer neglects due diligence in screening new hires."

There are many online websites offering criminal record search services; most charge a fee. Be aware that some sites include a disclaimer that they cannot guarantee the complete accuracy of their results.

Sex Offender Database. States maintain a registry of convicted sex offenders, which can be accessed online by the public. By law, these individuals are not allowed to be within a certain number of feet from schools and child care facilities, which might affect your business depending on the location of your commissary and/or whether you cater at events in these locations.

Motor Vehicle Records. For positions that require employees to drive company vehicles, employers should check for a valid driver's license, as well as whether it has ever been suspended or revoked.

Workers' Compensation Records. A number of states will provide information about whether a person has submitted a Workers' Compensation claim. In some cases, however, requests for this information are covered by federal and some state consumer credit laws. In addition, the federal Health Insurance Portability and Accountability Act of 1996 (HIPAA) includes extensive privacy laws that keep most medical and billing records private.

Federal and State Court Records. All federal judicial districts can provide information about civil, criminal, and bankruptcy cases. In most states, employers can find out whether a person is, or has been, either a plaintiff or a defendant in a lawsuit. In some states, you can review the court transcripts.

Educational Records. Virtually all colleges and universities will verify a job applicant's attendance and degree attainment for prospective employers.

Credit Information. Private companies can provide credit histories for a fee. As with Workers' Compensation records, this type of information may be obtained only in accordance with certain consumer credit protection laws. Typically, you must have the applicant's consent to receive this information, and a copy must also be furnished to the applicant, allowing him or her to challenge the findings and correct inaccuracies.

Employment Agreements

Some caterers use an employment agreement, a document that spells out job duties, work hours, days off, pay rates, the length of any introductory or training period, and so on. It includes conditions (known as *clauses*), such as:

- *Nondisclosure clause:* States that if a worker quits or is fired, he or she will not divulge names of customers, procedures, or methods of operation to any of your competitors.
- *Noncompete clause:* States that the worker will not go to work, whether paid or unpaid, for one of your competitors in the same geographic area for a period of 12 months after leaving your employ.

These clauses are common in the catering industry, particularly in markets where competition is fierce.

Another clause becoming increasingly common is a mutual agreement to arbitrate. This basically says that all claims and disputes regarding employment and termination will be arbitrated by a mediator, rather than taken to court—covering everything from discrimination, to contract and compensation terms, to injury claims. This clause generally does not cover Workers' Compensation and unemployment claims or employee benefits claims with a company plan because each of these includes its own arbitration procedure.

Arbitration is conducted in accordance with the rules of the American Arbitration Association, with the arbitration fees and/or expenses split equally by the parties and prepaid. Each party usually pays the fees and expenses of its own attorneys, experts, and witnesses. It's ironic, but representative of the times we live in, that any arbitration agreement should be carefully drafted by an attorney to avoid lawsuits that challenge the agreement itself.

Paying Catering Staff

When caterers gather, a sure topic of controversy is the issue of whether to pay catering staff as independent contractors or employees. The advantage to employing people with independent contractor status is that the caterer need not pay the employer's share of Social Security taxes (FICA), federal unemployment taxes (FUTA), Workers' Compensation insurance, and other expenses directly related to payroll. The amount of savings can be sizable, as high as 20 percent of total payroll expenses for some caterers.

Classifying Employees Correctly

Staff employed as independent contractors are pretty much self-employed—that means they are responsible for paying their own taxes and do not receive unemployment benefits when laid off or terminated. The Internal Revenue Service (IRS) has developed a series of questions to be used in individual situations when trying to ascertain someone's status as an independent contractor. The following questions are asked of the employer. The more "yes" answers, the more likely the person is an employee, not an independent contractor.

1. Do you provide the worker with instructions on when, where, and how work is performed?
2. Did you train the worker?
3. Are the worker's services a vital part of your company's operations?
4. Is the person prevented from delegating work to others?
5. Is the worker prohibited from hiring, supervising, and paying assistants?
6. Does the worker perform services for you on a regular and continuous basis?
7. Do you set the hours of service for the worker?
8. Does the worker work full-time for your company?

9. Does the worker perform duties on your company's premises?

10. Do you control the order and sequence of the work performed?

11. Do you require the worker to submit oral and written reports?

12. Do you pay the worker by the hour, week, or month?

13. Do you pay the worker's business and travel expenses?

14. Do you furnish tools or equipment for the worker?

15. Does the worker lack a "significant investment" in tools, equipment, and facilities?

16. Is the worker insulated from suffering loss as a result of the activities performed for your company?

17. Does the worker perform duties solely for your firm?

18. Does the worker not make services available to the general public?

19. Do you have the right to discharge the worker at will?

20. Can the worker end the relationship without incurring any liability?

Reviewing these questions makes it quite apparent that most catering staffers are classified as employees and should be paid as employees. It is highly unlikely that a caterer would win an argument with the IRS about this issue, so in our estimation, it is best to pay staff members as employees. Even in situations where workers are paid directly by clients, if the caterer is actually supervising the client's event, the IRS can argue that the workers are working for the caterer, not the client. Why hassle with it? Pay them as employees, including all the necessary deductions and taxes.

To determine a fair hourly rate or salary, off-premise caterers should review the wage rates of competitors and other local employers, the cost of living in the area, the existing supply of qualified staff members, and the caterer's ability to pay. As a general rule, wage rates in rural areas are lower than in metropolitan areas. In our experience, you get what you pay for in terms of employees—those who pay at least average, or above-average, wages for their geographical area are more likely to attract above-average staff. Paying less per hour, you'll be unlikely to attract the best job candidates.

Premium Pay

When employees need to travel long distances to party sites that are far from the catering commissary, compensation becomes an issue. Many off-premise caterers choose to pay staff members for those two or three hours they spend commuting to a party site—not for every commute, but for the really long ones. Others split the difference and pay for one-way travel to remote locations. Either way, it is wise to have a formula that is fair to both employer and employee, and stick to it. Policies on issues like travel time are made at the discretion of the caterer and are influenced by competitive factors, so find out what your competitors do—and do a little more, if possible.

Overtime Pay

We've already discussed the federal wage and hour law that includes overtime pay, or paying one- and one-half (1.5) times a person's regular hourly rate for hours worked in excess of 40 per week. Some states have enacted different laws, requiring overtime pay for hours worked in excess of 8 per day, so check with your state labor department for the particulars.

Most employees understand the need for working overtime, especially in an industry like catering, which requires intense planning and crazy hours. Many of them need and appreciate the extra money too. You may even have to require overtime work to meet certain production deadlines; however, overtime hours should be distributed as fairly as possible among your staff.

Whenever possible, overtime should be planned in advance. This way, workers can make the necessary arrangements at home to spend more time on the job, and as their employer, you can budget for the extra expense. Here's a tip from experience: It's important to have a policy stating that before anyone can work overtime, it must be approved in advance by management. Under no circumstances can employees decide on their own to work extra hours.

Sometimes, the hours of catered events extend beyond the planned stopping time. In this situation, most caterers pay their staffers extra hours of pay for those extra hours worked. This is not to be confused with overtime pay, which is for hours worked in excess of 40 per week. Do you see the difference?

Recording Hours Worked

The technology known as biometrics has allowed fingerprint or hand recognition and proximity cards issued to each staff member to replace the old time-clock system of "punching in" to record work hours. Even at off-premise events, there are portable models and systems that enable people to check in on the job with a cell phone call. Nonetheless, the event captain or supervisor should be observant enough to notice if someone shows up late or not at all, and to make a note of it on the event report. Some websites to peruse for state-of-the-art "time-tracking solutions," as they are now called, are Qqest's Time Force site and Avid Biometrics' site.

Staff members should not be permitted to begin work prior to their scheduled starting time unless approved in advance by management. Those who are late should be paid for the actual hours they worked, not for their scheduled hours. Some off-premise caterers even send staffers home if they arrive noticeably late; others give written or verbal warnings.

Tipping Policies

Off-premise catering staffers may receive a portion of their compensation in the form of tips provided by clients. Catering staff members must report tips given directly to them by clients on IRS Form 4070 (*Employees Report of Tips to Employer*) if the amount exceeds $20 per month. Employers, in turn, must deduct federal income tax and Social Security tax from the employee's paycheck on these reported tips and, of course, pay the employer's share of the Social Security tax.

If part of the caterer's service charge is distributed to staff members for their work at an event, the IRS considers this wages, not tips. No matter what you call such amounts or who collects them, money distributed to employees is still subject to all payroll taxes. Guidelines can be found in IRS Publication 531, *Reporting Tip Income*, which is available online.

Employee Benefits

Today's small businesses say hiring a full-time worker means adding 30 to 35 percent of his or her salary to cover the employee benefits. This section covers various types of benefits that may be offered by off-premise caterers. It is important to note that federal law requires none of these benefits, although some state laws require them and most caterers provide at least some of them:

- Employee meals and breaks
- Paid Time Off (combined vacation pay and sick pay)
- Holiday pay
- Employer-paid health insurance
- Pay for jury duty

Employee Meals and Breaks

For regular staff members, most caterers establish times for breaks and meals through-out a busy day and even during events. For staff working at lengthy off-premise events, the question of meals and breaks becomes more complex. As you will learn in Chapter 8, some caterers prefer to feed their staff members prior to the start of an event, and they bring separate box lunch–style meals specifically for this purpose. Still others do not feed the staff unless they are working a shift that is longer than five or six hours. Typically, breaks are 10 minutes in length; meal times are 30 minutes.

If your policy is to let workers eat after the guests have eaten and/or left the prem-ises, you might occasionally make use of the leftover food. However, it is important to remember that the people who paid for the event are the ones who paid for the food, no matter who is eating it. If it looks like there will be plenty of leftover food and your workers are going to be helping themselves to it, be absolutely certain that the host is okay with this. Some prefer that the leftover food be portioned and given to the party hosts and/or people they designate.

It is smart to offer brief breaks to staff members after the party is completely set up, but before the guests arrive. After the party begins, there certainly is no time for a staff break until after foodservice has come to a close. Most caterers allow those workers who arrived first to go on break first; those who came later take their breaks later. As long as guests are present, some staffers should always be on duty, no matter how late into the evening an event continues.

Paid Time Off

What was once tracked and calculated separately as paid vacation and sick leave for ill-ness or injury is now often rolled into a single category known as Paid Time Off (PTO). PTO is an "earned benefit"—that is, full-time employees accrue their time off based on how many hours they have worked for the company. For the first year of employment, amounts range from 40 hours (5 days) to 15 days a year, depending on what the time off may be used for. We've seen companies that offer 80 hours (10 days) after three years on the job, and 160 hours (20 days) after five years of eligible service.

PTO must typically be taken in eight-hour increments; otherwise the tracking can be too cumbersome. PTO systems work well for off-premise catering because they allow workers the freedom to use their time off as they wish.

No matter what the pay or time-off policy, one thing is certain: In off-premise cater-ing situations, workers who call in sick at the last minute create enormous complications.

Some caterers even require that staff members who are unable to work find their own replacements. In these cases, a written policy makes for clearer understanding of the rules, as well as the methods that can be used when the caterer feels the policy is being abused. The policy can include such provisions as:

- "Buying back" unused PTO when an employee leaves
- Discipline measures for staff members who abuse the benefit
- The possibility of bonuses paid for attendance

Legal holidays pose some interesting dilemmas for off-premise caterers because they are generally among the busiest times. How do caterers pay staff who work—or do not work—on holidays? Again, your PTO policy must clearly spell this out.

Some caterers choose not to book events on holidays. Those who cater on holidays may pay nothing extra, and others choose to pay double time and pass the costs on to the clients. For regular staff members who are given holidays off, most caterers pay their regular pay. Competitors' holiday pay practices should be noted—for instance, it is not unheard of in big cities to pay double the hourly wage, or even more, for staff members who work on New Year's Eve.

Health Insurance

Medical costs continue to skyrocket and, therefore, the cost of health insurance has done the same. More and more caterers are reevaluating their decisions to offer health insurance coverage to staff members. Some follow the lead of companies in other industries and split the costs with employees. Others obtain the group policy but require anyone who wants coverage to pay the full amount. Ultimately, it is the competition for employees that will help you make the final decision.

Jury Duty

From time to time, regular employees are required to perform jury duty. Most employers pay employees the difference between their regular pay and the pay they receive for jury duty (usually a pittance, only a few dollars) as long as the employees present documentation stating they were actually on jury duty at the time. Some employers make jury duty part of their PTO policy.

No matter what benefits you decide to offer to staff members, it is important to consider the true costs of each of them, and to be well aware of what your competitors are offering to craft the best benefits package to attract the best possible workers. Benefits must always be provided in a clear and consistent fashion so all workers understand what is being offered and feel they are being treated fairly.

Orientation and Training

The first day on the job determines, to a great extent, how well things will go in the future. It should be no surprise that turnover is highest among new employees. All too often, this is the fault of the employer for not properly acclimating new people and not making them feel welcome on the job.

Proper orientation is not "Go find Jim, and he'll show you what to do." For new employees, many caterers have found it works well to conduct orientation meetings at the beginning of each season. This gives part-time staff members, who work the parties but are not involved on a daily basis, a refresher course about the overall operation. For regular, daily employees, orientation should include such things as:

- A personal welcome for new employees.
- An introduction to coworkers.
- A look at how the new employees fit into the overall operation or a particular event.
- The purpose and history of the company.
- A brief tour of the event site or commissary operation, including where to store uniforms and personal belongings.
- A review of on-the-job rules and regulations, including any grounds for dismissal. Your policies may cover making and receiving personal phone calls during work hours, use of cellular phones during events, breakage, and behavior both before and after hours while on-premise (commissary or party sites).
- A review of pay rates, overtime rules, taxes that will be deducted, and scheduling procedures.
- An explanation and/or demonstration of major job duties.

At the orientation, each new employee should be assigned to another employee to *job shadow*, or follow, and time should be scheduled periodically with a new worker to see how things are going. Learning should include regular training sessions, usually conducted in groups, and individual on-the-job-training, which is an ongoing process. Some caterers have formal training programs for staff, and others conduct training more informally, choosing a topic or two for each employee meeting, for instance.

The higher a company's employee turnover rate, the greater the need for more and better training. However, all caterers should offer continuous learning opportunities if they are to provide first-class service. Ask yourself the following key questions when developing a training program:

- What specific policies and procedures do my staff members need to know to be successful?
- Who can best help them learn these things?
- How can training results be evaluated?

Ideally, group training sessions should last no more than 30 minutes, focusing on one or two topics related to keeping in mind the needs of guests and clients. Encourage staff involvement by allowing discussion during the sessions. Potential topics for off-premise caterers may include:

- Techniques for carrying trays and plates
- Cooking pasta at a pasta station
- Carving meats at a carving station
- Creating attractive displays
- Correct wine service
- Dealing with "problem" guests (drinking, loud, rude, etc.)
- Personal appearance standards and expectations on the job

Other sessions can be aimed at building enthusiasm and camaraderie among the staff. Progressive caterers have long used training videos with their own, supplemental materials to reinforce the video's important points. There are some excellent video series that deal with customer relations, responsible alcohol service, sales and marketing, and more. Online training has emerged as an even better alternative because the format offers interactivity. Online programs present information, ask questions to determine comprehension, record responses, provide reinforcement, and subsequently report on performance to the trainee and his or her managers.

No matter what the format, successful caterers constantly work with their employees to further their development. They are never completely satisfied with the way things are, always striving to improve. Regularly scheduled staff meetings are an important part of this process to make expectations clear to workers and address issues as they arise.

A Day in the Life of a Caterer: The Staff Meeting

The operations and kitchen staff meeting takes place every Tuesday at 10:00 A.M Present are the operations manager, the chef and assistant chef, the company president, the pastry chef, and the warehouse/delivery manager. (The sales staff has its own separate weekly meetings.) The agenda is informal, and the idea is to hear from everyone around the table with questions and concerns, update everyone on what went right and wrong the previous week, and review the events on the calendar for the current week. Depending on how much chatter prompts the congenial group to veer off course, these meetings last about 90 minutes.

The first item of business is procedural—a client was supposed to pick up an elaborate gift basket between 2:00 and 3:00 P.M. on the previous Saturday, showed up instead at 9:00 A.M., and was angry that it wasn't ready. Right or wrong doesn't matter so much here as how to prevent this from happening again. Additionally, as the warehouse manager puts it, "We're probably wasting money having a guy here on Saturday if he doesn't have to be. Wouldn't it be better to just deliver everything, no pick-ups, and charge a $10 fee?" The group discusses the pros and cons of this as a possible policy going forward. This leads to a discussion of the need for delivery and setup training, both for warehouse and kitchen staff, so that anyone can pitch in if necessary.

The warehouse manager also elicits chuckles when he reports that it "creeped him out" when they had to set up buffet tables at a funeral over the weekend—directly next to the open casket of the elderly deceased. "No food next to caskets!" is the vote for future funeral receptions.

The discussion of upcoming events includes reading over the menus, equipment lists, and staffing lists, with people chiming in if they note something that needs a clarification or change. Here's a sample of what was mentioned:

- At a breakfast event, will the French toast portions be large enough?
- At the same event, add extra worktables to the packing list.
- For a pre-wedding tasting for three people, butterfly the chicken to be prepared and serve the jicama salad, typically in a Martini glass, with clear glass plates under the glasses. This particular group has requested no cilantro—in anything.
- Put more mint in the coconut rice to be served—"as long as they don't think it's cilantro," is the quip.

- The pastry chef asks for suggestions for strawberry shortcake for 150. Should it be in hotel pans so people can serve themselves or plated individually? She also wants to know if three hotel pans will be enough berry cobbler for another event.

- They decide that, for all formal-service dinners, desserts must be served in Martini glasses; otherwise there's just not enough room on the table for all the florals, plateware, and so on.

- The event coordinators for a particular, popular venue are raising eyebrows, not only with the caterer's staff but also with guests at events held there. They don't dress appropriately, often pick at the food and/or ask to "eat early," and also order drinks at the bars during events. The discussion is about how (and to whom) to address this to make the venue managers aware of these problems without alienating the event coordinators and/or the venue managers' supervisors.

- The operations manager wants to see the per-person cost on a Western-theme barbecue recalculated to include prices for the elaborate décor—ropes, hats, saddles, and so on. This request will be forwarded to the salesperson who booked the event.

- There's some discussion about linens: The ivory crushed table linens probably should be replaced, but there's no money in the budget for it.

- The warehouse reports an overstock of paper napkins in a variety of colors. It's decided that these should be used in box lunch orders.

- There's some concern that the dishroom staff has been throwing away shot glasses and votive candleholders rather than washing the really dirty ones. The chef says that he'll talk with them.

- Plates are wrapped in sets of ten for transport, as this makes them easy to count. However, most of the tables at events seat eight. Is there a benefit to changing the count per set? Which number stows best in the packing crates? The warehouse manager will test a few and report his findings.

The meeting wraps up with cost percentage figures for a variety of categories, which are compared to the goals each manager has set for trimming them. For linens, for instance, the target cost was 21 percent, and the result is 19 percent—good news! But wages, which were supposed to be at 19 percent, have inched up to almost 21 percent.

Meeting notes are typed up and will be distributed to all attendees by e-mail.

Uniforms and Staff Attire

We believe the use of uniforms on the job is one way to promote teamwork, as well as a positive, professional image—for individual workers and for the company. Off-premise caterers should require specific uniforms for all staff members, to be worn prior to and during an event. This policy should be extremely specific; "white shirt" is not a sufficient description if caterers require a wing-tipped collar tuxedo shirt with black studs. A sample Uniform Policy for servers is seen in Exhibit 7.2. There will be different requirements for kitchen staff.

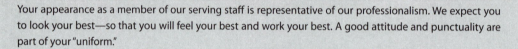

EXHIBIT 7.2 Sample Uniform Policy

Your appearance as a member of our serving staff is representative of our professionalism. We expect you to look your best—so that you will feel your best and work your best. A good attitude and punctuality are part of your "uniform."

Our dress policy for servers is as specified, with no exceptions, and we expect servers to conform to the exacting standards of personal hygiene and dress described in this policy.

Servers are responsible for supplying their own slacks, set-up shirt, socks, and shoes. If you need help finding or purchasing suitable attire, we will do our best to assist you. At more formal events, we will supply a clean, freshly ironed chef's coat in your size to change into at the event. At less formal events, we will supply a golf shirt with our logo in your size. Other requirements are as follows:

For formal events, ironed black dress slacks. Dress slacks are the only suitable option here! No Docker-style pants, cargo-style plants, leggings, jeans or capris. Nothing faded or torn. Slacks must be hemmed to an appropriate length, and a black belt can be worn with them.

For informal, outdoor or summer events, ironed khaki pants. In this case, Docker-style pants are recommended. Nothing faded or torn. No shorts or jeans unless specifically requested.

A black or white set-up shirt. Before guests arrive, we must still look uniform and professional as we set up the event. Wear either a black T-shirt (with sleeves, no logo) or long-sleeved black shirt for fall and winter. In summer, white T-shirts are acceptable. Health codes require that all shirts must have sleeves, so tank tops and halter tops are not allowed. It is not permissible to wear a sweater or hoodie over the set-up uniform.

Polished black dress shoes. Only black shoes are permitted. No sneakers, high heels, noisy shoes, casual shoes, sandals, or flip-flops, even during event set-up periods.

Black socks. No white or colored socks! Black, and black only.

Jewelry. These rules are for safety as well as uniformity. Women are allowed to wear one (1) set of stud-style earrings, no hoops or dangling earrings, and one (1) ring. Please refrain from wearing bracelets and, in general, bright or extravagant jewelry. We would prefer that men do not wear jewelry, but wedding rings and stud-style earrings are okay, with the exception of gauged ears. Nose rings and other facial piercings are also not acceptable, either for men or women.

Hair and hygiene. Come to work clean, fresh, and presentable. Men are to be clean-shaven. Pull long hair back, off the shoulders, and presented in a professional manner (no pigtails, childish barrettes, etc.) If you smoke, please use breath mints to cover the odor; no chewing gum. We recommend that you bring a comb, deodorant, and other toiletries with you as needed to events. Women's fingernails should be no more than one-quarter inch past the edge of the fingertip. Use of clear nail polish is best, so that dirt may be detected. Men's nails should be short, clean, and not extend past the edge of the fingertips.

Source: Courtesy of Cuisine Unlimited Catering and Special Events, Salt Lake City, Utah.

An on-the-job dress code should address accessories that may and may not be worn, the use of cosmetics, exactly how the uniform is to be worn, and who will purchase and clean the uniforms. Some employers provide the complete uniform, some pay for part of it, and others require employees to pay for the complete uniform. (Caterers and staff should talk with their accountants regarding deductibility of uniforms for income tax purposes.)

It is logical that you require staff members to keep their uniforms clean and to wear nametags, especially at event sites. It is also important to ask your employees' opinions when making uniform choices or changes. After all, it is the employees who will be wearing them. Consider the look, comfort, durability, purchase price, and availability for reorders, as well as the ease and cost of cleaning the uniforms.

Motivating Workers

Motivating catering staff members to perform to the best of their individual abilities and still work as a team to keep the client's needs at the forefront, is a never-ending challenge, no matter how experienced the caterer. Off-premise caterers develop their own styles of motivating people. Most understand all employees need to be challenged by their work and recognized for their good work, to feel they are an important part of the company, and to feel safe in the workplace. These underlying needs can be met in many ways:

- Offering wages that are commensurate with the work and competitive with the wages paid by other caterers in your area
- Offering adequate employee benefits, with clear rules that are administered fairly

- Running a well-organized workplace
- Displaying firm and fair leadership
- Never treating a client better than a staff member
- Rewarding people who do things right
- Fairly disciplining (and even terminating) those who continually do things wrong or are troublemakers
- Empowering employees to solve customer service problems themselves
- Being flexible about scheduling whenever possible
- Scheduling the best performers for the most and best shifts
- Allowing the best staff members to grow into supervisory and managerial positions
- Scheduling employee breaks and meals as appropriate
- Providing hot and cold beverages and meals for staff members at off-premise sites
- Holding briefings prior to each event about its purpose and importance, as well as management's expectations of the staff
- Conducting frequent and fair performance appraisals
- Allowing opportunities to attend pertinent seminars and conferences
- Allowing job rotation between positions
- Conducting upbeat meetings and including staff members in future planning

This list reflects some of the many ways to make an off-premise catering operation a truly hospitable place to work by projecting a lively image, showing respect and concern for your staff, and encouraging teamwork.

Baltimore caterer Jerry Edwards of Chef's Expressions, a former president of the National Association of Catering Executives, believes it is important to motivate staffers, particularly during busy periods. In his words:

When in the depths of overtime, work side-by-side with them, or at least make your presence known. If they see you working as hard as they, it lessens the chance they'll resent you for not doing the same. Do some dirty work! Not all of it, rather just enough to remind them that you can. It lets them know that you have done it and will continue to do so whenever necessary.

Listen to their problems. While it's likely you can't solve them, it shows that you are there for them to talk to and that you care enough about them to listen. And never forget to give recognition to your staff for all their hard work, especially during stressful and overbooked periods. Help them understand the "big picture" by letting them know that it can't happen without them.

There are plenty of ways, some of them offbeat, to prompt fun, as well as loyalty, among employees. Reward the younger staff members with things meaningful to them—help with college tuition, give gift certificates for clothing or CDs, or buy concert tickets. You can even exchange catering services with other local merchants to obtain the gift certificates to pass along to your workers. Hold a lottery with the prize being a round-trip commute from their home to work in a limo. Hire a masseuse to give chair massages during especially hectic times at the commissary. For a job well done, give bonuses or lottery tickets on employment anniversaries. Give employees their birthdays off—their own personal paid holidays! And, finally, there's nothing like a handwritten thank-you note to express your gratitude with meaning.

Employee Turnover

Staff turnover is a measurement of how long workers remain in the employ of a particular company. It can be computed by dividing the number of W-2 forms you issue at year's end by the number of staff members. For example, a caterer who issued 100 W-2 forms and has an average staff of 50 persons would have a 200 percent turnover.

For some caterers, turnover is practically nonexistent; for others, there's virtually a whole new staff every two years. The typical quick-service restaurant chain, for example, completely turns over its staff two or three times a year. In catering, with the complexity of work, this would be crazy.

Some percentage of employee turnover actually has advantages. It keeps workers from becoming too complacent in the performance of their duties. Yet catering an event with all new employees is not much fun either. Turnover created by people moving away, students who graduate, and other external reasons is unavoidable. Caterers who do not treat their staff members properly find that they soon defect to other employers. This type of turnover should be avoided at all costs through excellent hiring, training, motivation, pay, and benefits.

Performance Reviews

Employees require feedback about their performance, and professional managers see that they are given useful feedback on a timely basis. Performance reviews serve a dual purpose—as a basis for encouraging more effective work performance, and to provide dates for decision making about future job assignments and compensation.

Permanent employees should be evaluated at least once a year, except in the first year on the job, when evaluations should be performed no fewer than three times. It is advisable to establish probationary periods for all new employees, which can last from three to six months. During the probationary period, employees who are not meeting expectations may be terminated without warning. At the end of the probationary period, every employee should receive a performance review.

Progressive catering managers also take time to evaluate the performances of all staffers after each catered event, to identify problem areas and determine needs for further training. Many use these evaluations for future scheduling purposes. Excellent performers receive the best schedules and shifts; those whose work was mediocre will be scheduled less frequently. Those who performed poorly may not be rescheduled at all.

Exhibit 7.3 is a sample Staff Evaluation Form. It addresses such performance areas as quality and quantity of work, ability to follow directions, ability to interact with guests

---

EXHIBIT 7.3 Staff Evaluation Form

NAME OF EMPLOYEE_____

EMPLOYEE'S POSITION _____

NAME OF PERSON(S) RATING _____

DATE OF REVIEW_____

RATING SCALE OF 1 TO 5

1   UNSATISFACTORY
2   NEEDS IMPROVEMENT
3   SATISFACTORY
4   ABOVE AVERAGE
5   OUTSTANDING

QUALITY OF WORK   QUANTITY OF WORK

ACCURACY _____   AMOUNT COMPLETED _____
NEATNESS _____   COMPLETED ON TIME _____
ORGANIZATION _____   CONSISTENCY _____

ATTENTION TO DETAIL _____

FOLLOWING DIRECTIONS _____

COMPLY WITH INSTRUCTIONS _____

FOLLOWS RULES AND REGULATIONS _____

CARE AND USE OF EQUIPMENT _____

 FOLLOWS SAFETY AND SANITATION RULES _____

OTHER CRITERIA _____

PUNCTUALITY AND ATTENDANCE _____

GETS ALONG WITH GUESTS _____

GETS ALONG WITH OTHER EMPLOYEES _____

PERSONAL APPEARANCE AND HYGIENE _____

OTHER BEHAVIOR _____

DATE REVIEWED WITH EMPLOYEE _____

EMPLOYEE'S COMMENTS AND REACTION _____

_____

_____

_____

MUTUALLY AGREED-UPON STEPS TO IMPROVE PERFORMANCE _____

_____

_____

SIGNATURE OF EMPLOYEE _____

SIGNATURE OF PERSON REVIEWING PERFORMANCE WITH EMPLOYEE

and fellow employees, and so on. This form can be used for either full- or part-timers; you can adapt it as necessary.

Management and supervisory staff members should be evaluated with the use of additional criteria: their judgment, analytical and planning abilities, profit and cost sensibilities, effectiveness as a supervisor, and more. Above all else, the caterer should always use his or her own independent judgment and avoid the inevitable rumors that always seem to circulate in this type of close-knit work group. Also evaluate a staff member based on his or her typical behavior, eliminating both "good" and "bad" extremes. You might consider using peer group evaluations in which fellow staff members (often anonymously) evaluate their coworkers.

Discipline and Termination

In order to be effective, discipline must be consistent. It must be administered as a result of specific behavior problems, rather than personality conflicts. Appropriate workplace discipline normally follows a particular series of steps:

1. Verbal warning

2. Written warning(s)

3. Suspension without pay

4. Termination

Employees who steal, are insubordinate, or use alcohol or drugs while working should be terminated immediately.

Documentation of unacceptable behavior is imperative. For staffers who are frequently late, it is not enough for a manager to warn them by saying, "You're always late!" Taking the time to document exact times and dates is essential; jot notes and keep them.

Verbal and written warnings should include clear statements of expectations: "You must be properly dressed and at your workstation by 9:00 A.M. each day." If the infraction is not serious, it may be possible to put the employee on an improvement plan, with written goals agreed to by both worker and supervisor and a time line for accomplishing them. If additional training is needed, it can be part of the goals.

Finally, warnings should include the consequences for not doing what is necessary. Can the violation result in suspension, transfer, demotion, or termination?

There are two forms of termination: voluntary and involuntary. A voluntary separation occurs when an employee resigns. Smart managers always identify the reasons why employees leave and obtain letters of resignation, so employees who quit cannot receive unemployment benefits because claims of this type often directly contribute to an increase in the employer's unemployment rates.

Involuntary separation, or firing, should be considered a last resort after trying all else. In either case, and no matter what the reason, an exit interview should be conducted with every worker who leaves your employ. Make this part of a consistent exit process that is used uniformly with everyone who leaves the company, and stick to it. Some companies have two managers do the interview, enabling each to witness the process in case of a future legal challenge.

Letting someone go, or watching someone leave, is tough even if it is the best move for the worker or the company. Make sure the person leaves with his or her dignity intact.

The Employee Handbook

All off-premise caterers, regardless of business size, should have their employment rules, standards, and procedures in writing in an employee handbook. This document will not replace personal contact and can't possibly answer every potential question, but it can at least inform staff about the most vital company policy information.

Generally, the larger the company, the more information should be included. You can try writing the handbook yourself with the assistance of a good local freelance writer and input from your attorney. Ask executives in other industries if you can look at their manuals for ideas. Or you can hire a human resources consulting firm to craft a manual for your company. Many companies now keep their employee handbooks online, on their own internal websites, so they can be updated regularly, although it is advisable to have printed copies available. In addition to their employee handbook, off-premise catering companies should also have a server's handbook that details specific procedures for the serving staff. You will employ a fair amount of part-time people as servers and bartenders, and it is critical that they all become familiar with your expectations.

Ask new employees to sign a short statement affirming they have received a copy of the handbook, have read it, have had an opportunity to ask questions, and have understood its contents.

Every employee handbook should begin with a basic "welcome" and a policy statement that summarizes the way business is done by the company. Here's an example of a policy statement:

Hypothetical Catering is known throughout this area as a reputable, service-oriented firm that provides excellent food and service to its corporate and social clientele. Our goal is to astonish the guest by delivering more than promised on a consistent basis, and this can be accomplished only through teamwork within our company. All staff members are expected not only to perform their own jobs, but also to assist other staff members whenever needed.

At Hypothetical Catering, we put our staff first. We realize that an outstanding staff will deliver and produce the types of events that will exceed the guests' expectations, creating wonderful word of mouth that will generate future business.

Our staff is made up of friendly, caring, courteous, and concerned individuals who enjoy working for us. They smile; they keep their promises; they are always pleasant to our clients and guests. They listen attentively to guest requests and always exhibit a positive, "can-do" attitude. We try to empower our staff members to handle any special customer request quickly and courteously.

We produce special events and parties that are user-friendly for the guests and hassle-free for the clients. We treat clients and guests the same way we wish to be treated when we are out. Our staff members exhibit pride in themselves, pride in our food and service, and pride in our organization. We are pleased to welcome you to the Hypothetical team!

Following the policy statement, include a table of contents, and then detail your specific policies about a wide range of topics, whatever fits best for your company.

Employee Handbook Topics

- Alcohol and drugs (policy to prohibit use)
- Americans with Disabilities Act (company compliance)
- Attendance policies
- Automobiles (where to park, including a statement that the company is not responsible for personal vehicles or their contents)
- Breaks (when and where)
- Compensation (payroll deductions, signing in and out, minimum shift lengths)
- Courtesy (a statement regarding kind, professional treatment of others)
- Equal opportunity employer ("The company reaffirms its policy of treating all employees and applicants equally, according to their individual qualifications, ability, experience, and other employment standards. There is to be no discrimination due to race, religion, national origin, sex, age, disability, or veteran status.")
- Event etiquette
- Exit interviews (to be conducted for all terminated staff prior to leaving)
- Family and Medical Leave Act (company compliance)
- Gambling (on-the-job prohibition)
- Grievance procedures
- Holidays (and related pay policy)
- Hours of work (normal office hours, shift times, etc.)

- Instructions (for table setup, use of tray jacks, formal service, butler-passing, etc.)
- On-the-job injuries (All of these, regardless of their nature or severity, must be reported immediately to the supervisor. All employees are insured through Workers' Compensation. Those employees who do not report injuries are subject to disciplinary action.)
- Personal appearance and hygiene (possible policies on excessive tattoos, body piercings, dreadlocks)
- Personal phone calls, and cell phone and personal digital assistant (PDA) use
- Moonlighting (rules about working for other caterers, restaurants, etc.)
- Overtime policy
- Paid Time Off (PTO) policies (vacation, illness, jury duty, personal time)
- Payroll discrepancies (pay dates; adjustments for errors, advances, lost paychecks; reimbursement for out-of-pocket expenses at an event, etc.)
- Pension plan (if applicable)
- Performance reviews (who conducts them, how often, where records are kept, how the results can be questioned or challenged)
- Probationary or "introductory" periods
- Promotions and transfers
- Property (care of company property; statement that the company is not responsible for personal property)
- Rules and regulations (miscellaneous)
- Safety and sanitation rules
- Security (policy for checking employees' bags and personal property, policy on employees taking home leftovers, etc.)
- Sexual harassment (Potential problems must be reported to management, and management will investigate by interviewing the alleged offender and others; management will ask for legal advice in situations that are unclear and take appropriate disciplinary action if necessary.)
- Smoking (should be prohibited in all food production and service areas and on client event sites)
- Social media and e-mail use (including how the company is represented in employees' public social communications)

- Suggestions (are encouraged; how to submit them)
- Teamwork (importance of working together)
- Telephone courtesy and incoming calls (policies and procedures for answering phones, taking orders on proper forms, etc.)
- Termination policies
- Training programs
- Uniforms (specifics, who pays for uniforms, use of nametags, etc.)
- Vacations (how and when to request)

Summary

This chapter begins with a high-level overview of the federal employment-related laws, many of which have been put into place and amended over the years to ensure that employees receive fair treatment and fair wages from their employers.

After reading this chapter, it should be clear to you that off-premise caterers need to forge a relationship with an attorney who is familiar with labor laws and issues. Hiring has become a real minefield, in terms of finding the best people and getting them onto the payroll. Among the current issues: the growing backlash for companies that hire illegal immigrants (knowingly or unknowingly) and use of the E-Verify system for determining a person's immigration status; the fact that federal laws prohibit employers from asking some questions that once might have been considered part of a normal conversation when getting to know a job applicant; and the option of criminal background checks, sex offender registries, and the like.

Nonetheless, off-premise catering is a people-oriented and service-oriented business, and smart, personable workers are always in demand. The chapter includes guidelines for determining how many staff members you will need for particular events, and how to find, interview, and train them.

Pay and benefits are discussed, along with ways to motivate and retain good workers. For situations where it doesn't work out, the basic steps for discipline and termination are outlined. The chapter ends with information about the importance of creating an employee handbook and a long list of possible topics.

🍴 Study Questions

1. Research the hourly pay amounts of at least two off-premise catering companies in your area, and summarize your findings. Also ask about the benefits they offer full-time employees and what percentage these benefits add to overall labor costs.

2. Find out the latest information in your state about the use of E-Verify. Is it mandatory or optional? Ask at least three employers if they are using it, how it works, and if they are satisfied with it. Briefly summarize your findings.

3. Do you believe an off-premise caterer should perform criminal background checks on any employee? If so, how extensive do you think they should be? Explain your answer.

4. Would you institute a PTO plan at your off-premise catering firm or have separate rules for vacation, sick leave, and holidays? How would your plan accommodate jury duty or bereavement situations?

5. Suggest two additional topics for staff training that are not mentioned in the section on "Orientation and Training" (page 268). Explain the importance of these topics.

The Show 8

"We're not in the hamburger business—we're in show business." When McDonald's founder Ray Kroc uttered that famous line, he might as well have been talking about off-premise caterers. *The Show* is the term many caterers use for the event itself. All the planning, purchasing, and preparation lead up to a single event, and it's your job to make it everything the clients expect. This chapter is about delivering what you promise. We discuss the key elements of successful off-premise events, focusing on the following topics:

- The importance of good service
- The role of the event captain or supervisor
- Rules for setting tables
- Service tips for buffets and food stations
- Service techniques and procedures
- Tips for handling complaints

The Show is by far the most important time for off-premise caterers. This is the time when the clients and their guests receive what was agreed on in the planning and contract-signing phases of the negotiations. There is only one opportunity to perform, so it must be right the first time. Everyone who attends the event will evaluate the food, the service, and the off-premise catering company. Good reviews should bring future business, but bad reviews create negative word of mouth that can quickly spread, resulting in lost business.

Four out of five dissatisfied guests won't necessarily complain to the caterer or on-site staffers, but they'll tell others. Every dissatisfied guest or customer tells an average of four other people about a bad experience, according to research at the Wharton School of Business at the University of Pennsylvania. Therefore, the caterer must focus all of his or her attention on client satisfaction to remain successful and profitable.

Customer service is a delicate, intangible product. It cannot be stored for future use; once given, it is lost. It is a direct function of the customers' expectations and perceptions. The perceived level of service equals how closely the guests' experiences match their expectations. And, ironically, when the service experience matches their expectations, it is often unnoticed or taken for granted. You might say the customer's impression is neutral when the service is "neutral." On either side of neutral is the memorable experience—which may be good or bad.

To make a positive memorable impression, what has to happen? The service must be efficient and attuned to the mood of the event, as well as the cultural level of the guests. Staff members must be caring, courteous, concerned, and reliable. The people and surroundings must be clean, safe, and pleasant. Overall, the client must consider the outcome worth the investment.

Yet good service is often a matter of opinion or perception. It is not what is said, but what is seen and heard. Miscommunication is often at the heart of service problems. For example, suppose an off-premise caterer says that roast beef will be served on the buffet. The customer is accustomed to eating beef tenderloin and assumes that beef tenderloin will be served. The caterer serves a steamship roast. The caterer never said *beef tenderloin*, but the client heard *beef tenderloin*. Some caterers will say, "Not my fault, and not my problem." But it is! We are dependent on clients for future business, so we must at least meet their expectations and, ideally, exceed them. In this case, the caterer should have been specific about what type of beef would be served. Of course, the client could have asked, but that is not the point. We are considered the experts, so we must take the ultimate responsibility for clarification.

The five most common service-related complaints are:

- Broken promises
- Rudeness

- Indifference
- Not listening
- Negative attitudes

What do these complaints have in common? They are all, to a large extent, matters of opinion and personal perception. And they all occur when there is contact with clients and guests. These "moments of truth" occur thousands of times during an off-premise event—with the bartenders who serve the drinks, with the meal servers, with the person at the door who says "good night" and so on. The goal for caterers should be to create the entire experience so that guests float through the party, barely noticing the servers, having their needs anticipated. The experience should be user-friendly and hassle-free. Long waits for food and beverages, unpleasant servers, poorly prepared food, and disorganized or unclean surroundings are examples of situations that antagonize guests and ruin any chances for future business.

Everyone in the catering company must be motivated to create a wonderful experience for clients and guests. Everyone from the chef to the bus person must aim for guest satisfaction. Effective off-premise caterers empower their staff members to solve service problems on the spot, without involving a supervisor, which may take too much time. This could mean anything from obtaining a special meal for a guest, to helping a person who may have difficulty walking to a buffet.

An outstanding server is one who anticipates a need and takes action. It is someone who, when a guest drops a fork during a meal, notices and replaces it immediately, presenting the clean flatware on a tray. An attentive server folds the cloth napkin of a guest who has temporarily left his or her seat, so that the place setting always looks nice. An observant server looks for opportunities to add something positive to the guest experience.

In this regard, caterers who think that food quality is the most important aspect of an event are mistaken. In fact, clients are equally concerned with such things as the caliber of the service staff, the table appointments and buffets, and even the accessory services, such as the music. A band or deejay blaring loud tunes while guests are trying to dine and converse can ruin an event. The Disney organization perceives itself as providing a "fantasy experience" in its theme parks. It does not think of its facilities merely as amusement parks. In similar fashion, the successful off-premise caterer realizes that he or she provides a complete entertainment experience, not just food. It is the event—in its entirety—that creates a memorable experience.

Great customer service has to feel sincere, warm, and, most important, spontaneous. There is nothing worse than robotic service, delivered without enthusiasm. Great service makes everyone feel that he or she is truly special. Bumping good service up to extraordinary can be something as simple as reversing the place settings for left-handed guests.

Yes, there will be mishaps. Caterers should handle servers' accidental spills graciously, in a courteous and professional manner. Offer a clean towel immediately; offer to pay the cleaning bill. Other examples of extraordinary service include escorting guests to the restroom, rather than simply pointing, and giving them tours of your commissary or off-premise catering kitchen before an event.

The bottom line here is that extraordinary service will bring extraordinary sales and profits and will ensure that you will have repeat business. Service sells! In the rest of this chapter, we discuss how you can establish service standards and follow through to see that they are met and exceeded.

The Role of the Event Captain

Before discussing specific techniques for providing outstanding service, we will address the role and responsibilities of the event manager or supervisor on-site, commonly known as an *event captain*. This person's role is so important that, for very large or formal events, it is not uncommon for the off-premise catering company owner to fulfill this role.

In Chapter 6, we described the delivery of food, equipment, and supplies to the event location. At this point, we are assuming the catering truck(s) have arrived, one of them perhaps being driven by the event supervisor, and it's time to start setting up. The event captain, with some assistance, oversees the unloading and organizing of the equipment, so that the staff can find it. If there is rental equipment, this must also be organized, unwrapped, sorted, and counted. If there are problems with the equipment, the supervisor should call the rental company immediately to correct them.

The captain is also responsible for assigning setup duties as staff members arrive. (Check-in nowadays can be done electronically on-site, to accurately record each person's work hours, but staff members should also seek out the event captain and let that person know they've arrived on-site.) Depending on the size of the event, the staff may receive printed diagrams for the various bars, buffets, and stations and the off-premise kitchen. Many caterers prefer to stagger the arrival of staff members, scheduling a few workers early to help unload, organize the equipment, place and cover tables, and so on. Once things are organized, other staffers arrive to perform other functions, like setting tables, stocking the bars, arranging buffet decorations, and so forth. For those who will be setting the tables, the supervisor should set up a sample place setting.

As the crew sets up, the captain should meet with the client for a last-minute check: Are the various accessory service providers on schedule? How can the food service schedule be best coordinated with the program and the music? Event setup can be a hectic time, but never ignore the client. In addition, at an opportune time the event captain should briefly introduce the host(s) to every member of the staff and mention the function they will serve at the event. Particularly at a private function or in a private home, this puts the host(s) at ease.

The captain must also be aware of the kitchen setup to direct the service staff as to where food will be picked up and where soiled dishes will be placed. Normally, another person is in charge of the kitchen. The kitchen supervisor sees that the cooking facilities are set up as shown in the event diagram and operated in a manner that meets the client's needs. This person addresses the following issues:

- Is the kitchen set up properly, neatly, and safely for the particular function?
- Are all the necessary utensils, food, and supplies—from latex gloves to garnishes— on hand in sufficient quantity?
- Has the scheduled staff checked in and been assigned duties?
- Has everyone on-site been properly trained and briefed?
- Are the recipes on-site for preparing this menu?
- Are there any last-minute changes in the menu or service to be discussed?

If all is on schedule, the event site should be completely set up 60 to 90 minutes before the guests arrive. This gives the setup crew a chance to have a meal break, then freshen up and change into their uniforms, with sufficient time remaining for the event captain to conduct the staff meeting. At this gathering, the event captain checks everyone's appearance and uniform, explains the menu and beverage arrangements, and makes assignments for the various responsibilities during the event. For large events, handouts (such as the one shown in Exhibit 6.1, in Chapter 6) or even a large poster taped to a wall in the staging area can be very effective for this purpose. This briefing should include some information about the purpose of the event, the clients, and the guests, as well as any other information that will assist the staff in properly serving the event. It should also include:

- The schedule of events
- Restroom locations for guests

- Review of all serving procedures if necessary (how to pass hors d'oeuvres, serve the meal, and bus dishes, etc.)

- Making sure that staffers each have a few business cards to hand to guests who ask about the catering, and/or they know where to find the cards in the staging area.

For an event captain, it is important to answer any and all staff questions and to give your team an upbeat send-off for a great event. Tell them how much you appreciate their hard work and courtesy to the guests. Once the briefing is complete, the staff members report to their assigned stations, and the supervisor should begin a last-minute check of all stations, bars, the kitchen, the accessory service providers, and other details.

If the event is underway and everything is going smoothly, the event captain might be able to mingle a bit with guests, listening for comments and fielding guests' questions. However, event captains must not get so involved in any particular task that they lose sight of the "big picture"—literally. Their prime duty is to supervise the overall event. If a particular area needs attention, shift another staff member who is not so busy to the area to help temporarily.

When food service is complete, the event captain can see that staffers receive short breaks, in shifts. Although it is true that every event seems to have one last-minute crisis (small or large) to be dealt with, a good supervisor operates more like a mayor than a firefighter. He or she walks the floor, noticing every table, setting the pace for the staff, and assisting as necessary without getting stuck in one job. Great supervisors observe, anticipate, prioritize, and act. They must be capable of multitasking, keeping everything in perspective while never letting staff or guests "see them sweat."

Good supervisors not only observe the guests, but also observe their staff members, particularly during large or demanding, high-pressure events. Sensitivity to the needs of the staff ranks first for outstanding leaders. Good leaders nourish the staff. They give energy, rather than deplete it!

Breakdown of the event site can begin as soon as the guests leave. The event captain's main responsibilities at this point might include assigning staff members and/or pitching in to help with any of the following tasks:

- Count all equipment, and see that it is returned to a safe place or loaded into the catering vehicle.

- Bag trash and recycling, and ensure they are put in the proper place(s) for proper disposal.

- Deal with any leftovers in the manner decided by contract or by mutual agreement on-site with the client.
- Debrief staff members quickly before allowing them to leave the site.
- Collect any funds due from the client (if not already paid or arranged for).
- Pack and load all food, equipment, and so on.
- Safely return the catering vehicle to the commissary and help unload it.

Exhibit 8.1 is a multipage Event Captain's Report, on which the supervisor can make notes before, during, and after the event. It is important that it be completed promptly after every event, while memories are fresh. It can be a valuable indicator of what the caterer needs to work on in terms of staff training—or who needs to be congratulated for a perfect job at a perfect event. This report is reproduced with the permission of Cuisine Unlimited Catering and Special Events in Salt Lake City, Utah.

Setting Up for Meal Service

Most off-premise caterers allow two to three hours of setup time prior to an event. The amount of time will vary, depending on the size of the event, the complexity and location of the setup, and other factors, but it is always better to allow too much time, rather than too little, in case there are unforeseen problems during the setup. The setup crew can be a skeleton crew—maybe 25 to 50 percent of the total staff scheduled to serve the event. They should be attired in a setup uniform, designated by the caterer. It may be something as simple as a T-shirt or golf shirt with the caterer's logo, matching slacks or shorts, and comfortable shoes. Most pre-party work involves heavy lifting, so don't make it fancy. A uniformed, efficient, and well-organized setup crew is a signal to the client that things are already going well and will continue to do so.

It is advisable to have all the tables set at least one hour prior to the start of the event. Why?

- It reassures the client that everything will go as planned and enables the crew to take a short break before the event.
- It allows time for problem solving if something goes wrong.
- It gives staff time to freshen up and change into service uniforms.
- It leaves time for a staff meeting before the event.

EXHIBIT 8.1 Event Captain's Report

Client:

Event site:

Event Date:

Number of Guests:

Start times:
Packing for this event began at: _____
Loading vans began at: _____
Left commissary at: _____
Unload began at: _____
Setup began at: _____

Staff Name	Position	Time-in/out	Gratuity Capt., <u>Full</u> load, unload (Cuisine/Onsite), work, set & break, <u>On Site</u> load & unload (on-site), set and break, work, <u>Work Only</u> no load or no unload (on-site), break and work.
	Captain		
	Server		
	Server		
	Server		
	Bar		
	Bar		
	Bar		
	Bar		
	Chef		
	Kitchen		
	Setup		
	Preload		Document time taken to preload van. This time is in addition to scheduled time for event staff.
	Unpack		Document estimated time for packers to unpack event.

Uniform:

Items	Check-In	Check-Out
Ice		
Ice Rings		
Greenery		
Creamer		
Beverage napkins		
White Chef's Jacket or Black Turtleneck w/ bistro aprons		
Foil Pans		
Camera		
Garbage Cans w/ liners & linen		
Tray Jacks w/ tray & linen		
Full Glass–Disposable		

Centerpiece:

Beverage:
SEE ATTACHED LIQUOR LIST

Actual number of guests:

CHARGEABLE LINENS: (Seating tables, guest napkins, buffets, etc. Do not charge for "fufu," tray jacks, trashcans, or kitchen prep tables.)

TYPE	QUANTITY	TYPE	QUANTITY
72372		Radial	
90390		1200	
543120		Rentals	
Guest Linen Napkins		Overlays	

(Continued)

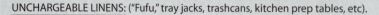

EXHIBIT 8.1 Event Captain's Report (*Continued*)

UNCHARGEABLE LINENS: ("Fufu," tray jacks, trashcans, kitchen prep tables, etc).

TYPE	QUANTITY	TYPE	QUANTITY
72372		Radial	
90390		1200	
543120		Rentals	
Fufu		Runners/Overlays	

CHARGEABLE TABLES: (Seating, Buffet, Tall Boys, Cocktails, Registration etc. Do not charge for kitchen prep tables.)

TYPE	QUANTITY	TYPE	QUANTITY
49		600	
69		Tall Boys	
89		Cocktail	
480		Serpentine	
Wooden Blocks		Rentals	

CAPTAIN'S COMMENTS (Please be thorough in your explanations.)

1. How was the overall event? Anything happen that we need to know about and/or discuss?

    Excellent   Good   Satisfactory   Problem Area
    Explain…

2. How was the overall presentation of the event including food? Was everything pretty?

    Excellent   Good   Satisfactory   Problem Area
    Explain…

3. How was the packing?

    Excellent   Good   Satisfactory   Problem Area
    Explain and List Missing Items…

4. How were the quality & quantity of food? Did you have enough food? Did it taste good?

Excellent   Good   Satisfactory   Problem Area

Explain…

5. Did you feel confident about the staff?

Excellent   Good   Satisfactory   Problem Area

Explain…

6. Did you have adequate time to execute the event?

Excellent   Good   Satisfactory   Problem Area

Explain…

7. Did you feel confident in your knowledge (details) of the event?

Excellent   Good   Satisfactory   Problem Area

Explain…

8. Were there any changes from the briefing information once you arrived on-site? Did you get a signed change form?

Explain…

9. Were there any specific comments/concerns by the event host(s) or guests?

Explain…

_____   _____

Signature–Event Captain   Date Signed

Source: Courtesy of Cuisine Unlimited Catering and Special Events, Salt Lake City, Utah.

Unlike at hotels, where nonservice staffers set up the tables, many off-premise caterers rely on their service staff to perform this function. A diagram of the room layout will show where tables are to be placed. The captain should designate someone to check that each table leg is properly locked for safety reasons and that there is at least 5 feet of space between the tables to allow room for chairs and walking space. When rolling round tables, staff members should keep the legs opposite their bodies and wear heavy work gloves to protect their hands from splinters and sharp metal edges. Tables must be carried, rather than rolled, over certain floors that may scratch, and over dirty or muddy surfaces.

When placing the linens on the tables, servers should be trained not to drag clean linens on the floor or ground, to see that they hang evenly from all sides, and to ensure that the hem sides are down and that the creases all run in the same direction for uniformity. Servers' hands must be clean before handling linens, and to set flatware they should wear latex gloves.

Although not always possible, it is advisable to place the centerpieces on the tables as soon as the linens are on, but prior to setting the tables. This shows the servers how much room is available for the place settings. When very large floral arrangements are placed on already-set tables, glasses may be knocked over or the place settings may have to be compacted to make room. For a damp floral arrangement, a napkin should be folded and placed under it to protect the more expensive cloth. Wet cloths can mildew quickly if not handled properly after an event.

The menu for a seated, served meal determines the place setting, and the event captain fully sets a sample table, so that staffers know how each table is supposed to look and can refer to the sample as they work. At the sample table, a "direction" is established such that all the tables and settings will look uniform. For instance, the podium or an obvious spot at the front of the room is designated the "12:00" spot. When linens are arranged, the center creases on every table will aim at that 12:00 spot. At round tables, the place settings are placed around the table as if they represented the spots on a clock dial. Later, that also comes in handy for service—at every table, the guest seated at 12:00 is the first to be served (if it is a woman); if it is a man, the first woman to his right is served.

Guided by the sample table, staffers may begin to set the tables once they are all in place. It is easier to set the tables without the chairs in place because they get in the way as servers are moving around the tables. If this is the case, how do the staff members know where to place the flatware? They can use the creases on the linens as guidelines, as shown in Exhibit 8.2. Using our clock-dial analogy, they place the knives at 12:00 and 6:00, and then evenly place the remaining knives according to whether the table is to be set for 8, 10, or 12 guests. The idea is that seated guests are able to distinguish which is their place setting.

The basic pieces of a place setting, and their purposes, include:

Dinner knife	For main course
Butter knife	For butter
Salad knife	For salad course

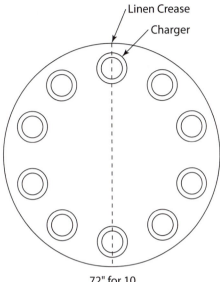

72" for 10

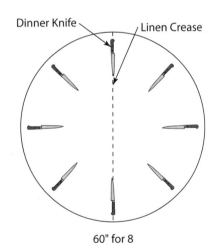

60" for 8

Step 1   Line up knife or charger on each end of the crease.

Step 2   For 10 settings, place 4 knives or chargers spaced
evenly between the 2 knives on the crease.
For 8 settings, place 3 knives or chargers spaced
evenly between the 2 knives or chargers on the
crease.

Exhibit 8.2 Setting a Round Table Without the Chairs in Place

Fish knife	For seafood dishes
Dinner fork	For main course
Salad fork	For salad course
Fish fork	For seafood dishes
Oyster fork	For shellfish
Soup spoon	For soups or pasta
Teaspoon	For desserts or sorbets
Iced tea spoon	For iced tea
Bread and butter plate	For bread and butter
Charger	Under any courses served before the main course
Water goblet	For water
Wineglasses	For wines
Champagne flute	For Champagne
Coffee cup and saucer	For coffee or hot tea
Napkin	

Of course, you will never put each and every one of these items in a single place setting all at once! We know of two efficient ways to set a large number of tables:

- The first method is to assign one particular item per setup person. This eliminates presorting into sets of 8, 10, or 12 for each table and assigns responsibility for a particular item to one person: Jane sets the dinner knife, Joe sets the dinner fork, Sue sets the salad fork, and so on. When each is finished setting his or her assigned utensil, the person starts with a new one until the tables are all set. It is very easy to misplace items when everyone is handling all of them—one server has extra teaspoons, momentarily sets them down, and forgets where. Another server is short of teaspoons and can't find any more. Setting tables in a more organized fashion can save significant time, effort, and frustration.

- The second method is to count flatware and leave a sufficient quantity at the center of each table; then do the same with the other items that belong on that table. Once all the tables have the proper numbers of utensils, glassware, chargers, and so on, one person sets that entire table. This gives a single person the responsibility for making sure the table is complete and looks perfect.

Once the place settings are on the tables, the chairs may be positioned at each place setting by just touching the front edge of the chair to the linen. The chairs should never be shoved under the table or pushed into the tablecloth, which makes the whole table look rumpled and unattractive.

Exhibit 8.3 is a sample place setting for a multiple-course dinner. Note that the utensils are placed in order of service from outside in. The bottom edges of the flatware and charger should be one inch from the edge of the table. Please note that

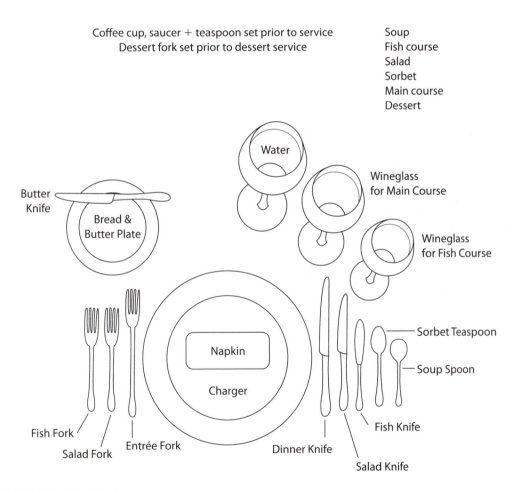

Exhibit 8.3 Place Setting

the coffee cup and saucer are not preset, which is standard for a meal of this caliber. In circumstances where speed is important, or for breakfasts and lunches, the coffee cup and saucer may be preset. Again, the saucer should be one inch from the edge of the table, and the cup handle should be angled at 4:00. Because this place setting is very full, the dessert fork and coffee teaspoon can be placed prior to the coffee and dessert service.

In addition to the items depicted in Exhibit 8.3, tables will also require salt and pepper shakers, sugar bowls, and creamers. The salt and pepper shakers are preset but are removed when the main course is cleared. The sugar and cream containers should be placed prior to the coffee service.

Standards vary from caterer to caterer, but a general rule for numbers of these "ancillary items" per table is:

Tables of 6	Two sets
Tables of 8	Three sets
Tables of 10/12	Three sets

In many parts of the country, placing a folded napkin in a glass is considered unsanitary and it is simply not in vogue to do this, even to save space on a crowded tabletop. Off-premise caterers should also remember that if the first course is to be preset, the napkin cannot go in the center of the charger. In this instance, it must go above the plate, or perhaps in a simple, flat fold underneath the forks.

When setting tables with small candles, supervisors must check that the candles are placed so as not to ignite a centerpiece or napkin. At one event, a quick-thinking, observant waiter discovered that a centerpiece was on fire and simply doused the fire with the water from a water glass, which averted what could have been a major disaster. When removing candles with hot wax after the event, servers must be instructed to wait until the wax is hard to avoid dripping wax on the linens or on themselves.

Exhibit 8.4 depicts a sample setup for a service table to be used by the service staff for storing items required during the meal. Service tables may be used in conjunction with served dinners, as well as with buffets and food station parties. One table is required for approximately every 100 guests. Most items are kept on top of the table. It used to be okay to store some items underneath to save space, such as racks of wrapped cups and saucers. However, this is now considered unprofessional and might well be unsanitary too. Extras of these items must be stored in the staging area and brought out as needed.

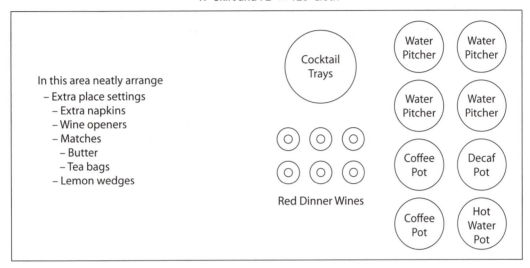

6' × 30'—Banquet Table
17' Skirt and 72" × 120' Cloth

In this area neatly arrange
– Extra place settings
  – Extra napkins
  – Wine openers
  – Matches
  – Butter
  – Tea bags
  – Lemon wedges

Cocktail Trays

Water Pitcher   Water Pitcher

Water Pitcher   Water Pitcher

Coffee Pot   Decaf Pot

Coffee Pot   Hot Water Pot

Red Dinner Wines

Exhibit 8.4 Service Table

Serving Procedures

Serving Butlered Hors D'Oeuvres

Frequently, prior to served meals, off-premise caterers serve hors d'oeuvres that are passed *butler-style*. Although this is a relatively simple procedure to learn, there are a few rules that servers must follow to make this part of the event most enjoyable for the guests:

- Do not hesitate to step into a group of people to offer them hors d'oeuvres. You need not stand back and wait for them to acknowledge you—they're most likely waiting for you!

- Know the name of the item and any accompanying sauce, along with the ingredients and method of preparation (fried, oven-baked, grilled, etc.). Be prepared to describe it, preferably with a bit of sales savvy.

- Warn guests if foods are very hot or spicy.

- Always smile and show courtesy toward the guests.

- Carry a supply of cocktail napkins in your free hand.

- Always return to the kitchen with dirty dishes and glassware.

- Keep the passing trays looking neat. It is smart to designate one server with an empty tray to keep an eye on the others, removing and disposing of any soiled cocktail napkins, bones, or picks they might have left on a food tray.

- When passing hot food during times that are not busy, return to the kitchen after five to ten minutes for a fresh tray as the food cools off quickly.

- Once a tray of hors d'oeuvres is depleted to the point that it does not look appetizing, return to the kitchen for a fresh one.

- Always pass to different guests during each "trip" around the room by going different routes.

Water, Bread, and Butter Service

The last 15 to 20 minutes before guests are served can be quite hectic. To minimize chaos, we recommend filling water glasses 30 minutes before the meal with ice, right to the brim. There will be some melting, but plenty of ice will be left and the glasses can quickly be topped off with chilled water just before guests are seated. Water glasses should be kept filled throughout the meal. Chilled bottled water is often not served until after the guests are seated since it is not served with ice to keep it chilled.

In this calorie-conscious age, there is not always a bread course. Sometimes, savory shortbreads are served with a salad course as an interesting alternative, or artisan breads are served with olive oil and balsamic vinegar for dipping. No matter what the choice, uniformity is key to making the table look attractive. Place all the individual dipping dishes in the same spot at each place setting, for example.

When bread is to be served, the traditional service style is that both bread and butter are placed on the individual bread and butter (B&B) plates—envision the plate as a clock face and position the bread and butter as uniformly as possible—prior to guests being seated. Warm rolls or bread can be placed in baskets on the table just after the guests are seated and can be preset in baskets or on the B&B plates if not served hot. However, the classiest way to serve bread is to have the server come around to each guest and offer it. For smaller events, a warm roll may be placed on the plate after the guests are seated. In the view of some caterers, serving rolls or bread individually also minimizes waste, as unused contents of breadbaskets must be thrown away after the event. Servers should make sure to replenish breads, rolls, and butter throughout the meal.

Seating Guests and Starting Service

Servers may assist the guests with seating, seeing that people are comfortable, placing the napkins across their laps, and serving a last-minute drink from the bar. Next, the bread should be served. If the first course was not preset, then the first course should be served. Some items (such as chilled soups) work well preset, but hot appetizers and mixed salads (like Caesars) must be served after guests are seated.

As a general rule, each course should take about 15 to 20 minutes to serve, consume, and clear. Most guests at parties prefer to dine at a moderate rate—that is, not rushed, but not made to wait 15 to 30 minutes between courses. Most meals can be served within 60 to 90 minutes, no matter how many guests attend.

As servers start serving a table, it is essential that the runners have supplied a sufficient number of orders to service all the guests at that table. Never should servers begin a table, serve only a few guests, and then have to wait for more meals. Be sure that everyone at a table is completely served before starting to serve the next table.

One method for serving large banquets is to divide the room into sections and assign a team of runners and servers who service only that section. For an eight-seat table, two runners each carry a tray of four plates. They deliver them to the section, place them on tray stands, and head back to the dish-up area for more. In the meantime, the servers serve the guests, moving the tray stands as needed and placing the empty trays on the stands. The runners pick them up, deliver a new set of full trays, return the empty ones to the dish-up area to be refilled, and so on. When all entrées have been served, servers and runners can turn their attention to table service duties, such as refilling beverages and clearing soiled dishes.

The key to excellent banquet service is the timing of the service of each course. Guests in the same area of the room should receive their food at approximately the same time. Aside from scheduling sufficient service staff, there must be sufficient kitchen staff, with an organized system for dishing up each course in the off-premise kitchen. Some cold courses may be preplated, which eliminates the pressure of dishing up to order. Hot food that is preplated and held in warmers is simply not as fresh or as good as hot food plated and served within a matter of minutes.

Off-premise caterers have developed their own systems for hot food dish-up, and some are better than others. Exhibit 8.5 is a proven dish-up system that, when properly staffed, will plate 200 hot meals in 15 minutes or less. Please note that this is a double-sided line, with plates being prepared on each side. This system involves the use of hot plates, hot food, and efficient dish-up staff. For it to work best, follow these guidelines:

- Food is kept warm in hot food cabinets. One staff member is assigned to pull pans of food from the warmer as needed. (*Chafing dishes* or *chafers*—pans with a heat source below them—are sometimes used, but cabinets work better.) Another can replenish hot plates if needed.

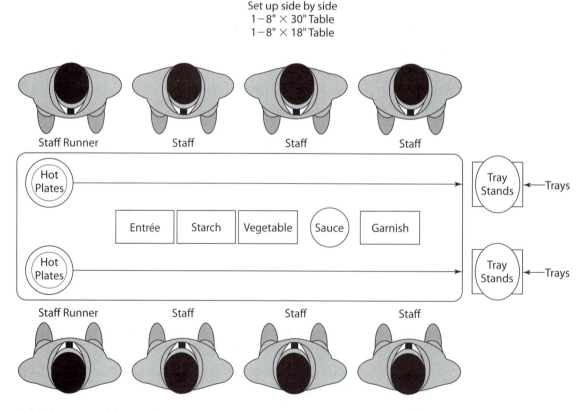

Exhibit 8.5 Double-Sided Hot Food Dish-Up Line

- The staff dishes food onto each plate and slides it down the line to the next person.
- The last people in line sauce and garnish the plate, wiping the plate rim if necessary to ensure consistency of presentation.
- As plates are finished, they are arranged on trays at the end of the line, for waitstaff to take and serve. Runners bring the empty trays back to be restocked.

Another method is to serve the hot food from linen-covered buffets set up around the perimeter of the area where the guests are seated. For this type of setup, the kitchen staff must be impeccably attired as they are in view of the guests. They stand behind the buffet lines and portion food onto plates carried by the servers. Each server carries one plate in each hand with a napkin and walks through the line just as a guest would (but at a much quicker pace). Then when the plate is complete, the server walks toward the supervisor, who directs the server to the table that is to receive the meal. The servers continue to return to the line and walk through it again, until everyone is served.

When hot food is plated, all plates should look the same. A sample plate should be prepared and shown as an example of how all plated dishes are to look.

Meal Service

Your servers are responsible for serving food and beverages to guests. Many off-premise caterers have found that each member of the service staff can be designated as either a *server* or a *runner*. The runners bring the food from the kitchen, assist in serving the guests if necessary, and return to the kitchen with soiled dishes. The servers stay with the guests at all times, serving and clearing. The ratio of servers to runners depends on the menu, the distance to the kitchen, and other unique factors. A ratio of one-to-one is a good place to start, and you may adjust this depending on the event and the skill of your staff members. The total number of people on the service staff will vary according to the level of service to be offered—anywhere from one staff member per 5 guests to one per 20 guests is standard.

There are a number of standard service procedures that never seem to go out of style, no matter the geographic area in which you work. For instance:

- Serve food from the left, with your left hand, while moving forward in a counter-clockwise direction around the table.
- Always serve the female guests at each table before serving male guests.

- Clear from the right, using your right hand, except for such items as B&B plates, side dishes, and unused silver that are on a guest's left. These should be cleared from the left, using your other hand.

- Serve beverages from the right with your right hand, moving clockwise around the table. (Some caterers consider soup a beverage.)

- Never reach across in front of guests, and if two guests are leaning toward each other talking, clear and serve from their outsides.

- Servers should not make unnecessary noise and should be as inconspicuous as possible.

- Service staff should never touch flatware that is on plates, nor put their fingers inside glasses when clearing a table.

- Water glasses should be replenished throughout the meal.

- Table numbers and unused place settings should be removed when all the guests are seated.

- Tables, chairs, buffets, and bars should not be broken down and removed until the guests have left the event.

The rules that relate to the actual serving of the food and clearing of the plates can be practiced in your weekly staff meetings, designating some employees as "customers" and others as servers. Your service personnel should learn to make every move count, to avoid wasting motions by anticipating their next moves. In short, a good server remains vigilant, plans ahead, rarely stops, and is always accomplishing something.

During the staff meeting prior to a meal service event, the supervisor must instruct the service staff if there is an order in which certain tables must be served. (For instance, if there's a table of guests who will be speaking at an event, they are typically served first so they can complete their meals and get ready to give their speeches.) An acceptable way to do this is to divide the seating area into sections of five to ten tables, with a lead server in charge of each area. The lead server will not only serve, but also ensure that the tables within the section are served in the correct sequence. The lead server knows that each table must be completely served before starting at the next table. For smaller events, the supervisor can direct the order of service. Of course, the head table is always served first, and then the other tables are served in designated sequence.

Other Service Styles

Military Service. This is a highly rehearsed, dramatic form of service that requires a great deal of precision—and one server for every two guests at the table. Each server carries two plates. When the captain nods, all servers take one step (counterclockwise) and, in unison, places one plate in front of one guest. Another nod and all servers step back, then take another step and serve the next guest, in unison. It is very impressive when it's done right, but appropriate only for the most formal occasions.

English Service. In the United States, we refer to this as *family-style service*, although there is a specific, traditional method for English service that keeps it from being a free-for-all. It involves the table host, as well as the server. The host dishes up each course—or sometimes, the plate contains an entrée, and the host fills the remainder of the plate with the side dishes—and hands each full plate to the server, who then places it in front of each guest.

French Service. The hallmark of French-style service is the use of a *rolling cart* (called a *gueridon*). It's about the same height as the table and contains cooked food that is being kept warm on a small warming stove (called a *réchaud*). Several different foods are offered, so the guests can select what they want. The server finishes and plates the dish at tableside, resulting in an elegant presentation and a bit of showmanship.

Guests may love the personal touch of having their food prepared in front of them, but it doesn't work well for every type of food. For large groups, French service is also impractical because it is slow. Even for small groups, it requires sufficient room for the rolling carts, which can be large. There are hot food and cold food carts, and some caterers like offering one course—perhaps the salad or dessert course—this way.

Russian Service. This service style is much like the French style, except that the food is prepared and cut into portion sizes in the kitchen, and typically placed on large silver platters. The full, beautifully arranged platter of food is shown to the guests, then placed onto individual plates by the waitstaff, using serving utensils. Russian service is a way to impress guests and ensures uniform portioning, although it is rarely used at off-premise events because it is labor-intensive and requires a highly skilled waitstaff, as well as expensive additional equipment and utensils.

Clearing the Tables

When everyone at a table is finished with a course, the dishes and flatware for that course must be removed, including flatware for that course that guests did not happen to use. If one or two people at a table have not finished a course and they are lagging behind the others, it is permissible to ask them if the course may be set to the side so that the next course may be served. However, remember that guests often arrive late. If their utensils have already been cleared, it's just more work to reset. For this reason, it is best not to remove unused place settings until after the entrée has been served.

Generally, clearing the table starts with a female guest's plate and continues clockwise around the table. And, of course, it always begins with the server asking, "Pardon me, may I take your plate?" Clearing should be done from the right, with the right hand. A plate should be kept below eye level until it is clear of the guest and in the aisle space. Then it may be transferred to the left hand.

Glassware is also cleared from the right side, with the right hand. Stemware should be held by the stem or bottom of the glass. Glasses, plates, and flatware should be carried to the dirty dish area on large waiter trays or in bus boxes. Bus boxes (or bins) should always be kept out of sight until they are needed. Bus boxes are an excellent choice when there are long distances to walk, when it is very windy, or when the service staff is unable to carry heavy trays. Broken glass should never be placed in a bus box and should be deposited into the trash. Glasses, china, and flatware should be placed in separate bus boxes to minimize breakage and loss.

Let's face it, used dishes are unsightly—but there are a couple of easy methods to minimize their unsightliness in the presence of guests. If trays are used, set flatware in one direction on the tray. As discreetly as possible, dump leftover food onto one plate and cover it with a napkin. Stack the rest of the plates and put the covered leftover plate on top of the stack for return to the kitchen.

At the end of a meal (particularly a dinner), set stemware in the center of the tray as you clear. Flatware, dessert plates, and coffee service items can be stacked around them on the tray.

When clearing the main course, clear the B&B plate and knife, as well as the salt and pepper shakers. Good service also dictates that the tables should be cleared of crumbs, preferably with the use of a small metal rod, known as a *table crumber*; a server should run a crumber gently and discreetly over the table linens while catching the crumbs on a small, clean plate.

Carrying fully loaded waiter trays can be dangerous. Million-dollar lawsuits have resulted from accidents involving dropped trays. Before lifting a tray, the staff member should make sure that it is properly loaded and balanced and that there are no items that may tip over. Before a tray is loaded with dishes and glasses, it should be clean; it should have either a nonskid surface or a damp napkin on its surface to keep items from sliding. Heavier items should be loaded in the center of the tray, and lighter items toward the exterior. Plate covers should be properly nested together. Servers should carry only trays that they can comfortably handle—there's no point in "showing off" how much you can carry.

When you carry a tray, you're looking out not only for the guests' safety, but for your own. Trays should always be lifted with a squat. One hand should go under the tray, and the other should support the tray as you stand up using your thigh muscles. The tray should be carried above your shoulder and steadied with your free hand if necessary. If you have to go through a door, carry the tray with the hand that is farthest from the door hinges, to ease entry and exit. It isn't always possible, but try to carry trays around, rather than through, crowds. The tray should be lowered, using the squatting technique, onto a service table, kitchen table, or tray stand, which should be opened up with the free hand before lowering the tray. When unloading trays, you should unload from the center out, or from opposite sides, so that the tray does not become unbalanced and tip over.

Tray stands should never be placed in the center of the room, other than just prior to serving or clearing. When not in use, they should be kept around the perimeter of the room away from guests' sight lines, if not out of sight altogether.

Beverage Service

When serving cocktails and other drinks from the bar, servers should always carry the cocktail tray in the left hand, and serve beverages from the right with the right hand.

When pouring wines at the table, the glass should be filled one-third to one-half full, depending on the glass size. The wineglass should never be lifted from the table when it is being filled. Normally, a four- to five-ounce portion is sufficient. There are an increasing number of nondrinkers, so servers should consider their needs as well and offer nonalcoholic beverage choices. When guests decline wine, their wineglass(es) should be removed from the place setting, indicating to the other servers not to offer wine.

Wines may be served at the tables by the foodservice staff or some of the bar staffers who are not busy during dinner. Specific assignments should be made as to who is responsible for wine service at each table.

Before coffee is served, there's a little extra work to do, and someone must also be appointed for this. Servers (or, often, their runners) must place creamers and sugar on each table, as well as the coffee cup, saucer, and spoon if they were not preset. The cups and saucers should be placed to the right of the place setting, with the edge of the saucer one inch from the table's edge and the handle of the coffee cup angled to about 4:00. The cup should be seated in the center of the saucer. For some events, cognac, cordials, and after-dinner drinks are also served at this time, in addition to dessert.

A growing number of people are enjoying hot tea at the end of a meal. One way to make them feel really special—rather than make them wait until everyone else has been served coffee—is to offer tea first. The server at each table might ask, "Ladies and gentlemen, we are about to begin our coffee service; but first, who would prefer hot tea?" Then a tea box is presented, offering several tea choices. Hot water, in individual pots, soon follows.

Many guests prefer to have their coffee or tea with their dessert and cordials, and caterers should try to coordinate these activities, so that guests receive desserts and beverages at about the same time. This can be accomplished by assigning different duties to different servers. For example, at a party for 50 guests with six servers, two can pour coffee for everyone, two can serve cordials, and two can be runners and serve dessert. Of course, all servers should start at the same table and serve tables in the same order.

Coffee should be poured from the right, with the right hand. Servers should not remove the cup and saucer from the table when pouring coffee. They should use a clean napkin, held in the left hand next to the left of the coffee cup, to ensure that coffee does not splash on the guests while they are pouring. Extreme caution should always be used when handling and serving hot beverages.

Decaffeinated coffee must always be made in the industry-standard pot that clearly differentiates it from regular coffee. When serving, a nice little trick we learned at the Inn at Little Washington in Washington, Virginia, is to place regular coffee in cups on patterned saucers, and decaf in cups on plain saucers. That way, the server isn't always having to interrupt guests to ask, "Regular or decaf?" And please make servers aware that people who ask for decaffeinated coffee actually deserve to get it. When you're busy, it is certainly easier to pour whatever's handy, but many people have a specific health-related reason for wanting decaf. Don't serve them regular coffee just because it is convenient for you.

As coffee is served, servers should replenish cream and sugar as needed.

Buffets and Food Stations

The service for buffets and food stations differs from served meals in that guests generally serve themselves. There are some exceptions to this—perhaps a preset first course, followed by guests going to buffets, or dessert and coffee being served at the table. Place settings may or may not be provided for buffets and, in most instances, food station menus are designed so that the foods can be eaten on small plates and require only forks instead of full table settings. There may not be seating for everyone, and guests may eat standing up. When there are no place settings or seats, the flatware and napkins must be provided on the buffets or food stations.

Setting up buffets and food stations can require additional time because of the time-consuming process of designing and decorating the food display. If there is a theme for the event, there may be specific items to be included in the displays. If these items are provided by clients or decorators, off-premise caterers must be certain that they are delivered on time for the setup. Ice carvings are the exception, although the container for the carving may be preset.

As we have mentioned in other chapters, creating a diagram to ensure correct placement of your buffets and stations is a critical step in achieving a smooth setup, so that staff may work without continually having to ask questions of the event captain. The diagram of the buffet or station should include:

- The name and location of each component or area
- The number and size of the tables, cloths, and skirts needed for each area
- A list of all equipment, china, flatware, and serving utensils needed at each area

When you pack at the commissary, these items may be grouped together in containers, with removable labels on the containers. Food items may be grouped the same way, by station. Before you start the setup, everything necessary, as shown on the diagram of the buffet or food station, should be placed next to the location for the buffet or food station. This makes the setup process much faster.

On-site, your staff should be instructed about how much overall "creativity" is allowed in designing the displays. Some clients prefer a clean, simple look, while others appreciate a profusion of colors and textures.

No matter how elaborate the décor, there are a few generic procedures regarding food stations and buffets:

For Planning

- The number of food stations and buffets may vary, but approximately one buffet or type of food station should be provided for every 50 to 75 guests.

- In general, each main dish will require 18 to 24 inches of space on the buffet table or food station.

- The backs of buffets and food stations should be covered with table linens if guests will see them.

- Bring extra bowls, display props, utensils, dishes, platters, cassette au feu stoves and fuel, chafing dishes, and chafer fuel. These items will be essential if items are broken in transit, misplaced, or out of order.

- Determine replenishing methods for foods, and provide the necessary containers and utensils.

- Check to be certain that all equipment works properly. Remove and label any equipment that is in need of repair, so that it is not used (at this event or any other) before being repaired.

For Setup

- Cassette au feu stoves and heating appliances should be tested to make sure they work properly as they are placed, long before the guests arrive. Extra fuel should be stored beneath the station.

- Staff members who use cassette au feu stoves for tabletop cooking should be thoroughly instructed on their proper use and how to replace fuel safely and properly.

- The water pans beneath the chafing dishes should be filled with hot water as soon as they are put in place. Chafer fuel tops should be loosened but not removed, and the fuel should be installed under the water-filled pans. Most chafers have fuel holders; for those that do not, fuel should never be placed directly on the table. A small plate should be used. Servers must be able to easily and quickly locate matches and extra fuel for the chafers if needed.

- Chafer fuel should be lit 30 to 45 minutes before the chafing dish full of hot food is brought out.

- Fire extinguishers should be placed near buffets and food stations with open flames.

- Plates for the guests' use should never be stacked more than nine inches high. Taller stacks detract from the appearance of the table.

- Votive candles should never be placed next to napkins or any other flammable item.

- Candelabras should be positioned so that hot wax will not drip onto food, napkins, or serviceware.

- Food in chafing dishes must be kept hot, and this means it must be very hot before it is placed in the chafer. Chafers are not designed to warm food but to keep it hot. Ways to keep food hot include:

  1. Place solid food items only one layer deep in the pans.

  2. Cook fried foods only as needed.

  3. Keep lids on the chafers until the guests arrive, unless they contain fried foods, which will become soggy if covered.

  4. Avoid setting chafers in drafts or in the wind.

  5. Use custom-made plastic shields that stand up around the perimeter of the chafers to protect the fuel from drafts.

For Serving

- Instruct the staff about proper portion sizes, particularly for high-cost items.

- Servers should know what they are serving, as well as the ingredients of each item in case a guest wishes to know.

- Carvers should be instructed as to the number of orders they should be able to cut from each piece of meat.

- Any kitchen staff member who is cooking foods to order must be trained about ingredients and procedures.

For Replenishing Fuel and Food

- Staff should be instructed about how long "canned heat" fuel burns and trained in how to replace it safely. Extreme caution is required here. When fuel is replaced, it should be recapped with its own lid or extinguished with the top of the chafer fuel holder. Used cans of fuel should never be touched barehanded because they can be very hot and the flames are often tiny or invisible. Staff should be instructed to use tongs that will grasp the can tightly, and then place the can on a small china plate. Once this is accomplished, a new can of fuel can be properly placed beneath the chafer and lit.

- Chafing dishes full of food and water are very hot and heavy. When you remove a pan of food from the chafer, extreme caution must be used to keep hands, arms, and faces away from the rising steam.

- Specific staff members must be assigned to bring food from the kitchen to the food stations and buffets. Bowls, hot food pans, or platters should not be removed from buffets or food stations until their fresh replacements are ready to be set down; there's nothing more unsightly than a gaping "hole" on a buffet table where a full dish should be. In some cases, food may simply be added to the existing container. Once a container of food is half-depleted, it should be replenished.

For Breakdown

- Staff members should never break down food stations and buffets until specifically directed by the event captain. This is a sensitive area, and staff should not be permitted to make this decision. When most guests have eaten, some duplicate food stations may be discreetly disassembled, with foods consolidated at those that remain open. Where there is only one food station or buffet, it is always best to leave it open until it is evident that everyone has eaten; even then, check with the client before beginning disassembly. Dessert and coffee stations are normally kept open until the very end of the event.

- After extinguishing all chafer fuel, the food pans should be removed from the chafers and carried to the off-premise kitchen, along with other foods from the buffet. Extreme caution must be used when carrying chafing dishes containing hot water, so as not to splash hot water on anyone. To be safe, many caterers simply cover the dishes on the buffet line and leave the water in them until guests have left.

- The kitchen should be ready to receive the buffet items. Advise the kitchen supervisor in advance so space can be arranged for receiving chafers, bowls, baskets, and the like. Be aware when laying out your kitchen that this requires a lot of landing space.

- Linens should never be removed from buffet tables or food stations until absolutely all the guests have departed.

Handling Complaints

When events are executed properly, complaints should be few. In those rare situations when complaints arise, there are some basic ways to handle them:

1. Allow the complainer to blow off steam. In other words, let the person say what is on his or her mind. Never interrupt unless the person needs to clarify a certain point or perhaps provide more details.

2. An excellent way to diffuse a guest's anger is to ask politely, "Have I done something personally to anger you?" This tactic, in most cases, will calm the person down because most complaints are not of a personal nature, but rather about some specific aspect of the food or service.

3. If you are not the supervisor, tactfully get the event captain involved as soon as possible.

4. Try to identify the problem, and let the person know you understand the problem by repeating what you heard him or her say.

5. Offer a brief apology, let the person know the alternative solutions and resolutions, and tell the person what you intend to do.

6. Follow up if necessary, and always remember to be polite and courteous at all times, regardless of how you really feel.

7. No matter how minor the situation, jot a note about it when you have a moment. If your company has an Incident Report form (which it should), fill it out as soon as you get a chance. The event captain should also note the incident on the Event Captain's Report. Even if there is no particular legal liability, the incident may be a learning experience for others on the staff.

Summary

Properly supervised and executed, off-premise catered events are guaranteed to create positive word of mouth, which will generate future business. The Show is your time to shine! Nothing in the catering business is more important. There are no second chances to get it right.

Every event has an on-site manager or supervisor, commonly known as an event captain. This person's responsibilities are formidable as the company's reputation is on the line. This chapter outlines and explains those duties, which often are performed by the catering company owner if events are especially large, complex, or formal. After an event, the captain is also responsible for summarizing the event on a report that can be used to pinpoint problems, as well as to note outstanding individuals and work well done.

The most common rules for setting up dining rooms and buffet tables are covered in detail, with brief mentions of other forms of service. Serving procedures are discussed, with rules for butler-passing, serving and clearing seated meals, organizing and replenishing buffets, and the basics of beverage service. The chapter ends with tips for handling customer complaints at an off-premise event.

Study Questions

1. Should an event captain pitch in wherever and whenever busy servers or kitchen staffers need help or should the captain maintain a strictly supervisory role? Explain your thoughts.

2. Why does it matter that the creases on table linens all face the same direction for a catered meal?

3. Which courses is it permissible to preset on dinner tables before guests arrive? Explain your answer.

4. Describe the proper way to carry a waiter's tray, whether it is full or empty.

5. What are the keys to a successful dish-up process for catered food?

Marketing

One of the biggest challenges you will face as an off-premise caterer is obvious: You probably will not be the only caterer in your area. Marketing is the process of creating a strategy to convince prospective customers to choose *your* company and *your* services over the others—and it includes following through, with plans that fit the strategy.

Here's a critical distinction: Marketing is not selling. It's a lot more. It is creating name awareness for you or your company, through advertising, having a positive presence in your community, developing high standards, communicating these to prospective customers, and charging fair prices for the food and service you provide. Together, all these steps work to build an image for your name or brand—which builds trust that, in turn, builds customer loyalty.

Marketing can seem rather mysterious until you break it down to its essence. Marketing means using various tools or methods to:

- Attract prospective clients
- Qualify those prospective clients, separating the casual inquiries from those that can lead to business
- Sell your services to the qualified clients

In this chapter, you will learn how to, literally, "cater to the customer." In addition to the three points just mentioned, this includes learning about the following:

- Corporate versus social catering
- Marketing tools that will make up your plan
- How to design a marketing plan
- How to create a marketing budget

The end results of these efforts should be satisfied clients and satisfying profits, which, of course, are easier said than done. Customers are becoming more demanding and selective when shopping for catering services, and it takes more to be a successful caterer than being able to cook and serve excellent food. The simple reality is that clients can't buy from you if they don't know you exist.

Competition for off-premise business is increasing as more and more caterers enter the field. Supermarket delis, national foodservice management chains, hotels, restaurants, private clubs, and others look to off-premise catering as a way to increase their own sales.

Smart caterers must find ways to increase sales through better marketing, starting with making sure the market knows you're around, and then showing prospective clients how your company differs from competitors, and how clients can do better by doing business with you.

Catering Markets

There are two major off-premise catering markets: corporate and social. Let's look more closely at each of them.

Corporate Catering. These are business events, such as grand openings; holiday parties; groundbreakings; retirement parties; employee parties; receptions to promote business, give awards, and unveil new products; and so on. This category also includes catering business meals for meetings and seminars.

Corporate catering is generally more profitable than social catering, although caterers of high-dollar society weddings may disagree. However, for the most part, corporate event planners generally have predetermined budgets larger than those of social event planners, with leeway for add-ons. They tend to be more experienced in planning these events and usually know exactly what they need. Many of them also have limited time and prefer to work with off-premise caterers on whom they can rely to handle all the details—and are willing to pay premium prices for this level of service.

Social Catering. This category includes personal parties at homes, fund-raisers, wedding receptions and anniversaries, reunions, bar and bat mitzvahs, baptisms, graduations, proms, birthday parties, and holiday or other theme parties. And while you'll often work with professional social event planners, social catering often includes dealing one-on-one with clients or charitable committees whose budgets are smaller than those of corporate clients, who have no leeway for add-ons, whose knowledge of event planning varies greatly, and who frequently want to be "hands on" in every aspect of the event.

A key difference between corporate and social catering is the guests themselves. For the most part, corporate events have a more uniform crowd that tends to act in a more, well, corporate fashion. They tend to be more or less professional and restrained, especially when it comes to going overboard with food or adult beverages. Social catering, on the other hand, often includes the additional challenge of serving a wider variety of guests, who are there not for career reasons but for the sole purpose of eating, drinking, and partying as much as possible.

Corporate catering is more businesslike, too, in the sense that corporate clients want caterers whose service, food, presentation, and personnel reflect their corporate culture and professionalism. More specifically, some of the qualities corporate event planners seek include:

- People on the other end of the phone line, not voicemail
- Detailed proposals, often on short notice
- Sensitivity and attention to their specific needs
- Food tastings or sample presentations to confirm that you can in fact provide what your proposal offers
- Assurances that you can handle details, details, details
- The flexibility to go with the flow of an event and provide "extras" at little or no charge to ensure its success
- References

Finally, the stakes are higher when catering corporate events. Not only do they tend to be bigger moneymakers—making it more important to cultivate each account—but their planners also tend to be highly networked and talk to each other regularly. This means if you do a great job, you'll get referrals that will increase your business. The flip side, of course, is that if you don't do a good job, everybody in the corporate event planning community will hear about that, too.

Social catering, on the other hand, is by definition less professional and more—well, "social." Most of your customers will be individuals who are not in the events business per se, so word of your performance, good or bad, will not travel as far as it might with a corporate or charitable event that attracts a large crowd and media attention. And even though the professional planners do network with each other, they are often also in direct competition with each other, so they're less willing to share information than their corporate counterparts.

Beyond these significant differences, however, corporate and social catering clients have much in common, starting with their mutual interest in high-quality service, food, and presentation that stays within their budget. Let's look at each of these elements in detail.

Service. This is the heart of successful catering—yes, even more so than great food— because, at its heart, the definition of cater is to *serve, provide, and/or attend to the needs* of those to whom you cater. If you treat your clients and their guests like royalty, they will fondly remember their experience—and your company, even if your food and drink offerings were just average. Conversely, you can have the greatest food ever, but if you and your staff are rude, rigid, or otherwise provide poor service, your clients will remember their unpleasant interactions with your company far longer than their taste buds will remember your otherworldly filet mignon and tortes. They'll remember this too: There are always legitimate reasons why the food or presentation might suffer at an event, but there's never any excuse for your company to not provide first-rate service with a first-class smile.

Food. If first-rate service is the heart of successful catering, then great food is the life-blood that keeps it all going, and the closer your food matches your first-rate service, the better your clients and guests are going to like your company. Great food doesn't just mean preparing it properly and serving it at the right temperature; it also means varied menus that can accommodate a variety of personal tastes and diets, and gastronomic diversity within those menus, to surprise and delight even the most experienced of partygoers.

Presentation. Getting the service and food right gets you a long way toward the referrals and repeat business every caterer seeks, but if you don't have a good presentation for your service and food, an event can still fall apart on you. The essence of a high-quality presentation can be summed up in one word, repeated for emphasis: details, details, details. Presentation is about showing up on time in clean, shiny vehicles manned by enough immaculately dressed staffers with enough event-appropriate containers and other equipment, and enough food and drink contained therein to last for the duration of the event, all arranged at the venue to look good and work so smoothly that neither your client nor their guests give you a second thought. Sounds simple enough, but if you don't attend to the details, details, details that make the above description possible—it won't be. We get into those details more in other chapters, but for now suffice it to say that the better you handle the small presentation details, the better the big picture will look.

The other key element common to both corporate and social catering is the budget, which basically determines the general outline of what you'll provide for a given client. And while corporate catering budgets are usually larger and more flexible than their social catering counterparts, there's plenty of overlap. For example, a small company's Christmas party may cost a fraction of a large private wedding, so for each market it's a good idea to rough out a plan for budget, midscale, and upscale offerings.

Budget Events. A budget event for a corporation could entail dropping off luncheon platters, and one for a social client may be a child's birthday party. Budget parties are low-priced and, thus, usually focus more on delivering food than providing service.

Midscale Events. Midscale events are more expensive than budget events mostly because they usually involve more service. A midscale event may be a retirement dinner for a middle manager or a modest wedding reception held at a community center.

Upscale Events. Upscale events are the most expensive, involve the most intensive service, and are typically the most profitable. An upscale corporate event might be a grand opening for a fine jewelry store. For a social client, it could be a bar mitzvah with seven food courses, three bands, the finest crystal and linens, and one server for every five guests.

Marketing Strategy

Off-premise caterers frequently overlook the need for a marketing strategy. They simply respond to clients' demands and, as long as there are enough customers to generate a satisfactory profit, everything's fine. But running a business without a marketing strategy is like sailing a ship from port without a destination; you'll end up cruising around with no particular place to go and no reason to get there.

That may work for awhile, of course, but off-premise caterers who achieve long-term success do so by developing a marketing strategy, which starts with clearly defined financial goals. They determine their financial needs and aspirations, and then create a strategy to reach those goals. There's also a practical short-term reason for long-term planning: If you need financing, any reputable financial institution will expect you to have a detailed business plan based on your marketing strategy.

For example, some start-up off-premise caterers want to earn an annual profit of $100,000 per year after five years in business. This is a lofty goal, but it is also realistic if you use an incremental strategy to reach it. For example, you could plan for your first-year profits to be $20,000; your second-year profits, $40,000; third-year profits, $60,000, and so on. (We discuss budgeting in Chapter 14.) The point is that these caterers realize that if they earn 20 percent profit on their sales, they can make projections like these:

Year	Projected Sales	Projected Profit	Percent Profit
1	$100,000	$ 20,000	20
2	$200,000	$ 40,000	20
3	$300,000	$ 60,000	20
4	$400,000	$ 80,000	20
5	$500,000	$100,000	20

Most caterers learn by trial and error which marketing tools produce the best results. As they gain experience, they hone their marketing strategies to be more effective, and they always think in terms of the bottom line when evaluating their plans. If one form of marketing does not bring the desired results, they discard it and look for better alternatives.

One way to reduce your trial-and-error learning curve is by designing your marketing strategy before you start spending your marketing dollars. There are many strategies to use and many ways to approach your market, so the general marketing strategy that follows is just an example that can guide you as you figure out how best to show prospective clients how your company differs from your competitors and what specific benefits you can provide your clients.

Start by listing the benefits you will offer, no matter how obvious you think they might be to a customer. For instance:

- We are always professional and easy to work with.
- You will receive the best in service from our caring, courteous, and friendly staff, which is empowered to meet all your catering needs.
- Our events are turnkey and hassle-free.
- Our "no surprises" contract means you'll know exactly what you're spending and why.
- At our events, there are never long lines and there is always plenty of food.
- We provide a money-back guarantee that you will be satisfied with our services.
- We can help you with other areas of your event, such as music, flowers, photography, rental equipment, and valet service.
- You can be a guest at your own party!

An underlying theme of marketing is to intelligently use time and money to bring the greatest return on your marketing investment. For example, if personal contact with potential clients is one of your marketing tools, remember that five visits to a major corporation to get a contract for a large catered event will bring in more revenue than five visits to a social client planning one house party for 30 guests. Both are important, but one is a lot more profitable.

Market Research

The first step for the beginning caterer is to conduct a market survey to see what's out there, in terms of competitors and potential customers. This includes determining a variety of things: the size and population of the target market, the demographics and income levels of the area, the potential demand for the services, and the numbers and types of competitors. This type of information can be gleaned from:

- County population, density, and distribution figures
- Maps of major trading areas
- Articles on area businesses in local newspapers and magazines

- Online searches
- Local chambers of commerce
- The state's Department of Commerce

Local colleges, universities, or business schools may have a marketing department with students willing to assist you in compiling data. Just as important as demographics are the *psychographics*, which are the habits and preferences of your target customers. This kind of information may be harder to obtain, but with it, you can more accurately decide what types of food and services to provide, as well as how much money to charge for them.

As you glean this information, be on the lookout for the signs of positive growth in an area. Are stores and restaurants opening regularly—and thriving? Is the Chamber of Commerce an active, progressive organization? Who's moving into the area, and why? Are there good schools, good public transportation systems, and good public services?

Another key task is to evaluate the competition for catering dollars. This can be done by talking to rental dealers, surveying local companies who use caterers, attending catered events and asking questions, and even posing as a potential customer to analyze your competition's advertisements, menus, contracts, and sales pitches. If you're planning your own party, why not hire a competing catering company and see what it does? Armed with this knowledge, successful off-premise caterers can position themselves in the market to fit a potentially profitable niche that others have failed to see or take advantage of.

It's important that the market you choose to enter fits well with your image as a caterer. A new catering company whose specialty is fabulous barbecue could market to both social and corporate clients for budget or midscale events, but it might not be successful in marketing itself as an upscale caterer to the same clientele. In short, you can't be everything to everyone. A catering company's image reflects its reputation, style, and personality, and these are the elements that, together, can be used to create a vision for the company. Knowing who you are, and whom you wish to reach, will greatly assist you in creating your marketing strategy.

Marketing Tools

There are a variety of marketing tools you can use to start, maintain, and expand your business and the first of these is your marketing budget.

You might not think of a budget as a "tool," but think again—how much you are able to spend determines what you can (and cannot) afford to do. Some off-premise caterers spend very little on marketing, while others earmark as much as 5 percent of their gross sales. Before you decide, ask yourself a few basic questions:

- Is there available cash to spend on advertising?
- How quickly do we want business?
- Are we ready to handle the business?
- How much business can we handle?
- If it is a discount we plan to offer, how much can we afford if the response is big?

After you've answered these questions, you can set aside the appropriate portion of your overall budget for marketing.

Now it's time to examine the various types of advertising, publicity, promotions, and actions that off-premise caterers might use as part of their marketing strategy. We'll make sense of the many tools you have to choose from and discuss how to decide which ones will work best for you, whether your company is well established or just starting out.

Company Name and Logo

In the days when telephone books were king, many business owners believed that, if at all possible, it was best to begin your catering firm's name with the letter *A* to be listed first in telephone directories, as well as on lists of approved caterers at various off-premise catering sites, such as historical places, museums, and other facilities. "A Michael Smith Culinary Production," for instance, was far superior to "Mike's Catering."

With the rise of the Internet and the subsequent decline in marketing importance of telephone books, having an *A* (or *AA* or *AAAA*) at the front of your name is not so important, but no matter what letter or name you start with, be sure to choose your business name carefully because this is what becomes the "brand name" of the firm. In our example, clients will expect a higher level of catering from "A Michael Smith Culinary Production" than from "Mike's Catering." And, of course, with the classier name, Michael can achieve higher price points for his products and services, particularly if he is located in a metropolitan area. In a small rural area, the fancier name may be detrimental to business as folks might assume the prices are too high for them.

You'd do well to narrow a list down to three or four names and consult an advertising or design professional for advice on the final choice. The name should be convertible into a simple but eye-catching logo that isn't too complicated or expensive to reproduce on signs, vehicles, uniforms, cocktail napkins, and so on. You should also do some research to make sure the name isn't the same as—or too similar to—that of some other type of business, to avoid potential legal challenges. And in Chapter 2, you learned about the need to register the business name with the state.

Website

Business owners today must have a company website because, in today's marketplace, if you're not on the Web, you don't exist. A website lets potential clients know that you're there, and it's convenient for both you and prospective customers. You can use it to give people many more details about your catering services than you ever could in a networking setting or a brochure, and customers can access your website whenever they want, stay as long as they like, and e-mail any questions they have back to you.

The primary costs of Internet marketing include:

- Designing the website (writing copy, physically programming the site, putting photos and other graphics on it, and so on). This may seem expensive at first, depending on how fancy and interactive you want the site to be. You will also want to maintain a relationship with your site designer, so the site can be updated regularly, which costs less than the original design and content.

- Registering a domain name (the "_____.com" that people type in to access your site) that hasn't already been taken by someone else.

- Placing your website on search engines (Google, Yahoo!, AOL, and others), so that people who are looking for catering services can find it even if they don't know the company or domain name.

- Buying "links" on other websites (your city's chamber of commerce, Web-based business directories, etc.), so that people who are searching on those sites will find you.

The advantage of a website over social media is simple: You have control of the information on it. Most company websites are "static," rather than "dynamic"—that is, people won't be getting onto your site to have online discussions or debates. If they leave a negative comment, it is not automatically "out there" for all to see publicly and/or make additional comments.

That said, you certainly should give clients a reason to visit your site and leave their e-mail addresses. Prompt clients to leave this contact information by offering something free that will be e-mailed back to them. It may be recipes, interesting articles, or handy hints, such as "Ten Secrets for a Successful Party, Wedding, or Event."

If people don't know about you, how will they find your website? They will use key words to search for "Idaho caterers," or "Boston caterers," or "weddings Detroit." There are online marketing specialists who excel at getting top search engine placement for their clients. It's also important to see that your catering firm is listed under "catering" and other key words, as well as the name of your city and state.

A website should be a reflection of the unique personality of your company, and the content should be updated regularly to keep the site fresh and interesting. This also helps keep it at the top of search engine lists because there is technology that can detect when a site is "static" for certain time periods, which can affect its ranking in a search. If you won't be able to do this regular updating on your own, you will need to budget for a freelance writer or marketing company to do it.

Also be sure that your website is linked to as many other websites as possible. The more links, the closer your site is placed at the top of search engine lists.

Remember to include the basics on your site: your company's physical address, phone and fax numbers, and e-mail address. We've noticed a number of catering websites that do not include an e-mail address and/or force the visitor to complete a lengthy form to contact them by e-mail.

One big "content" question for your website is: Should you list prices for your services? Some caterers do and some don't—and there are good arguments for and against both ways. We like the middle course: giving price ranges for your offerings, while at the same time making it clear that these price ranges are guidelines that are flexible and can be adapted to meet the specific needs of a given client. That way, your potential customers know generally how much your services will cost, and then they can decide whether that fits within their budget or not.

Your website should also include news about the company, menus, recipes, and trends, along with professional photos of food, staff, weddings, and events. Many companies include this information as a blog, a running compilation—whether it's a series of articles or written diary-style—of interesting trends, facts, and impressions. If you're going to blog, plan to do so at least every other week, even if you have to hire someone to keep up with it or split the duties among staff members. The idea is to show customers that, as a business, you're always thinking, always observing, and always involved in something fun and exciting.

The website should be constructed so that it can be easily updated and expanded (at least seasonally) and very easy to navigate. Keep in mind that the attention span of a potential client is very short. If a site does not capture a person's attention in a few seconds, he or she will move on to a competitor's site.

Social Media

Social media is the twenty-first-century version of word-of-mouth advertising, and it can exponentially expand your market reach if you learn about it and make effective use of it. Nearly two-thirds of American adults who use the Internet use social networks, according to the Pew Internet and American Life Project. In its 2011 survey, women ages 18 to 29 reported the highest usage (69 percent on a typical day), but even baby boomers are catching on—32 percent said that they use a social networking site daily, up from 20 percent a year earlier. By the time you read this, the numbers will probably have grown.

New social media sites crop up frequently, but as of this writing, here are some of the major options that a small business can use to connect with potential customers:

- On Facebook (www.facebook.com), a business can create a page and post content that viewers can say they "like," and comment on; you can then respond to those comments. You might answer questions, offer recipes or advice, or post special deals that people can only get if they view your Facebook page.

- On Google Plus (www.plus.google.com), a feature called "circles" enables you to send messages to specific groups.

- LinkedIn (www.linkedin.com) is a business-to-business networking site. You create a profile as an individual—in this case, as the owner of an off-premise catering company. Then you list your previous places of employment and schooling—some people post their résumés, as it is often used for job hunting—and LinkedIn suggests other people with those places in their profiles and suggests that you "link up" with them. You can link to people whom they know, too, to expand your network further. On your profile, you can list your company website, Twitter address, and more, so that anyone "linked" with you can see them. You can also state what you're "looking for," so to speak—referrals, new business, and so on.

- Twitter (www.twitter.com) is a microblogging site, for messages (called *tweets*) of up to 140 characters. It's a place to send people to an interesting article (by "tweeting" a link) or announce a discount or special offer. And when you receive a tweet worth passing along, you can "retweet" it to others in your network.

- Tumblr (www.tumblr.com) is also a microblogging site, but it includes music, photos, and video in addition to text and links. The company says that its typical user creates 14 original posts per month and reblogs three posts from other sources.

- On YouTube (www.youtube.com), you can post videos for all to see. The video might be a speech or cooking demonstration that you'd like to share with the world, or a video about your company's capabilities.

As you can see, there are plenty of ways for information from these sites to feed off each other, so to speak. Post a video on YouTube, and then "tweet" to customers that it's there for them to take a look at. Ask them to share their comments about it on your Facebook page . . . and so on.

If there is a problem with social media, it's that it can take a great deal of time to keep up with it—time that you'd probably rather be spending catering events.

Dave Green, whose company Readywebgo builds websites and assists companies with online planning and marketing, says that it is important to determine what you are trying to achieve before you launch into social media. Here's what he suggests for the relative novice, in catering or any small business:

- *Start by dabbling.* Set yourself up with a personal Facebook page and LinkedIn and Twitter profiles. Follow people, "like" groups, and just observe. Take careful note of who is interesting and who is annoying. Spend some time accessing online resources to learn more about these methods and their uses.

- *Continue by planning.* How can you measure success if you have not mapped out where you are trying to go? Social media is an inherently distractive arena. Without a plan, you may become disillusioned, lose track of your purpose, waste time, or even worse, damage your reputation.

- *Be a storyteller.* All of your communications should unite to tell one, coherent story about who you are and what you do. Your communications should create a consistent and compelling vision of what you do and how it is different from what others are doing.

Green suggests using your primary online presence—for most companies, this is their website—as the focal point and anchor for online activities, including social media. In short, what happens in the social media world should work to interest people in your website enough to check it out and learn more about your company.

 Social Media Tips

Website. Use this medium to allow users to quickly control their own journey through information that you present to them, through well-thought-out content and navigation. Clarity, usability, and transparency are keys to a website's value, always.

Facebook. Use this medium as your first chance to move from "broadcast" mentality (you give information but people can't react) to interaction with the public. Ask questions, start discussions, and remember that the stakes are relatively low. Do not post more than one item each day. Also, don't forget that Facebook is all about people; don't be faceless. Think of ways to let the personality of people in your organization shine through.

Twitter. Compare Twitter with real life—if you walked into a room and yelled out how great you are and then left, most people would think you're an idiot. They might be right. If you remember that Twitter is a social network, you will be on the right track to success. Recommend, respond, "retweet," share interesting content. And be personal—building networks around a fictional persona is not sustainable.

(From SoMe Start Up Notes, 2011, used with permission of Dave Green and Readywebgo, Boise, Idaho.)

Positive Word of Mouth

Compared to all the social media forms, word of mouth sounds downright old-fashioned. However, it is the simplest and best form of marketing, and many caterers have "marketing plans" based pretty much on nothing more than the positive comments of satisfied clients and guests. They realize that one successful party leads to another, and another. They also realize that they're only as good as their last event; therefore, they dedicate all of their energies to making each catering assignment the best it can be.

The problem for start-up firms is that it's tough to generate this positive word of mouth without a track record. It's kind of like job hunting as a teenager with no work experience. One way to surmount this hurdle is by catering charity parties or events at cost, or even at a loss, to generate goodwill and grow your business reputation. Another strategy is to deliver baked goods regularly to good clients during slower times of year— say, Halloween treats or shamrock-shaped cookies for St. Patrick's Day—with a note of appreciation for their business and perhaps a new menu for the coming season. If you hear that a big local company has won an award, send those cookies!

When you receive positive comments or letters after an event, always remember that they can be used as testimonials to generate more business. Ask those who send letters if you can quote them on your website or in a brochure. Testimonials are a proven way to market to new clients. Potential customers love to read or hear what others have said about a caterer. You can use testimonials in many ways: in brochures, on websites, or in direct mail pieces and newsletters. One South Florida catering firm includes verbal testimonials from actual customers in its "on-hold" telephone message!

Just remember to always get written permission to use the remarks from the persons who made them, and keep these written permissions on file. (Lest you think we're being too cautious, we've seen instances in which people wanted to be paid for using what had been their genuine compliments, freely given.) Along with these forms, it is also good idea to keep hard copies of the nice letters you've received in a notebook or file. In a busy office, items like that tend to scatter and can't always be found when you need them.

Another facet of word-of-mouth advertising is asking your existing customers to refer you to their friends and business colleagues. This is a powerful way to expand your customer base. It's not a good idea to ask them for a referral list since that's putting the workload on them. Instead, just ask, "Do you know of anyone who could use our catering services? Would you mind if I use your name as a reference when I speak to them?" This is a terrific way to obtain good prospects.

Networking

Networking is meeting and talking with people. It could be other local business owners, a woman in the supermarket produce section, or a person you meet at church or strike up a conversation with on a flight home.

The idea is that, sooner or later, any of these people may need catering services or know someone who does. The more folks who know you and what you do for a living, the greater the chance that one or more of them will call you when they have catering needs. However, it's not enough to just meet these people; you need to stay in touch with them.

A popular way to hone your networking skills with potential buyers of off-premise catering is to join and be active in such groups as:

- Chambers of commerce
- Civic clubs (Rotary, Kiwanis, Eagles, Lions, Elks, etc.)
- Church or synagogue groups
- Special-interest groups (like "Leads Clubs" for salespeople of all types)
- National Association of Catering Executives (NACE)
- Meeting Planners International
- The International Special Events Society
- Convention and visitors' bureaus
- The Society of Incentive Travel Executives
- Memberships at local museums or other arts groups

A main advantage of networking is that it focuses on establishing relationships with people first. You're not going directly to these people and asking them, after the initial handshake, to buy your catering services. Instead, you get to know them and keep in touch with them casually.

When they are ready to buy, they will contact those they know. Good networking concentrates on building long-term relationships, with long-term benefits. Doing business with people you know is one of the best ways to do business.

Don't discount your supplier relationships as sources of good networking opportunities. The farmer who supplies your locally grown produce or the artisan dairy where you get those delicious local cheeses might appreciate having a caterer use their fresh ingredients to make the samples to be served at their farmers' market booth—a partnership that benefits both of you.

Publicity

Publicity is free media exposure, which directly and indirectly produces revenue. In most cases, publicity is an editorial recommendation, an unbiased opinion that says an off-premise caterer is good. Publicity can help establish off-premise caterers as leaders in their field.

The basic way to generate publicity is to write and submit a *news release* (also called a *press release*) to your local newspaper, radio, and/or television stations. If you hire a person or company to do this, the task of getting publicity is known as *public relations*.

According to David F. Ramacitti, author of *Do-It-Yourself Publicity* (New York: American Management Association, 1994), "Virtually any small business could legitimately send out a minimum of six press releases per year, and many could easily double that number . . . In today's increasingly competitive marketplace, you should be taking advantage of every opportunity available to receive positive public exposure, especially if it doesn't cost anything."

Some events that are worthy of news releases for off-premise caterers are:

- Your company's grand opening or anniversary
- An exciting party or unusual challenge (The underwater wedding? The skydiver wedding? Catering for a unique themed event? Teaching grade-school kids about nutrition?)
- An expansion or renovation
- A hiring (new chef, etc.) or staff change within the company
- The appointment of a person in your company as an officer in an affiliated group (NACE, etc.)
- Catering for a celebrity or charitable cause
- Winning an award for business or culinary skills

The thing about news releases is that they truly are a crapshoot: A reporter may or may not call. Your recent award, or the hiring of an excellent new chef, may merit a single paragraph in the business section of the newspaper, a front-page feature article in the local food section, or both—or nothing at all. However, this should not deter you from writing and sending news releases.

Great Performances, a New York City–based catering firm, has received coverage from *People* magazine and numerous other publications, but to get this type of publicity, it needed a unique story to tell. Great Performances' story was that it conducted training to teach its staff, composed mainly of actors, actresses, writers, and musicians, service techniques for serving the Passover seder dinner. This caught the eye of local and national press and contributed to the rapid rise of Great Performances as one of the nation's top catering firms.

Caterers need to develop what reporters call a *hook*, something that will attract the media's attention. This is the difficult part. Simply catering an event for charity may not be enough, but making the world's largest pizza or paella may create the hook you need to generate interest. Helping improve the cafeteria food at your local elementary school, and teaching the kids how to properly set a table, would be a terrific feature story, as would catering for an exclusive group aboard a privately chartered jet that entertains corporate clients who fly from Los Angeles to Paris and back.

You can also become known as an approachable "source" that local (or national) reporters can call on for information. Maxine Turner of Cuisine Unlimited is a perfect example of this. Newspaper and magazine reporters contact her regularly for her thoughts on food trends, budget-minded parties, cooking with kids, food safety, and even running a small business. She hosted a cooking show for years on a local television station (in Salt Lake City, Utah) and still makes guest appearances and does cooking segments on talk shows.

A final thought on publicity: "Free media exposure" really isn't free because there are costs involved in producing the news release, following up, and taking the time to show up for a guest appearance. Caterers should also consider investing some marketing dollars to hire a public relations firm to help them identify publicity opportunities. Virtually every famous chef in the country does this, as do many restaurants. Caterers on a limited budget could consider going to a local university and finding students in a marketing curriculum to help.

Printed Media

There are many forms of printed media, including brochures, newsletters, letterheads, and business cards. Most forms of printed media have declined in marketing importance as websites and e-mail become ubiquitous, but they all still have a place in your marketing toolbox. Here's a look at some of them.

Brochures. Many off-premise caterers rely heavily on brochures. A caterer in Canada identified the major businesses in his area that employed more than 200, called each firm and obtained the names of the catering decision makers, and then produced a sales brochure that he mailed to 900 companies. This generated more than $100,000 in sales.

Successful brochures must not look like typical pieces of "junk mail." A first-class brochure should include colorful, high-quality photos and interesting text. When it comes to the format of the brochure, there are a couple of options:

- The *trifold*, which is produced on standard 8½- by 11-inch paper and can be folded in thirds and easily sealed for mailing.
- The *press kit–style pocket folder*, which can be "stuffed" with different types of information, depending on the recipient. It includes a slot for a business card and/or Rolodex card and pockets in which to place news releases, proposals, menus, price lists, and so on. These cost more to mail than trifolds, of course, because they are full-sized (8½ by 11 inches).

Here are some tips for brochure contents:

- Establish credibility by telling readers about your number of years in business, prominent clients, awards, memberships, and other significant facts.
- Brag a little! Tell readers how they will benefit from doing business with your firm.
- Guarantee your work. Inform readers that you will not overlook any detail and that their events will be perfect.
- Deliver your message in as few words as possible, and make sure that the writing is descriptive, but not overblown or verbose. Brochures should be easy to read and interesting, but not too cluttered.
- Brochures and other pieces of direct mail should be addressed to a specific person.

Personalized, handwritten envelopes are opened more frequently than those with computerized labels addressed to "Occupant" or "President." Interestingly, items with unusual or colorful postage stamps also attract more attention than those stamped by a postage meter.

Newsletters. Sending newsletters has proven to be one of the best ways for caterers to establish, maintain, and reinforce awareness of their services; gain new clients; and generate repeat business.

Newsletters can be sent via regular mail or e-mail, the latter being more economical. In fact, it's smart to offer both and give clients a choice. Publishing a newsletter is a major task and should not be taken lightly. Larger caterers may wish to outsource this project to a professional writer; a local freelance "foodie" can handle most of the legwork (and brainwork) for a reasonable price, as long as you provide the ideas and tone for each issue. Smaller caterers with limited budgets may need to produce newsletters internally to keep costs low.

Either way, the first step in producing a newsletter is to determine its tone and content. The best newsletters for caterers are warm and friendly, presented as a way to get to know the caterer and his or her services. Often, the newsletters contain several regular columns by the same author (the owner, the chef, or a wine expert) or a feature on a local food grower or producer whose wares the caterer uses and recommends.

Of course, anything newsworthy that's coming up for the company should be mentioned, whether it's a guest appearance on a local TV station by the owner, or a charitable or unusual event you're catering. At the start of a particular season or holiday, feature a roundup of seasonal recipes. Include information about food and menu trends, interesting new ways to use catering services, tidbits about celebrities who've hired you, food trivia, and humor. Do a short profile of a different member of your kitchen or serving staff in each issue. Quote some of your customers who just loved what you did for them. You might include a coupon or promotion in the newsletter, which will also help you track its usefulness as you see how many people respond to it. And always include contact information (e-mail, phone, physical address, website address), as well as a small form new readers can send to you to sign up for the mailing list or to update their address information.

Letterhead and Business Cards. Letterhead and business cards are still necessities for all off-premise caterers, and in today's computerized world, this includes both "e-stationery" and printed materials. They should reflect the caterer's image and should make good use of the logo you've designed. A caterer who markets budget events does not need to go to great expense; no multicolored or gold-lettered business cards are necessary. A simpler approach will be less costly and just as effective.

Some experts recommend against using unusually shaped business cards or those that fold over as they are not easily stored in standard business card cases; however some businesses use "gimmicky" cards with great success. All catering staffers should be given cards to hand out, not only to people they encounter while working, but also to people they meet outside work. At catered events, cards should be given out only if requested by guests.

Men should carry business cards in their shirt or jacket pockets for quick retrieval; women in a purse or briefcase, as long as the cards can be easily located. It is awkward waiting as a person rifles through a wallet or handbag. For men and women, there are some good carrying cases available, and some caterers give a nice case and a supply of cards to each of their staff members.

Remember that "letterhead" includes more than just stationery for correspondence. Use your logo on contracts, proposals, and any other type of printed or e-mailed form you have created for regular use, whether it is the clients or the vendors who see it.

And what do you put on that letterhead stationery? One excellent selling tool, although admittedly time-consuming, is a personal note written to a potential client or a handwritten thank-you to clients after a party, wedding, or event. Handwritten notes show a personal touch, and those that are signed by a number of key catering staff members are even more effective. The best ones are written as if the writer is talking, not writing. They evoke gratitude and surprise from the reader because so few people take the time to handwrite things, and the writer's thoughtfulness will be remembered when catering services are needed again.

Photos, Awards, and Plaques. Photos, awards, and plaques are excellent marketing tools for establishing credibility with clients. They show the client some of the caterer's past successes. Many off-premise firms display these items in the lobbies leading to their offices, or in their offices or tasting rooms. Nicely made copies of photos and awards can be put into albums that customers can look through, posted on your website or social media, or reproduced in your newsletters, brochures, and direct mail pieces.

We believe one real asset for an off-premise caterer is a good relationship with a professional photographer. It is worth hiring these pros specifically to take photos of important events that you can use on your website, in brochures, in newsletters, and so on. By hiring them, you have greater access to the images.

If a photo comes from a source outside your company, be sure to get written permission if you plan to use it online or in printed materials circulated outside your office. This protects you legally and, even if the photographer doesn't care, it's a nice gesture that shows respect and appreciation for the value of the work.

It is important to get copies made while the award or photo is new, clean, and unwrinkled (this also goes for letters of praise or recommendation). Keep the copies filed in a safe place. One corollary of Murphy's Law is that when you really, really want to show an item to someone, you can't seem to find it anywhere.

E-mail or Direct Mail?

When you have a new menu, newsletter, or special offer, how you send the message can be just as important as the message itself. In today's world, you have two choices: electronically (by e-mail) or by direct mail, mailed "directly" to prospective clients. Which should it be?

For those on a budget, e-mail is the least expensive way to send information, cutting out the U.S. Postal Service and heading straight to the in-boxes of your customers.

However, in a 2007 survey by International Communications Research (ICR), 73 percent of consumers said that they prefer direct mail for receiving new product announcements or offers from companies they do business with. Only 10 percent said that they prefer to receive such offers by e-mail. More than 53 percent said that they delete unsolicited e-mail messages about new products, while only 31 percent said that they discard unopened mail, including brochures, catalogs, and other advertising materials.

There are a couple of interesting reasons why direct mail "won out" over e-mail. Respondents said that direct mail is "less intrusive"—that is, it doesn't interrupt other activities—and more convenient because it can be set aside and considered when there is time to do so.

These results may be colored by the fact that Pitney Bowes, a company that offers direct mail services to its clients, commissioned the survey. But the conclusions make sense: People often receive mountains of e-mail in a day, and it becomes all too easy to press the Delete key without ever opening items you know are ads.

Direct mail experts say there are four components to a successful direct mailing. We'd go so far as to say that all four apply to e-mailed advertisements, as well.

- *The mailing list.* Your own customer list, compiled by you, is always more effective than renting a list—at least half of your future business comes from current customers. However, any mailing list is only as good as its upkeep. If a list is not regularly checked and updated, only half the names and addresses will be valid within three years, including postal zip code changes.

- *The offer being made in the mailing.* What do people or companies get for doing what you're asking them to do—a discount on their next catered event? An ice sculpture, a visit from Santa Claus, or half off their floral order if they book their Christmas party by a certain date? Make it fun, practical, and tempting. Don't just tell people what you will do—tell them how it will help them.

- *The creative aspects of the mailing.* How does it look? Does it prompt the receiver to open it right away, and why? For e-mail, of course, you're limited by what the reader can see at "first glance" in the subject line, so the subject line had better be both compelling and truthful.

- *The "call to action."* What exactly is it that you want the reader to do? Sign up for a drawing? Return a postage-paid card? Download and print out a menu? Visit your website by a certain date?

Two key differences in your message will help determine whether e-mail or direct mail is right for that particular message:

- *The complexity of the offer.* By e-mail, make it short and simple—just one topic, one quick note, and a deadline prompting the reader to "take advantage of" the offer right away. Longer pieces that contain more photos and/or detailed information—a ten-page holiday planner or wedding planner, for instance—deserve to be printed and mailed.

- *The timing of the offer.* How quickly do you have to get this message or offer out to customers? It takes a week to ten days to deliver a piece of third-class mail—although statistically, sending it first class (with higher postage costs) does not guarantee any better results.

Most off-premise caterers use a mixture of e-mail and direct mail. The key is to remain top of mind with customers, without annoying them. There is plenty of online advice for both kinds of campaigns, so take advantage of it.

Telephone Directory Advertising

Despite the growing importance of the Internet as a means of marketing and a source for directory listings, many off-premise caterers still advertise in at least one local phone book, whether it's the venerable Yellow Pages or one of the many competing directories that have sprung up over the years.

Telephone directories remain an important marketing tool because, even in the twenty-first century, there are many people who do not own or have routine access to a computer. The only drawback is that, while line listings in directories may be free or low cost, the display ads necessary to generate interest and set your company apart from others can be expensive.

For example, a caterer who invests $20,000 in an annual phone directory ad, and whose profit margin on catered events is 40 percent, needs to generate $50,000 in additional sales just to break even on the ad costs. (See Chapter 14 for accounting details.)

In many metropolitan markets, upscale caterers with established clienteles either skip this type of advertising altogether or take a low-key approach with a small ad, leaving the half-page and full-page ads to caterers who appeal to more budget-conscious clients who are more likely to shop around.

According to catering industry consultant Mike Roman, founder of Chicago's CaterSource (www.catersource.com), excellent directory ads should differ from the rest—and the can't-miss way to do that is by putting the owner's picture in the ad, along with text that might read: "I'm Joseph Dough, president of ABC Catering. Let me invite you to discuss your catering needs. I know my team of friendly professionals will be able to please you and your guests! And I promise you that our service is 100 percent satisfaction guaranteed." You may also want to use such words as "casual," "corporate," and "social"—and mention that "prices will be gladly discussed by phone."

A good way to become familiar with the telephone directory advertising space is to check out the advertising—not just for caterers, but for all kinds of businesses. The best ads are uncluttered but full of useful information, with strong headlines and complete descriptions of the products or services. They also include the business's addresses (physical, website, e-mail), phone numbers, and business hours.

Photographs and graphics are fine, but only if they reproduce clearly. Timing is also critical in placing an ad because missing a deadline can result in one full year with no exposure in that particular directory.

An advantage of phone directory ads is that, like websites, they are available anytime, day or night. They are there when the client is ready to buy.

Using Menus

As first discussed in Chapter 3, a complete listing of the foods you serve or menus for particular "sample events" are excellent sales tools that can be mailed and given to prospective clients. With today's emphasis on fresh, seasonal ingredients (and continual price fluctuations, if you're going to include prices), it probably makes more sense to produce these in-house on your own laser printer than to hire a printing company.

Further, we suggest publicizing your skills and signature dishes by producing colorful booklets or brochures that give people a reason to keep them—great ideas for summer picnics and parties, weddings, or holiday gatherings. Include planning tips, host checklists, menu suggestions, and décor ideas. These can be professionally printed and mailed, or designed electronically and e-mailed at customers' requests.

Whatever you share with the public, be sure it is easy to read, not too cluttered, and has all words correctly spelled. Your menu can (and should) also be used on your website.

Some descriptive copy about menu items is helpful to readers and helps to sell offbeat or ethnic items. In today's nutrition-oriented environment, everyone wants to know about ingredients and preparation techniques. If a dish is "heart healthy" or if foods can be adapted for certain groups (foods for those on low-calorie or diabetic diets and "fun foods" for kids), add a line about this or create your own "heart-healthy" symbol to highlight appropriate offerings.

Signage and Billboards

We've already discussed choosing a name and logo that can set the tone for your business, attract attention, and help create your image in the public eye. Now let's talk about what to do with them.

You'll need several types of signage, depending on your business. Be prepared to pay for signs and logos that are professional looking and large enough to be easily seen. This is not an area where you can cut corners; you're trying to impress clients. An advertising agency can help transform your logo into signage, as can a custom sign shop.

Signs can be used on your office or commissary site and on vehicles. You'll also want to have smaller, portable signs for use at food tastings, booths, fairs, and other events at which you may advertise your business. In Wisconsin, Miles Theurich of Theurich Catering has found that silk-screened signs purchased in quantity for present and future trucks are far more economical than hand-painting the vehicles. He also suggests magnetic signs for sales vehicles and vans because they do not destroy the value of the vehicles for resale or trade-in.

Billboards are not commonly used by caterers, primarily because they are usually too expensive compared to the business they generate. However, prime billboards located on major thoroughfares can bring off-premise caterers significant name recognition, and you may be able to barter a portion of the cost in exchange for catering services for a billboard company.

Paid Advertising

There are many places to advertise, ranging in price from inexpensive to astronomical. Let's look at the most common options.

Event Programs and Newsletters. These range from local opera or theater production programs handed out at performances to civic and church group newsletters. The audience is small, and, generally, so is the advertising price. Your decision to advertise here should be based on whether the printed piece actually gets into the hands of your target customers because, after all, they won't consult a theater program the next time they're looking for a caterer. For the most part, advertising in these venues is done more to build goodwill and name awareness than to actually get business. Some caterers advertise only in the programs of events for which they are actually catering, like charitable fund-raisers.

Magazines. Many city or regional magazines have relatively small circulations but high-end readers. In our experience, these are good advertising vehicles for caterers because, in addition to the ads, your involvement with the magazine staff often generates some form of editorial mention. You also build a relationship with the magazine, so you may be contacted for an occasional story idea or "expert" quote in feature articles about food or entertaining. Ads in these generally glossy magazines may be pricey, but they also look classy and thus help build your high-end business. Many magazines also offer "back-page" advertising, which looks more like classified ads. The back-page space is smaller and therefore priced more reasonably. We know caterers who take ads out in trade, in exchange for catering the magazine's staff parties or other events.

Newspapers. Caterers in small to medium-sized communities may find that newspaper advertising generates substantial revenue. No matter where you live or work, you may find newspaper ad rates rather shocking at first, so here's what you need to know.

Prices are charged by the column inch, with larger ads having lower per-inch rates. You'll want to specify which sections and days of the paper your ad should appear in, depending on the type of reader you're trying to reach. Sunday is the universally biggest readership day for any newspaper, so it will cost more to advertise on that day.

In larger markets, some papers have special advertising sections for smaller firms and special sections and editions. The rates for these sections are often discounted, and you should take advantage of them. Newspapers have sales staff members who can guide you through the process, and the paper can also create the ad for you if you don't have one *camera-ready*, as the papers call it. The main thing to remember, though, is that ad rates are almost always negotiable because ad spots are like hotel rooms; they're worth exactly nothing if the sell deadline passes without a sale.

Radio and Television. These mediums are available, but they are generally expensive and require that the advertisement(s) be written, narrated, produced, edited, and then placed on certain stations to attract your target clients at the "right" times of day when they might be listening. All this is even more complicated than it sounds, which is why larger catering companies usually outsource this work to advertising agencies.

The cost of running an ad depends on how often it airs and at what times of day. Some stations will produce an ad for you at no additional cost if you commit to buying a certain amount of airtime. One caveat, though: Try to avoid insisting on being the star of your own advertisements unless the professionals think it will work. We all know about local owner-pitchmen who do a great job selling their companies, but for every one who's good, there are 50 more who don't have the voice or, shall we say, "star quality," to do a good job. Our feeling is that this type of advertising is for large, well-financed catering companies. Smaller ones usually do better when they spend their limited marketing dollars elsewhere.

A final note here: Most advertising experts say consistency is the key to effective advertising. In other words, it's better to regularly place smaller ads in publications that produce results than randomly place larger ads in several publications and hope for a response.

Advertising Specialties

Advertising specialties are useful items that bear your company name, address, logo, website, phone number, and/or message or slogan. They include items such as key chains, calendars, pens, wine openers, and coasters. Your logo may be stitched or printed onto staff members' uniforms or nametags or printed on disposables like cocktail napkins, plastic cups, and (as discussed in Chapter 4) custom labels for bottled water. There are some 15,000 articles of merchandise classified as "specialties" and numerous catalogs full of them from companies willing to personalize them for you.

If these are going to be part of your marketing tool kit, they should be handy and of good quality. They can be handed out as little niceties with catering proposals, at tastings and other events, as a thank-you to customers with final invoices, or as a conversation starter with a prospective customer. They're not necessities, and their use will not make or break your marketing strategy, but if you can afford them, advertising specialties are small courtesies that can be used in a variety of ways.

Food Tastings

Whenever off-premise caterers gather to discuss common needs and problems, the topic of food tastings always generates discussion. Some caterers allow prospective clients to taste the foods they've chosen for their party menu, while others strictly refuse to do so, claiming their reputation speaks for itself. Some caterers report that they do food tastings only for major events or for clients who have requested an unusual item or recipe that the caterer hasn't previously prepared.

Still others offer tastings at a per-person charge, which is refunded as a credit on the final invoice if the client books an event as a result. We like this approach. In our experience, tastings are a cost of doing business because today's clients generally expect to be able to taste food in advance, based on what they read in bridal publications and on websites. One Miami-based caterer has built three tasting rooms into her facility.

It is true that private tastings are expensive and take time. The advantage is that when caterers actually sit down with prospective clients and spend time discussing the menu and the clients' needs, they significantly increase their chances of closing the deal.

When conducting food tastings, here are a few rules to follow:

- The chef should be present for the tasting to directly receive feedback from the clients.
- Tastings should be limited to no more than three "tasters." More people than that create a food happening, not a decision-making meeting.
- For the same reason, supply everyone at the table with a form so they can take notes. (Exhibit 9.1 is an example of such a form.)

EXHIBIT 9.1 Tasting Notes

Name of Event: _____

Date of Event: _____   Date of Tasting: _____

Number of Guests: _____

Chef at Tasting: _____

Salesperson at Tasting: _____

ITEM	Hot or Cold	Client Notes	Chef Notes
Hors d'oeuvres			
Sauces			
Salads			
Entrées			
Starches			
Desserts			
Beverages			
Dietary Restrictions			
Photos			
Miscellaneous			

Source: Courtesy of Cuisine Unlimited Catering and Special Events, Salt Lake City, Utah.

- The dishes should be presented exactly the way they will be served at the event. Take photos of each dish for the prospective client to use as a reference and so you will know (sometimes weeks later) exactly how it was garnished and presented and can reproduce it to the clients' expectations.

- Listen to the tasters. Some may have a great knowledge of foods and will offer valuable insights and feedback. Others may simply say that a particular dish "just needs something . . ." but can't tell you what. In these cases, quiz them or make suggestions to see if they're onto something—or not.

Another type of food tasting is designed to generate new business rather than to close a sale. You simply invite current and prospective clients to your commissary, once or twice a year, to sample a new seasonal menu, check out a new chef, and ask questions. John Berryhill of Berryhill & Company did this for years in a small space he rented in a trendy shopping area in Boise, Idaho. The walls were lined with nicely framed photos of his catered events, and his business license allowed him to sample wines as well as food with customers. Business was so brisk, and the location was so good, that Berryhill eventually decided to make the place into a small (ten-table) restaurant in addition to his booming catering business.

A third option is to partner your food-tasting site with another business trying to gain marketing exposure, such as an office building wishing to lease space or an automobile dealership—or make a commitment to offer tastes or tidbits (not entire meals) for two or three charitable food-related events per year. No matter where you host them, tastings should be part of almost every caterer's marketing because they are effective marketing tools when properly targeted and managed.

Barter

Barter is an excellent way to conserve cash flow and increase business. Caterers can barter catering for needed services, such as dry cleaning, printing, plumbing, and more. Have your signs made by a local sign company and, in exchange, cater the grand opening of its new location. All kinds of "trades" like this are possible. You can also barter for employee incentives, like movie tickets and clothing.

The best time for barter transactions is during slower catering periods, and it's usually better not to barter for the total bill, just for the projected gross margin. For example, if a party's "retail price" is $2,000, and the direct operating costs are $1,000, have your client pay the $1,000, and then provide you with products or services worth $1,000, at no cost to you.

There are numerous barter exchange groups across the nation. These can be found through the International Reciprocal Trade Association. One other point: Remember that barter sales are taxable income, so make sure that you keep your accounting straight—and avoid bartering with anyone who uses bartering as a sales or income tax dodge.

 Pick Up the Phone!

We're not talking about telemarketing here, but about telephone manners. Thousands of catering sales are lost every day because caterers (or poorly trained employees) have poor phone manners:

- They don't answer the phone promptly—or at all.
- They provide an inaudible or otherwise unprofessional recorded message.
- They answer the phone rudely or abruptly.
- They just say, "Hello," without identifying the company. (This can cause prospective clients to wonder if the caterer is working illegally from home.)
- They don't make follow-up calls.

Telephone manners are more critical to success in catering than in many other businesses because poor phone manners can lead prospective clients to ask themselves, "If this company can't even answer the phone politely, how are they going to treat my guests?"

Caterers who answer their phones politely and personally—or at least have a warm, pleasant, professional-sounding recorded message—are sure to increase their revenues, and one of the best ways to upgrade your telephone procedures is to make sure you forward your office phone to your cell phone if no one's in the office, or your staff is busy preparing for an event. That way, you can either answer personally or respond quickly to messages. Nothing pleases potential customers more than talking to a real person who is polite, helpful, and courteous—or gets back to them within a few minutes of their call.

Naturally, "telephone tag" is a by-product of modern telephone technique, so another key element is leaving good follow-up messages in case your return call goes to the prospective client's voice mail or answering machine.

Remember too that polite, professional follow-up calls after an event can not only lead to future sales and referrals, but also provide valuable feedback. Clients can't always give you accurate feedback at the event itself because they're busy or don't really know how it's going themselves. Call soon after the event, however, after they've had time to reflect and get feedback from their guests, and they may provide compliments or constructive criticism (or both). This is useful as a learning experience, or as an opening to pitch a discounted future event. And if they say something nice, be sure to ask if you can use them as a reference.

In short, pick up the phone and be nice! It's one of the most overlooked yet least expensive tools to market your catering business.

Catering for Charity

Caterers are besieged with calls to cater charitable events, either for free or at significantly reduced prices. The caller usually mentions that the cause itself is important, a lot of important guests will be at the event, and the caterer will generate significant future business from the exposure. Perhaps this is all true, but many caterers find that the more "nonprofit" catering they do, the more charitable requests they receive.

These types of events are important for exposure and for the goodwill gained by assisting in a good cause. However, the sheer number of requests necessitates a written charitable policy that can be put on your website. Such a policy should contain:

- Specifics about the types of organizations or causes you want to support, including a requirement that they must be actual charities, with 501-C3 tax-exempt certificates with the Internal Revenue Service. Some caterers select two or three groups every year and change each year; others select causes (education, the arts, and senior citizens, for instance) and stick with those. Ask your staff to help with the selection.

- A short list of the types of events you do not wish to support. ("We have chosen not to pledge money for walks, marathons, or telethons." "We have chosen not to support individuals seeking personal financial or medical assistance." "We do not supply gift certificates or baskets for silent auctions.") This will help cut down on requests.

- Exactly what you are willing to do "for free." Some caterers offer a substantial discount to charitable groups. Others charge regular prices but promise a donation and ask that they be listed and treated as any other sponsor of the event.

You are a business, not a religious order, so here are additional tips to help you handle charitable requests:

- Get the request in writing, on letterhead, to weed out scam artists, or offer a form on your website that the group can download, fill out, and return to you.
- Keep careful track of how much "charity" you provide each year and to whom.
- Create a buffer by appointing someone (a secretary, for example) who is familiar with your guidelines and limits and can handle and track the requests.
- Donate wisely by catering for charities associated with or recommended by your best customers.
- Put the onus on the charity to bring you paying business first.
- Avoid charitable events during busy times of the year.
- Consider your staff schedules too. If you have to bring workers in on a day they're scheduled to be off, you have to pay overtime, which increases your unreimbursed costs.
- Be sure that the food reflects your corporate image. Do it right, or don't do it!
- Contribute to events that draw major corporate executives.
- Contribute to groups to whom you wish to cater. For example, for a barbecue caterer, a blue-collar crowd is perfect.
- Make the most of on-site marketing when catering these events. Use your portable signs. Distribute brochures and other marketing materials at the event.
- Ask your suppliers for discounts and donations for these events because they will also benefit from any increased business. If a supplier consistently refuses to give you items at cost or to donate anything, look for a new supplier.

Another important step is to establish a budget each year for charitable events, and stick to it. Further, be pleasant when you must turn someone down (see "Pick Up the Phone!" on page 346). You can always say, "We've already used our charitable budget for this year, but please contact us earlier next year." Other good answers are variations on the following:

"We don't have the resources to accommodate your event."

"We've reached our nonprofit event quota for this month/season/year."

"Your organization is not on our list this year. (Here's how to be considered in the future . . .)"

"Our schedule is full for that time frame."

Other Marketing Tools

Before you do any type of marketing, ask yourself two questions:

- Will it effectively reach my target customers?
- Will it benefit my company, even if we won't make any money from it?

To conclude this section on marketing tools, here's a quick roundup of some effective ideas you might make use of that were not covered in detail:

- Make public appearances, speaking to groups about food-related topics.
- Create a PowerPoint presentation so you can make laptop or smartphone sales pitches.
- Write a food column for a local newspaper or magazine.
- Pitch yourself to be the regular "guest chef" on local radio or TV shows.
- Offer special promotions and discounts during slow periods.
- Offer a referral bonus—perhaps a discount to existing clients on their next event—for recommending a new client that ends up booking a party with you.
- Invite a well-known culinary author to your town; have an event at your commissary, or cater one at the local bookstore where the guest autographs copies of his or her book(s).
- Hire a freelance camera crew to help you produce a video that shows party styles and locations. (Often, local news people will "moonlight" these on their days off.)
- Use customer comment cards to generate feedback and mailing list information.
- Offer free seminars for those who plan special events, such as fund-raisers, employee picnics, and corporate client entertaining.

The Marketing Plan

Now that you have a working knowledge of your marketing tool kit, you can use it to create a marketing plan. You may be full of ideas—this plan is a way to get them organized and put them on a timeline. It should be based on your knowledge of:

- The local catering market
- Your competition
- Your budget for marketing-related expenses

There is no universally accepted marketing plan or formula, but any marketing plan must be based on a realistic budget and should not exceed that budget. For example, if start-up off-premise caterers plan to spend 5 percent of projected first-year annual sales of $100,000, that means there is $5,000—and only $5,000—to spend on first-year marketing efforts. Prioritize your needs and you might come up with this basic list:

- Name and logo
- Business cards and stationery
- One nicely printed brochure
- One food tasting (at your facility) for prospective clients
- A quarterly newsletter
- A small ad in one local phone directory
- Signs for your building and vehicles
- Do-it-yourself cold-calling of five new potential clients per week
- A direct mail piece to send to those who have been cold-called

The next step is to put each item on a calendar. Give it a deadline and put someone in charge of it if necessary, so it will get priority amid all your other start-up plans. Discuss the progress in your sales meetings.

Plans for forthcoming years will be based on the relative successes and failures of each of these marketing tools. Half of great marketing is making the plan and deciding what to spend, but the other half is keeping good track of how effective each item on the list is for you, once you actually do it.

Selling Catering Services

Some people in the catering business subscribe to what's known as the "80/20 Rule": 20 percent of your business comes from 80 percent of your clients, and 80 percent of your business comes from 20 percent of your clients. It makes a sound case for gearing the greater part of your marketing plan (and budget) toward capturing the more lucrative 20 percent.

One way to do this is by marketing not to prospective clients specifically, but to "intermediaries," such as:

- Independent meeting planners, who are hired by small and medium-sized companies and government agencies

- Special event producers, who specialize in events for large gatherings

- Independent party planners or wedding consultants, who work with noncorporate clients

- Ground transportation companies and/or destination management companies that handle arrangements for convention groups and/or hotel guests

- Travel agents and representatives of convention and visitors bureaus

These types of service providers generally represent major pieces of business and must be seen as prospective clients in the same way as your "end user" clients, and as an excellent source of referrals to the "20 percenter clients" you seek. By directing your marketing to these intermediaries, you can generate more revenue and build a different kind of customer loyalty. You can further enhance their value to you by offering a nice commission or fee when one of their referrals results in a paid job.

Up to this point, we have addressed those marketing efforts that will produce inquiries and buyers for off-premise catering services. We are now at the stage where we have some interested prospects ready to discuss catering and specific parties with a knowledgeable person. Enter the catering salesperson, who can put himself or herself into the buyer's shoes. A successful salesperson is one who is willing to serve before trying to collect and who always remembers that the client's message is, "Can you help me? Can you fix it? Am I important?"

Successful catering salespeople always:

- *Put the client first.* They know that if they satisfy the needs, wants, and desires of the prospective client, they will ultimately gain the client's business.

- *Take a sincere interest in clients.* They do their homework before meeting with clients, ensuring that they understand all there is to understand about a particular event. They know that when prospective clients interrupt, it means that the point under discussion is a key point in the decision-making process.

- *Stay in touch with clients.* They show appreciation for clients' support on a regular basis.

- *Keep things in perspective.* They remember that there will be good days and bad days, so they look at the long-term, not just day-to-day operations. They take their business seriously, but they also have fun and never take themselves too seriously.

To paraphrase Mike Roman, founder of CaterSource, a Chicago-based catering consulting firm, catering can be very difficult to sell because it is not tangible; it can't be taken from the shelf and examined. A catering contract is a piece of paper that contains a series of promises. In fact, many buyers of off-premise catering have never bought catering services before and don't require these types of services on a regular basis. The occasions are important enough, however, to enlist the caterer's expert assistance.

Smart salespeople are quite aware of these inherent disadvantages and know how to turn them into advantages by:

- Showing pictures or laptop presentations of previous events
- Guaranteeing their work will be executed to perfection
- Providing references and testimonials
- Providing explicit details in all catering proposals

Cold-Calling

Cold-calling means contacting someone without invitation or prior contact and asking that person if he or she has use for your services. It can be done in person, over the telephone, or even through e-mail, texting, or social media. New off-premise caterers and their salespeople should definitely cold-call prospective clients within their market area, if for no other reason than to use the great built-in opening line, "Hi, I'm Joseph Dough, owner of the new ABC Catering company a few blocks from you, and I wanted to introduce myself to the neighbors."

This is also the way you learn the names and titles of the people who plan the catered events at these businesses. If the person is not in when you call or drop by, you can leave information or mail or e-mail it later, and plan a follow-up contact on the spot.

On the other hand, established off-premise caterers who cold-call need to be aware of the practice's negative effects. Current or prospective clients may perceive it as annoying or indicative of business problems: "Why else would it be necessary for them to call door-to-door?" they may wonder. So approach cold-calling carefully, and with class.

Jeffrey Gitomer is president of BuyGitomer, Inc., a Charlotte, North Carolina, company that trains and motivates salespeople. Gitomer wrote in the *South Florida Business Journal* that one way to view cold-calling is not as a way to make a sale, but as a way to learn to sell. With this approach, rejection is just part of the learning process, not a personal failure—plus, to make the experience even more valuable, you will occasionally make a sale. Some of the objectives of cold-calling, according to Gitomer, include:

- Developing a fast opening that grabs attention
- Building instant rapport
- Gaining acceptance
- Finding and/or qualify the decision maker
- Developing powerful questions
- Gaining a prospect's interest
- Learning to persuade quickly
- Learning persistence
- Learning to "think on your feet"
- Learning creativity in your sales presentation
- Learning the "Joy of Rejection" (yes, that's what he calls it!)

"Add a dose of humor to rejection," Gitomer counsels. "For example: Thank people for telling you 'no.' Tell them they're helping you get one step closer to 'yes!' Tell the prospect that only one in four people buy. Ask them if they know anyone else who might not be interested because you still need two more 'no' responses before someone says 'yes.' It'll blow them away, and make them laugh. Make me laugh, and you can make me buy." (Learn more about Jeffrey Gitomer's sales style and advice on his website.

For caterers who prefer not to make their own sales calls, there are telemarketing firms that will do this. For a fee, they'll call businesses in any part of the country, find the person who makes the catering decisions, and set up an appointment for the caterer to make a personal contact or sales presentation. One such firm that we have used with success is Access Direct Marketing.

Truthfully, it is a rare individual who likes to make cold calls and can do so successfully. The most you can hope for is to learn some patience, refine your sales skills, and hope for that elusive "yes."

The Catering Salesperson

How do you find salespeople who will cold-call, keep in touch with clients, stay motivated and well organized—and more? In many off-premise firms, the owner or manager sells the majority of events and, frankly, many prospective clients prefer to deal with the person in charge. Off-premise caterers who do the selling themselves feel this increases their chances of closing the deal. They also know that the business they book will meet their standards and, of course, they need not worry about turnover in their sales staff if they do it themselves.

Before hiring a person specifically to sell catering services, determine if perhaps hiring someone to answer the phone will be a good enough start. Some owners and managers truly enjoy the selling process and, if that's true in your case, you should never give that task to others. However, if you don't feel that selling is your strength, then you may wish to hire someone part-time or appoint a family member in the business who is better at it than you are. Hiring someone for a full-time position is a major step that must not be taken lightly. During busy periods there is great need for help, but at slower times the need diminishes.

It's tough to hire and train an effective salesperson. Those who come highly trained demand commensurate salaries and may not be particularly loyal. Those with no experience require intensive training in food preparation and presentation, etiquette, local traditions, entertaining locations and trends, staff relations, client relations, organizational skills, food and beverage service, and numerous other details. The catering company owner or manager usually trains the salesperson personally as this job is too important to delegate. Training is, and should be, the main investment you make in a new person.

The brand new salesperson can't be expected to create new sales immediately but can start by responding to existing requests. An excellent beginning is to allow him or her to answer phones and obtain basic customer information and event details, such as time, date, location, number of expected guests, and projected budget. Next, make sure that the new salesperson sits in on meetings between off-premise caterers and clients, attends walk-throughs at event venues, and so on. He or she can then begin to arrange small, simple parties in accordance with the company procedures.

We have achieved moderate success by engaging the services of independent contract salespeople who work on a straight commission, with no "pay draws" or advances. It is, indeed, difficult to find folks like this, but it can be an excellent way to grow a catering business without an up-front financial commitment. A good way to start a program like this is to provide these types of salespeople with *warm leads*, defined as former clients with whom the caterer has not recently worked. The best candidates for commissioned sales positions should also have their own network of clients.

How much business should a catering salesperson sell, and how much should a catering salesperson be paid? This depends on the size of the catering firm and the prices the firm charges. Some catering salespeople sell in excess of $1 million per year; others, much less. In sales, employees are paid by various methods, each with its advantages and disadvantages:

- *Flat salary:* This is easy to administer but offers no incentive for the person to produce or increase sales.

- *Hourly rate:* There's little incentive to produce sales here, either, and there's a tendency for salespeople to "expand" their hours to receive overtime pay.

- *Partial commission:* A combination of base salary with a commission for some types of sales offers a level of income security for the salesperson, as well as some incentive to increase sales.

- *Strict commission:* There's little security for the salesperson, and this system is more complicated to administer, but it does create the ultimate incentive for the salesperson: "You don't sell, you don't eat—and if you do sell, you eat well."

There's no perfect or one-size-fits-all answer to the payment question; off-premise caterers must make such decisions based on their individual circumstances. Much will be determined by the payment practices of other caterers within the market and the sheer supply of (and demand for) talented salespeople in the area. Any pay plan must also comply with all federal and state laws, as described in Chapter 7.

Qualifying Prospective Clients

An effective marketing plan will produce numerous catering inquiries each day. Some callers are interested in planning a specific event, whereas others are shopping for general information. Experienced caterers can all attest to the countless hours that can be wasted if prospective clients aren't properly screened. Some caterers have spent half a day driving miles to meet with a client, only to learn that the event is unworkable for the caterer because of the size of the party, the budget, the date, or the location.

Astute off-premise caterers all have learned the secret of qualifying callers to determine if they are truly prospective clients. They know how to separate the "time wasters" from the potential revenue producers. There are four key qualifying points, and we'll discuss each of them.

Event Date. This will almost immediately determine an off-premise caterer's availability, as well as whether the caller is inquiring about a specific party or just shopping. The date also reveals the caller's sense of urgency. Is the party next week or next year? Acting quickly on a party for the following week will more than likely gain the contract. The date also may be on a holiday, when prices may be higher or the caterer has chosen not to work.

Number of Guests. The answer to "How many guests are you expecting?" reveals whether the event is too big or too small for your company—and if the caller has no idea, this tells you that the person either is not a serious shopper or is in the very early planning stages of the event.

Event Location and Type. This information helps establish the caller's budget. A cocktail party at an exclusive private villa will most likely require a bigger budget than a barbecue at a city park. If the party's at a private home, the address may reveal the caller's lifestyle and income level, which often (though not always!) gives you an idea of the budget. The same holds true for some business addresses; an exclusive downtown law firm planning a grand opening of new offices, for instance, will have a larger budget than an inner-city manufacturing plant planning a retirement dinner.

Budget Estimate. Getting the answers you'll need to prepare a budget for clients can be a real challenge. First, many people honestly don't have a clue about how much they want to spend, especially if it's early in the event-planning process. Others are just being cagey; they know the numbers but don't wish to reveal this information because they think it gives them some type of advantage over their vendors.

Ask the question anyway, listen to the answer for clues, and ask pertinent follow-up questions or make suggestions. You may hear things like: "I really don't know, but I want it to be perfect." "Last year we spent $___." "I want it all to look elegant, but I don't want to spend too much." When you think about it, each of these responses provides a bit of budget information.

Charlotte Williams, president of The Events Organization, Ltd., in Columbia, Maryland, wrote in *Event Solutions Magazine* that she uses what she refers to as the "Ouch Test." She explains:

At my company, we will not start to prepare a preliminary event plan without a budget guideline from a client. Of course, many are hesitant to give a figure, especially if they are not the final decision maker. So I ask the following, "Somewhere in your company there is someone with decision-making authority who will say 'Ouch!' when they see a certain number. Tell me what you think that number is, and our plan will not exceed it." If they still are hesitant, I will float some numbers to select from. Using this approach, I always have gotten a number to start from.

Similarly, you can find out a budget for a party, wedding, or event by suggesting various prices to clients and getting their reactions. Tell them, for example, "Well, a party like the one you're describing will cost somewhere between $8,000 and $11,000." If the client indicates some discomfort, you can respond with a lower price range or suggest changes that can be made to bring the figure into line with their budget.

Mary Tribble, CSEP, president of Tribble Creative Group in Charlotte, North Carolina, another contributor to *Event Solutions Magazine*, wrote that the important thing is "to make the conversation a dialogue, one with an outcome that benefits your client, not you. This way, they will understand that your motivation is not to help spend their money, but to help them invest it wisely."

The Next Step

The answers to these basic questions can be obtained within a few minutes. At this point, it is up to the off-premise caterer to decide on a next step, which could be any of the following:

- Continue the dialogue by scheduling an appointment with the caller.
- Offer to submit a written proposal that includes a budget.
- Offer to send the caller some general written information.
- Thank the person for calling but explain that you cannot cater their event because (fill in the blank) won't work for you.
- Establish a time for a follow-up call if the caller needs to provide more information.

The key point to remember here is that time is money and you must use your limited time marketing and selling your services to the most qualified potential clients.

There are times, too, when caterers should refuse a party, such as when they are already too busy or when the party will not generate enough profit. There are also times when the prospective client seems too difficult, indecisive, or overly demanding. It is often best to gracefully decline working with such people, because the resulting frustrations and hassles are not worth the effort.

The Sales Interview

After you qualify prospective clients, the next step is an in-person meeting to discuss the specific elements of the event to prepare a written proposal. During this meeting, off-premise caterers must establish their credibility with prospective clients by discussing prior events, showing photos and letters, and providing references. (This is where your event scrapbook, video, PowerPoint presentation, and nice brochures help you sell.) A client is often nervous about the forthcoming event, and the professional caterer must dispel that nervousness. Do this by reassuring the client that you will do an outstanding job, as well as by guaranteeing your work.

Clients also want to see suggested menus. Some will ask to see actual parties, and others ask about food tastings. Smart clients will ask off-premise caterers about their licenses and their insurance, so bring these documents (or a summary of them) along. Most will ask exactly what other arrangements you can handle in addition to food and beverages, such as rental equipment, flowers, music, and décor. Others will want to know which manager will supervise their party, and how many parties you commit to at one time. One client question for which you must be ready is: "What if you run out of food?" Off-premise caterers can never stress enough that there will be more than adequate amounts of food for the guests.

In addition to knowing what questions prospective clients will ask, smart salespeople know to ask such questions as:

"What type of party do you imagine?"

"What message do you wish to give your guests?"

"What is the overall goal of the event?"

"Who will be making the food and beverage decisions?"

"Is there a theme?"

"Was there a similar event last year? If so, what worked—and what could be done better?"

Another key to a good sales meeting is to really listen to what your prospective clients has to say. Focus on what they are telling you. Let them finish their sentences. Make good eye contact without staring, nod encouragingly, and don't fidget when they talk.

Part of even the most preliminary meeting includes negotiation, and this involves prioritizing the prospective clients' needs and wants. What will they be willing to pay for and, if they balk at something, where can you afford to scrimp?

When clients say they "want to think it over," zero in on exactly what it is they wish to think about. Is it the food, the service, the rental equipment, the overall cost? Meet price objections by stressing quality, and negotiate by reducing menu choices, beverage choices, or rental equipment choices in exchange for a less expensive price. The key to this process is to never arbitrarily reduce the price without reducing or eliminating something from the event. Choose your words carefully; here are some terms to use that should make the sales interview go more smoothly and help you close the deal.

- "paperwork" instead of "contract"
- "investment" instead of "price"
- "approval" instead of "sign"
- "opportunity" instead of "deal"
- "visit" instead of "appointment"
- "areas of concern" instead of "objections"

A good salesperson will also be on the lookout for opportunities to *up-sell*—that is, to suggest an additional service or a more upscale treatment that is more profitable for the catering company. Up-selling is recommended only after the event is booked, rather than when it is still in the negotiating stages. After all, giving a client too many choices and multiple prices for each can result in confusion and frustration. However, once a date and budget are in place, it's fine to offer additional ideas—an ice carving, a martini bar, valet parking, or higher-end florals or china.

To make these add-ons and upgrades more appealing, you can offer them at reduced markups. After all, you are already making most of your profit from the initial package. Up-selling is a chance to delight the client for not much extra cost—and more cash in your pocket.

EXHIBIT 9.2 Special Event Information Sheet

(This form can be referred to during sales interviews to ensure that all of the necessary details are addressed prior to preparing a catering proposal.)

Name and address of client(s): _____

Name and address of client(s): _____

Name and address of client(s): _____

Phone numbers: _____

Fax number(s): _____

Exact location of the event: _____

Day and date of the event: _____

Minimum number of expected guests: _____

Starting and ending times: _____

Proposed menu: _____

_____

_____

_____

_____

_____

_____

_____

_____

_____

_____

Type of beverages to be served (liquor, wine, beer, Champagne, cordials): _____

_____

Number and location of bars: _____

_____

Equipment

Tables for guests (number and size): _____

Type of chairs and chair covers: _____

Napkins and linens (color, sizes, number): _____

Banquet cloths and skirting: _____

China color and pattern: _____

Type of glassware: _____

Number of service tables: _____

Size and location of cook's tent: _____

Tenting for guests (size, location, lighting, plants, floor covering): _____

Size and location of dance floor: _____

Size and location of platforms and staging (skirting, railings, and steps):
_____

Audiovisual equipment required: _____

Other Services

Staffing to set up, serve, and clean up the event: _____
_____

Music and entertainment: _____

Floral requirements (for guest tables, buffets and foot stations, passing trays, and other areas): _____
_____

Photographer and videographer: _____
_____

Wedding or other specialty occasion cake: _____
_____

Valet parking: _____
_____

Security: _____
_____

Uniforms for staff: _____
_____

Location Layout and Planning

For weddings and receptions

Ceremony: _____

Receiving line: _____

Gift table: _____

Guest book table: _____

Escort table (for place cards): _____

Wedding cake table: _____

Location of cocktail reception _____
_____

Locations of buffets and food stations _____
_____

Location of seating for guests _____
_____

Rain plan _____
_____

The Written Proposal

As soon as possible after the sales interview, the catering salesperson should prepare a written proposal. Many salespeople are creative procrastinators, usually a result of their fear of rejection. Just remember, your company will not be able to cater everyone's party, and all you can do is the best possible job of convincing prospective clients that they should hire you. The ultimate client turnoff is to delay providing the proposal or not to submit it on the date promised. It's also much easier to prepare a proposal when all of the details are fresh, so get it done immediately!

Catering proposals are basically unsigned contracts. Some off-premise caterers prepare them in a business letter format; others use preprinted forms that are simply filled in. Proposals can be powerful sales producers. All proposals should include the elements discussed in Chapter 2, such as date, time, and number of guests; menu, beverage service, service staff, equipment, and other services; and methods of payment and other legal details as appropriate (see "Components of an Off-Premise Catering Contract" on page 50).

As Mike Roman of CaterSource discussed with us during an interview:

Words such as "fresh" and "imported" are excellent if they are accurate. Clients should be informed of portion sizes, product origins, grades and cuts of meat, and method of preparation and service. All words should be completely spelled out with correct spelling. Pricing should be accurate, with no surprises at a later time. In order to separate themselves from the competition, off-premise caterers make their proposals unique by:

- Personally delivering them
- Delivering promptly, by overnight or courier service
- Using attractive stamps, rather than a postage meter
- Putting the proposal in an elegant binder
- Creating a sense of urgency by giving the proposal an expiration date for approval by the client

---

Catering proposals, as well as sales presentations, should sell benefits to prospective clients. Let them know how they, and their guests, will benefit from the services that are offered. Use such statements as:

"Your guests will love the food, and we guarantee there will be plenty of it."

"Your guests won't wait in long lines for food."

EXHIBIT 9.3 Sample Proposal Form

(ON YOUR COMPANY LETTERHEAD)

Date of proposal

Client Name
Address
City, State, Zip

Dear (name of client):

Thank you for the opportunity to provide you with this proposal for your forthcoming (name of event). I enjoyed meeting with you (include here the names of others at the meeting and any other specific things about the meeting, such as time, location, and any other things that will make the proposal more personal). The specific details as I understand them are as follows:

>   DAY AND DATE OF EVENT: (Fill in)
>   MINIMUM NUMBER OF GUESTS: (Fill in)
>   EXACT LOCATION OF THE EVENT: (Fill in)
>   STARTING AND ENDING TIME OF THE EVENT: (Fill in)
>   PURPOSE OF THE EVENT: (Fill in)

You can be assured that we will do an outstanding job for you and your guests. We rely on satisfied clients and guests for our future business! Unlike other caterers, at least one owner of our firm will oversee each detail of your event from setup to breakdown. We guarantee perfection in the execution of each and every detail.

We proudly submit the following proposal that has been created exclusively for your event:

MENU (Include all menu items to be served.)

BEVERAGE SERVICE (Include details of beverages to be served, number of bartenders, and nonalcoholic items to be provided by off-premise caterer.)

EQUIPMENT PROVIDED (Include a listing of all items, such as tables, chairs, linens, china, flatware, glassware, and other equipment.)

SERVICES (Include details regarding music, photographers, and other services to be provided by off-premise caterer.)

[Note: It is also advisable to include, in the equipment and services section of proposals, details of equipment and services that clients intend to provide themselves.]

PRICING Pricing for the food, equipment, and services is as follows: (Include all pricing details, including policies regarding gratuities, service charges, other charges, and sales taxes.)

Other pertinent information regarding our policies is included on the attached page.

Please feel free to call me with any questions, comments, or changes. We are in the service business, and we wish to provide you with the best of service and food.

Sincerely,
(Name and title of off-premise caterer)

"You can be a guest at your own party."

"All you need to do is be there!"

"We'll handle all the details."

"Your guests will rave about this party for months."

Closing the Sale

After the proposal is delivered, prospective clients usually want to review it before making a final decision. Often, others are involved in the decision-making process, such as committees, bosses, future spouses, family members, and so on. Some caterers give their clients a certain number of days to reply, usually by guaranteeing the price if the proposal is accepted by a given date. If clients go past the deadline, the price may increase. This is an excellent opportunity for you to go over a few basic rules, as noted in the sidebar, "Catering Policies"—the all-important price guarantee, and other policies that need to be emphasized, and clearly understood by the client, long before the week of the event.

Most catering sale "closings" occur automatically, without the salesperson having to ask directly for a decision. The clients realize that the benefits offered by a particular caterer meet their wishes at a price they can live with. They may ask a few additional questions or request some clarification. Then they just sign the proposal and return it.

Training in this area never hurts, and there are a number of powerful DVDs and CDs available to teach proper sales and closing techniques. Off-premise caterers should develop a habit of viewing or listening to these and providing them to sales staffers. They are an outstanding marketing investment.

Watching training DVDs when you have time or listening to audio CDs in the car, during exercise, or whenever your mind is free are outstanding ways to learn, and smart caterers realize that investing in knowledge always pays dividends. Those who take advantage of motivational programs to improve their selling skills report increased sales, as well as increased job satisfaction.

No matter how good you are at selling, the very nature of sales involves some percentage of failure and rejection. Nobody closes a sale with every client, every time, and part of what good sales training courses teach is how to handle discouragement by seeing the failures as learning experiences (and opportunities to develop a sense of humor). And, yes, in retrospect, some of your sales negotiations will be truly hilarious!

Catering Policies

As you will see, policies are some of the most critical components of your contract, and they may vary among catering companies. If you take the time to go over them in a friendly way with your clients, you will set a professional tone for the entire event. In parentheses, we've included brief explanations of why the policies are necessary, in the form of suggested responses to clients' questions.

1. Advance deposits are not refundable in case of cancellation. ("This is the cost for planning and advance purchasing, and for booking that date and turning down other business during that time.")

2. A common practice is that wedding catering invoices are paid in full, five days before the ceremony. ("Brides, grooms, and their families have enough to think about that day! This way, no one at the ceremony or reception has to worry—it's already taken care of.")

3. Your per-person price for the event is based on a minimum guaranteed number of guests. If the final guarantee is less than the minimum guarantee, we reserve the right to increase the per-person price. ("This is why it's important to confirm the number of guests as accurately as possible.")

4. We will need a final guarantee of the number of guests no later than four working days prior to the party. ("That's what we're basing all of our food and service on, so it can't be reduced.") You will be billed for that number, unless more people show up at the event.

5. We absolutely will not serve alcohol to minors or to anyone who appears to be intoxicated. ("If you foresee any problems we need to watch for, please let us know early.")

6. Clients must agree to a start time and stop time for the event. Service provided before or after these hours may result in additional charges. ("This also affects our food and service costs.")

7. There may be a surcharge if changes to the guaranteed minimum are made 48 hours or less prior to an event. ("The idea is for everything to go smoothly, which means we really plan ahead in terms of food and service. We can be somewhat flexible—but we're not magicians!")

Summary

Marketing is a critical factor in determining whether your off-premise catering business becomes and remains successful. Your marketing efforts are just as important as the quality of your food, service, and staff because if prospective clients don't know you are around or how your company provides service second to none, they won't know to call in the first place—or to choose you over a competitor even if they do know you exist.

In this chapter, we begin with a discussion of corporate and social catering, looking at their similarities and differences. We then climb the steps of creating a marketing plan and budget, and examine the specific activities and strategies that can be used to fill that plan with meaningful actions to not only achieve sales, but also build the catering company's name recognition, reputation for quality, and overall status in the community. Today, this includes a vibrant online presence, as well as involvement in networking, charitable pursuits, and traditional media.

Readers are advised to ask of any tool in the marketing tool kit: Will it effectively reach my target customers? And will it benefit my company, even if we won't directly make any money from it?

The discussion continues with guidelines for caterers and their salespeople to qualify prospective customers and work with them to discover exactly what they need; an information sheet for event details and a sample proposal are included.

Study Questions

1. What are the two primary catering markets, and how do they differ? Describe which one you would prefer to target in your catering firm, and why.

2. What is the starting point for developing an effective marketing strategy?

3. Select the three marketing tools you believe are the most important for a beginning caterer; explain your answers. Do the same for a well-established off-premise caterer who is trying to grow a business.

4. What is the "80/20 Rule," and how does it affect the way you design your marketing strategy?

5. What is the biggest "time waster" in off-premise catering, and how do you avoid it?

Pricing Off-Premise Catered Events

10

Apparently, even Congress has a tough time understanding how catering is priced. An Inspector General's report in September 2011 accused the Department of Justice "extravagant and potentially wasteful" spending, citing "$16 muffins" served at law enforcement conferences. Some federal lawmakers were quick to jump onto their soapboxes and criticize the department for its pricey snack selection.

Within a couple of days, the caterer—in this case, Hilton Worldwide—issued a rebuttal statement. "The contracted breakfast included fresh fruit, coffee, juice, muffins, tax, and gratuity, for an inclusive price of $16 per person," it said. The service charge in this case was 20 percent, well within the industry standard.

Whether or not your event is being paid for with taxpayers' dollars, deciding how much to charge for catering any off-premise event is a balancing act for sure, even for the most experienced caterer. How much will you have to spend up front to make the event meet your standards and the client's? How much do you think the client is willing to pay? How much flexibility do you have in estimating your own costs? How many other caterers in your market are, even as you ponder this price, preparing competing bids? This chapter may be short, but it is packed with information about the various theories for pricing off-premise events. Indeed, there is no right or wrong way to do it. Rather, you will learn about the components of a fair and profitable pricing structure:

- Common percentages for expenses and markups
- When and how to discuss costs with clients
- Pre-costing methods
- Pricing food and labor
- Options and strategies for offering price discounts
- Common pricing methods and strategies
- Service charges, gratuities, and taxes

Many caterers think of pricing as a sales tool, knowing that events priced fairly (for both client and caterer) will create sales that result in positive word of mouth and loyal customers. When clients achieve their budget objectives and caterers make satisfactory profits, everybody is happy.

Pricing for Profit

The main goal of all pricing strategies is to maximize the caterer's bottom line. The art of pricing entails learning the amounts to charge that will produce sales, and then taking a long-term view and creating a reliable pricing system that works for you in most situations. While every proposal for every event will be unique, each one should not cause you to completely rethink your pricing strategy.

When you do market research, you might find caterers whose pricing makes them seem very exclusive. Their high prices may earn them large profits on the events they cater, but the number of events might be very small. These caterers might be content with the lack of volume—or may be scrambling because their income isn't enough to cover overhead expenses and make a nice profit. Bargain-priced caterers may have the same problem but for different reasons. These caterers may be scrambling to meet the demands of multiple clients—and earning insufficient income from each event to cover overhead expenses and make a profit. Either way, it's the caterer who loses financially.

The goal of fair pricing is to charge enough to earn an overall profit but not so much that most sales proposals are lost. The middle ground is where most off-premise caterers are found. As a rule, somewhere between 50 and 75 percent of all your catering proposals should result in contracts. If they do not, the problem is frequently pricing.

It is not uncommon for a client to ask a caterer to reduce a quoted price. Let's say, for example, that a caterer quotes a price for an event that will generate a $1,000 profit. The client (not having any idea what the target profit amount is) decides to negotiate a bit.

"I'll work with you if you can lower the price by $250," he tells the caterer.

Since food and labor costs have already been realistically and fairly computed, what this most likely means is $250 less profit for the caterer. Should the caterer accept the lower offer? This depends on the caterer's philosophy. Some believe that 75 percent of the pie is better than no pie at all. Others say, "Clients either do business on my terms, or we don't do business."

A good philosophy is never to reduce a price without "reducing" something in the proposal as well. In this example, the caterer might agree to the reduced price but serve less expensive top sirloin instead of beef tenderloin. Another might compromise by catering the party for $125 less and making one or two minor changes in the menu to reduce food costs.

What should off-premise caterers expect to earn for their efforts, and what are the common percentages? These figures vary dramatically, depending on pricing structure, local market conditions, and other factors. However, these are some common ranges:

Food cost percentage	30 to 33% of gross sales
Payroll and benefits	32 to 34%
All other expenses (overhead)	23 to 25%
Net profit percentage before federal income tax	8 to 15%

Prime cost is a term used widely within the foodservice industry. It is the total of the company's food costs and direct labor costs. Some operations may have low food costs but high labor costs, or vice versa. For example, caterers serving steaks will more than likely have higher food costs but lower labor costs, inasmuch as little labor is needed to cut, season, and broil steaks. Conversely, caterers serving upscale menu items that require significant labor to produce will have higher labor costs and lower food costs. For caterers, prime cost will normally be less than 60 percent of sales. Therefore, caterers with higher food costs (say, 40 percent of sales) should strive for labor costs of no more than 20 percent of sales to stay within the range. Those with lower food costs will normally have higher labor costs.

"How Much Will It Cost?"

Creating an event proposal is about more than dollars and cents. Caterers and their salespeople should also look for clues about the clients and their needs. A corporate client who, on a moment's notice, requires a very specialized service will not be very price sensitive—however, a bride on a limited budget whose wedding is two years away has a year to shop around. The bride's situation is much less urgent than that of the corporate client, so most brides tend to shop for the best price.

All too often, the first open-ended question asked by a nervous bride or her parents is something like, "How much do you charge for a wedding?" It may be a frustrating moment for the caterer or salesperson, but it's understandable. A lot of folks just don't have much experience using caterers, so there are numerous potential clients whose main concern is cost.

Remember, smart caterers do not directly answer cost-related questions until they ask their own qualifying questions (as discussed in Chapters 2 and 9) regarding the date, number of guests, location, and entertainment goals, and other questions that reveal the client's true perception of the event. Firm prices should not be given until these questions are answered to the satisfaction of the caterer and the pre-cost of the event has been computed. It is extremely poor policy to quote erroneous prices, only to later advise clients that there are additional charges "not originally estimated." It's tough news for you to deliver, and it creates an atmosphere of distrust in the entire negotiation. Clients will then question your credibility, and some may even refuse to pay, leaving you with the decision of whether to absorb the difference or decline to cater the event.

Pre-Costing Catered Events

Pre-costing an event is the term for estimating all expenses in advance that will be incurred to produce the event. These include:

Food costs

Commissary labor cost to produce the food

All costs to deliver, set up, prepare food on-site, serve, and clean up

Equipment costs (rental and owned)

Other costs (flowers, décor, music, miscellaneous)

Computing Food Costs

The first step is to accurately estimate the cost of the food necessary to produce the menu. To do this, you need to know the costs of each ingredient in any dish you prepare. Several computer programs have been created to assist in this effort, but every caterer needs to take the time to initially input product costs and then accurately update these costs to account for fluctuations. It is not an easy process, but it must be followed to accurately estimate food costs.

Costs for major items like meat and seafood are volatile and can change dramatically in a matter of days. Beef prices always increase prior to and during the Christmas holidays, and seafood prices change depending on weather and fishing conditions. Since your calculations will only be as good as the accuracy of the information in the database, it is useful to calculate an average price, gleaned from recent invoices and suppliers' price quotes. Avoid using sale prices to reach your cost figures per item.

Standardized recipes must be maintained in the database; it helps with cost computations if they are also standardized in terms of numbers of servings. Costs must be computed for each recipe ingredient, no matter how miniscule the amount used. Exhibit 10.1 shows this procedure.

EXHIBIT 10.1 Costing a Recipe

Item: Baked Rice (serves 110)

Ingredient	Recipe Quantity	Price	Total Amount
Rice, long grain	8 lb.	$0.70/lb.	$5.60
Butter	1–½ lb.	2.00/lb.	3.00
Onions	2–½ lb.	0.40/lb.	1.00
Chicken stock	8 qt.	0.25/qt.	2.00
Salt	⅛ lb.	0.20/lb.	.03
	Total cost		$11.63
	Number of portions		110
	Cost per portion		0.11

Source: Courtesy of Cuisine Unlimited Catering and Special Events, Salt Lake City, Utah.

In the following example, the cost for each item on the menu was computed on the basis of the caterer's standardized recipe cards, and the total food cost was computed by adding the costs of all menu items, as follows:

Menu Item	Food Cost	Portion Size
Shrimp raw bar (18–24 ct.)	$8.00	4 per person
Caesar salad	1.28	4 oz.
Beef tenderloin	4.44	8 oz. (raw)
Baked rice	.11	5 oz.
Grilled vegetables	.85	4 oz.
Garnish and sauce	.50	
Rolls and butter	.60	1
Coffee, decaf, cream, and sugar	.65	
Chocolate pecan torte	2.00	1
Total dinner price	$18.43 (per person)	

This total food cost per person is then multiplied by the number of expected guests plus a planned overage, which is generally a percentage of the total number of guests. The larger the number of guests, the smaller the percentage, and vice versa. In Chapter 3, 10 percent is used as a planned overage for a dinner party for 100 guests. Using this as a guideline, the total cost for this meal for 100 guests is:

$$\$18.43 \text{ per person} \times 110 \text{ guests (100 plus 10\% extra)} = \$2,027.30$$

Many caterers prefer to round up, which is always a safe bet. So, in this case, the food cost totals $2,050. And this is just the starting point—only the food cost.

Computing Labor Costs

Labor costs for an off-premise event typically have three components:

- The commissary labor to prepare the food, and pack and transport all the necessary supplies for an event

- The kitchen staff on-site at the event

- The event captain and service and bar staff on-site at the event

In the preceding example, many preparation tasks will be completed in the commissary: cleaning and cooking the shrimp, washing the salad greens, trimming meat, peeling vegetables, and so forth. The labor required to perform these functions must be accounted for and included in the cost of producing the party. The ideal way to compute the labor costs is to actually time each process. For example, if it takes one cook (who is paid $10 per hour, including payroll benefits) six hours to cook and clean the shrimp for the raw bar, this would equal $60. Labor costs should be computed for all items and totaled. In this case, let us assume the commissary labor costs to produce the rest of the menu are $240; the total is now $300.

After you compute food and commissary labor costs, the next step is to compute the other labor costs necessary to produce the party; for instance:

- Cost to pull, pack, deliver, return, clean, and store food and supplies
- Cost of kitchen and prep staff at the party site
- Cost of service and beverage staff at the party site

Most caterers use estimated figures based on past events to estimate the cost of pulling, packing, delivering, returning, cleaning, and storing. Smart caterers know not to underestimate these costs, as they are considerable and can amount to hundreds of dollars for each event. In our example, let's assume that it takes 20 hours to perform these functions, and that the staff members are paid $10 per hour, including payroll benefits. Twenty hours times $10 per hour equals $200.

Kitchen labor at the party site is computed by estimating the actual hours necessary. In this case, for example, six staff members are required for seven hours of labor at $10 per hour, including payroll benefits:

$$6 \text{ staffers} \times 7 \text{ hours each} \times \$10 \text{ per hour} = \$420$$

Finally, the cost for service and bar staff must be computed. This is done, again, by simply multiplying the number of staff members times their hourly rate, times the number of hours worked. Assume that there will be ten servers and two bartenders for this event, each earning $15 per hour, including payroll benefits. Six staffers will work seven hours, and six will work five hours. The cost is computed as follows:

6 staffers × 7 hours each× $15 per hour =	$630
6 staffers × 5 hours each× $15 per hour =	$450
Total service and bar staff =	$1,080

Now we know the total labor cost to produce this event:

Commissary labor to prepare the food	$300
Labor to pull, pack, deliver, etc.	200
On-site kitchen labor	420
Service and bar labor	1,080
Total labor	$2,000

Computing Equipment Costs

Off-premise caterers frequently provide equipment such as china, glassware, flatware, tables, chairs, linens, and the like. In some cases these items are rented from party-rental companies, in others they are owned by caterers, and sometimes there is a combination of the caterer's equipment and rented items. So how do caterers charge clients for equipment?

Rental Equipment. Most off-premise caterers add markups to their costs for rental equipment. In addition, most rental companies offer discounts from list prices to caterers. This means that off-premise caterers produce profits from rental equipment. To compute the cost of the rental equipment, caterers simply add the costs of all rental items. Once the rental orders are placed, these costs may be verified with the rental companies.

For example, assume that the list price of all equipment necessary to produce this party is $2,000, and the rental dealer offers caterers a 10 percent discount. Therefore, the cost to the caterer of the rental equipment is $1,800.

How much is an acceptable markup for rental equipment? Again, this varies widely between caterers. All catering companies must invest time to order, receive, handle, rinse or wash, and repack this equipment. For most large parties, there's also some loss to figure in due to breakage, burns, and pilferage by guests. You can certainly add in a small allowance, automatically, for losses—but, politically, it's probably smarter to absorb these costs in the overall markups. Passing them on to clients directly can result in disputes. ("Prove that three of those were stolen!" "If they were broken, I want to see them!") Then again, major losses that are due to a client's negligence must be charged directly to the client after the event, with or without a separate loss allowance in the contract.

Among the items in our sample $2,000 rental order, there will more than likely be minor losses, even with the most professional staff. Novice caterers have been known to sacrifice all their profits from an event because of equipment losses. Some off-premise caterers may charge clients the rental equipment dealer's discounted price plus a small allowance for losses, while others may apply liberal increases to the prices charged by the dealers.

If the rental equipment cost would normally be $2,000, note the profit options, depending on what the client is charged for its use:

Equipment List Price	Discounted Price	"Selling Price" To Client	Margin
$2,000	$1,800	$1,800	$ 0
2,000	1,800	2,000	200
2,000	1,800	2,200	400
2,000	1,800	2,400	600
2,000	1,800	2,600	800
2,000	1,800	2,800	1,000

Please note that in these examples, the margins are prior to any losses due to missing items or damaged merchandise.

Owned Equipment. Off-premise caterers also own equipment that they provide to clients for their events. Some do not directly charge for it, and others charge just as if it were equipment rented from a dealer—because, indeed, the client is renting the equipment from you. The charge may vary based on the situation and, in fact, owning equipment can be a useful tool in the pricing process. It can allow you the ability to "discount" the rental prices you would otherwise charge for the equipment. Since the equipment is yours, you are making something off its use no matter what you charge.

For a small home party, the caterer may charge the full local retail rental price, but when bidding on a large event, the caterer may chose to charge little or nothing for the equipment, content with profits from the food and other services.

Pricing Accessory Services

Many off-premise caterers assist clients by arranging for so-called *accessory services*—everything from music or entertainment, to floral design, valet parking, security, photography, and wedding and special-occasion cakes not made in their commissary. We discuss each of these in greater detail in Chapter 13.

Some caterers include these services in a package plan. Some price them separately. Some ask clients to pay the vendors directly, and others charge a markup on some or all of these services. They reason that, as the professional who recommends these services, the caterer shares some of the responsibility for the results. In addition, they spend time arranging for these services (and supervising or overseeing them on-site), and their expertise in knowing whom to recommend is worth something. Therefore, they add a markup when billing clients for these services.

How much markup is proper? This, like the markup for rental equipment, varies from caterer to caterer, but it is invariably less than markups applied to food costs. Markups in the range of 10 to 25 percent are fairly common. Sometimes, in an extremely competitive situation, caterers may simply provide these services at cost to gain a pricing edge.

Where the clients deal directly with the accessory service providers, is it ethical for off-premise caterers to receive commissions from the suppliers they recommend? This is a touchy subject that will spark debates from coast to coast. The main point is that commissions received from accessory service suppliers must be reported as income to the catering company.

Pricing Beverage Services

In every state, there are liquor laws that dictate who can (and cannot) profit from selling beer, wine, and liquor. In some states, a caterer is not allowed to make a profit on liquor sales and, therefore, can purchase beverages on behalf of clients but cannot mark up the cost.

However, it is common and perfectly legal to make a small profit from the other items required for beverage service: mixers, soft drinks, ice, and other bar supplies. The handiest way to price these items is to charge a flat amount per guest. The average is between $1 and $2.

For this example, we will estimate that the costs of mixers and ice are $100, and we'll charge a flat $200 for them.

Here is a summary of the totals we have estimated for food, labor, equipment, and beverages in the last few pages:

Food costs	$2,050
Labor costs	$2,000
Equipment rental costs	$1,800 (if you don't own it and have to rent it)
Beverage mixers and ice	$ 100
Total cost	$5,950

Pricing Food

With the estimated pre-costs computed, the next step is to determine the various markups and food cost percentages. There are several formulas that will give the same results. With a goal of a food cost in the range of 20 to 50 percent, let's examine two ways to calculate the markup for our sample menu with that $2,050 food cost. The first way is to divide the food cost by the desired food cost percentage to get a selling price. For example:

Food Cost	Divide By Food Cost Percentage	Selling Price	Margin
$2,050	25% (÷ .25)	$8,200	$6,150
$2,050	30% (÷ .30)	$6,833	$4,783
$2,050	35% (÷ .35)	$5,857	$3,807
$2,050	40% (÷ .40)	$5,125	$3,075
$2,050	45% (÷ .45)	$4,555	$2,505
$2,050	50% (÷ .50)	$4,100	$2,050

By subtracting the food cost from the selling price, you can determine the amount of gross margin produced from the food sales. For instance, in the 25 percent food cost example, the gross margin from the food sale is $6,150 ($8,200 minus the original food cost of $2,050).

Another way to price food is to multiply the food cost by a markup factor:

- A markup factor of 5 will produce a 20 percent food cost.
- A markup factor of 4 will produce a 25 percent food cost.
- A markup factor of 3 will produce a $33^1/_3$ percent food cost.
- A markup factor of 2.5 will produce a 40 percent food cost.
- A markup factor of 2 will produce a 50 percent food cost.

For example:

Food Cost	Markup Factor	Selling Price	Margin
$2,050	4.0	$8,200	$6,150
$2,050	3.0	$6,150	$4,100
$2,050	2.5	$5,125	$3,075
$2,050	2.0	$4,100	$2,050

Again, the gross margin is computed by simply subtracting the estimated food cost from the selling price.

Pricing Labor

Some off-premise caterers add the labor cost to the food cost, and then apply a markup factor to the total. In our example, the combined food and labor cost, or prime cost, is $4,050 ($2,050 + $2,000).

Food and Labor Cost	Markup Factor	Selling Price	Margin
$4,050	1.5	$6,075	$2,025
$4,050	2.0	$8,100	$4,050
$4,050	2.5	$10,125	$6,075

Notice in this example that the markup factors produce greater margins because we are marking up not only food cost, but also labor cost.

Some caterers mark up the food and labor; others simply mark up the food and charge for the labor. However, many operate on the theory that all cost centers should also create profit.

Determining the Markup

Thus far, we have discussed the math involved in pricing, but not the "art" of determining the amounts of markup to use. There are no easy equations for this purpose. Most caterers learn pricing by trial and error within their markets—they quote a price too high and don't get the job, or they quote too low, get the job, and lose money on it. Those who survive the learning process learn the art of pricing for profit.

Several *market factors* influence pricing:

- What are the competitors' prices for similar events?
- What are the previous prices charged to clients?
- How many guests are expected?

- How badly is the business needed?
- Is this a bidding situation, or not?
- If so, who else is bidding on the event?
- What is the customer's perceived value of the party?
- Once the price is quoted, will these clients expect to negotiate it?
- Once it is quoted, will these clients expect a discount?

Sometimes the location of an event affects the profit margin. To be included on their list of "preferred vendors," many venues require that the off-premise caterer pay them a percentage of food and beverage sales. This can dramatically affect the profit margin of caterers on these lists, and should be factored into the event proposal.

Before you submit your proposal, you should always ask if the client is getting other bids. In some cases the answer is no, but if the client is asking other caterers for bids, it is fair to ask against whom you are bidding. Often, the client will tell you, and you then learn where you stand in the competitive arena and are better able to decide whether you want to bid or not. If the other bids are coming from low-end caterers and you're strictly upscale, you can't compete on price alone, so you may choose to emphasize other factors, such as quality and service.

Even if the client selects another caterer for the event, it is good practice to look at the lost bid as a learning experience. Try to determine the reasons for the client's selection—the deciding factor may not have been price, but it may have been other factors that may be important to know. This information may also help you further develop key marketing strategies to capture new clients or replace business you have either lost or failed to win.

Pricing the Event

With the knowledge of pre-costing techniques, we are now prepared to price an event. Using the particulars of the example in the text, here is one way to price this event. It isn't the *only* way to price it—it is only *one* way to do so. Discussion of a few common pricing philosophies follows.

Charges to Client

$2,050 food cost (times markup factor of 2.5)	$5,125
Labor (at cost)	2,000
Equipment (10% markup)	2,200
Beverage mixers, ice, etc. ($2 per person)	200
Total price	$9,525

Total Costs (For the Same Event)

Food	$2,050
Labor	2,000
Equipment	1,800
Beverage mixers, ice, etc.	100
Total cost	$5,950
Total projected profit	$3,575

One way to check your calculations is to do a *cost-out* for each event—that is, compare your actual costs after the event (food, labor, etc.) to see if your proposal was accurate. Aim for a gross margin of 50 percent after all direct costs are deducted from revenues.

Common Pricing Methods

Off-premise caterers do not use one universal pricing method. Caterers have various methods for pricing that fit their styles and needs. However, all successful caterers have one thing in common. They charge prices that not only produce sufficient profits, but also generate repeat business. In no particular order, the following are some of the available pricing methods.

Budget Pricing Method. With the budget pricing method, the client sets the price by giving the caterer an overall budget for the event. It may be just for food, staff, and equipment, or it may also include accessory services like music and décor. For example, a client tells a caterer that the budget for a forthcoming event is $5,000 for 100 guests, and only for food, staff, and equipment. Astute caterers first determine their desired profit for the event, and then budget for the expenses as follows.

Assume that the off-premise caterer wants to earn a profit of $1,500 from this event. When deducted from the total budget of $5,000, this leaves $3,500 for all expenses, including food cost, labor, and equipment. At this point, the caterer simply computes the menu, staff, and equipment needs at costs that will result in expenses of $3,500. Please note that these are computed at cost, not at retail, because profit was budgeted first.

Cost-Plus Method. From time to time, off-premise caterers may be requested to cater a special event where the client wishes to provide some or all of the food. An example is the grand opening of a supermarket, for which the supermarket provides the food but requires the off-premise caterer's expertise in executing the event. In this case, the caterer may charge a flat fee for time, expertise, and profit. The amount should be at least what the caterer would normally earn on an event of similar magnitude. Above the flat fee, the caterer would simply charge the client cost for labor, equipment, miscellaneous food expenses, and other specific costs for the event.

Range Pricing Method. This method is used when off-premise caterers are quoting prices for an event in the distant future, when costs may be uncertain. For example, when quoting a price for a Florida stone crab dinner or a Maine lobster dinner two years in advance, there is no sure way of knowing the cost of these fresh seafood items two years out. In such instances, a caterer might simply quote a price range, high and low.

Package Pricing Method. A package price includes all components necessary to produce an event, including food, beverage setups, staffing, equipment, music, flowers, and so on. Package prices should be designed for a minimum number of guests because the price is determined per person. If there are fewer people than the minimum, there will be insufficient revenue to cover costs and produce profits. Here's an example of a package price for 100 guests:

100 dinners at $15 per person	$1,500
100 beverage mixers and ice at $2 per person	200
Staffing	750
Equipment	1,000
Band	750
Flowers	300
Total (before tax and other charges)	$4,500

Here, the caterer may wish to price this package at $44.95 per person, for a minimum of 100 guests.

Strategies for Successful Pricing

Whatever pricing method you choose, there are a number of important considerations to keep in mind when considering the right markup factor and final price to offer.

Higher Markups for Smaller Parties. For example, a markup factor of 2 for a chicken dinner that costs $5 each for 20 guests will produce a margin of only $100 ($5 × 20 × 2 = $200, less $100 cost). Is this sufficient profit? It is certainly not for a full-service caterer who is cooking at the party site. In this instance, a larger markup factor would be appropriate.

Higher Markups for Lower-Food-Cost Parties. In the preceding example, the food cost for chicken is low compared with the food cost of a lobster dinner, which may be $15. A markup of 2 on the chicken produces a $5 margin, whereas a markup of 2 on the lobster produces a $15 margin ($15 × 2, less $15). This approach only works, however, when the menu is not labor-intensive.

Markups Based on the Number of Expected Guests. With more guests, smaller markup factors may be sufficient. The $5 food margin on the chicken dinner for a group of 1,000 will produce a food margin of $5,000. Many caterers charge less per person for larger events. Some take a sliding scale approach (without describing it thusly to clients), with "regular" prices for small groups, slight discounts for larger ones and deeper discounts for very large groups.

Markups Based on a Particular Date. Special holidays and other major events, such as New Year's Eve, the last Saturday before Christmas, or the Super Bowl are generally busy days for off-premise caterers, with a large demand for catering services. Astute caterers realize that they can charge more on these days than during slow periods. Moreover, because these days and nights are generally busy, when pricing, off-premise caterers should remember that there may be additional, unexpected expenses, such as renting extra vehicles and paying premium pay to staff on New Year's Eve.

Markups Based on the Probability of the Need to Negotiate or Discount. In some instances it is better to price a party higher, realizing you will later need to reduce the price or offer other concessions to satisfy a particular client. As we have mentioned, it is not advisable to reduce the price without deleting something from the party or receiving a concession from the client. For example, a $2-per-person price reduction will result in the elimination of some food.

Some caterers offer discounts for parties held during slow seasons or for those held at certain times of day. Others offer discounts for clients who sign contracts months or years in advance or who agree to engage them as the "preferred vendor" for all their parties.

Pricing for Future Business. Generally, inexpensive parties "breed" more inexpensive parties. When pricing events, every off-premise caterer has learned not to give a low price to clients who say that there will be many people at their events who will buy in the future. There may be, but these folks will inevitably expect the same bargain prices. Beware!

Pricing Based on Value of Time. Most off-premise caterers reach a point in their careers when they ask themselves, "What is my time worth?" It isn't a rhetorical question. Situations crop up that will prompt you to make this kind of decision: "Do I sacrifice a long-awaited day off to earn a meager profit?" For a regular client, the answer may be yes. In other situations, perhaps by quoting a higher price, you can earn a sufficient profit to make the sacrifice worthwhile.

Pricing When Cost Isn't a Factor. There are clients who look beyond the price to such factors as top quality in food presentation and service. They are excited about an off-premise caterer who really works to come up with dazzling party themes and unique food displays. Some clients take pride in saying, "So-and-so is 'my' caterer." Some, rare as they may be, even enjoy telling others how much they paid for an upscale party. We're certainly not suggesting you "gouge" such customers. However, in these cases, your proposals can be more lavish—and the client might even expect as much.

Service Charges, Gratuities, and Sales Taxes

Every state has laws regarding whether to charge sales tax on labor, and they vary too much to summarize here. Some obvious confusion occurs because catering is a service, but the products being served are, well, products. Sometimes, the products (food) are taxed but the services (labor) are not.

Each state also has specific laws regarding gratuities (tips) and service charges, and it is incumbent upon caterers to learn and comply with them. Penalties for violations are often severe.

In most states, service charges are subject to sales tax since they are not voluntary. But tips, which are voluntary, are not generally taxed.

Prospective clients (and, with the beginning of this chapter in mind, congressional representatives) may question the purpose of a service charge, and they have every right to do so as these vary from 15 to 25 percent. Spend a half hour online and you will see a great deal of misinformation floating around about the service charge. Many people incorrectly assume it is a mandatory "tip" split among the on-site staff, much like the amount that restaurants tack on to a bill automatically for large parties. This is unfortunate because those who believe that might skip tipping servers they otherwise would have rewarded for excellent service.

In fact, service charges are how off-premise caterers cover the myriad overhead expenses involved in delivering and serving food at a remote location without cutting into their profit for the event. Some calculate the service charge based on the invoice total; others include a service charge only on the food and labor totals.

Based on our "sample event," let's look at two ways to do it. Note that we have rounded some figures to the highest dollar amount:

$$15\% \text{ for entire invoice} = \$9,525 \times .15 = \$1,429$$
$$\text{Total event price for client} = \$9,525 + \$1,429 = \$10,954$$
$$15\% \text{ for food and labor only} = \$4,050 \times .15 = \$607$$
$$\text{Total event price for client} = \$9,525 + \$607 = \$10,132$$

One of the best explanations we've heard for service fees comes from Nathaniel Neubauer, owner of Contemporary Catering in Los Angeles, California. His company refers to it as an "event production fee."

We do not charge for tastings, walk-throughs, meetings, CAD diagrams, insurance certificates, etc. This fee offsets all of these costs to ensure our clients aren't worrying about asking for help in these areas, as many of our clients have had experiences, or have heard of others' experiences, in which they were billed for these things. We like to ensure that the planning process is as easy as possible, with nothing to worry about once clients have us on board.

Reports from around the nation indicate that the majority of caterers include a service charge in their proposals. However, Mike Roman, catering industry consultant and founder of CaterSource in Chicago, Illinois, notes that most buyers would rather spend money on anything but a service charge:

A buyer getting a chance to purchase two identical menu packages from two different caterers will always buy the one with more value. Look at this scenario: One caterer is charging $24 per guest plus an 18 percent service charge, while another caterer is charging $27 per guest with a 14.5 percent service charge. Which do you think the client buys?

Roman thinks caterers should become more inventive with their service charges. For example:

- Charge a flat 20 percent service charge instead of 15 percent or 18 percent.
- Change the name. We've also seen it referred to as a "support fee," an "event coordination fee," or an "administration fee."
- Change the percentage. The higher the menu price and/or the larger the group, the smaller the percentage.
- Charge a smaller service charge on slower days.

Pricing for Charitable Events

Most charities or nonprofit groups are able to negotiate very low prices because there is always a novice caterer who is willing to work for a reduced rate to obtain exposure. For newcomers to this field, these events can be great launching pads. However, most experienced caterers have learned that they must charge a realistic price that will not only result in a modest profit, but also ensure a sufficient budget to produce excellent food and provide excellent service.

We first introduced you to the possibilities and limitations of catering for nonprofit groups in Chapter 9, including the importance of having a written policy about the types of causes and requests you will consider—or not—and how much you are willing to do for them.

Within these parameters, charitable catering can be a wonderful way to raise your public profile in the community and introduce you to the board members and major donors that could have need for your services. Therein lies the pricing dilemma for catering charitable events: You cannot afford to reduce quality or quantity, regardless of the discounted price you may be offering, as your goal is to ensure that the event reflects your excellent reputation and attracts new clients.

Most charitable groups are encouraged to get multiple bids. Handle your bid just as you would any other, with a professional written proposal and the same pre-costing steps for the menu, labor, and services. Whether or not you are going to charge full price for catering the event, you should track expenses just as diligently and even let the group know the "actual value" of what they are getting. Some possibilities for discounting events include the following:

- As mentioned in Chapter 9, this is the time to ask your suppliers for discounts and/or product donations to minimize your food costs.
- Consider charging the group only for food and labor.
- Eliminate the service charge or include all the rentals at no charge.
- Charge for everything except dessert, and offer an interesting and generous dessert selection.
- If a board member of the charitable organization has a service you could use, consider a barter arrangement for part of the cost.
- As with any other client, if the first reaction is, "It's a little high . . . ," you can offer to reduce the price—with a commensurate reduction in a food item or other cost.
- Cater at a smaller profit margin and/or offer to make a cash donation directly to the organization.

Catering an occasional charitable event has upsides in addition to good publicity and exposure. With proper documentation, you can receive a tax deduction for your actual costs of food and labor, and you have the satisfaction of helping an organization you believe in. Just be sure that you receive the good publicity you deserve for your good work.

Delivery and Overtime Charges

For drop-off catering jobs that do not require a serving staff, some off-premise caterers include a delivery charge to cover the costs of delivering food to an event site. With gas prices today, it is hard to imagine that some clients object to this fee and won't buy from caterers who charge it. To avoid this situation, you could simply add the cost of delivery into the food cost, rather than record it on the invoice as a separate charge.

And what happens when a party continues beyond the specified ending time? How should caterers charge for this type of overtime? Normally, overtime charges are specified in the catering contract, so that there are no surprises if an event runs longer than planned. These charges are usually based on the hourly rate paid to staff, the number of staff members, the amount of extra food and beverages served, and some form of markup to these costs. Most overtime costs are usually for labor because, by the end of the event, most guests have had their fill of food and drink. In circumstances where off-premise caterers are providing such accessory services as music or valet parking, overtime fees for these must also be added to the final bill.

For example, assume that a party goes one hour past its scheduled ending time and there are three staff members working the event who will stay. They are each paid $18 per hour—remember, this is overtime pay—including payroll benefits. In this case, no extra food or beverages are being consumed. Three staff members at $18 per hour equals $54 in extra payroll expenses. The caterer may wish to mark up the labor two times (to $108) or three times (to $162), thus generating an additional profit.

An important note: If overtime is caused by the caterers' inability to fulfill their responsibilities on schedule, it is considered unreasonable to charge clients the additional costs.

🍴 Summary

The first subhead in this chapter says it all: "Pricing for Profit." It might seem from these pages that there are as many ways to accomplish this as there are off-premise caterers, but the methods all can be summarized with the few simple steps that are discussed herein.

You cannot price an event unless you know your costs up-front. Catering software makes it easier than ever for a company to calculate food costs, labor costs, and equipment-related costs for an event, down to the penny. However, to help you understand the process, the chapter breaks it down and includes examples on paper. The examples reflect the expenses a caterer will incur to prepare and serve specific menu items at a specific event. As food costs can vary seasonally, someone at the catering company needs to be responsible for updating the figures in the database to ensure accuracy.

With the cost information in hand, there is a great deal of flexibility in setting a price. The caterer can *mark up* (charge a small additional percentage for) accessory services, food, labor, and rental equipment. Guidelines for markup percentages are discussed in the chapter. The location of an event will also affect the bid because many venues demand that caterers share a percentage of food and beverage sales with them. No less than a dozen different pricing theories and strategies are mentioned. Off-premise caterers who have their own tables, chairs, glassware, and other items that they would normally have to rent have an additional advantage as they can charge for these items and make money, or reduce a price by not charging (or not charging as much) for their use.

The difference between gratuities and service charges is explained, and information is provided about catering for charities and the use of delivery and overtime fees.

Study Questions

1. When pre-costing a recipe, should the water required—say, for a soup—be priced along with the other ingredients? If so, how would you do that?

2. Should an off-premise caterer mark up the cost of rental equipment that the catering company does not own or simply pass the costs on to the client? Explain your answer.

3. Why should you care if other caterers are preparing bids for the same event you are bidding on?

4. How do you feel about the service charge? What percentage do you think would be fair in your market, and do you believe it should be charged on a client's entire order or just on certain components of the order (food, labor, accessories)? How did you come to that conclusion?

5. Which of the "Common Pricing Methods and Strategies" on pages 380–383 make the most sense to you? Explain your answer.

11

Purchasing, Receiving, and Storing Foods

Timothy Jones, an anthropologist at the University of Arizona in Tucson, spent ten years measuring food loss throughout the supply chain in the United States. He released some shocking findings in 2004: that even a partial correction of the waste in agriculture, food production, transportation, retail, consumption, and waste disposal could save consumers and manufacturers tens of billions of dollars each year. Jones said that the average American household, for instance, wastes 14 percent of its food purchases, and that the value of household food tossed out unnecessarily totals $43 billion a year.

Imagine, then, how much food an off-premise catering company could waste, and how much money this would represent in terms of lost profit. That's why it is important to learn techniques for purchasing, receiving, and storing foods. Poor execution in these areas can mean the difference between financial success and failure. This chapter will provide readers with the knowledge necessary for competence in these areas:

- Determining how much and when to order
- Using product specifications
- Selecting and working with suppliers
- Receiving and storing foods properly
- Taking inventory

In addition to documenting wastefulness, researchers, including anthropologists like Jones, archaeologists, and ethnographers, have been measuring trash output since the 1970s for clues about our society's culture and psychology. If they looked in your catering commissary dumpster, what conclusions might they reach?

Purchasing

As first mentioned in Chapter 3, those who purchase foods for off-premise catered events need to know how to compute yields. For instance, how many Caesar salads can be produced from one case of romaine lettuce? How many heads of romaine are there in a case? Without knowledge in this area, you will not know how to purchase a sufficient quantity of romaine for a dinner party of 50 guests with a Caesar salad as a first course.

The goals of purchasing should be:

- To order the right product
- In the correct quality and quantity
- At the best possible price
- To be delivered at the right time
- From a reputable supplier

Product specifications, such as Prime and Choice beef, are specific descriptions that define the various qualities and forms of products. For example, when preparing shrimp salad, purchasing shrimp pieces or broken shrimp will be less expensive than buying whole shrimp. For beef stew, stew meat is more practical and less expensive than top sirloin butt.

Learning to correctly time your purchases is another important element of the purchasing function, and today's intense focus on fresh, locally grown, and locally made foods makes this even more critical. Purchasers should know the shelf lives of products and understand how the culinary staff will be using them. A whole frozen turkey received on the day of the party for which it will be cooked will create turmoil in the kitchen; more lead time is needed so that the turkey may first be thawed properly and safely. Fresh strawberries to be used with a sabayon sauce, however, should not be received until the day of the party.

Determining Purchasing Needs

Purchasing for off-premise catered events differs from purchasing for restaurants because caterers know the number of guests that are expected and their menus. Purchasing needs are determined by reviewing the catering menus for a certain period of time. Many off-premise caterers work on a week-to-week basis for major meat, poultry, seafood, and dry-store items, and a daily basis for breads, produce, fresh fish, and other perishables. For example, each Monday morning, a purchasing agent may review the needs for the forthcoming week, starting with the following Wednesday, through the weekend, and for parties on Monday and Tuesday of the following week. All major needs for various parties are consolidated, and bids are received for these items. Produce and other perishable items should be ordered and received as close as possible to the time of use.

A typical purchasing mistake is the failure to check the amounts of products on hand in inventory before ordering. Frequently, purchasers order items that are not truly needed. It takes only a few minutes to check current inventories. Another mistake is ordering in too large a quantity. If the party requires only six heads of romaine, why order a whole case (24 heads)? If you use only 3 dozen eggs for a two-week period, why order a 30-dozen case from a wholesaler? It is normally better to pay a few cents a dozen more at a supermarket than to pay a bit less per dozen but have 27 dozen extra eggs taking up refrigeration space and tying up capital. In these and other cases, off-premise caterers are often better off going to a local supermarket or wholesale club and picking up these products, rather than ordering from suppliers who deliver only in larger-than-needed quantities.

Savvy off-premise caterers maintain very low inventory levels. They buy only the products they need. They realize that unneeded foods in inventory represent money that could be needed elsewhere. They also realize that the more foods they have on hand, the more likely it is for theft to occur. It is simply much easier to control and inventory smaller supplies of foods.

Some large-volume caterers buy certain foods in bulk, but only when savings are significant, when they have available cash to pay for these items, and when they have sufficient, secure storage for these products. No matter how good the deal may appear to be, set limits for yourself: Buy in bulk only when you are able to save 20 percent or more on the regular price, and only if you plan to use the items within a three-month period.

Purchasing Specifications

Purchasing specifications, like those shown in Exhibit 11.1, must be developed in writing for each menu item. Although this is time-consuming, the results can save off-premise caterers thousands of dollars annually. Purchase specifications for products should include:

- The intended use of the product
- Both general and detailed descriptions of the product to be purchased

  The exact product name

  The brand or manufacturer's name

  The U.S. product grade (or equivalent)

  The size of the product (container size, number of items in a carton or package weight)

  For produce, the color, degree of ripeness, and type of trim

- Any other exact specifications

  The way you want the product packaged ("16-ounce resealable containers," "moisture-proof fiberboard containers," "packed in ice in reusable plastic bins")

- Storage requirements ("unrefrigerated," "frozen," etc.)

The key point to remember when developing purchasing specifications is to buy sufficient quality to meet the menu needs—no more, or less. For example, caterers who specialize in Prime beef must buy USDA Prime beef, whereas other caterers who specialize in deli platters will not need to order Prime beef. Caterers who specialize in pasta will produce their own rather than buy prepared pasta products.

For more information about specifications, we recommend a book from a fellow John Wiley & Sons author. *SPECS: The Foodservice and Purchasing Specification Manual*, by Lewis Reed (Hoboken, NJ, 2006), contains information on purchasing policies, foods, and quality controls, as well as storage and handling procedures.

Ethics in Purchasing

Many off-premise caterers purchase food and other products themselves since they realize the importance of savings in this area. Others concentrate on other areas of their businesses and delegate this function to a staff member. In the latter case, the

EXHIBIT 11.1 Sample Product Specs

Note how the specifications vary slightly, depending on the type of product being requested.

Red Delicious apples	Cauliflower, white
Used for fruit plate item	Used for side dish for all entrées
U.S. Fancy	U.S. No. 1 (high)
Washington State	12 count
30- to 42-lb. crate	18- to 25-lb. carton
Moisture-proof fiberboard	Moisture-proof fiberboard
Layered arrangement, cell carton	Loose pack or slab pack
Whole apples	Pretrimmed heads
Fresh, refrigerated	Fresh, refrigerated
Fully ripened	Fully ripened

Examples of fresh produce product specifications.

Fresh shell eggs	Broiler/fryer, raw
Used for fried, poached, scrambled eggs	Used for fried chicken lunch entrée
U.S. Grade A (high)	U.S. Grade A
Large size	Quarter chicken parts, cut from whole
30 dozen (full case)	birds weighing between 2½ and
Moisture-proof carton	3¼ lb. dressed weight
12 flats per case, 2½ dozen per flat	No variety meats
White shell	Ice packed in reusable plastic tubs
Refrigerated	Approximately 30 lb. per tub

Examples of egg and poultry product specifications.

Australian lobster tails	Beef loin, strip loin steak, boneless
Used for dinner entrée	Used for dinner entrée
U.S. Grade A (or equivalent)	IMPS Number 1180
16/20 count	USDA Choice (High U.S. Choice)
25-lb. moisture-proof, vapor-proof	Cut from USDA Yield Grade 2 carcass
container	Dry-aged 14 to 21 days
Layered pack	12-oz. portion cut
Frozen	Individually wrapped in plastic film
	Layered pack
	10- to 12-lb. case
	Refrigerated

Examples of seafood and meat product specifications.

(*Source: Purchasing: Selection and Procurement for the Hospitality Industry*, 8th Edition, by Andrew Hale Feinstein and John M. Stefanelli, 2011. Reprinted with permission of John Wiley & Sons, Inc.)

caterer and his or her representatives should abide by ethical purchasing practices. These include:

- Purchasers should be prohibited from accepting personal gifts of more than a specific dollar value. For example, during the holidays, a purchaser may accept a gift valued at no more than $50 from a supplier.
- Purchasers should show no one supplier favoritism and should buy from the best-qualified suppliers.
- Purchasers should not make personal purchases from suppliers for themselves or other catering company employees.
- In a bidding situation, the order should be awarded to the lowest bidder who meets the company specifications for the product.

Selecting Suppliers

When selecting suppliers, caterers generally have a large number to choose from. To select the proper suppliers, learn whatever you can about their honesty and business reputation, product knowledge, inventory lists (will they have what you want, or can they get it quickly enough?), and pricing policies.

Off-premise caterers should choose suppliers like they would choose any other merchant with whom they do business: by checking their references and their reputation for product quality and service. One advantage of doing business online is that it is easier than ever to get information, both positive and negative, about a potential supplier.

In this age of e-procurement, with product catalogs, pricing information, and order forms all available online, it is still important to be able to reach a human being on the phone when there is a problem or an unusual situation. Great customer service is paramount, and you should expect nothing less.

Reliable delivery is crucial to off-premise caterers, who are always working with deadlines, and this includes convenient delivery times. A meat delivery promised and expected at 9:00 A.M. will do no good if it arrives at 2:00 P.M. Excuses about traffic and mechanical problems cannot usually be tolerated. Timing is everything!

Many successful off-premise caterers think of their suppliers as partners. The relationships between such partners should be honest and up-front. Each should share their policies and respect the policies of the other. When requesting quotations, off-premise caterers should give reasonable purchase estimates. For example, a caterer who expects to spend $20,000 per year for dry goods should give this estimate to the supplier, rather than overestimate to receive a potentially lower price. Suppliers and their drivers should be treated with respect and courtesy. They are indeed partners in an off-premise caterer's success.

How many suppliers are enough? The answer to this question will vary from one caterer to the next, and there are several different types of supplier relationships to consider:

- *Multiple sourcing* means a product is available from many different suppliers. You may choose to deal with only a few of them, but these situations enable you to shop for the best deals, which should give you greater flexibility and savings, and ensure that you'll never run out of the item. For large purchases, it is smart to request bids from several suppliers who meet your product specifications, and you'll probably go with the least expensive. These relationships can be touchy as the suppliers work to please you even as they realize you're not especially loyal to them.

- *Single sourcing* means you could get the product from a number of suppliers, but you have chosen a single company to deal with. It's more of a partnership, often built on mutual trust. You may even have a contract with this supplier.

- The term *sole sourcing* applies to artisan products and many (but not all) locally produced foods. These are brand-named, high-end, or otherwise one-of-a-kind products that you cannot get anywhere else. Of course, the trade-off with these small suppliers is that their deliveries might not be as fast or frequent as you would like, and they may sometimes be out of products when you need them, requiring you to plan accordingly.

- You will probably have all three types of relationships as part of your purchasing function.

In addition, there are times when an off-premise caterer can get the best deals simply by shopping, like any other retail customer, at wholesale clubs, office supply stores, and restaurant supply stores. The potential savings make these worth your while, as long as you are willing to devote the time necessary to search for these outlets, select the merchandise, and transport it to the commissary yourself. Large-volume caterers are also able to save money on purchasing by negotiating volume-purchasing agreements with major foodservice suppliers. Smaller caterers do not have that kind of leverage, so they are better off buying from wholesale clubs.

Purchasing Meat

Off-premise caterers purchase meat from three basic sources:

- Local retail markets are good for emergency purchases but comparatively expensive.
- A local butcher can buy meat by the case, break up the case lot, and cut the meat to satisfy a caterer's requirements. Such purveyors are responsive to caterers' needs and are less expensive than local retail markets but more expensive than meat distributors.
- Meat distributors buy meat directly from the meat packer and then sell it to off-premise caterers by the case. They do not break up case lots.

In meat purchasing, it is recommended that the caterer ask the date the animal was slaughtered, to determine freshness. This isn't the kind of detail most people find appetizing, but you'll have to get past that to ensure that you are ordering the freshest product. Experts recommend that no more than six days pass from slaughter to packing to shipping.

One extremely handy resource for caterers is the book *The Meat Buyer's Guide*, from the North American Meat Processors Association in Reston, Virginia. The latest edition, published in 2011, is a single volume that contains information in both English and Spanish. This pictorial guide will enable you and your kitchen staff to readily identify all cuts of beef, lamb, pork, and veal.

Purchasing Produce

Fresh fruits and vegetables are available from a variety of produce distributors, who buy directly from farming companies, produce packers, and local produce markets. These distributors deliver most orders that meet their minimum quantities, and they offer competitive prices. Most cities have at least one wholesale produce market where buyers may go and select fresh produce from a variety of wholesalers who display their products for viewing. Those who buy in this fashion can easily save 30 percent or more; however, the caterer must make time to shop and must have a vehicle in which to transport the produce. An alternative for the busy caterer is a *wagon-jobber*, who buys directly from the produce market based on the orders received from clients, and then delivers these orders to catering companies and other clients.

For more information on buying and using fruits and vegetables, visit the What's Cooking America website, which we have found to be very helpful.

Purchasing Fish and Seafood

Frozen fish and seafood are available from the major national wholesalers; fresh fish and seafood are sold by local companies that specialize almost exclusively in these products. Caterers located in cities that border oceans, gulfs, and rivers may buy fresh fish from local fishermen who sell their daily catches at the wharfs. It is always more desirable to use fresh rather than frozen fish when budgets permit, but it's hard to price—fish costs depend on the season, weather conditions, and overall demand. Some of the more popular fresh fish include salmon, swordfish, halibut, grouper, dolphin (the fish, not the mammal), haddock, snapper, trout (both freshwater and saltwater), bass (both freshwater and saltwater), tuna, and scrod (young cod). The popularity of fish varies from region to region, based on local preferences and availability.

Most off-premise caterers purchase at least some of their seafood in a frozen state—usually scallops, lobster tails, and shrimp. Whole Maine lobsters and stone crab claws are always purchased fresh. Sea scallops are sold by size, such as 20–30 count, which means there are 20 to 30 scallops, on average, per pound. Lobster tails are sold by size: 4- to 6-ounce tails or 6- to 8-ounce tails.

For most off-premise caterers, shrimp is the most frequently used seafood. Like scallops, shrimp are sold by size, also called *counts*. For example, "16–20 count" means that there are 16 to 20 shrimp per pound. The range goes from "U-10," under 10 per pound, the largest shrimp, to 300–500, the smallest. The most common product form is known as green, headless shrimp, which is raw, with head off and shell on. Off-premise caterers with limited facilities should investigate cooked shrimp for use in cold shrimp cocktails and hors d'oeuvres. There are some excellent products on the market that taste as good as fresh-cooked, cost no more, save labor, and are consistent. (Every off-premise caterer at one time or another has overcooked shrimp.) These shrimp are always cooked to perfection.

The editors of *Seafood Business* have a comprehensive guide to sourcing, buying, and preparation called *Seafood Handbook*.

Using Purchase Orders

A *purchase order* (or PO) is a written order form used by off-premise caterers to document and verify orders placed for food and supplies. It is most highly recommended as a means of control for large-volume caterers. Smaller firms may also wish to use purchase orders to keep track of their orders and receipts. Most firms at least have an in-house form listing their purchasing needs by categories that can be used as an order form, but these forms do not replace purchase orders as a form of control.

Purchase orders used to be four-copy forms (and some probably still are), although today's software allows a caterer to place most orders electronically. When printed copies are required, the distribution typically works as follows:

- Original copy   Mailed or faxed to supplier.
- Second copy   Sent to accounting for control.
- Third copy   Sent to Receiving Department and kept until foods arrive. Upon receipt of goods, this copy is signed and forwarded to accounting with the invoice.
- Fourth copy   Kept in Purchasing.

Purchase orders should always be numbered in advance to ensure control over the number of purchase orders issued by the company and to prevent employees from issuing unauthorized purchase orders. And, no matter how it is generated, a purchase order should include the following information:

- Date the order was placed.
- Payment terms.
- The supplier's name, address, and fax number.
- The off-premise caterer's name, address, and address for delivery.
- Description, quantity, and quoted unit cost of each item ordered.
- Blank column for the person receiving the merchandise to document the quantity of each item received.
- Quoted prices. These should be extended and totaled on the purchase order after the merchandise has been received, and compared with the invoice; discrepancies should be reconciled with the supplier immediately.
- Signature of the purchaser and that of the person receiving the merchandise

Exhibit 11.2 is a sample purchase order form. Any office supply store will have purchase order forms already made up, or you can easily create your own template on a computer. Another good source for information about purchase orders and other purchasing functions is *Purchasing: Selection and Procurement for the Hospitality Industry*, 8th Edition, by Andrew H. Feinstein and John M. Stefanelli (Hoboken, NJ: John Wiley & Sons, 2011), from which our sample product specs were taken.

EXHIBIT 11.2 Sample Purchase Order Form

PURCHASE ORDER NUMBER 0001

ORDERED BY:
ABC OFF-PREMISE CATERING FIRM
MAIN STREET
ANYWHERE, USA
FAX NUMBER

ORDERED FROM:
BEST SUPPLIER
MAIN STREET
ANYWHERE, USA
FAX NUMBER

ORDER DATE _____   DELIVERY DATE _____   PAYMENT TERMS _____

QUANTITY ORDERED	DESCRIPTION	QUANTITY RECEIVED	UNIT COST	TOTAL COST
		GRAND TOTAL		

SIGNATURE OF AUTHORIZED PURCHASER _____
RECEIVED AS NOTED ABOVE _____

(RECEIVING AGENT)

Tips for Effective Purchasing

Generally speaking, the purchaser wants to pay as little as possible, the seller wants to receive as much as possible, and the agreed-upon price is somewhere between these two extremes. Market prices for food items are based on the general supply and demand for any given product—as Christmas approaches, the demand for meats may increase while supplies either remain constant or decrease, resulting in higher meat prices.

There are a few good overall practices that should result in lower food purchasing costs.

Edible-Portion Cost. A sharp caterer realizes that the lowest price is not always the least expensive. Think about it in terms of an item's true cost per serving, or *edible-portion cost*. For example, when you purchase meats, the least expensive cuts also contain more fat and bones and must be trimmed, which involves a labor expense to perform the additional butchering chores. Other inexpensive cuts may be too tough to eat or take too much time (and waste energy) in slow-cooking them to compensate. You may be wiser to buy cuts that are trimmed of fat and bone and are ready to cook, thus saving labor and energy expenses and resulting in a lower edible-portion cost.

The Make-or-Buy Decision. Off-premise caterers should carefully analyze their menus and determine which items to make in-house and which items to buy from suppliers. This question applies to foods like pasta, breads, desserts, mayonnaise, dressings, and some sauces. For example, the cost of ingredients to make bread and pasta is a fraction of the price paid for prepared products; however, other factors enter into the make-or-buy decision:

- Is the necessary equipment available to make the product?
- If equipment is not available, what is the cost to purchase it?
- Is there skilled labor available? What is the cost?
- What are the quality considerations? Will a product made in-house be of superior quality to that which can be purchased?
- Is this product so unusual that the only alternative is to prepare it in-house since no supplier handles it?
- How does producing products in-house relate to the overall operation?
- What impact will preparing the product in-house have on other commissary functions?

Competitive Bidding. It is critical to obtain competitive bids from at least three suppliers for most purchases, as well as to buy from the lowest bidder who meets your written specifications for a product. Exhibit 11.3 is a sample competitive bidding form for produce. Many caterers become comfortable dealing with certain suppliers, and soon

EXHIBIT 11.3 Quote Sheet

PREPARED BY _____

DATE _____

ITEM	GRADE	UNIT OF PURCHASE	PRICE QUOTES		
APPLES, EXTRA FANCY, 88 COUNT		DOZEN/CASE			
AVOCADOS, HASS, 48 COUNT		DOZEN/CASE			
BANANAS (40# PER CASE)		POUND/CASE			
BROCCOLI, CALIFORNIA, 14 COUNT		POUND/CASE			
CABBAGE, RED, LARGE HEADS		POUND/50# BAG			
CABBAGE, WHITE, LARGE HEADS		POUND/50# BAG			
CARROTS, CALIFORNIA, JUMBO		POUND/50# BAG			
CAULIFLOWER, CALIFORNIA, 12 PER CASE		POUND/CASE			
CELERY, CALIFORNIA, 24 COUNT		STALK/CASE			
CUCUMBERS, SUPER SELECT		POUND/BUSHEL			
EGGPLANT, FANCY		POUND/BUSHEL			
GARLIC, JUMBO (30# PER CASE)		POUND/CASE			
GRAPEFRUIT, PINK, FLORIDA, 18 COUNT		DOZEN/CASE			
GRAPES, RED, CALIFORNIA, EXFANCY		POUND/CASE			
GRAPES, WHITE, CALIFORNIA, EXFANCY		POUND/CASE			
LEEKS, CALIFORNIA		BUNCH/CASE (24 BUNCHES/CASE)			
LEMONS, SUNKIST, US#1, 165/CASE		DOZEN/CASE			
LETTUCE, LEAF, DOLE CALIFORNIA, FANCY		HEAD/CASE			
LETTUCE, ICEBERG, DOLE CALIFORNIA, FANCY		HEAD/CASE			
LETTUCE, ROMAINE, DOLE CALIFORNIA, FANCY		HEAD/CASE			
LIMES, US#1, 150–160/CASE		DOZEN/CASE			
MELONS, CANTALOUPE, FANCY, 15/CASE		EACH/CASE			
MELONS, HONEYDEW, FANCY, 15/CASE		EACH/CASE			
MUSHROOMS, US#1, WASHED, 10# BASKET		POUND/BASKET			
ONIONS, JUMBO, SPANISH		POUND/50# BAG			
ORANGES, CALIFORNIA, 56/CASE		DOZEN/CASE			
PARSLEY, CALIFORNIA		BUNCH/DOZEN			
PEARS, ANJOU		POUND			
PEPPERS, GREEN BELL		POUND/CASE			
PEPPERS, RED		POUND/CASE			
PINEAPPLES, DOLE, 7/CASE		EACH/CASE			
POTATOES, BOILING		POUND/50# BAG			
POTATOES, IDAHO, 90/CASE		POUND/CASE			
RADISHES, POLY BAG		BAG/DOZEN			
SCALLIONS, BUNCH		BUNCH/DOZEN			
SHALLOTS		POUND/5# BAG			
SPINACH, CALIFORNIA, FLAT LEAF		POUND/10# CASE			
TOMATOES, VINE RIPENED, 536		POUND/18# BOX			
WATERCRESS		BUNCH/DOZEN			
WATERMELON, EXTRA LARGE, JUBILEE		EACH			

they stop obtaining bids. Once preferred suppliers realize that there is no bidding for business, they are free to increase their prices. Competitive bids will help keep food costs under control.

Focus on Center-of-the-Plate Items. Because time is money, it makes sense to spend more time negotiating prices for the "major" items—seafood, meat, and poultry—than for salt or sugar (unless, of course, you're making potato chips by the ton or candy by the truckload).

Determine Par Stock. After tracking your usage of food items over a period of time, you will become familiar with the product flow in storage, which enables you to determine the minimum amount of each product that you must have on hand for a specific time period. If your par stock level of yellow onions is two cases and there's one in storage, you'll need to order another case—no more, no less. Another term for par stock is a *build-to amount*—that is, you have a number in mind and you "build up to" that number with your order.

Can You Do Better? In a purchasing situation, it never hurts to ask certain suppliers if they can do better. This practice gives suppliers an opportunity to offer an extra incentive or give a discount. The worst case is that the supplier will say no, but you may be surprised at how frequently suppliers will negotiate a better deal. Remember, your business and trust are valuable commodities to them.

Less Service, Lower Price. Certain suppliers will offer lower prices as long as deliveries are limited to certain days. Some paper goods suppliers offer lower prices but deliver only once or twice a month. Frequently, supermarkets and wholesale clubs offer better prices than suppliers who deliver. An example is the price of soft drinks, which are invariably less expensive at supermarkets and wholesale clubs. Off-premise caterers must determine if the savings are worth the time spent shopping for and transporting these bargain-priced items.

Less Expensive, No Adverse Effect on Quality. Purchasers should buy the least expensive product that will not reduce the quality of the dish to be served. Remember those broken shrimp pieces for dishes like shrimp salad? They're less expensive than whole shrimp and the end result is just as tasty. Random-packed boneless chicken breasts (which are not of uniform weight) can be used for many chicken dishes, rather than breasts of uniform size, which are significantly more expensive. Ungraded tomatoes can be used for marinara sauce instead of paying extra for those that are graded.

Seasonality. Caterers and chefs should know the seasonality of particular items. For example, there are times during the year when it is less expensive to use limes than lemons. In the late fall, fresh strawberries are expensive and generally not of good quality.

Pay with Cash. Certain suppliers offer discounts for cash purchases.

Price Trend Speculation. Some off-premise caterers who use large quantities of certain items become successful at speculating on prices. Let's say you expect to use 2,000 pounds of shrimp in the next three months. If you have the cash flow to make the purchase and the freezer space to store the shrimp, you can consider buying all 2,000 pounds now if you learn that the price is expected to increase.

Purchase in Larger Units. Larger units of purchase are usually less expensive than smaller units. Flour sold in 100-pound bags is less expensive per pound than in 10-pound bags. However, be careful not to overbuy. You can't afford spoilage and high inventory levels.

Special Promotions. Frequently, suppliers offer special promotions that can result in significant savings. Also ask your suppliers for value-added services, such as marketing and promotion ideas, recipe and presentation suggestions, and so on. This, too, is part of building a feeling of partnership that, in turn, builds business for both caterer and supplier.

Go to the Market. Significant savings are available to those who shop at wholesale clubs, local volume-purchase markets, and farmers' markets. Caterers who do this need time and transportation, but many report purchase savings of 50 percent or more.

Take Advantage of Rebate Programs. Many major brands offer rebate programs. These are available through distributors, as well as through such outlets as Restaurant Depot.

Many caterers are not aware of these programs because sales reps are reluctant to take on the additional paperwork.

Buy Generic Products. Many generic products are produced by the same manufacturers who produce the brand names but at a fraction of the cost.

Receiving

In purchasing, the term *receiving* means accepting the shipments you have ordered for your business. It requires both verifying the quantity and quality of every incoming order and checking that the price you are being charged for it is correct.

In most cases, this means the person who orders merchandise should not be the same person who receives it, unless he or she is the sole owner of the catering company. There are just too many opportunities for collusion between the purchaser and the supplier when the purchaser is also the receiver. A purchaser may indicate that certain goods were received when they were not, and then receive a kickback or other reward from the supplier; "extra" goods can "disappear" without being accounted for on purchase orders; and so on. It is essential to have at least two people involved in the all-important receiving function.

Many off-premise caterers make the mistake of not employing a qualified receiving employee—qualified, that is, to be sure that the goods that were ordered are actually the goods that are now being delivered, with no scrimping on quantity or quality. The receiving person may have other duties (not purchasing) but should be thoroughly trained in product knowledge by the chef, catering company owner, or purchaser. When in doubt about the quality of a product, the receiver should consult with the chef, owner, or manager before signing for receipt of the merchandise because it is always easier to reconcile problems with the supplier's delivery driver present. The driver can return the inferior or incorrect product, rather than leave it at the commissary, where it must be stored or could even be used in error.

Those who receive food, supplies, and rental equipment should be extremely particular about checking and inspecting for quality and quantity. Successful caterers do not accept products that do not meet their standards. Even when receiving rental equipment, they check all items to make sure that the correct quantity is being delivered. They open containers and inspect glassware and china for cleanliness, chips, and cracks; flatware for corrosion or tarnish; chairs for cleanliness and stability (any cracked wooden chair legs, or missing screws, nuts, or bolts?); linens for snags and tears; and portable dance floors and stages for missing pieces, rough edges, and other unsafe conditions.

There are two reasons for being so particular: First, you expect to get exactly what you ordered, and in good condition. Second, after an event, you don't want the supplier to charge the catering company for causing damage to goods that were already damaged upon arrival. Thus, the receiver can never be too particular. For this reason, deliveries should always be scheduled during slow periods of business, so that all products can be carefully examined, weighed when necessary, and quickly moved to their proper storage areas.

In many cases, correct receiving can only be accomplished with the right equipment. The commissary must have a designated receiving area, usually a loading dock that can accommodate delivery trucks. Receiving requirements include:

- Sturdy scales that are large enough to weigh items that arrive in bulk.
- A variety of thermometers and temperature probes to check temperatures of incoming fresh foods.
- *Pallets* (low, raised wooden platforms) on which cases or boxes can be stacked and stored. Pallets keep products off ground level and can be moved with a pallet jack or, in larger operations, a small forklift.
- Utility carts and hand trucks for moving small stacks of cases.
- Extra boxes and bags in case questionable items must be stored and kept out of inventory until a supplier can be contacted.
- Shelves and/or metro racks on which to organize and stack items.
- Marking pens. If you need to write a date in prominent letters on an incoming package or case of perishable food, do so.

The temperatures of foods received in refrigerated shipments should always be checked. Chilled products should be at least 45 degrees Fahrenheit and frozen products below 0 degrees. Frozen seafood should be checked for excessive glazing (the ice encrusted on products like shrimp and lobster). Excessively glazed products should be returned because your business does not include paying premium prices for frozen water, which increases the cost per pound of these already expensive commodities.

When receiving produce, inspect for ripeness, color, and cleanliness, as well as bruises, spoilage, and other adverse factors. Counts of produce items (like lemons and limes) are very important, and caterers should frequently count to ensure proper sizing. Items that do not meet or exceed standards should be returned, and the receiver must insist that their supplier deliver the proper quality in time for the event. Of course, the best indication of produce quality is taste.

Off-premise caterers must first weigh all meat, fish, seafood, poultry, and any other product sold by weight. Often, short weights can result in direct losses on a catered event or perhaps even running out of food. Packing ice should be removed before weighing poultry and fish (which are usually packed in ice). Short weights should be corrected by either a credit or delivery of additional product. After weighing, meats should be inspected to ensure that they comply with specifications (your own written specs and those documented in *The Meat Buyer's Guide*).

All meats should have been federally inspected, and the supplier should confirm their USDA stamp or verification if necessary. Meats that arrive in dirty, torn, damaged, or broken wrapping or boxes may be contaminated and should not be accepted. Any that smell sour or rancid should be rejected. Meat texture should be firm and elastic. Any meat that feels slimy, sticky, or dry should be rejected.

Fresh poultry should be kept below 45 degrees Fahrenheit and should be packed in crushed ice. Poultry that is purple or greenish in color should not be accepted, nor should any that smells bad, has darkened wing tips, or has soft, flabby, sticky flesh.

Once fresh fish is weighed, it should be inspected for freshness, appearance, damaged flesh, and other signs of quality. Fresh fish should always be packed in crushed ice and kept between 32 and 45 degrees Fahrenheit. Signs of freshness include clear eyes; bright skin; tight scales; bright red gills; firm, elastic flesh; and a fresh, not "fishy," odor.

Fresh and frozen seafood must be checked for quality and proper sizing. Often, the size on the label is not what happens to be in the package. For example, 5-pound boxes of raw frozen headless shrimp that are graded 16–20 count should contain between 80 and 100 shrimp per box, with an average of 90 per box. This number is obtained by multiplying 5 pounds (in the box) times the minimum, average, and maximum counts of shrimp per pound (16, 18, and 20, respectively). These counts are important because they ultimately determine menu costs and selling prices for shrimp. If there are too few shrimp in the box, it may mean that the shrimp are larger than they should be or that when they were frozen, too much water was frozen along with them. In this instance, the caterer's actual cost per shrimp will be more than specified. If the shrimp are too small, the costs will be lower per shrimp, but the client will not receive the size of shrimp promised by the caterer.

The standard pack for green headless shrimp (*green* is the term for any raw shrimp in the shell) is a 5-pound net weight block. With ice and packaging, the gross weight is generally 6 to 7 pounds. Two-kilo blocks are also sold, and off-premise caterers should be aware of paying for 5 pounds when they are receiving only 2 kilos (4.4 pounds). Cooked, individually quick-frozen (IQF) shrimp are packed in plastic bags weighing from 1 to 30 pounds, and they should also be checked for weight and proper sizing upon receipt.

Milk and dairy products should be checked for temperature (40 degrees Fahrenheit), expiration dates, smell, and appearance. Cheese should be rejected if it is discolored, excessively moldy, or dried out. Cheese rinds should be undamaged.

Eggs should be checked for cracks and excessive dirt. Check eggs' temperature (it should be 40 degrees Fahrenheit) by breaking one and measuring the yolk temperature. Acceptable eggs will have firm yolks and no noticeable odor, and the whites will cling to the yolks.

Frozen foods should be checked for signs of thawing and refreezing: large ice crystals, ice at the bottom of a carton, and deformed containers. All frozen foods should be received at temperatures below 0 degrees Fahrenheit.

Canned foods should be checked for leakage, broken seals, dents along seams, rust, and missing labels—not only upon receipt, but again before using. Dry foods, such as sugar, cereal, flour, and dried beans, should be completely dry when received, and their packages must not have any broken seals or holes.

A common receiving discrepancy is a difference between the invoiced amount and the amount received. For instance, the invoice is for an order of 70 pounds of Choice beef tenderloin, but the incoming package weighs only 68 pounds. This must be noted on the invoice, initialed by the receiving agent and the delivery driver, and immediately reported to the supplier for proper credit.

Some suppliers will not refund or replace spoiled or damaged items if the receiver signed a purchase order accepting them without noting the discrepancy on the invoice. Carelessness in this area is very costly and cannot be tolerated. (Two pounds of tenderloin at $6 per pound is $12, so more than $600 per year would be saved by proper verification if this discrepancy occurred once a week.) There are many similar situations, and your receiving person must have a combination of people skills and professional knowledge to handle them without alienating the suppliers.

Receiving personnel should be required to submit all invoices daily to the bookkeeping office, because discrepancies can be resolved more easily as they occur, or within a day or two. Trying to reconstruct what occurred on December 1, when it is January 10 of the following year, is virtually impossible.

Storage

The online supplier Food Service Warehouse (www.foodservicewarehouse.com) says that most food waste problems could be eliminated if commercial kitchen operators would adopt this simple mantra: "Label, date, rotate, and consolidate." We heartily agree.

To that end, we have adapted the following storage guidelines for foodservice businesses from the National Assessment Institute's *Handbook of Safe Food Service Management,* Second Edition (Upper Saddle River, NJ: Prentice Hall, 1997). Off-premise caterers should comply with all of them to meet normal sanitation and food-handling standards. In addition, we suggest you create a shelf-life chart to be posted in your walk-in cooler and freezer, with the numbers of days common items can be stored safely. Similar charts come in handy for produce and baked goods too, as reminders to the staff to minimize waste.

Refrigerated Foods

HACCP guidelines require that refrigerator temperatures be kept at or below 40 degrees Fahrenheit. (The initials stand for Hazard Analysis Critical Control Points; the guidelines are discussed further in Chapter 12.) Place thermometers in several areas of the refrigerator where they can be easily read and checked often. Check the internal temperatures of refrigerated foods on a regular basis to make sure that the foods are kept at 40 degrees Fahrenheit or lower. In addition, follow these guidelines:

- Always refrigerate fresh meat, poultry, and fish.
- Cover stored foods to prevent contamination from other products or direct contact with refrigerator shelves.
- Store fresh fish in crushed ice and keep it well drained.
- If possible, provide separate refrigerators for different types of foods. If different foods must be stored in the same unit, store meats, fish, and dairy foods in the coldest part.

- To prevent cross contamination, be sure that prepared foods are stored above raw foods.
- Do not store packaged food or wrapped sandwiches where they can get wet.
- Do not overload the refrigerator. This can raise the temperature of the entire unit to unsafe levels.
- Do not store refrigerated foods on the floor of a walk-in refrigerator.
- Store food packages so that cold air can circulate around all surfaces of the containers.

Frozen Foods

- Keep the temperature range for frozen foods between −10 and 0 degrees Fahrenheit.
- Never thaw and refreeze frozen foods.
- Do not thaw foods at room temperature.
- Keep frozen foods in moisture-proof packaging.
- Use the *first in, first out* (FIFO) rule, also discussed in Chapter 12.
- Store frozen foods to allow for air circulation between packages.
- Do not freeze large quantities of unfrozen foods. This can raise the temperature of the entire unit and damage the foods being stored.
- Defrost freezers regularly.
- Be sure that foods do not thaw during the defrost cycle of self-defrosting freezers.

Dry Goods

- Apply the FIFO rule here too.
- Keep foods in dry storage tightly covered and protected from contamination.
- Remember that cereals deteriorate rapidly, as do canned foods containing products that are high in acid, such as tomatoes.
- Keep these storage areas well ventilated and well lit.
- Store foods at least 6 inches off the floor in a way that allows adequate air circulation.
- Store items on ventilated shelves.
- Install window coverings or frosted glass to reduce heat and exposure to light.

- Cover all interior surfaces with easy-to-clean, corrosion-resistant materials.
- Do not allow smoking, eating, or drinking in dry-storage areas. Check with the local health department for specific rules.
- Do not store trash in dry-storage areas.
- Seal walls and baseboards to keep out pests. Keeping the area clean and well maintained will also discourage pests.

Inventory

Dozens of products are received and used by a catering company every day, and it is important to track them for many reasons: to determine quantities for the next order, to budget and forecast based on usage patterns, and to prevent theft, to name a few.

Inventory is the process of counting the items in storage, and it should be performed weekly. If possible, have the same two people perform this task. (There should be more than one person responsible for inventory counts, as an obvious security precaution.) This way, they become familiar with the process, as well as the location of items in your dry and refrigerated storage areas, and the task can be performed more quickly.

Taking inventory is a labor-intensive process in which items are counted by hand and by sight, but your accounting software will include forms that you can customize (see Exhibit 11.4), so the inventory team knows what they are looking for and how many of each item the system lists as currently in stock. If the theoretical count (on the list) and the actual count don't match up, this is known as a *variance*. There are multiple reasons for variances, from sloppy receiving practices to people who grab goods from storage without checking them out (ignoring a control system that may be in place), to theft. The latter, unfortunately, is all too common. Your inventory system should also include a way to account for wasted food, from a burnt steak to dairy products that went bad before they were used. Observant kitchen managers, committed to minimizing food waste, are a critical component of a good inventory process.

As a new business, one of your inventory-related goals should be to get an idea of how long each item sits in storage from the time it is delivered until the time it is used, a time period referred to as a product's *inventory turnover rate*. You want to have sufficient supplies in stock to meet current catering orders and a little to spare "just in case" but not too much stock sitting around. It takes up space and means you have tied up capital paying in advance for things you aren't using.

EXHIBIT 11.4 An inventory document can be 50 pages or more. This is a single sample page

LOCATION	COMP	Item Code	ITEM & DESCRIPTION	PK SIZE	Qty	Cost	Total
A1		4862967	PASTA-CAPELLINI	CS		$25.20	$0.00
A1		7981251	PASTA-SPAGHETTI	CS		$25.63	$0.00
A2		5309547	PASTA-BOWTIE	CS		$15.29	$0.00
A2		4913117	PASTA-ELBOW	CS		$26.85	$0.00
A2		4933164	PASTA-LASAGNA RIDGED	CS		$19.62	$0.00
A2		2603496	PASTA-ORZO LABELLA	EA		$2.21	$0.00
A2		5776893	PASTA-PENNE	CS		$23.46	$0.00
A2		4786943	PASTA-WIDE NOODLES KOSHER	CS		$1.67	$0.00
A2		5807094	POLENTA BERRETTA	LB		$1.71	$0.00
A3		4862843	PASTA-FETTUCINE LABELLA	CS		$22.39	$0.00
A3		4862959	PASTA-LINGUINE	CS		$24.55	$0.00
A3		5559604	PASTA-OCCHEITTA	EA		$1.88	$0.00
A1		4246336	CRACKERS-CARRS	CS		$4.38	$0.00
A1		6700637	CRACKERS-LAVOSH	CS		$50.17	$0.00
A1		1841188	VEG-SWEET YAMS	CS		$36.26	$0.00
B2		1079193	VEGETABLE-JICAMA ROOT	LB		$1.20	$0.00
A4		1039304	VEGETABLE- SWEET POTATOES	CS		$36.85	$0.00
A5		8313967	VEGETABLE-ONIONS-RED	LB		$0.67	$0.00
A5		8313918	VEGETABLE-ONIONS-YELLOW	LB		$0.47	$0.00
A5		8485013	VEGETABLE-POTATOES-RED-B	CS		$39.31	$0.00
A5		1008465	VEGETABLE-POTATOES-RUSSETT (90 ct)	CS		$21.88	$0.00
A5		990960	VEGETABLE-SQUASH BUTTERNUT	LB		$0.61	$0.00
A5		1450204	VEGETABLE-YUKON GOLD	CS		$45.10	$0.00
B1		3236569	STUFFING-CORNBREAD MIX	EA		$10.49	$0.00
B2		3236569	STUFFING-TRADITIONAL	LB		$10.49	$0.00
B2		3616455	COUSCOUS-MIDEAST	CS		$17.59	$0.00
B2		5685441	COUSCOUS-MORROCAN 6/36OZ	EA		$5.23	$0.00
B2		5534011	DEMI-GLAZE KNOR SWISS	EA		$16.55	$0.00
B2		3616620	WHEAT-CRACKED BULGUR	LB		$1.47	$0.00
B3		4341954	HONEY 5#	EA		$11.50	$0.00
B3		7359627	LENTILS-BLACK BELUGA	LB		$3.57	$0.00
B3		7420151	RICE-ARBORIO SUPERFINO	LB		$1.69	$0.00
B4		4939302	RICE-BAMBOO	LB		$5.44	$0.00
B4		5364559	RICE-BASMATI	LB		$1.33	$0.00
B4		Indian Harv	RICE-BLACK	LB		$6.38	$0.00

(Continued)

EXHIBIT 11.4   An inventory document can be 50 pages or more. This is a single sample page (*Continued*)

LOCATION	COMP	Item Code	ITEM & DESCRIPTION	PK SIZE	Qty	Cost	Total
B4		8402302	RICE-BROWN	LB		$0.60	$0.00
B4		Indian Harv	RICE-CONFETTI BLEND ½#	BAG		$7.50	$0.00
B4		Indian Harv	RICE-JASMINE	LB		$0.76	$0.00
B3		5848056	RICE-LONGGRAIN & WILD BLND	EA		$7.46	$0.00
B4		CHIEFTAIN	RICE-MIDWEST MEDLEY ½#	BAG		$7.80	$0.00
B4		4671368	RICE-PARBOILED	LB		$0.80	$0.00
B4		CHIEFTAIN	RICE-SPRING BLEND	BAG		$7.40	$0.00
B3		7657451	RICE-SUSHI BOTAN	LB		$0.46	$0.00
34		CHIEFTAIN	RICE-QUINOA	LB		$8.20	$0.00
BIN 1		5495460	BREADING-PANKO	CS		$4.50	$0.00
C2		923MUIR	CHILI-CHILI ANCHO (PACILLA) DRY	LB		$9.71	$0.00
C2		945MUIR	CHILI-GUAJILLO DRY	LB		$8.47	$0.00
C2		956MUIR	CHILI-NM DRY	LB		$8.96	$0.00
H3		4971038	BAKING SODA	EA		$1.00	$0.00
H3		4032991	CORNSTARCH	LB		$0.87	$0.00
C2		6040760	SALT-KOSHER	EA		$1.96	$0.00
C2		4540373	SALT-TABLE IODIZED	EA		$0.22	$0.00
C2			SPICE-ASIAN SPICED SEA SALT	EA		$12.17	$0.00
C2		8532810	SPICE-GARLIC ROSEMARY RUB	EA		$8.82	$0.00
C2		8487698	SPICE-SMOKEY CHILI RUB	EA		$12.41	$0.00
							$0.00
C2		4590121	SPICE-BAY LEAVES	EA		$15.34	$0.00
C2		5229299	SPICE-BLACK PEPPER CRACKED	LB		$64.90	$0.00
C2		8932576	SPICE-CARAWAY WHOLE	EA		$9.06	$0.00
C2		5228499	SPICE-CELERY SEED GRND	EA		$9.99	$0.00
C2		5228564	SPICE-CHILI POWDER (20 oz)	EA		$10.60	$0.00
C2		5228655	SPICE-CLOVES GRND	EA		$21.00	$0.00
C2		5228655	SPICE-CLOVE WHOLE	EA		$21.00	$0.00
C2		5074661	SPICE-CRAB BOIL	EA		$1.42	$0.00
C2		5228697	SPICE-CREAM OF TARTAR	EA		$16.44	$0.00
C2		5228770	SPICE-DILL WEED	EA		$13.50	$0.00
C2		5228796	SPICE-FENNEL SEED WHOLE	EA		$12.58	$0.00
C2		8941965	SPICE-GUMBO FILE	EA		$1.83	$0.00
C2		9806480	SPICE-LEMON PEPPER	EA		$12.38	$0.00
C2			SPICE-MED SPICED SEA SALT	PK		$12.17	$0.00
K-SPICE		9765561	SPICE-MESQUITE BBQ SEASONING	EA		$11.97	$0.00
C2		6923874	SPICE-MONTREAL CHICKEN SEASONING	EA		$11.11	$0.00

LOCATION	COMP	Item Code	ITEM & DESCRIPTION	PK SIZE	Qty	Cost	Total
C2		5229067	SPICE-NUTMEG GRND	EA		$17.14	$0.00
C2		5229109	SPICE-ONION GRAN.	EA		$9.25	$0.00
C2		5156068	SPICE-OREGANO WHL	EA		$18.90	$0.00
C2		5229265	SPICE-PARSLEY DRIED	EA		$15.64	$0.00
C2		Shriebers	SPICE-PEPPER CHERE	EA		$7.46	$0.00
C2		5517073	SPICE-PEPPERCORN MELANGE	EA		$22.80	$0.00
C2		5229562	SPICE-POULTRY SEASONING	EA		$13.86	$0.00
C2		5229612	SPICE-ROSEMARY (1LB)	EA		$9.89	$0.00
C2		7228943	SPICE-ROTISSERIE CHICKEN	EA		$13.14	$0.00
C2		5229653	SPICE-SAGE RUBBED	EA		$12.16	$0.00
C2		5229737	SPICE-SESAME SEEDS	EA		$37.20	$0.00
C2		4825192	SPICE-SMOKED BLACK PEPPER	EA		$26.36	$0.00
C2		6202638	SPICE-SMOKED SEA SALT (35 OZ)	EA		$36.25	$0.00
		9798323	OIL-OLIVE OIL BLENDED 80/20	EA		$13.51	$0.00
		5005418	PEPPER-CHERRY MILD	EA		$13.89	$0.00
		4249322	PEPPERONCINI GREEK GOLDEN	EA		$7.95	$0.00
C3		4002499	DRESSING-COLE SLAW	EA		$14.50	$0.00
C3		6172118	KETCHUP-FCY JUG	EA		$5.73	$0.00
C3		6600157	MUSTARD-DIJON W/WINE TIN	EA		$31.01	$0.00
C3		6206551	MUSTARD-JUG PREPARED	EA		$4.67	$0.00
C3		4064986	MUSTARD-WHOLE GRAIN TIN	EA		$18.45	$0.00
C3		5778071	SAUCE-BBQ	EA		$13.68	$0.00
D4		4069373	VINEGAR-APPLE CIDER	EA		$7.19	$0.00
D4		5889654	VINEGAR-BALSAMIC 2/5LTR	EA		$34.46	$0.00
D4		651828	VINEGAR-BALSAMIC GLAZE	EA		$6.08	$0.00
C3		5492640	VINEGAR CHAMPAGNE	EA		$20.66	$0.00
D2		4113049	VINEGAR-DIST. WHITE	EA		$4.56	$0.00
D4		4042479	VINEGAR-RED WINE	EA		$9.08	$0.00
E5		4086195	VINEGAR- RICE SEASONED	GL		$11.55	$0.00
C4		4007621	KITCHEN BOUQUET	EA		$9.60	$0.00
C4		7783467	SEASONING-LIQUID SMOKE	EA		$17.36	$0.00
D2		3554490	ARTICHOKE HEARTS	EA		$13.87	$0.00
F1		2503597	GRAPE LEAVES	EA		$9.71	$0.00
E2		Smith's	CACTUS STRIP NOPOLITT0 12/28OZ	EA		$2.33	$0.00
E2		4432068	CAPERS-BERRIES	EA		$4.70	$0.00
E2		1743681	CAPERS-NON-PAREILS	EA		$8.53	$0.00
E2		4163788	CHUTNEY-MAJOR GRAY	EA		$6.01	$0.00
E2		4146668	COCONUT CREAM	EA		$2.03	$0.00
E2		5525639	COCONUT-MILK 24/13.5OZ	EA		$1.83	$0.00

(Continued)

EXHIBIT 11.4 An inventory document can be 50 pages or more. This is a single sample page (*Continued*)

LOCATION	COMP	Item Code	ITEM & DESCRIPTION	PK SIZE	Qty	Cost	Total
E2		9695560	GINGER-GRATED (6.7oz)	EA		$3.16	$0.00
E2		5097761	HEARTS OF PALM (#5 CAN)	EA		$6.98	$0.00
E3		5757091	CHIPOTLE IN ADOBE SAUCE 12/7OZ	EA		$2.24	$0.00
E3		4628087	PEPPERS-PIQUILLO PEPPERS	EA		$17.91	$0.00
E3		6179758	PEPPERS-ROASTED RED	EA		$8.70	$0.00
E3		1126655	PEPPERS-ROASTED YELLOW	EA		$3.41	$0.00
C4		4007894	WORCESTERSHIRE SAUCE	GL		$4.73	$0.00
E3		9153982	SAUCE SOY JADE MT 4/1GAL	GL		$9.38	$0.00
E3		9153982	SAUCE SOY SWEET ABC	EA		$7.98	$0.00
E3		4356382	SOY SAUCE DISPENSER BOTTLE	EA		$18.75	$0.00
G4		5985759	TAHINI	EA		$8.03	$0.00
E3		4280343	TOMATO PASTE	EA		$1.63	$0.00
E4		5882717	CHILES-WHOLE GREEN (2.5LB)	EA		$9.36	$0.00
E4		4007530	SAUCE 57 5OZ	EA		$1.87	$0.00
E4		4007498	SAUCE-A-1 5OZ	EA		$2.10	$0.00
E4		6984306	SAUCE-FISH	EA		$1.71	$0.00
A4		4948741	TEMPURA BATTER MIX	EA		$5.19	$0.00
E5		5354881	SAUCE-CHILI SAUCE 24OZ	EA		$3.20	$0.00
E6		5881776	SAUCE-HOISIN	EA		$6.19	$0.00
E5		8357818	SAUCE-HOT SAUCE (FRANK'S)	EA		$11.58	$0.00
E5		9158908	SAUCE-MOLE BASE 12/8.25OZ	EA		$2.63	$0.00
E6		3252178	SAUCE-OYSTER	EA		$6.82	$0.00
E5		5344031	SAUCE-PLUM	EA		$9.57	$0.00
E5		6770440	SAUCE-SRIACHA CHILI	EA		$2.84	$0.00
E6		539664	SAUCE-STIR-FRY	EA		$11.41	$0.00
E5		4936530	SAUCE-SWEET & SOUR	EA		$7.58	$0.00
E5		228510	SAUCE-SWEET CHILI SWT THAI6/2.2KG	EA		$9.78	$0.00
E5		4232682	SAUCE-TERIYAKI GLAZE	EA		$6.78	$0.00
E6		4014304	TUNA-WHITE SOLID 24/12OZ	EA		$3.70	$0.00
E6		4181947	WINE-MARSALA COOKING	EA		$11.35	$0.00
B3			ASIAN-BAMBOO SHOOTS	EA		$3.78	$0.00
E5			ASIAN-CHESTNUT WATER SLC	EA		$2.73	$0.00
B3		5343405	ASIAN-NOODLE-RICE STK MED	EA		$1.82	$0.00
B3		5160108	ASIAN-NORI-SEAWEED	EA		$6.38	$0.00
E5				EA			$0.00
B3		7926575	ASIAN-SOY WRAPS	CS		$57.54	$0.00
B2		Asian Mark	ASIAN-SPRING ROLL SKINS	EA		$1.00	$0.00

LOCATION	COMP	Item Code	ITEM & DESCRIPTION	PK SIZE	Qty	Cost	Total
B3		4816007	ASIAN-WASABI POWDER	EA		$6.36	$0.00
#10 CANS		4062097	APPLE SAUCE FANCY	EA		$5.42	$0.00
#10 CANS		3686979	APRICOT HALVES	EA		$6.66	$0.00
#10 CANS		4850954	BAMBOO SHOOTS STRIPS	EA		$3.79	$0.00
#10 CANS			BEETS-SLICED	EA		$7.48	$0.00
#10 CANS		8342602	BEANS-BAKED	EA		$5.44	$0.00
#10 CANS		5844220	BEANS-BLACK	EA		$4.84	$0.00
#10 CANS		4062337	BEANS-GARBANZO	EA		$4.09	$0.00
#10 CANS		4062360	BEANS-GREAT NORTHERN	EA		$4.18	$0.00
#10 CANS		4014973	BEANS-KIDNEY RED	EA		$5.19	$0.00
#10 CANS		5882311	BEANS-REFRIED VEGETARIAN	EA		$5.70	$0.00
#10 CANS		4306833	CARAMEL TOPPING	EA		$8.12	$0.00
#10 CANS		5050729	CHOCOLATE SYRUP (Hersheys)	EA		$7.71	$0.00
#10 CANS		4107520	CORN KERNELS	EA		$4.74	$0.00
#10 CANS		5393600	DARK SWEET CHERRIES	EA		$10.82	$0.00
#10 CANS		4184461	GRAPE JELLY	EA		$9.27	$0.00
#10 CANS		3435823	HOMINY-WHITE	EA		$4.61	$0.00
#10 CANS		4904223	MALLO CREAM TOPPING	EA		$4.78	$0.00
#10 CANS		5989538	MARINARA SAUCE	EA		$5.91	$0.00
#10 CANS		4334082	MARMALADE-ORANGE	EA		$12.05	$0.00
#10 CANS		103564	OLIVES-SLICED	EA		$10.13	$0.00
#10 CANS		6060048	OLIVES-WHOLE	EA		$11.02	$0.00
#10 CANS		3548385	ORANGES MANDARIN	EA		$7.13	$0.00
#10 CANS		4261889	PEARS-SLICED	EA		$5.90	$0.00
#10 CANS		6346134	PIE FILLING-CHERRY	EA		$18.61	$0.00
#10 CANS		4205555	PRESERVES-APRICOT	EA		$19.60	$0.00
#10 CANS		4341269	PRESERVES-RASPBERRY	EA		$21.81	$0.00
#10 CANS		4184636	PRESERVES-STRAWBERRY	EA		$15.33	$0.00
#10 CANS		4111498	PUMPKIN SOLIDS	EA		$8.02	$0.00
#10 CANS		964809	SAUCE-CHILI	EA		$5.26	$0.00
#10 CANS		5882782	SAUCE-ENCHILADA RED	EA		$9.47	$0.00
#10 CANS		4189171	SAUERKRAUT	EA		$4.93	$0.00
#10 CANS		4001921	SAUCE-TOMATO	EA		$3.83	$0.00
#10 CANS		4113684	TOMATOES-DICED	EA		$3.48	$0.00
#5 CANS		4111217	APRICOT NECTAR	EA		$2.22	Total
B1		4101481	MARSHMALLOWS LARGE	CS		$22.73	$0.00
B1		4899845	MARSHMALLOWS MINI 4/5LB	EA		$7.12	$0.00
F1		5398953	MIX-MILK POWDER 25#	LB		$3.64	$0.00
F3		4008769	SYRUP-PANCAKE	EA		$6.27	$0.00

Source: Courtesy of Cuisine Unlimited Catering and Special Events, Salt Lake City, Utah.

Summary

Off-premise caterers will develop relationships with multiple vendors to supply their businesses with everything required to cook and serve food. This chapter describes the processes for ordering, receiving, and storing the ingredients and supplies, with examples of some of the common forms (product spec, purchase order, price quote sheet) used to accomplish these steps.

The chapter begins with purchasing, which involves an accurate determination of the amounts of products needed. The importance of exact product specifications is discussed, and tips are provided for purchasing meat, produce, and seafood.

From whom will you purchase? Guidelines are included for selecting vendors and building good relationships with them. For some types of products, price and availability will be the deciding factors; for others, such as specialty and artisan products made locally, closer relationships are required, and perhaps even contracts.

The chapter contains advice and strategies for purchasing the correct amounts of products and supplies to meet your needs without overstocking and tying up storage space and money. Procedures are discussed for receiving the merchandise and double-checking it, and the invoice, when it arrives at your facility, and for handling discrepancies.

Proper storage will ensure the longest shelf life for your inventory, and the chapter includes guidelines for refrigerated and frozen foods, as well as dry goods. An explanation of inventory procedures and their importance ends the chapter.

Study Questions

1. Briefly explain why it is important for a caterer to maintain a low inventory.

2. Describe the three types of supplier relationships and give examples of the types of products you might purchase in each.

3. Select the three "Tips for Effective Purchasing" in this chapter (pages 399–404) that you think you would be most likely to utilize, and explain why.

4. Why is FIFO important in storing food? What does it accomplish?

5. Why is it important to designate a person to be in charge of Receiving?

Sanitation and Safety

The headline of the MSNBC article on July 30, 2010, was enough to make any off-premise caterer feel a little queasy: "Caterers Dish Up More Cases of Food Poisoning." The writer detailed several recent cases of food-borne illnesses from wedding receptions, banquets, and other events, and a spokesperson for the Centers for Disease Control and Prevention (CDC) explained that proportionately, outbreaks from catering are higher than from home kitchens or restaurants. The supposition is that, since more people eat the same foods at the same place at a large catered event, when someone becomes ill, he or she is more likely to report it.

Avoiding this type of publicity is only one reason that sanitation and other food safety procedures are of paramount importance in your off-premise catering business. The health and safety of customers and staff members must always come first. Legal liability is also a concern in such cases. To assist you in avoiding problems, the examples and procedures in this chapter focus on the following topics:

- The causes of food-borne illnesses
- Employee hygiene
- Safe food handling procedures
- The HACCP system

- Sanitation
- Creating a safe work environment
- Responding to food safety complaints
- Insurance coverage for caterers

A widely touted study by an Ohio State University professor, released in 2010 and funded by the Pew Charitable Trust's Produce Safety Project at Georgetown University, estimated food-borne illness costs to the U.S. economy at $152 billion each year in lost productivity, hospitalization, long-term disability, and fatalities.

The average cost of a food-borne illness outbreak to a foodservice operation exceeds $100,000, including the cost of legal representation and financial settlements to victims, so caterers should not skimp in this important area. Before identifying procedures for safe food handling to avoid these crises, let us examine the various types of food-borne illnesses and how they occur.

Common Causes of Food-Borne Illness

In a single year (2008), 1,034 food-borne disease outbreaks were reported in the United States. Almost half had a single cause or food source, and, according to the CDC, the top "problem foods" in 2008 were beef (14 percent), fish (14 percent), and poultry (15 percent).

Based on information from the CDC and the University of Florida Department of Food Science and Human Nutrition, here is a brief rundown on the more common types of food-related problems and information on whether they are prevalent or rare.

Bacteria. The main causes of food-borne illnesses, bacteria are found in many foods—milk, milk products, eggs, meat, poultry, fish, shellfish, and edible crustaceans—that have not been handled, inspected, or prepared properly. Most bacteria grow best at temperatures between 45 and 140 degrees Fahrenheit.

- *Bacillus cereus:* This is the basic bacterium type that causes some types of gastroenteritis—cramps, stomachache, vomiting, and diarrhea. It lives in soil and shows up in foods that begin as agricultural crops: potatoes, rice, pasta products, and vegetables, as well as milk and cheese products. The CDC says that it is difficult to track infection numbers because this type of food poisoning exhibits the same symptoms as *Clostridium* and a virus, *Staphylococcus aureus.*

- *Campylobacter:* This type of bacterium lives in the intestines of healthy birds and infects poultry. The most frequent cause of this infection is eating undercooked chicken or other foods contaminated by contact with raw chicken. Using the same cutting board for chicken and then for vegetables without sanitizing it between uses is a common cause of campylobacteriosis. The CDC says this infection is more common in the summer months and typically causes diarrhea. It affects more than 2.4 million people every year.

- *Clostridium:* The effects of bacteria in this genus include the deadly illness botulism, usually associated with improperly canned foods. Food from cans with severe dents, cans or jars with bulging tops, and cans with ends that spring back when pushed in should not be used, even if the food inside appears normal. The CDC says fewer than 150 cases a year of botulism are reported, and only 15 percent are food-borne.

- *Escherichia coli:* Most strains of this bacterium, commonly known as *E. coli*, are harmless, but one strain (*E. coli* O157:H7) produces a powerful toxin that can cause severe illness, through meat or milk products contaminated with tiny amounts of feces. Hamburgers, roast beef, and unpasteurized milk are the primary sources of human infection. Cooking beef to an internal temperature of 155 degrees Fahrenheit kills *E. coli* bacteria, and the CDC says that proper hand-washing procedures are also critical to prevent infections from spreading. Symptoms, which occur 12 to 24 hours after ingestion, include severe diarrhea, cramping, and dehydration; in toddlers or frail elderly consumers, the bacteria may also kill red blood cells and cause kidney failure. The CDC estimates *E. coli* O157:H7 causes 265,000 food-borne illnesses annually in the United States. (That's up from 73,000 when the last edition of this book was published in 2005.) In 2009 to 2011, the CDC reported eight multistate *E. coli* outbreaks; seven of them were *E. coli* O157:H7.

- *Listeria monocytogenes (L.m.):* This bacterium is found in both processed and uncooked vegetables, as well as meats and dairy products. It grows in the soil and is also found in animal manure (which is sometimes used as fertilizer). Symptoms of the illness, called listeriosis, include stomach cramps, diarrhea, nausea, and fever, and it causes about 500 deaths per year in the United States. The *L.m.* bacterium was the culprit in only one multistate U.S. outbreak in 2011. Cantaloupe grown on a single farm in Colorado caused about two dozen deaths and more than a hundred serious illnesses in what the CDC termed the deadliest outbreak since 1985.

- *Salmonella:* These microorganisms live in the intestines of birds, reptiles, and mammals, and they are passed to humans in poultry, red meat, shellfish, and eggs, as well as in prepared foods such as chicken, egg, and ham salads. Salmonellosis is the name of the illness; symptoms start 12 to 26 hours after eating the contaminated foods and include nausea, vomiting, cramps, and fever, and, in young children and elderly persons, other potentially fatal infections like septicemia and typhoid. Children under age five have the highest rates of this type of infection, according to the CDC. Poor personal hygiene by food workers and use of equipment and utensils that have not been properly sanitized may cause salmonellosis, which sickens about 40,000 people in the United States each year. From 2009 to 2011, there were 19 multistate outbreaks.

- *Shigella:* These bacteria can be acquired by drinking (or swimming in) contaminated water or eating contaminated food. A person infected with shigellosis will have fever, cramps, diarrhea, and bloody stools for about a week but may be infectious for another two weeks after the symptoms end. This is another reason hand washing is extremely important to prevent the spread of infection. The CDC says that about 14,000 shigellosis cases are reported annually in the United States, but estimates the actual number could be 20 times greater.

- *Vibrio:* There are several strains of *Vibrio* bacteria found in seawater, which can infect those who eat raw or undercooked shellfish. One type (*Vibrio cholerae*) causes cholera. *Vibrio vulnificus* can infect the bloodstream, and the disease can be fatal if contracted by someone with an immune system or liver deficiency. *Vibrio parahaemolyticus* is less serious and is most commonly associated with raw oysters; it causes typical food poisoning symptoms for about three days. The CDC says that *Vibrio* illnesses are underreported; they total about 4,500 a year.

- *Yersinia enterocolitica:* This bacterium is passed to humans through raw or undercooked pork, untreated water, or milk that has not been pasteurized. Symptoms of yersiniosis include fever, cramps, and diarrhea; they may take four to seven days to surface and last up to three weeks. The CDC says that the infection is rarely reported and is more prevalent during the winter months.

Viruses. Food handlers can spread viruses if they do not wash their hands well after using the restroom, sneezing, coughing, and touching their mouths with their hands. Foods that are not heated after handling are most likely to transmit viral illnesses.

- *Norovirus:* This is a whole family of highly contagious viruses, also called "Norwalk" or "Norwalk-like" viruses, or calciviruses. Each type of norovirus is named after the place where it was discovered, such as Taunton (in the United Kingdom), Sapporo (in Japan), and Snow Mountain (in the United States). As a group, they cause fairly mild food poisoning symptoms, which are often diagnosed by doctors as gastroenteritis. But they are prevalent enough to account for more than 20 million infections each year, and victims can be contagious for several days to two weeks after symptoms have passed.

  These viruses are not found in animals. They are passed strictly by human contact, usually via unwashed hands that come into contact with leafy greens, raw food, or shellfish. The CDC says about a third (31 percent) of norovirus outbreaks occur at parties, events, and restaurants; a little more than a third (36 percent) occur in nursing homes. Cruise ships and school cafeterias have also been outbreak sites.

- *Staphylococcus aureus:* "Staph" is a common food-borne illness, caused by toxins in protein foods (ham products, cold meats, mayonnaise-based salads) and dairy products (custards, milk-based products, cream-filled desserts). Unfortunately, staph germs resist drying and freezing, and cooking or freezing will not always kill them.

  Foods most likely to be contaminated by *Staphylococcus* bacteria are the ones that require a lot of prep work, so proper hand washing and hygiene are critical. Even healthy people carry harmful staphylococci, usually in the nose and throat and on their hands. Therefore, no one with a skin infection should be doing prep work; sores or cuts must be bandaged and the bandaged area must be covered with a finger cot or clean glove.

Parasites and Toxins. The good news about parasites, which live in animals and fish, is that they are killed when food is heated to sufficiently high temperatures in the cooking process.

- *Ciguatoxins:* These toxins cause a troublesome but rarely fatal poisoning called ciguatera. Ciguatoxins are produced by microscopic sea plants that are eaten by small fish, which are then eaten by larger fish, and so on. Large predatory reef fish like barracuda, sea bass, snapper, grouper, amberjack, and mullet have been associated with ciguatera. The illness produces all the "usual" food poisoning symptoms, plus some others—weakness, itching, unusual taste sensations, and even hallucinations—that take one to four weeks to subside.

- *Cryptosporidium parvum:* This parasite infects herd animals, both domestic (cows, goats, sheep) and wild (deer, elk). It lives in their intestines and is released in feces that can infect soil, water, and the produce grown in or irrigated with them. "Crypto" is tough to kill and chlorine resistant, so it can live even in swimming pools and hot tubs. The illness it causes, called cryptosporidiosis, is very contagious. Symptoms include upset stomach, diarrhea, and a slight fever. They last about two weeks, but not everyone infected has these symptoms. Birds and mice also often have a type of *Cryptosporidium*, but it is not thought to be infectious to humans.

- *Cyclospora cayetanensis:* Similar to *Cryptosporidium*, this parasite is spread by people who ingest food or water that has been contaminated with infected animal droppings. It affects the small intestine and usually causes diarrhea in humans.

- *Scombrotoxins:* Scombroid fish poisoning (also called histamine fish poisoning) is what happens when people eat fish that is spoiling—that is, when bacteria are breaking down the fish proteins. Symptoms, which can begin within a few minutes, include rash, diarrhea, headache, nausea, and sweating. The mouth may also swell or feel a burning sensation. These symptoms usually last only a few hours and may improve if the person takes an antihistamine. Between scombrotoxins and ciguatoxins, the CDC reports only about 30 cases a year, adding that because most cases are mild, many more go undiagnosed and/or unreported.

- *Trichinella:* This parasitic worm sometimes infests pork products (like ham and sausage) and game meats. Nausea, chills, fever, and diarrhea are the first symptoms of trichinellosis (also called trichinosis), occurring within a day or two after infection, but other symptoms—headaches, joint and muscle pains, extreme fatigue and weakness—start from two to eight weeks after eating the infected meat and can last for months. The illness is not contagious between humans. Fewer than 40 cases a year are reported, usually in people who have eaten wild game. Precautions include cooking meat products to internal temperatures of 170 degrees Fahrenheit, freezing meat (in cuts less than six inches thick) for at least 20 days at a temperature of 5 degrees Fahrenheit, and cleaning meat grinders thoroughly between uses.

Chemical Contamination. Certain food additives can cause chemical contamination: sulfites; pesticides used to kill bugs, either by growers or in a foodservice operation; preservatives to lengthen freshness of produce; toxic metals such as copper, brass, cadmium, lead, and zinc (used in galvanized food containers) that come in contact with certain acidic foods; and cleaning products in accidental contact with foods. An example of the latter occurred in a New England restaurant, when a careless cleaning employee contaminated raw lobster tails with detergent when they were stored on shelves beneath the steam table.

Food Allergens

We should also mention a category of symptoms that are not infectious but may also be life threatening because of food allergies. An allergic reaction happens when a person's body responds as if something he or she ingests is harmful, even when it's not. Some people break out in hives or a rash. The tongue or throat may swell, causing breathing problems. The people may cough or sneeze, their blood pressure may drop, or they may feel a tingling sensation in the mouth when they eat a particular food. They may get cramps, feel nauseous, or have diarrhea. In the most severe cases, they can lose consciousness. According to the Food Allergen and Anaphylaxis Network (www.foodallergy.org), allergic reactions prompt 30,000 emergency room visits and cause as many as 200 deaths each year in the United States. More information can be obtained on the website of the Asthma and Allergy Foundation of America (www.aafa.org).

There are two important points here. First, your catering staff should learn how to recognize an allergic reaction, and know what to do about it, as part of ongoing emergency training. Second, there are "trigger" foods that cause up to 90 percent of all allergic reactions. You cannot possibly protect everyone, but if your recipes contain any of these items, they should always be very clearly labeled and identified—or not served at all, in some cases, rather than pose a health risk. As first noted in Chapter 3's discussion of dietary and nutritional claims on menus, food scientists refer to these as the "Big 8":

- Eggs
- Fish
- Shellfish (clams, mussels, oysters, scallops)
- Milk
- Peanuts
- Tree nuts (almonds, Brazil nuts, cashews, filberts, hazelnuts, macadamia nuts, pecans, pine nuts, pistachios, walnuts)
- Soy
- Gluten (a protein found in wheat, barley, and rye)

Clients should be asked if there are any known food allergies or sensitivities before the menu is planned, but don't expect them to be familiar with each and every guest's special needs. On-site, the caterer should always be prepared to accommodate allergic guests with something as simple as a fruit plate or an egg-free dessert, if requested.

In addition, we mentioned sulfites as a chemical contaminant. In fact, these sulfur-based preservatives are used in many cooked and processed foods. They also occur naturally in beer and wine as a result of the fermentation process. The U.S. Food and Drug Administration (FDA) estimates that about 1 in 100 people is sensitive to sulfites, and about 5 percent of asthma sufferers are also sulfite sensitive. The FDA takes the issue seriously enough to require that the presence of sulfites be disclosed on food and beverage labels.

 ## What About Hand Sanitizers?

A couple of years after alcohol-based hand sanitizers appeared on the market as a convenient "water-free" way to clean hands, the controversy began. People asked, "Are they as effective as good old soap and water?"

The answer is, it depends on the product you use and how you use it.

If you use a sanitizer, it must contain at least 60 percent alcohol to kill most harmful viruses and bacteria. The type of alcohol may vary (ethanol, ethyl, isopropanol), but the concentration must be between 60 and 95 percent to be effective.

Hand sanitizer is not the best choice if your hands are visibly dirty. The CDC and Prevention point out that soap and water is more effective if hands have "dirt, soil, blood, feces or other body fluids" on them because these substances can interfere with alcohol's ability to sanitize.

According to the Mayo Clinic, it is also important to use the hand sanitizer correctly:

- Apply enough of the product to the palm of your hand to wet your hands completely.
- Rub hands together, covering all surfaces, for up to 25 seconds or until they are dry.
- Make sure that hands are dry before touching anything.

In short, use hand sanitizers as a supplement to, not a replacement for, soap and water—and only when they are strong enough to do the germ-killing job. Antimicrobial wipes or towelettes are better than nothing, although not as effective as liquid alcohol-based sanitizers.

Employee Hygiene

Poor personal hygiene is a major cause of sanitation problems in the catering profession. Off-premise caterers should insist that health-related procedures be posted in catering commissaries and in the kitchen or staging area at event sites; they should also be included in training programs and written training materials. These are absolutely critical to prevent the spread of food-borne illnesses. Employees who fail to follow them consistently should be disciplined and/or terminated. *These rules are not negotiable!* It takes only one careless person to ruin a successful catering company with a food-borne illness scare. They should be included in your employee handbook and should become part of your employee evaluations for kitchen, receiving, and serving staff.

Everyone picks up germs as they touch objects, surfaces, and other people throughout the day. Health experts say that frequent hand washing is the best way for people to avoid spreading illnesses to others and to keep themselves healthy.

Caterers and their employees should follow these health-related rules:

- Many caterers prefer hand washing to the use of gloves, inasmuch as many people don't use gloves properly. Workers should wash their hands before starting work and after:
  - Touching their hair, nose, or ears
  - Touching an open cut or sore
  - Sneezing or coughing (even if using a tissue or handkerchief)
  - Smoking
  - Handling trash
  - Using the restroom or changing a diaper
  - Handling soiled or used tableware
  - Gloves become torn or soiled

  Hand washing should be done with hot water and soap for at least 20 seconds, using a nailbrush. (Experts say that antibacterial soap is no more effective at killing germs than regular soap.) The arms below the elbow should be washed, and single-use towels should be used for drying purposes. When turning off restroom faucets or opening restroom doors, staff members should use a clean paper towel, not their newly washed hands.

- If disposable gloves are used when handling foods, employees must be taught to use them correctly. This includes changing gloves whenever they change tasks (or every four hours even if they don't change tasks), and removing them properly (inside out) before throwing them away. If a worker's hands are not clean in the first place, he or she will contaminate the gloves. There are nonlatex gloves for people with latex allergies, and cut-resistant gloves for kitchen work. Instructions for glove use should be printed on the glove dispenser.

- Gloves cannot be worn when working around open flames or other heat sources because they can melt or catch fire. Cut-resistant gloves should not be used while operating electric slicers or using serrated knives as these activities are more likely to pull at the internal fibers of the gloves and tear them.

- Jewelry should not be worn when working on back-of-the-house tasks because items like rings can catch dirt and other types of jewelry can easily fall into the food. Front-of-the-house staff may wear minimal jewelry, but only if it is in keeping with the caterer's image.

- For the same reasons, artificial nails are not permitted. Natural nails should be neatly trimmed and kept scrupulously clean, with the use of a nailbrush when washing hands.

- Any cut, burn, boil, or even a hangnail, must be kept clean and covered with a suitable bandage while working with food or food-contact surfaces—in addition to wearing gloves. There are also individual *finger cots*, one-finger guards that can be worn over a bandage to keep it clean and dry.

- Hats or hairnets should be worn in all food preparation areas, or hair must be tied back if it is long enough to do so. (We've noticed that many caterers are awfully lax on enforcing this policy.)

- Kitchen garments should be light in color so as to reveal stains. An apron should be removed when the employee leaves the kitchen (to use the restroom, take out trash, etc.).

- Clean shoes with closed toes and nonslip soles should be worn. Some caterers supply their employees with safety shoes or require that these be worn instead of tennis shoes, which can be slippery on wet surfaces. Steel-toed shoes are also a good idea for added protection from falling knives and heavy objects. Check the websites of Shoes for Crews and Chefwear for information on sturdy shoes.

- Catering staff should never touch the "eating ends" of flatware or the rims of glasses, bowls, plates, and cups.
- Smoking, gum chewing, and eating are never permitted in serving areas or in kitchens. (Some city health codes do allow kitchen employees to sip from a closed container, with a straw, while working.)
- Employees who say they are "fine" but come to work coughing and sneezing should be shifted, at least temporarily, to jobs other than food preparation. They can scrub floors, clean restrooms, remove trash, or perform other tasks.
- Food left on plates or that has dropped on the floor even for an instant should never be reused. (We can hardly believe we even have to include that rule, but there you have it.)
- All dropped flatware, napkins, and tableware must be replaced with clean items.
- Food should not be touched with hands. Use disposable gloves.
- The tops and bottoms of serving trays should be kept clean at all times.
- Hard-working food handlers should be careful that perspiration does not accidentally come into contact with equipment or food.
- Staff must be trained regarding food allergies and know what to say if a guest inquires about whether a certain food contains a specific ingredient. (If you don't know, it's best to tell the customer that you are not sure and will find out, before serving the item to him or her. Also be prepared to offer an alternative if the guest is allergic.)

Food Storage

Safe storage is the first key to safely prepared foods, and we covered many of the rules in Chapter 11. Upon arrival from purveyors, meats and poultry should be stored immediately at 41 degrees Fahrenheit or below. Frozen meat and poultry should be stored at a temperature that keeps it frozen, usually 0 degrees Fahrenheit. Raw meat and poultry should be wrapped and kept airtight because it will turn brown when exposed to air. Meats that show signs of spoilage should be immediately discarded—and remember, you have every right to refuse products that come in from vendors looking less than perfect. Raw chicken that is received packed in ice can be stored in that ice; however, the ice bin must be self-draining and changed regularly with fresh ice.

Fresh fish should be stored at 41 degrees Fahrenheit or less and used within 48 hours. Fillets and steaks should be kept in their original packaging or kept tightly wrapped and free from moisture. Whole fish can be stored in flaked or crushed ice for up to three days. Again, ice beds must be self-draining, and the ice must be changed and the container sanitized regularly. Fish that is meant to be eaten raw must be delivered frozen, or must be frozen before serving, to kill any parasites.

Eggs must be stored at 41 degrees Fahrenheit (or colder) and kept in their original containers. Produce should not be washed before storing. Most produce can be kept at 41 degrees Fahrenheit or less, but whole citrus fruits, hard-rind squash, eggplant, and root vegetables (potatoes, sweet potatoes, rutabagas, and onions) may be stored in a cool, dry storage area at temperatures of 60 to 70 degrees Fahrenheit.

Preparing and Serving Food

Bacterial growth in food occurs when food temperatures are between 40 and 140 degrees Fahrenheit. Within this range, there is a heightened danger zone—from 70 to 125 degrees Fahrenheit—in which bacteria can grow more rapidly. Catering personnel must be trained to thoroughly understand that foods must be brought "through" this zone, either from cold to hot or from hot to cold, as quickly as possible. The longer foods stay in the danger zone, the faster bacteria will grow. The current understanding of food science experts is that food must not stay in the danger zone for a total of more than four hours, including every moment from its arrival at your kitchen, to the time it is cooked or otherwise prepared, to the time it spends being held and/or reheated. Foods that exceed the four-hour rule should be discarded.

Frozen Foods. Frozen foods should never be thawed at room temperature and should be thawed as follows:

- Gradually, under refrigeration (at a temperature of 41 degrees Fahrenheit or lower)
- By cooking immediately after removal from the freezer
- In a microwave oven (but only if it will be cooked immediately after thawing)
- Submerged under potable running water for no more than two hours, with the water temperature at 70 degrees Fahrenheit or lower

Cooked Foods. Foods must be cooked to the following minimum temperatures, with internal temperatures checked in more than one spot. The temperature reading must be steady for at least 15 seconds or the food is "not quite done." These minimums are suggested in the ServSafe program of the National Restaurant Association Educational Foundation (www.nraef.org):

Type of Food	Degrees F
Poultry, stuffing, and stuffed meats	165
Steaks, roasts, and chops	145
Ground meats	155
Dishes that combine cooked and uncooked foods (like casseroles)	165
Cooked vegetables	140
Dishes containing eggs	165
Reheating foods	165

Cooked foods may be held before serving for only short periods of time, and at temperatures of no less than 140 degrees Fahrenheit. Holding equipment (like a chafing dish) is designed to keep already-hot food warm but should never be used to heat food that is cold. It simply doesn't work fast enough to keep the food out of that danger zone. Foods should already be at safe temperatures of 140 degrees Fahrenheit or more when placed in holding equipment.

When cooked foods must be cooled, it's important to chill them as quickly as possible to 40 degrees Fahrenheit to get them out of the danger zone. This is not accomplished by plunging the hot food into a refrigerator or freezer as these appliances are not designed for cooling. They are designed to keep cold foods cold and frozen foods frozen. This is critical, because hot foods stuck in the fridge can form a thin layer of ice on top. This *igloo effect* does exactly the wrong thing—it insulates the interior part of the food, keeping it at higher temperatures for too long. It also endangers other cold foods by raising the temperature inside the refrigerator.

Instead, food should be divided into portions small enough to put into shallow containers (no more than two or three inches deep) and placed in a *blast chiller*, an appliance made specifically for quick-cooling foods. The shallowness of the containers prompts quicker chilling. As an alternative, you can place a shallow container in a larger container filled with ice and ice water to precool the food before putting it into a regular refrigerator. Either way, the quick-chilled food must be moved to normal refrigeration within three hours.

Cold (Uncooked) Foods. Because so many different raw food items are cut and diced in a kitchen, the risk of cross contamination is great. This occurs when a knife or other utensil or a cutting board is used for more than one food item without being properly sanitized between uses. Here's how you can prevent cross contamination:

- Clean and sanitize utensils, equipment, and work surfaces after each use.
- Use color-coded cutting boards for different types of foods (and make sure that your employees understand what color board is used for what food). There are also color-coded containers, knives with color-coded handles, and color-coded kitchen towels for use in different prep areas.
- If a kitchen towel is used for wiping up spills in a particular area, use it only for that purpose. Store soiled towels in a sanitizing solution before washing. Alternatively, use disposable towels.
- Make sure employees know and use the proper hand-washing procedures.

Produce items, like salad greens, should be washed under running water, but there are also several brands of sanitizing additives that allow you to "dunk" fruits or vegetables in treated water for an extra bit of protection. (The prep sink, of course, must be properly cleaned and sanitized before using it for this purpose.) As salad ingredients are cleaned and chopped, they can sit in the prep area at room temperature as long as they are soon destined for refrigeration at a temperature of 34 to 38 degrees Fahrenheit. Store salads in shallow containers of no more than 10 pounds each to allow faster chilling. Cover them tightly with plastic wrap or foil, making sure that there is no layer of air between the cover and the salad.

Miscellaneous Precautions. Caterers should use only pasteurized milk and milk products, stored at temperatures below 41 degrees Fahrenheit and poured for use from their original containers. Ice cream must be served with a clean, dry scoop or one that is located in a dipper well in running (not standing) water.

Raw eggs should not be used in Caesar salads or other dishes that require little or no cooking. Only pasteurized eggs should be used in these dishes.

Ice used to cool stored food cannot be served to guests. Ice for human consumption should be dispensed only with clean ice scoops or tongs. Many people are under the mistaken impression that ice is cold enough to automatically be sanitary. Not true! Instead, the cold temperature essentially preserves whatever pathogens may have been in the water before it froze. Glasses, hands, or cups should never be used when the ice scoop is misplaced—have extras on hand!

Buffet-style service and self-service situations bring their own challenges. For buffets, most health departments require *sneeze guards* or food shields. Buffet foods should be labeled, not only so guests can identify potential allergens, but so guests don't feel the need to "sample" or return foods they have picked up. Serving staff should check food temperatures frequently on a buffet. The catering staff should offer a clean plate to those returning to food stations or buffet lines for seconds, as this prevents guests' use of a "contaminated" plate near the buffet foods.

Supplying tongs, long-handled spoons, and ladles for every serving dish ensures that guests do not have to touch the food. Caterers should never reuse ice, vegetable garnishes, or plants used to decorate the buffet if they have been touched by the buffet food.

Cold foods on buffets should be put out in small quantities, and replenishments should not be mixed with food that has already been sitting out on the buffet. It is better to use two small bowls—one on the buffet and one on ice in the prep area or refrigerated. When the bowl on the buffet runs low, it can be removed and the fresh, cold bowl can replace it.

For self-service condiments or coffee, off-premise caterers find it is more sanitary to use individually packaged items (sugar, ketchup, etc.) than bulk containers with spoons—not only for safety reasons, but also for the overall appearance of the table.

The HACCP System

The standard on which most foodservice safety regulations are based is the HACCP system. (The initials stand for Hazard Analysis of Critical Control Points.) HACCP has been used since the 1960s, and the system consists of seven basic steps:

1. Identify hazards and assess their severity and risks.
2. Determine critical control points (CCPs) in food preparation.
3. Determine critical control limits (CCLs) for each CCP identified.
4. Monitor critical control points and record data.
5. Take corrective action whenever monitoring indicates a critical limit is exceeded.
6. Establish an effective record-keeping system to document the HACCP system.
7. Establish procedures to verify that the HACCP system is working.

From *Design and Equipment for Restaurants and Foodservice*, 3rd Edition, by Costas Katsigris and Chris Thomas (Hoboken, NJ: John Wiley & Sons, 2009), here is a brief explanation of each step:

The first step is to decide what hazards exist at each stage of a food's journey through your kitchen, and decide how serious each is in terms of your overall safety priorities. On your own checklist, this may include these items:

- Review recipes, paying careful attention to times for thawing, cooking, cooling, reheating, and handling of leftovers.

- Give employees thermometers and/or temperature probes and teach them how to use them. Correctly calibrate these devices.

- Inspect all fresh and frozen produce upon delivery.

- Require hand washing at certain points in the food preparation process and show employees the correct way to wash for maximum sanitation.

- Add quick-chill capability to cool foods more quickly in amounts over 1 gallon or 4 pounds.

The second step is to identify critical control points (CCPs). This means any point or procedure in your system where loss of control may result in a health risk. If workers use the same cutting boards to dice vegetables and debone chickens without washing them between uses, that is a CCP in need of improvement. Vendor delivery vehicles should be inspected for cleanliness; product temperatures must be kept within 5 degrees of optimum; expiration dates on food items must be clearly marked; utensils must be sanitized; and the list goes on and on.

The third step is to determine the standards and limits for what is acceptable and what is not, in each of the CCP areas, for your kitchen.

The fourth step in the HACCP system is to monitor all the steps you pinpointed in Step 2 for a specific period of time, to be sure each area of concern is taken care of correctly. Some CCPs may remain on the list indefinitely, for constant monitoring; others, once you get the procedure correct, may be removed from the list after several months. Still others may be added to the monitoring list as needed.

Step 5 kicks in whenever you see that one of your "critical limits" (set in Step 3) has been exceeded, and corrective action must be taken.

Step 6 requires that you document this whole process. Without documentation, it is difficult at best to chart whatever progress your facility might be making. If there is a problem that impacts customer health or safety, having written records is also very important.

Finally, Step 7 requires that you establish a procedure to verify whether the HACCP system is working for you. This may mean a committee that meets regularly to discuss health and safety issues and to go over the documentation required in Step 6.

Transporting Foods Safely

Your company's food safety procedures should be as "portable" as the foods themselves; these procedures should be second nature to all employees at an event site, just as they are at your commissary. These include the same personal hygiene standards: tie back hair, use protective gloves, adhere to the same hand-washing practices, and so on. In addition to the information in the Food Holding Equipment section in Chapter 5 (page 153), we have included more tips here for storing, transporting, and handling food:

- Prechill any foods that are to be served cold before you transport them. Keep them at a temperature of 41 degrees Fahrenheit or below, both for storage and for service.

- All food, serving equipment, and utensils must be carried in tightly covered containers or securely wrapped packages to protect them from contamination. Use insulated carriers packed with ice or frozen gel-packs for cold foods. For hot foods, preheat to temperatures above 140 degrees Fahrenheit and pack the hot containers snugly into carriers to hold the heat in during transport.

- Always store cooked foods separately from raw and/or ready-to-eat foods.

- Have your dairy delivery person bring perishables like milk directly to the event site in a refrigerated truck.

- If fresh drinking water is not available on-site, bring your own water supply.

- Be sure that there is enough electrical power at the site for the cooking and holding equipment you plan to use.

- Label all food containers with their contents, storage requirements, and cooking or reheating instructions, so there is no confusion at the event site.

- Pack food thermometers so internal temperatures can be checked upon arrival.

- In case a hand sink or traditional hand-washing setup is not available at an event site, always bring alcohol-based hand sanitizers and antibacterial kitchen wipes for workspaces and utensils.

- Clean and sanitize all insulated carriers between uses.

- Clean and sanitize the delivery vehicles regularly too.

More Sanitation Tips

Refrigeration. Refrigerator temperatures should range from 38 to 40 degrees Fahrenheit. These may vary according to local regulations. Refrigerators should be clean and sanitized inside and out. Condensation should never drip on foods, and fans should be kept clean.

Equipment and Food Surfaces. From cutting boards and worktables to your largest mixer, everything in your kitchen should be washed, rinsed, and sanitized after each use—as frequently as possible. To thoroughly clean some types of equipment, a sanitizing solution must be pumped through them. Manufacturers usually provide both cleaning instructions and cleaning product recommendations. For stationary equipment, the National Restaurant Association Educational Foundation recommends the following steps:

1. Turn off and unplug equipment before cleaning.

2. Remove food and soil from under and around the equipment.

3. Remove detachable parts and manually wash, rinse, and sanitize them, or run them through a warewasher, if permitted. Allow them to air-dry.

4. Wash and rinse fixed food contact surfaces, and then wipe or spray them with chemical sanitizing solution.

5. Keep cloths used for food-contact and non-food-contact surfaces in separate, properly marked containers of sanitizing solution.

6. Air-dry all parts, and then reassemble according to directions. Tighten all parts and guards. Test equipment at recommended settings, and then turn it off.

7. Resanitize food-contact surfaces handled when putting the unit back together by wiping with a cloth that has been submerged in sanitizing solution.

Dish Machines. Proper water temperatures are part of the story; an adequate rinse cycle is the other part, to keep guests from tasting (and ingesting) dish detergent. If there's a presoak or prewash cycle, the water temperature should be at least 120 degrees Fahrenheit. Wash water temperature should be 140 to 180 degrees Fahrenheit (for chemical or "low temp" machines, 120 degrees). Final rinse water should be 180 to 200 degrees Fahrenheit (165 degrees for stationary rack, single-temperature machines; 120 degrees for chemical or "low-temp" machines). For all cycles, sufficient water pressure is required—at least 20 pounds per square inch.

Cleaning and Pest Control. Off-premise catering facilities must be cleaned regularly, in accordance with established cleaning procedures. All utensils and equipment must be stored at least six inches above the floor. Spills should be wiped up immediately. When floors are being mopped, warning signs should be posted. Many caterers use a cleaning and sanitizing setup with two color-coded buckets: green for detergent and red for sanitizing solution. A white cloth is used for the detergent, and a blue disposable cloth for the sanitizing agent. A discard bin for soiled cloths makes them easy to toss without accidentally reusing. Dispensing systems for the cleaning chemicals are handy, and they save money by dispensing the proper product in the correct amount, thus preventing waste.

Pest control is a huge sanitation priority for caterers, and the best method is to leave it to the experts. Hire a professional, licensed pest control operator who can develop an ongoing pest control program that includes prevention, repairs, pesticides and/or traps, and related training for your people about what they can do to assist in the program, day to day. To find out more about commercial pest control, check out the websites of Orkin, Pest World, and Pest Control Technology.

To reduce the chances for chemical contamination of foods, poisonous or toxic materials may not be stored near food preparation and serving areas and must be clearly labeled. Detergents, sanitizers, polishes, chemicals used for maintenance, insecticides, and rodenticides are permitted in foodservice areas, but only if storage and labeling requirements are followed.

Trash. Garbage should be deposited in garbage cans lined with heavy-duty plastic bags and removed frequently from the commissary. It should be deposited in containers or dumpsters outside, preferably in a lockable enclosure. There should be enough covered containers to hold all garbage and refuse, and there should be separate containers for recycled items, preferably also covered. About 70 percent of restaurant kitchens participate in recycling programs. They can generally save you some money on trash pickup fees. Dumpsters with sloped fronts should be equipped with safety legs to keep them from accidentally tipping forward. The trash area should be lit for safety if employees take trash out after dark.

At off-premise event locations, especially outdoors, be sure that the trash receptacles are convenient but locate them away from food prep or cooking areas so as not to invite insects.

Handling Customer Complaints

Off-premise caterers are not immune to food-borne illness outbreaks; therefore, they should know what to do if a crisis arises. Food poisoning is less likely to occur at an à la carte restaurant, where each guest chooses from a variety of dishes; food poisoning at an off-premise catered event usually involves many people eating the same foods.

When someone complains, alleging a food-related illness, it is very important to determine the facts (versus the opinions). A telephone caller should always be referred to the catering company owner, who should have a preprinted sheet of questions, so that he or she will know what to ask the caller. Exhibit 12.1 is a sample of this type of form.

Anyone calling with such a complaint should be taken seriously. Samples of any foods in your commissary that may be suspect should be kept, never thrown away, and certainly not reused. Employees who were at the event should be interviewed, and all supplier records of where raw materials were purchased should be kept. In fact, one of your suppliers may be at fault and may have to recall some products. Some caterers may wish to conduct an investigation using an independent laboratory. It's good to know, well in advance of when you'll need them, what laboratory testing resources are available in your area. Your state health department and food processors in your area are good places to inquire.

An off-premise caterer should never immediately admit liability or offer to pay anyone's medical bills. Instead, show concern by saying, "I'm sorry you're not feeling well."

EXHIBIT 12.1 Call Sheet for Incoming Complaints of Illness or Injury

1. TELL the caller you "have a few questions that need to be answered to confirm all the facts." Ask for the person's patience in answering each question as completely as possible.

Date and time of call _____

Who received the call? _____

Name of person who is calling _____

Contact numbers for this person _____

Name of person who is ill (or injured) _____

Does this person have any known illnesses or allergies? _____

_____

Describe the problem _____

_____

_____

Is there a particular item (a dish, specific food or beverage) you are complaining about?

_____

Date and time of the meal (or food) eaten _____

List the exact symptoms, and when they appeared _____

Did this person eat anything after the suspect meal? _____

What, and when? _____

_____

Has this person seen a doctor for the problem? (If so, when?) _____

Was there a diagnosis? _____

Name and phone number of doctor _____

Have you reported this to anyone else? (If so, whom?) _____

Do you still have any of the product (leftovers) in the original container? _____

May we send someone out to pick it up for testing? _____

Address _____

_____   _____
Signature of person who took this report   Date and time

2. THANK the caller for his or her concern.

3. TELL the caller the complaint will be investigated, and that if the catering company has any further questions, someone from the company will call him or her.

4. DO NOT PROMISE ANYTHING other than that the company "will look into the complaint."

(*Continued*)

EXHIBIT 12.1 Call Sheet for Incoming Complaints of
Illness or Injury (*Continued*)

FOLLOW-UP ACTION

This complaint given to _____

For follow-up investigation on (date and time) _____

Date of follow-up action _____

What was done? _____

_____

_____

Further contact with caller was made (date and time) _____

_____

Never say anything like, "I'm sorry our food made you sick." You can show dismay but certainly not guilt. When you have obtained the information with the use of your preprinted question sheet, it is very important to notify your insurance carrier, who will generally pursue an investigation or settlement as appropriate. Even if a customer threatens to sue, or acts on that threat, you should continue to be polite. Just remember, you and your company have rights too, and you are entitled to a proper defense against what may be an inflated or spurious claim.

However, a valid complaint from a concerned guest can alert you to a possible problem with your food-handling methods or with the raw materials purchased from a supplier. Make sure that your suppliers are informed if you receive complaints that involve their products. They may need to recall a hazardous product from the market.

Occasionally, you will be part of a recall or even perhaps a full-blown outbreak of a food-borne illness. In these rare cases, caterers are advised to hire a public relations firm skilled in crisis management. Trying to deal with the news media yourself can cause further damage if, as happens in so many instances, you are asked leading questions or quoted out of context in interview situations. Your objective at this point is to minimize the losses and save the business. Protecting your business is worth every penny you will spend on professional public relations.

Safety on the Job

Each year there are more than 250,000 on-the-job accidents in the foodservice industry that, on average, mean 35 lost workdays while the employee recovers. The majority of these are slip-and-fall accidents, but there are also muscle strains, burns, and cuts aplenty. So it's important to do whatever possible to make the workplace safe and comfortable for employees. Even at off-premise sites, a caterer must be able to quickly recognize unsafe conditions and take corrective action immediately.

Here are some standard practices that should reduce accident risks for both employees and clients:

- Floors must be kept clean, dry, and in good repair. Spills should be wiped up immediately, and "caution" and "wet floor" signs should be used as appropriate.

- Dance floors at party sites must be checked for cracks in which a woman's heel could get caught. Honoring requests from clients and guests to make the dance floor "slicker" can result in a serious slip and fall. Floors should be smooth but still provide traction.

- There should be adequate lighting in all areas where guests and employees walk, including parking lots. Dimly lit walkways at off-premise sites should be lit with temporary lighting. Employees never should be permitted to run, and they should be cautioned to use extreme care when working at off-premise sites with which they are not familiar. Better yet, there should be enough time in the setup phase of an off-premise event for a short "walk-through" tour of the space for the staff members who will be working there.

- Employees should be instructed in correct lifting and transporting methods. When you lift, it is best to lift twice, first mentally and then physically. By lifting mentally, you think, "Is the item too heavy or too bulky to see around? Is the path clean, and is there a place to put the load?" Lifting heavy objects should be accomplished with these steps:

  1. Establish solid footing, and check to see that the floor is dry and clean.
  2. Stand close to the load, and spread the feet to shoulder width.
  3. Place one foot slightly in front of the other to establish a focal point for the weight of the load.
  4. Keep the head over the body, and bend at the knees to reach the load.

5. Grip the load with the whole hand, not just the fingers, and pull the load close while it is still on the ground.

6. Tighten the stomach muscles. Arch the lower back in by pulling the shoulders back and sticking the chest out.

7. Lift slowly, keeping the load close to the body with the legs taking the weight of the load.

8. To set the load down, reverse the procedure.

Lifting belts are highly recommended for employees who are responsible for loading, unloading, and receiving area duties. The belts should be stored in the receiving area and also carried routinely in the catering delivery vehicles.

• Only staff trained to operate specific machinery should be permitted to use it. They should follow these procedures:

1. Use equipment only for its designated use.

2. Make sure the plug is disconnected and visible before disassembling, repairing, and/or cleaning the equipment.

3. Use equipment only with its safety guards in place.

4. Remove jewelry, avoid loose clothing, and restrain hair. Wear protective goggles, gloves, or other suitable clothing for that task.

5. Turn off the equipment if you get distracted.

6. Use proper tools to feed food into the equipment—not hands!

7. Never operate equipment with loose wires or damaged switches or plugs.

8. Report any maintenance problem immediately to management.

• Knives should always be kept sharp, since dull knives easily slip off foods and can cut the person using them. Be sure that everyone knows how to handle knives, including these rules: Cut away from the body, and cut foods with fingers curled under. If a knife falls, don't grab for it—get out of the way! Knives should never be used to open containers, and they should be stored in a knife rack.

• Keep beverages away from fryer stations because the cold beverages, if spilled into the hot grease, can cause a major eruption of the grease. Deep fryers should not be set up in high-traffic areas. And it is imperative to train inexperienced fry cooks—they have been known to reach into hot grease with their hands for an accidentally dropped article!

- Ovens, broilers, and grills fueled by large propane tanks should never be used indoors or in any area lacking adequate ventilation. In some parts of the country, caterers also need special permits to use butane fuel and Sterno indoors. Check with the local fire or health department about such regulations.

- Folding tables and chairs should be checked for damage before each use. Folding table legs should be locked in place to ensure that the table does not collapse while in use. Chairs should be inspected for splinters, loose or missing screws and bolts, and other unsafe conditions.

- All cords should be taped down and covered with floor mats or some other protective covering, so that staff and guests do not trip on them. Orange cords are common because they are the most visible. Warning signs should be placed in areas where staff members and guests could possibly trip.

- The service staff should be trained in proper tray-carrying procedures. Injuries to guests caused by careless staff members have resulted in million-dollar lawsuits.

Fire Safety and Burn Prevention

The Burn Foundation (www.burnfoundation.org) says that about 12,000 burn accidents are reported annually in foodservice settings, the highest number of any employment sector. And little wonder, when commercial kitchens are full of hot surfaces, hot liquids, and steam-generating appliances. We have rounded up these burn prevention tips from a number of sources, including the Burn Foundation; *Restaurants and Institutions Magazine* (a publication of Reed Business Information, a division of Reed Elsevier, Inc.); RCM&D, a corporate insurance and risk management company based in Baltimore; and our own experience.

- Remove lids from pots, pans, kettles, and chafers carefully, allowing steam to escape away from the face and hands.

- Use dry, flameproof pot holders.

- Turn the handles of pans inward on the range, so that pans cannot be knocked off. Make sure that the handles are not placed too near the heat.

- Avoid reaching over or across a hot surface.

- Move heavy or hot containers with enough help, and know where the containers are going before picking them up. Never carry or move a container when the cooking oil inside it is hot or on fire.

- Be careful when filtering, changing, or discarding shortening in fryers. Wait until the oil cools before handling.

- Keep range tops and hoods free of grease.

- Keep oven doors closed when ovens are not in use.

- Do not clean ovens or ranges until they have cooled.

- Be sure that all personnel who will be using Sterno or propane at off-site events know how to do so safely.

- Keep papers, plastic aprons, and other flammable materials away from hot areas. Don't store combustible materials in or around cooking areas.

- When working with charcoal, spray charcoal lighter fluid on the coals prior to lighting. Never spray lighter fluid on charcoal that is partially ignited because the flame can travel up the stream of fluid and cause a severe burn or explosion.

- Avoid serving flaming drinks and tableside flambés as numerous burn injuries resulting from these have been reported. The best policy is simply not to offer these types of items.

- In walk-through inspections of off-premise sites, note the locations of fire exits and fire extinguishers.

Fire prevention involves routine inspections of your facilities, an occasional fire drill, and training staff members to think about fire safety and follow these guidelines and/ or procedures:

- Frequently check gas appliances for proper maintenance, and always check for a gas odor before lighting a match (which may signal a gas buildup).

- All smoke alarms should be properly maintained and regularly checked.

- Grease to be discarded, oily rags, and other flammable or combustible materials should not be stored in the catering commissary.

- Take trash out regularly, not only in kitchens, but also in receiving areas. Don't let items like cardboard boxes and wooden crates accumulate.

- Allow adequate clearance between major cooking appliances to reduce heat buildup.

- Fire suppression and alarm systems generally are designed for automatic operation, but employees should know how to manually activate them if necessary. The devices for doing this should be clearly marked and readily accessible.

- Power cords should be checked for damage, and water should never be splashed around electrical outlets.

- Hoods and exhaust filters should be cleaned at least weekly, and hot ductwork should be cleaned at least twice a year by a professional company. (Your insurance company, in most jurisdictions, will send an inspector to look at your fire protection system at least annually, if not every six months.)

Fire extinguishers are classified by the types of fires they are designed to put out and rated by the size of fire they can extinguish in a single use. Use only extinguishers that have the Underwriters Laboratories (UL) or Factory Mutual (FM) approval logo on them. The most common extinguisher classifications are:

- *Class A:* Cloth, paper, wood, and some types of plastic
- *Class B:* Flammable liquids
- *Class C:* Electrical equipment
- *Class D:* Combustible metals
- *Class K:* Commercial cooking-related fires

There are also "clean agent" fire extinguishers that can be used on fires around computers and other more sensitive types of mechanical equipment. Older fire extinguishers may not be effective and may even cause injuries. Those containing carbon tetrachloride or soda acid are no longer considered safe and should be discarded. Consult local fire and/or health department authorities for the number and types of extinguishers required, correct placement, and maintenance requirements. You are also responsible for having an evacuation plan in case of fire, both for the commissary and at off-premise sites. Most local fire departments are happy to offer suggestions and participate in employee safety training.

First Aid and Emergency Procedures

The law does not require off-premise caterers to provide emergency assistance, but it does not forbid them from taking emergency action. No establishment or employee will be held liable for civil damage for an action that could be expected of any reasonably prudent person under similar circumstances.

First aid kits should be located in all catering commissaries and at all off-premise locations. All catering staff should be trained in the Heimlich maneuver, and some states require that an instructional sign with the Heimlich steps be posted in a conspicuous place in the catering commissary. Staff members are not always required to be trained in cardiopulmonary resuscitation (CPR) techniques, but it is an excellent idea to have at least some of your staff members trained, and this can be part of your employee training regimen.

When emergencies arise, the caterer or event manager must remain calm, determine the seriousness of the problem, and quickly decide whether to call for help. Meanwhile, the accident victim must be made as comfortable as possible and basic first aid must be administered in accordance with a first aid guide, which you should always keep in each catering vehicle. Staff should follow these basic guidelines:

- For burns, first remove whatever is causing the burn. Use cool, running water to soothe minor burns; never apply ointments, sprays, antiseptics, or home remedies. Seek medical assistance in case of serious burns.

- For wounds, first rinse with clean running water. Apply pressure with a clean towel or napkin. Using a first aid kit, apply a water-resistant bandage (covered with a plastic glove, for hand wounds of staff members handling or serving food). Have severe wounds treated by medical personnel.

A written accident or incident report must be completed for all accidents, at the commissary or off-site at events. Make your own form or ask your insurance company for one. Copies of these reports may go to most, or all, of the following:

- Your own insurance-related files
- The employee's personnel file with your company
- The catering company's Workers' Compensation insurer
- The Occupational Safety and Health Administration (OSHA)
- The claims agent for your general business insurer

After an accident (and as promptly as possible, within reason), it is important to ask the injured person exactly how he or she thinks the accident happened. Obtain witness reports and inspect the scene for conditions—lighting, cleanliness, wet or dry floors, fallen objects, outdoor weather conditions—that may have contributed to the accident. Note the condition of the person's shoes and clothing. Be alert for signs of alcohol or drug use. When a mishap like this occurs, you've got to think fast but remain calm. It is absolutely never advisable to:

- Argue with the injured person over the cause of the accident
- Reprimand any employee at an event site
- Offer to pay all medical expenses
- Admit any type of responsibility
- Mention insurance coverage
- Discuss the accident with strangers, at the site or afterward
- Permit photographs by anyone other than your own, or your insurance company's, representatives

Government Agencies and Inspections

The foodservice industry receives a lot of assistance, and a lot of oversight, from a wide range of government organizations. Here are just a few you may deal with:

- Your local health department may be a city or county agency. This is the department that sends out health inspectors to check safety and sanitation conditions periodically, often unannounced.
- The health department of your state may become involved if an outbreak of foodborne illness has been reported.
- There are a number of federal agencies that deal with food-related issues. Their functions can range from tracking and investigating illness outbreaks; to inspecting meat, eggs, seafood, and imported foods; to upholding safe workplace laws. These agencies include the following:
  - U.S. Food and Drug Administration (FDA)
  - U.S. Department of Agriculture (USDA) and its subagencies, like the Food Safety Inspection Service (FSIS)
  - Centers for Disease Control and Prevention (CDC) and its subagencies, like the Foodborne Diseases Active Surveillance Network (FoodNet)
  - Environmental Protection Agency (EPA)
  - National Marine Fisheries Service
  - Occupational Safety and Health Administration (OSHA)

State and local health departments enforce most of these agencies' regulations. The Code of Federal Regulations (CFR) is a massive federal database of laws that includes the FDA's extensive food product definitions and regulations. Most state and local health department rules and standards are based on this document.

Inspectors can cite, fine, and even close a food-related business for failure to comply with these requirements. It's a good idea to ask in advance for a blank copy of an inspection form, so that you'll know what the inspectors look for and can work on total compliance. Also take a look at the Internet websites for these agencies. Most have a wealth of food safety and compliance-related information. In most areas, health inspectors do not have to call before visiting your commissary or even an off-premise site; they can show up unannounced. What will they be looking for? Our thanks to the University of Florida Department of Food Science and Human Nutrition for sharing this basic checklist from its *Food Recall Manual*, published in 2004.

- Food protection—whether containers are properly stored, sealed and labeled.
- Proper food temperatures during storage, preparation, holding and serving.
- Safe handling of food and ice; correct use and sanitation of utensils and food contact surfaces to prevent cross-contamination.
- Hygiene practices of employees, and restriction of any infected or ill employee from working with food.
- Construction and installation of equipment for maximum safety.
- Adequate ventilation, especially in cooking and dishwashing areas.
- Safe temperatures of dishwashing machines.
- Safe water sources; adequate hot and cold running water.
- Proper disposal of sewage and wastewater.
- Adequate numbers of toilets and sinks, and separate hand-washing sinks.
- Clean, covered interior trash receptacles, and exterior dumpster facilities that are properly constructed and enclosed.
- Insect, rodent, and animal control (with written records available for inspection).
- Floors, walls, ceilings washable and in good repair; working floor drains in food preparation areas; lighting adequate and fixtures shielded in case of bulb breakage.
- Toxic items (like cleaning materials) properly labeled and stored.

- Proper storage of both clean and soiled linens, dishtowels, etc.

- A no-smoking policy, or designated smoking areas, which must be clearly marked.

- If a *grease interceptor* (grease trap) is used, its clean-out records must be available to inspectors.

- Emergency procedures (Heimlich maneuver, etc.) must be posted prominently in many foodservice work areas, along with any permits the city, county, or state requires of the particular type of business.

It is a busy caterer's typical first reaction to view health inspections as either a nuisance or a threat, but neither is really the case—at least, not if you have a food safety plan in place that combines common sense, local laws, and ongoing training. It is more helpful to see an official inspection as another safety measure, some objective eyes that can take a look at what your employees are doing and make improvements and suggestions.

Federal OSHA inspectors look for different sorts of things than local health inspectors: accessibility of fire extinguishers, adequate hand railings on stairs, ladders that are properly maintained and used, proper guards and electrical grounding for foodservice equipment, safe use of electrical extension cords, lit passageways that are free from obstructions, readily available first aid supplies, and so on. Again, fines are levied for serious violations.

So what happens when the inspector shows up at your commissary? It's important not to lose your cool but to maintain a mutually respectful relationship with any inspector. The best kind of business you can be is one that is well organized and receptive to his or her requests. Here are some tips for accomplishing this:

- Always be polite and professional, and instruct your staff to do the same.

- Ask questions; ask for the inspector's assistance or opinion. Don't make excuses.

- Don't be defensive or argumentative.

- Accompany the inspector as he or she tours your facility.

- Correct any violation immediately, if you can, in front of the inspector who points it out.

- Never offer food, discounts, or any type of favor to the inspector.

- When answering the inspector's questions, be honest and to the point.

- It's okay to converse and make small talk with the inspector. It makes the situation more comfortable for everyone.

Periodically, you may want to hire a food safety consultant to help you plan and improve your safety practices in a variety of ways. These experts can save time in finding areas for improvement and can offer a fresh perspective. With their calibrated probe thermometers and flashlights, they'll check areas most commonly missed during cleaning—potato wedgers, can openers, ice machines, shelves under prep tables, floors under the food prep counters, mop/broom closets, and walk-in cooler fans. Using an outside consultant demonstrates to your staff, your customers, and your local health department that you take food safety, and the safety of your employees, seriously. Your insurance company may be able to recommend a consultant. For information on food safety specialists, try these websites: www.nsf.org, www.apha.org, and www.fcsi.org.

Security Procedures

The following news report appeared in the *Sacramento Bee* on July 23, 2010:

Two armed men wearing disguises and food-service uniforms walked into an unguarded money-counting area at the California State Fair in Sacramento and hit the mother lode—$100,000 in cash. The robbery took place late Wednesday as the fair was closing down. Police suspect the robbers worked for the catering company that was targeted, or knew there wouldn't be guards present when workers counted money from the day's take . . .

Norb Bartosik, general manager of the fair, told *The Sacramento Bee* that it was up to the vendor, Ovations Food Services, to provide its own security in the counting room and did not know why none had been arranged.

Whether or not cash collection is part of an off-site event, today's caterer not only needs to be concerned with employee and guest thefts, but also must perform rigorous security checks prior to catering certain types of high-profile events, from celebrity-studded social functions to political conventions.

According to Carl Sacks, owner of Event Creators Group, LLC, in Woodland Park, New Jersey, caterers who plan and/or work at high-security events should:

- Perform employee background checks on all job applicants.
- Photograph all employees in a digital format that can be e-mailed to a third party to verify identity.
- Create picture ID cards for full-time and delivery employees.
- Identify their catering trucks with prominent logos.
- Send out all deliveries with proper paperwork.
- Send staff members to events dressed and ready to work, with no duffel or garment bags.
- Allow plenty of extra setup time because of the high level of scrutiny expected and the resultant delays.

On your own premises, the costs for security systems—closed-circuit televisions, time-delay safes, and perimeter alarm systems—are high, but they will deter at least some burglars and embezzlers and lower your insurance premium costs. You can examine some of your options on the website of the National Burglar and Fire Alarm Association (www.alarm.org). On the same website, the organization suggests simple but effective security policies that can become part of your everyday business practices, such as creating a visitor management policy for when people visit your commissary, creating policies for Internet usage, and managing your company's external reputation with guidelines for what is (or is not) allowed to appear in its social networking sites and posts.

Loss-prevention tactics include depositing excess cash in a safe, varying your cash-handling routines, counting money only in a locked office, and never admitting any unauthorized personnel into the catering commissary. Put internal controls into place: The person who counts the end-of-day cash cannot deposit it without verifying the total with the company owner or another preauthorized employee. Keep a written record of all people who have keys to your building(s) and vehicle(s), and get those keys back when they leave your employ for any reason.

Many robberies are triggered by security leaks from current employees or committed by former employees who learn the security system, and then quit and return to rob the business. However, almost 43 percent of robberies happen on the street, when someone going about his or her business is stopped by a stranger with a weapon. Another 13 percent happen at residences. In the 1990s, Round Table Pizza's San Francisco locations began posting a list of safety tips for their delivery drivers. We've kept them in the book because they are still excellent advice and can be adapted for catering staff members as well:

1. Enter and exit the commissary through the front entrance after dark.

2. Drop excess cash after every delivery run in a secured drop-box located in the delivery area.

3. Carry only a minimum bank, no more than $20 or $30. This bank might include two $5 bills, 10 $1 bills, and a few dollars in change. Order takers should tell delivery customers that drivers will not accept bills larger than $20 for payment of food. (Of course, this point won't often apply to caterers, but there is a chance that an employee would be carrying petty cash.)

4. Always carry a cell phone.

5. Always lock vehicles and leave headlights and emergency lights on, and use a flashlight for a night delivery. After exiting the vehicle, scan areas around the house, especially in darkened areas to the sides of the home.

6. Use extra caution in case of darkened homes or areas. If the situation seems threatening, do not make the delivery. Call the restaurant and have the restaurant phone the customer again, requesting he or she leave the front light on.

It isn't just money that disappears from catering companies. Controlling in-house theft of food products, tableware, and other items is another concern of every caterer. Some caterers use security cameras, and others spot-check bags, purses, and employee lockers. When hired, employees should be informed about how their activities will be monitored and asked to sign a statement acknowledging that they know and understand this policy.

Another pesky problem is that guests at catered events seem to love to take off with "souvenirs." Your staff members should be alert for these sticky-fingered guests. A South Florida caterer recovered eight Champagne flutes from a female guest's purse when alerted by an observant staff member who saw her stuff them into the oversized handbag.

This is just one reason that an inventory of equipment at the end of each catered event is a must. As mentioned in the discussion of catering contracts in Chapter 2, clients should be made aware that if there are excessive losses of napkins, flatware, or glassware, they will be billed for these losses. The same goes for table linens damaged by spilled wax or burns from client-provided candles or sparklers.

Insurance Coverage

We touched on the importance of insurance coverage in Chapter 6, and we continue the discussion here. When purchasing insurance, the off-premise cater should evaluate the size of the potential loss, the probability of the loss, and the resources to meet the loss if it should occur, keeping in mind that risks involve everything from thefts to weather-related disasters. Minor risks can be absorbed with the use of deductibles, but major risks should be covered. A good basic rule is to never risk more than you can lose.

Off-premise caterers should cultivate a good relationship with several reputable insurance brokers who deal with the following types of insurance. Some of these may not apply to every caterer, or may apply only in some situations, while others are required by law.

- *Property* or *business property insurance* includes everything owned by you in your business. It covers losses that are the results of fire and/or water damage, and theft.

- *Business interruption insurance* is a type of property insurance that covers expenses (salaries, rent payments, taxes, interest, utilities, and lost profit) in case your business must close temporarily because of a fire or other disaster.

- *"Property of others" insurance* might be necessary if you use anything routinely in your business that belongs to someone else—leased equipment, for example.

- *Liability insurance* covers the caterer's liability for injuries or damage that occurs either on the caterer's property or off-premise at event sites. It may also include product liability (in case of a food-borne illness) and liquor liability (in case of alcohol-related accidents). An off-premise site often requires the caterer to include that specific site on his or her policy (as an "additional insured") for an event. Liability coverage is an absolute requirement in the catering industry. Get as much as you can afford.

- *Personal injury insurance* gives caterers the funds to protect themselves against libel, slander, defamation, and false arrest.

- *Glassware insurance* covers breakage of dishes and glasses.

- *Vehicle insurance* should cover employees who are using their own vehicles for company business, as is often the case in off-premise catering jobs—in addition to the company-owned vehicles.

- *Equipment insurance* covers damage to equipment while it is being transported and during its use at off-premise events.

- *Food spoilage insurance* covers losses incurred when refrigerators and freezers fail. If your area is known for power outages or brownouts, you'll want to look into this type of coverage.

- *Workers' Compensation insurance* is required by law and is typically administered by your state insurance commission. If you don't pay for coverage, your business can be shut down. "Workers' Comp" covers employees for job-related accidents and injuries.

- *Disability insurance* pays at least a portion of a person's income when he or she is unable to work for a long period of time after an injury or accident. Because an off-premise caterer is self-employed, he or she should be insured in the event of a disability.

- *Umbrella coverage* is an extra option that gives a company more coverage than the standard, general liability limits—hence the name "umbrella." It is designed to protect a business from an extraordinary loss. Your insurance agent or broker can discuss its appropriateness for a particular business.

Crime insurance (also known as *fidelity insurance*) is a fairly recent addition to the lineup of insurance possibilities. It sprang up in the insurance industry because many property insurance policies do not cover theft, embezzlement, and other "insider" losses perpetrated by employees. Crime insurance also covers counterfeiting and computer fraud.

Crime insurance is an alternative to bonding your employees. There are several types of fidelity bonds, and their goal is to absolve the employer from legal responsibility for the dishonest acts of bonded employees. Depending on the bond, these acts can include everything from theft and forgery, to destruction of property, to outright disappearance of the employee. A bond can cover one person, all employees, or only persons with particular job titles. The cost of bonding varies widely, depending on the type of coverage and number of bonded individuals.

It is always best to obtain bids from three or more brokers; you might also look into the various insurance programs offered by associations, like your state restaurant association or the National Association of Self-Employed Persons (NASE). Where insurance is not available, or if it is inordinately costly, restaurant owners sometimes pool their resources and become their own insurers. You may be able to participate in such a group.

🍴 Summary

The first half of this chapter contains what is likely the least appetizing portion of a book about off-premise catering, with an extensive discussion of the many types of food-borne illnesses. The millions of people who suffer from gastrointestinal distress every year are not the only victims here; a catering company faced with such a scandal may never be able to recover its good reputation and will surely suffer financially, even if the illness itself was minor.

Prevention strategies include a combination of strictly enforced employee hygiene standards and practices; safe food storage for hot and cold products and ingredients; sanitary preparation, holding, and transport methods; proper sanitation of equipment; and vigilance to keep all of these rules and systems in full force. All are discussed in this chapter, with emphasis on the HACCP system in wide use today. A closer look is also provided at the most common food allergens.

Often, an off-premise caterer does not realize a food safety problem existed until days after an event has taken place. A form is provided to guide the person at the catering company in obtaining as much information as possible from a caller with such a complaint.

A wide range of on-the-job safety topics are covered in this chapter. There are tips for safe lifting, use of kitchen knives and equipment, fall prevention, fire safety, and burn prevention, to name a few. In addition, we summarize the types of problems that inspectors look for and offer advice about how to deal with an unannounced health or safety inspection.

Today's off-premise caterer must be aware of the potential for security breaches at events or within their own facilities. The chapter ends with information about avoiding these problems and insuring against the damage they might cause.

Although some people consider topics like insurance and workplace safety to be mundane, we cannot sufficiently stress their importance in today's litigious society. Mistakes in these areas can cost an off-premise caterer his or her reputation and livelihood. Yet most of these problems are surprisingly easy to avoid with the assistance of your local health and fire departments and your insurance carriers. You owe it to your customers and employees to ensure that the highest standards of sanitation and safety are being met, day in and day out.

Study Questions

1. Select one of the "Big 8" food allergens. Find out what the symptoms are of an allergic reaction to this substance and what, if any, first aid steps should be administered.

2. How and when do you use disposable gloves, and how often should you change them?

3. Can ice be considered sanitary if it has not started to melt? Explain your answer.

4. Describe the considerations necessary to create a safe trash enclosure outside a catering commissary.

5. Look into the costs of bonding versus crime insurance in your area and explain why you would choose one or the other for employees who are responsible for handling money and financial records.

13

Accessory Services and Special Themes

One of the hallmarks of a great off-premise caterer is the ability to "take care of everything," so that the hosts and their guests enjoy a well-planned and perfectly executed event. This chapter encompasses the "everything" portion of that statement.

As we have mentioned, most people are not especially familiar with the catering business—and if they trust you enough to hire you, they often need your advice about many of the elements other than catering, known as *accessory services*, that are part of most banquets, weddings, and other events. Off-premise caterers soon learn that these types of specialized services can be profit centers. They seek out the best purveyors of these services, handle the contractual arrangements with them, or, in some cases, add this service to the catering company's repertoire. It is not unusual to see an off-premise catering company with its own floral department, event designers, and wedding planners on staff.

In addition, clients often expect the caterer to suggest themes for an event and/or to be familiar with the etiquette surrounding a wedding or bar or bat mitzvah. With these topics in mind, this chapter serves as an introduction to the following:

- Working with musicians and entertainers
- Florals and décor
- Working with photographers and videographers

455

- Lighting and audiovisual services
- Transportation and parking services
- Creating event themes
- Kosher catering
- Weddings and wedding receptions

We encourage you to read as much as possible elsewhere about the topics covered in this chapter, but remember that experience is the best teacher. You will gain confidence when you resolve to learn as much as possible from each event you cater. Take detailed notes, observe, and evaluate the suppliers you use to provide accessory services.

Accessory Services

Accessory services are those additional touches that contribute to the overall success of a catered event. The term *accessory* hardly means they are unimportant. Wonderful food and perfect service at a wedding reception can be completely overshadowed by an inappropriate band, an impossible parking situation, or inadequate sound or lighting. At minimum, caterers need to know whom to recommend for these services. Out-of-town clients often depend on the caterer to recommend and book all facets of an event. Local clients usually choose to engage at least some of their own services, but they may still come to you for advice. The key point in either case is to be able to recommend only those suppliers who are professional, dependable, and able to meet the needs of each particular client.

Before discussing each area of accessory services, let's consider how you, as the off-premise caterer, should charge for your expertise in these areas. It is a somewhat controversial topic in the industry. The most common practices, and justifications for them, are as follows:

- Some caterers simply make recommendations—they give clients a list and let them do the selecting and hiring. No fee is paid for the recommendations; these caterers feel that they make their money from the food and service and that clients can negotiate their own prices for the other services, possibly at a lower price.
- Some caterers receive a small commission or referral fee from the supplier who gets the business. These caterers feel that they are, in effect, acting as sales representatives for the suppliers and that they are entitled to the referral fee.

- Many caterers hire the accessory providers, then mark up their services slightly and add them to the overall invoice for the event. Their feeling is that they spend time screening, contracting, and paying the providers and that they are, in effect, responsible for the performance of the providers' services. The amount of markup will vary, depending on the situation. Such factors as overall budget and the amount of profit to be made on other areas of the party (food, beverages, rental equipment, etc.) will affect the markup.

Off-premise caterers must base their policies on their own unique situations. For the most part, good caterers who have been in business for any length of time have developed excellent working relationships with certain accessory suppliers. They have created a select team of winners who work well together to produce superb events. How the client is billed for these services depends largely on how the caterer feels about charging for that professional expertise.

Now let's examine the different types of accessory services and the caterer's role in booking and/or providing them.

Music and Entertainment

Music is the heartbeat of a party. It can transform spectators into participants and can truly make or break some types of events. A deejay playing the songs everyone loves to hear will certainly make the party more enjoyable. However, we recall at least one large party that was ruined when the party planner hired a Michael Jackson impersonator to perform for a group of soft drink company executives, when, at that time, Michael was promoting a competitor's soft drink.

There are three general types of music:

- Background music is a good choice during cocktail hours and dinner parties.
- Music for dancing is best after dinner.
- Music for listening is usually found at events where the entertainer is the "show" and people are there to see that specific person or band

Music at catered events can range from background music provided by clients' stereos to the live sounds of large show bands. Harps and string quartets produce excellent background music and are always appropriate for wedding ceremonies. Deejays play a wide variety of prerecorded music at economical prices. Some deejays are also personalities who entertain between songs by chatting up the audience and acting as master or mistress of ceremonies. Party bands are always popular, with their wide range of cover tunes that appeal to all age groups.

Whether a client hires musicians or asks the caterer to hire them, the following advice should be heeded:

- Be sure that the music fits the event. A string quartet at a country-western party is not appropriate. All too often, people make musical selections because they "know somebody who's in a band" or because somebody's relative offers to play for free. That can be a big mistake if the type of music doesn't fit the crowd.

- Absolutely go to hear and see the group in advance. Any band worth hiring has a CD of its music, which should also be shared with the clients, but they need to see the performers in action if at all possible.

- Music should appeal to the group as a whole rather than just satisfying the clients' own personal tastes. Included in the musical equation should be the purpose of the event, the average age of those in attendance, the range of ages, the region of the country where the guests live, and where the party will be held.

- Always obtain and sign a written contract, whether it is with the musicians them-selves or their agent. It should include these essentials:

  The exact price for a certain amount of performance time

  A specified time by which setup will be completed (this should be long before the guests arrive)

  The start and end times of the performance (not the event!)

  Scheduled break times (how often and how long)

  The exact location of the event

  The type of event

  The type(s) of music to be played

  The names of the musicians who will be playing (some leaders have a number of different groups playing under the same name) and their instruments

  The musicians' attire (dress code or not?)

  Overtime charges, and who is authorized by the client to approve them if the event runs long

  Cancellation charges, deposit amounts, and payment terms

  A guarantee of work (that the musicians will be there, will perform, etc.)

- There may be other areas to outline. We think it is best to offer musicians a meal at the event—will this be a special meal or the same food that is served to the guests? Additional concerns that should be spelled out in the contract include:

Where instrument cases and personal belongings will be kept

Whether the musicians can bring guests and/or potential clients who wish to hear them

Whether they can drink alcohol during the event

Whether there is a changing and/or break area

Insurance requirements, depending on the venue

Be sure that the entertainers have directions to the event site. A general rule that applies to every event is that music should be playing when the guests arrive. Strings may play softly as guests assemble for a wedding ceremony; rock music may be blasting as guests arrive for an outdoor barbecue; trumpets may herald guests' arrival at an upscale dinner at a prestigious location; mariachis may greet guests at a Latin-themed event; the orchestra might be belting out an upbeat tune as guests enter the ballroom for dinner. The late Lester Lanin, referred to in the *New York Times* as "the quintessential society bandleader," said that the preferred number of musicians should depend on the size of the crowd at an event. We agree with his suggestions:

Group Size	Number of Band Members
125	5–7
250	7
500	12
750	12 plus strings
1,000	15–20

Now led by Music Director Spencer Bruno, Lester Lanin Music maintains an office in New York City's Empire State Building. Its services include live music and deejays "at correct decibel levels."

Off-premise caterers should also be familiar with certain terms when dealing with musicians and their agents:

- "Pre-heat" means cocktail hour music.

- The term "noncontinuous" generally refers to the time musicians will play and the duration of their breaks. Usual examples are playing for 40 minutes and resting for

20 minutes, or playing for 45 minutes and resting for 15 minutes. (Too bad the caterers don't get breaks like this!)

- "Continuous" means there will be music throughout the evening—either no breaks or very short ones lasting no more than 5 minutes. The musicians in larger bands and orchestras will take their breaks at different times throughout the party. It's a good idea to request that recorded music be played while they are on break. Typically, the musicians supply this music.

No matter who hires the musicians, the off-premise caterer is responsible for working the musicians' requirements into the event. This means determining the amount and costs of seating, staging, and tenting. How many extra chairs will they require? How about music stands? (They should bring their own.) Portable stages can be expensive, and so are tents, but most performers with electrical equipment (sound board, amplifiers, etc.) will not play if they are unprotected from rain and other elements.

The cost of musical entertainment depends on several factors, including the size of the band or group; the season, night of the week, and time of day; and other regional factors.

Whenever live human beings are hired to perform an important service—like entertaining—problems are bound to arise. A savvy off-premise caterer is always prepared. Carolyn Luscombe, CSEP, president of Eclectic Events International in Toronto, Canada, offers these additional tips:

- Always have a backup plan in case of cancellation.
- Consider cancellation insurance for major acts.
- Don't "beat the entertainers down" on pricing. However, if the budget needs to be trimmed, ask them to accommodate you.
- For major acts, review the contract rider, which covers such topics as dressing rooms, meals, and other amenities.
- Choose a corporate entertainment agent for major acts. An agent can negotiate better prices, as well as handle the other details (insurance rider, travel arrangements, preperformance sound check, etc.) The best agents are licensed by the American Federation of Musicians of the United States and Canada.

Weddings have their own built-in musical challenges. The bride and groom may have their favorite songs, but at most weddings the guests are of all age groups. To achieve a mix that works best for the couple, as well as the crowd, Miami bandleader Simon Salz (www.simonsalz.com) provides his prospective clients with a Wedding

Music Planner, which he has graciously allowed us to reproduce as Exhibit 13.1. It pins down all the information the musicians need to do their part, both at the ceremony and the reception.

Florals and Décor

Off-premise caterers are often consulted about floral design and the use of other items to decorate an event site. One of the reasons you are hired is typically because you have a sense of design and décor in addition to great recipes—you can make a party look as good as the food tastes! Some caterers choose to create their own floral designs, which can be a highly profitable part of the business, rather than referring the work to others. Other caterers recommend floral designers or work regularly with a few they know and trust.

As with music, prospective clients want an off-premise caterer who understands at least the basics of floral design and décor. Here are just a few guidelines:

- On dining tables, floral centerpieces should never be more than 14 inches high, or they should be elevated on stands so as not to obstruct guests' views of each other across tables.

- For upscale events, a few exotic flowers are much nicer than a larger number of inexpensive blooms.

- When budgets are limited, a large, striking arrangement at the entrance is much more effective than a number of smaller arrangements placed around the party area.

- For weddings and receptions, the emphasis should be on the reception flowers and bouquets, rather than those at the church, because guests will enjoy them much longer at the reception than at the church.

- Whether the caterer or the client selects the florist, the florist should always visit the event site before preparing a proposal and price estimate.

- Whenever possible, the flowers used at a ceremony should be reused on buffet tables or in other areas at the reception site.

- Off-premise caterers and their clients should be aware of extra charges typical of florists, such as delivery and setup fees. Also, as with wedding cake fixtures, arrangements must be made between caterers, clients, and floral designers for the safe handling, storage, and return of items like mirrors, special vases, and arches after the event is concluded.

Wedding Music Planner

Music plays an important role at your wedding, setting the atmosphere and providing memories for many years to come. Each family has its own unique tastes in music—as well as pieces that have special meaning for the participants. This planner is a guide to the musical decisions you will be making as well as a way to gather the information needed to provide fitting music for each part of your event. Once completed, this planner will be invaluable in making your special day 'note' perfect.

The Wedding Ceremony

Wedding Date _____ Start Time _____ Approx. Length of Ceremony _____

Location _____

Approx. # of Guests _____ Will a sound system be needed for the music? ___ no ___ yes

Attire for Musicians _____

Religion/Ethnicity/Style of Wedding Ceremony _____

Instrumentation _____ Will you want a vocalist? ___ M ___ F

Special Musical Requests _____

_____

Music to Avoid _____

Prelude: Start Time _____ Approximate Length _____

Musical Selections

Prelude _____

Processionals —

   Bridal Party _____

   Groom _____

   Bride _____

   Other: _____   _____

Ceremony

   When in service?

   _____   _____

   _____   _____

   _____   _____

Recessional _____

Exhibit 13.1 Wedding Music Planner

(Courtesy of Simon Salz Productions, Inc.)

The Wedding Reception

Bride's Name _____ Groom's Name _____

Time of Reception: from _____ to _____

Location of Reception _____

Type of Music Preferred During Cocktail Hour _____

Type of Music Preferred During Dinner _____

Type(s) of Dance Music Preferred (check as many as you like):

__ Big Band/Swing __ Latin __ Rock/Pop __ Ballroom __ Line Dancing

__ Klezmer/Jewish __ Country __ Disco __ R&B Other: _____

Instrumentation _____

Persons To Be Introduced for Grand Entrance:

Name	Relationship
_____	_____
_____	_____
_____	_____
_____	_____
_____	_____

Upon Entrance of Newlyweds, Introduce Them As _____

Song for First Dance _____

Other Important Songs _____

Songs or Things to Avoid _____

_____

Please indicate who will be brought up to dance after the bride and groom. It is traditional to invite up the parents, then the wedding party, and then the rest of the guests. As this is not always the case, we need to know your preference.

_____

_____

_____

When will the toast be given? _____ Who will give it? _____

Will you have a cake cutting? _____ A bouquet/garter toss? _____

Other rituals, announcements, or events _____

_____

NOTES:

Exhibit 13.1 *(Continued)*

- Always look for florists who understand the needs of the off-premise caterer, as well as the client, and will stick to the budget.

- Live plants, such as areca palms and ficus trees, add dimension to certain off-premise locations. They work well to disguise tent poles, act as a backdrop for the stage and musicians, fill in otherwise empty or awkward-looking corners of rooms, and line entrances to create an aisle-like effect.

- The newest "green" trend is to decorate with bamboo. It looks great and is considered eco-friendly because it takes only a few years to mature. It also comes in all sizes, from tall canes to potted "lucky bamboo" for guest gifts and centerpieces.

In terms of prices, some off-premise caterers recommend that the budget for flowers should be approximately 10 percent of the food cost for an event. Smart caterers and their clients also realize that flower prices change dramatically according to the time of year. Flowers are usually less expensive during spring and summer and most expensive between Thanksgiving and Christmas. Roses are extremely expensive around Valentine's Day and Mother's Day unless ordered months in advance. Many florists refuse to do weddings or other catered events during these holiday weeks because that's when they are swamped with traditional holiday business.

Contracts for florals and décor are relatively simple, but they should include:

- Particulars about who will show up, when they will show up, and where they will show up. (If an event is going to be photographed, it is critical that the flowers arrive before the photographer.) Also, will the florist stay at the event site until you approve the work?

- A complete listing of everything that is required. This includes the small items, such as flowers to garnish the hors d'oeuvres trays and ferns around the wedding cake. Never assume.

- The size, shape, color, number, and types of flowers for each arrangement, as well as where they will go.

- Deposit and cancellation terms.

- Information on whether the designer guarantees the work. What happens if, at the last minute, you or the clients are not pleased?

There should always be a plan for distributing fresh flowers at the conclusion of events. Some groups hold drawings for them, hiding stickers under the chairs or tying a small ribbon on a piece of flatware to signify "winners" of tabletop arrangements. At charitable events, the centerpieces can be sold to benefit the organization. A very nice touch is to suggest that florals be taken to a nursing home and distributed among the residents.

When flowers are left behind, off-premise caterers should control their distribution, rather than simply let the staff take them at random. In many cases, caterers can reuse the flowers, perhaps rearranging them for another event the following day. Under no circumstances should the staff be allowed to remove floral arrangements from the tables until approved by the caterer or event supervisor.

Aside from using florals and plants, caterers can enhance the décor of a party, wedding, or event with ice carvings, balloons, and props. Caterers are limited only by their imagination when it comes to decorating. Both brides and corporate planners are becoming increasingly interested in the "looks" of their parties, and this trend is expected to continue. Creative caterers can separate themselves from their competitors by offering in-house floral and other décor services that they control, instead of leaving these services to contractors.

In most markets, caterers can arrange for ice carvings in all shapes and sizes. These work well for cold food presentations, particularly raw bars, so it is important to know a couple of vendors who can provide this service.

The use of balloons is an inexpensive way to decorate. Balloon centerpieces and arches add color, excitement, and a festive feel to any party and provide a good way to fill up a large room on a moderate budget. "Balloon walls" can be used to hide a person or products—on a stage or platform, for instance—and can be cued to explode all at once to reveal what's behind them. Again, these are services that some caterers provide and some subcontract to others.

Many caterers have accumulated all sorts of props to enhance buffets, dining tables, and the event itself. We know one South Florida caterer who travels to Europe each summer, buying items to enhance her displays and create a unique look.

A variety of machines may be employed to produce special effects. Scent machines can produce up to 1,300 different scents. Bubble-, snow-, and fog-making machines can enliven any party. Visit Global Special Effects' website to learn more about these special options.

Photography and Videography

Off-premise caterers should establish relationships with several good photographers and videographers. These professionals may be recommended to clients, and, in turn, most of them will also provide the caterer some good photos and videos from the caterer's events to show prospective clients.

In our experience, the best photographers and videographers for events are those who are calm, efficient, and have a sense of humor. They are able to keep things moving, so that the pace of an event—or in the case of a wedding, the photo session—does not stall. It is important that guests are not left sitting, waiting for a meal, while a photographer is still shooting photos. A professional photographer will want input from the clients on how they wish the event to be remembered. The photographer can shoot dozens of "candids" of guests as they enjoy the event, or focus on more formal, group shots—or both.

Décor and other details should not be ignored. We know of one married couple who spent a tidy sum on a beautiful custom-decorated cake but do not have a single photo of it; the photographer showed their faces as they were cutting the cake, but didn't bother to get the cake itself in any of the pictures! If there are certain people who absolutely must be in the photos, the client or a person they designate (in some cases, the caterer) should be able to point them out during the event.

Off-premise caterers should evaluate a photographer's work before recommending him or her and can share these suggestions with clients as well:

- Check out the photographer's website.
- Ask to review complete albums of work, rather than the best shots from a number of albums. This will give you a better sense of the photographer's style from start to finish.
- If a price list is not on the website, ask for one, including costs for extra prints, and deposit and refund policies.
- Select a particular photographer rather than a large studio that will simply send out one of its "associates" with a camera.
- Inspect photographs for sharp shadows in the background (not good) and look for detail in such areas as the wedding cake icing and the wedding gown (good).

Additional tips come from renowned wedding photographer Joe Buissink of Beverly Hills, California, coauthor (with Skip Cohen and Denis Reggie) of *Wedding Photography from the Heart* (New York: Amphoto Books, 2009).

- Do a walk-through of the wedding and reception sites with the photographer prior to the wedding to determine where the formal shots will be taken.
- Be sure to go over the wedding day time line with the photographer. Make him or her aware of any photo restrictions in the church or temple, as well as rules at

the reception site—where to park and unload, where to plug in equipment, and so on. (Older or historic sites sometimes have limited power, and circuits can easily be overloaded.)

- Be sure to pay the photographer in advance.
- If a hair and makeup person has been hired, make sure that he or she stays through the formal shots in case touch-ups are needed.

As with florists, it is important that contracts with photographers or videographers be specific about who is going to be on-site at the event, what time they will arrive, and how long they will stay—including pay considerations if more time is required.

One of clients' main concerns with photography is, "How soon can we see the pictures?" Make sure that you ask about the time line for viewing proofs and, after photo selection, delivery of the finished photos or albums. With videographers, ask about how long it will take to edit and duplicate the video, and what formats are available. And, if the final product doesn't show up on time, determine in advance how to handle that situation. Also ask how the photographer or videographer guarantees his or her work.

The relationship between caterer and photographer has the potential to be extremely beneficial to both. Separate from the discussions and/or contracts for specific events, you must sit down and discuss copyright issues for reuse of the images. Photographers might want to use shots from your events in their marketing; you might want to use photos and/or video clips on your website and in your marketing. Be very clear about who pays whom for these arrangements or, if no money will change hands, at least agree on specifics so that neither party feels taken advantage of.

Lighting and Audiovisual

Lighting is one of the most neglected elements at catered events. The beautiful food displays are inadequately lit or dangerous steps and other obstacles are barely visible. If an event is to be held after dark, the off-premise caterer should plan a visit during that time period to accurately assess the lighting needs.

Good lighting is truly "invisible." It can highlight attractive features, hide flaws, and provide for guests' safety, all without calling attention to itself. Many off-premise caterers handle some of their own lighting, and others work with lighting specialists.

A caterer should at least have "a basic knowledge of lighting, so as to be able to professionally assist clients in this area," says South Florida lighting specialist Stephen

Pollock. Pollock and Nicole Pierce Fraser, director of business development for Media Stage (Sunrise, Florida, and Bayamon, Puerto Rico), offer these illuminating tips:

1. Theatrical-type light fixtures can work wonders for buffets. These fixtures are easily mounted, adjustable, and can hold colored *gels* (a gel is a film placed over the bulb to make the light a certain hue). They can be purchased or rented and can provide illumination ranging from soft, diffuse lighting to a hard-edged, focused pattern. This type of lighting can also be created by *pipe-and-base*, a weighted base with an upright pipe and light source attached to it. Most people don't pay attention to where the light originates—they just notice that it's there.

2. For buffet lighting, a good instrument is the six-inch Fresnel light, which puts out a soft light that can be narrowed to a spotlight or "flooded" to wash a wide area with light. The perfect color for lighting food is generally a *no-color* pink, which is a pale pink that is almost white, but adds a rosy glow to a buffet. Buffet centerpieces can be lit with another color, such as lavender. It is best to light buffets from the front, top, and back whenever possible.

3. Lighting is only as good as the power sources available. You usually cannot illuminate a whole room by plugging into a simple wall outlet. Using separate circuits in other rooms, or even renting an electric power generator (be sure that it's a silent model), can solve this problem.

4. Caterers should also be sure that additional lighting sources have dimmers on them, so that the lighting can be adjusted to fit the mood.

The Lighting Terminology sidebar on page 469 was prepared by Stephen Pollock. It is also important to be familiar with the terminology used regarding *conventional* and *intelligent lights*. Many people throw these terms around without knowing what they really mean.

- *Conventional lights* have no motors and do not move once they are installed and focused. Of course, their colors can still be changed by changing the gel colors.

- *Intelligent lighting*, which can be motorized or programmed, is more expensive, but it is essential for events that require high-impact lighting. These lights work well to highlight people in the room (at an awards program, for example) or for doing *ballyhoo effects* at the entrance to create a mood. They also work well when directed at people when they are dancing and having fun. In fact, *ballyhoo* is a commonly used term for a rotating searchlight.

Lighting Terminology

Fresnel: A lighting instrument named for the Fresnel lens it uses to produce a diffused, soft-edged beam. The spacing between the lamp and the lens can be adjusted to alter the beam spread, from soft to flood.

Gobo: A template inserted into a focusable lighting fixture that defines the pattern of the light as it is projected. Gobos can be made of either metal or glass; metal gobos give a "two-color" look (black and one other color), and glass gobos can provide more color. Glass gobos provide a great look for empty walls and entrances.

Leko: A device containing an adjustable lens that allows a beam to be focused with either a soft or hard edge. A group of internal shutters allows the beam to be cropped, and many Lekos have an adjustable iris to allow a variation of the beam's diameter. Lekos can accommodate a *pattern holder* (containing a gobo) for projection of a specific image. Lekos are used for specific lighting situations, such as buffets or podium spots. Keep in mind that they must be mounted somewhere.

Par light: Short for "parabolic aluminized reflector" light. Unlike Fresnels and Lekos, the reflector and lens are built right into this lamp. Par lamps are available ranging from very narrow spotlights to wide floodlights. These are fairly inexpensive and versatile. By simply changing the gel color, you can change the whole mood of a room. They work well for uplighting and can be set on the ground or floor, to point upward.

Pin beam: A small, 25-watt lamp that projects a narrow beam of light up to 20 feet. It is often used to light banquet tables and can make a simple centerpiece look stunning. (Keep in mind that the pin beam must be mounted directly over the centerpiece to avoid an angled beam that may cast undesirable shadows.) Pin beams are also used to highlight mirrored balls and dance floors.

Wash: A broad, even, soft form of lighting over all (or part of) a room or stage. It is created by a group of floodlights set up to provide general illumination in one or more colors. More than one "wash" can be set up to cover an area, blending multiple colors attractively.

Frequently, off-premise caterers are asked to provide audiovisual (A/V) equipment. This might include podiums; microphones; slide and overhead projectors; movie screens; videocassette, DVD, or CD players; rear-screen projectors; and so on. Many of the event sites you work with regularly will have such equipment and an A/V staff person to work with.

For other situations, a caterer should establish relationships with one or more audiovisual suppliers. Many caterers add markups to their costs for these equipment rentals, creating additional profits in exchange for the time it takes to deal with these matters. Others simply recommend A/V companies and let clients contact them.

Don't think of A/V technology as something to be used only for speeches and presentations. It can be useful for many aspects of special events: to enhance a theme with music or visuals, to add a personal touch to wedding receptions or birthdays with photo montages of those being honored, and so on. Technology changes constantly, and off-premise caterers should at least be familiar with the basics in these areas to be able to recommend enhancements to their clients.

Ground Transportation and Limousines

Off-premise caterers should be prepared to arrange ground transportation for clients, usually for out-of-town corporate clients or for wedding parties at destination wedding locations who require transportation to and from the event site. They may also schedule transportation for wedding couples on the day of the ceremony—limousine service, a horse and carriage, a trolley or rickshaw ride for the wedding couple and their guests. In Dallas, Texas, the city's trolley system even allows children's birthday parties on moving trolleys.

In our experience, it is better to be familiar with transportation vendors and to make informed recommendations than it is to actually book these services. Most caterers have learned that their time should be devoted to the event itself rather than worrying about whether the buses or limousines arrive on time. You should also give the following advice to clients using buses for transportation to event sites:

- Be sure that there is a person to meet and greet the guests, both as they board the bus and disembark.

- Each bus driver must have a map with detailed directions to the event. (We've seen buses full of guests get lost and arrive an hour late!)

- Refreshments should be on board if the trip will be longer than 30 minutes.

- Movie star look-alikes, fortunetellers, magicians, or palm readers can provide entertainment during longer trips.

- Written or verbal travel guides along the way will create interest.
- An end-of-party pickup time should be reconfirmed so that the transportation is present when guests are ready to leave the party site. (Some guests like to leave early, so it's important to have at least one bus for early departures.)

When you recommend ground transportation providers, the main criteria are dependability and reliability. You may also keep on file the types of transportation each company can offer. For instance, there are now "stretch" limousines that seat up to 16 passengers, and most come equipped with a telephone, television, and beverage service. According to Lynn Campanile of Bayshore Limousines in South Florida, Lincoln Town Cars are popular, partly because of their comfort and elegant, conservative look. However, it's fun to have vendors that offer vehicles like Hummer limousines or stretch limousines. And in Texas, the limo with a set of Texas longhorns affixed to the front is practically a staple. For weddings, many couples prefer elegant vintage cars like the Rolls-Royce and Mercedes-Benz. As their caterer, you must be prepared to offer options.

Valet Parking

From time to time, off-premise caterers are asked to assist clients with valet parking services. Self-parking can be a hassle at many locations, and clients may wish to provide valet service as an accommodation to guests. Before recommending a valet parking service, caterers should investigate the following:

- Is the company properly bonded and/or insured? One million dollars is a good minimum for broad-spectrum liability insurance. Harm done to a vehicle while the valet is driving is the responsibility of the valet service. Theft or vandalism that occurs when the car is parked is usually not covered.
- How does the service handle claims, and how long does the claims process take?
- Does the service carry a business license and a valet permit to operate in the municipality where the party is to take place?
- Are the people who work for the valet company clean-cut, well-groomed, and immaculately attired?
- Are the valet attendants courteous? These are usually the first people guests talk to when arriving at an event. The first impression should always be outstanding.
- Is there a policy on tips for the attendants?

- Can the company provide references or letters of recommendation? Be sure to call the references.
- If possible, observe the company in action. Is there is a long wait for cars, is sufficient staff provided, and how well are the vehicles treated?

We think it is always smart and courteous to provide the valets with a meal. They work hard and are doing their part to create a polished overall impression. The number of parking staff members necessary for any event depends on these factors:

- The number of expected vehicles. On average, there will be two to three people per car.
- The timing of guests' arrival. Will they "trickle in," as is common before a wedding ceremony, or will there be a rush as most guests arrive at the same time for a wedding reception?
- The distance that the valet attendants need to take the cars to actually park them.

Professional valet companies will evaluate each situation and be able to recommend an adequate number of parking attendants to service an event. When waiting in line for your car to be either parked or returned to you, one minute always seems like ten. Keeping this in mind, it is usually better to have too many, rather than too few, valet parking attendants.

The valet attendants should assemble at the party site one hour in advance of the arrival of the first guests. It's the caterer's responsibility to check the attendants' appearance and discuss the details of the event. Provide the valets with a written script, just a couple of lines telling them exactly how to welcome the arriving guests. For example, they might say, "Welcome to the Smiths' wedding reception! Please be sure to take your valuables with you, and follow the sidewalk to the reception."

Some classy perks can be part of the valet service. We've seen valets wash car windows (at no charge to the guests, of course) while the guests are at the event. Another idea is to provide a party favor for each vehicle, a little surprise as the guests depart. A small box of chocolate truffles on the dashboard or driver's seat, beautifully wrapped and including the catering company's card, might even gain some new business for you. For Saturday night events, a complimentary copy of the following Sunday's local newspaper is a nice touch.

Fireworks and Laser Lights

Add Fire Inc. in Miami Shores, Florida, has been among the nation's leading fireworks firms for 30 years, providing effects for everything from barge shows to live theater performances, to television ads. According to President Ted Walker, "The use of pyrotechnics [fireworks] can cause the level of excitement of any event to heighten and continue throughout the event. There are three ways to maximize the use of fireworks: outdoor aerial displays, outdoor ground displays, and indoor pyrotechnics."

Most people are familiar with outdoor displays. These are launched from the ground, produce their effects high in the sky, and require a large amount of space. Outdoor ground displays—meaning fireworks that are not shot into the air like an aerial shell—are normally used in conjunction with aerial displays to add "dimension" to the overall production. They can be custom-made to call specific attention to a logo, trademark, or business phrase or message. A ground display can safely be placed not only on the ground, but also on a hot air balloon, helicopter, stadium wall, mountainside, ocean float, or cruise ship. The Add Fire website contains some spectacular photos, along with an extensive glossary of fireworks terminology.

Fireworks companies will inspect the site for safety and the feasibility of aesthetic positioning of the fireworks in the environment, secure the necessary permits, and provide insurance and bonds as required. The local fire inspector may request a "trial run" before the event, which fireworks companies are accustomed to providing. This should be part of the contract and included in the overall cost.

Today there also are a variety of flameless "fireworks" made specifically for indoor use. These can add color and excitement to events without the fire hazard. They release streamers and confetti for up to 90 seconds at a time and can be "choreographed" to music; confetti cannons work with a simple carbon dioxide cartridge. There are also plug-in confetti blowers. The X-Streamers website is a good place to check these out. Another related product that's popular for indoor use is the Glitzzz Super Sparkler. These sparklers are great in birthday or anniversary cakes and can also be hidden in centerpieces and activated remotely.

Laser light shows can also add excitement to a catered event. *Laser light* is a solid beam of light that, when coupled with computer choreography, creates complex and colorful visual displays that can be synchronized to music. Indoor lasers, which include such models as Variscan, DualScan, and Smart Scan, look like lasers but are less expensive. When this type of laser is used with a smoke machine, the audience can't tell the difference between this and a "real" laser. Lasernet's website is one place to get more information; for a look at laser light shows in action, the website of Lightwave International is a must-see.

Another alternative to laser light effects for groups on a budget is to suggest "ballyhoo" rotating spotlights.

Themes and Theme Parties

Most types of gatherings—from weddings to charitable auctions to cocktail parties—can be even more fun and memorable if the client or caterer has a theme to unify all aspects of the event.

Think of a theme as the "umbrella" that encompasses every aspect of the event. Each part or "rib" of the umbrella is an important part of keeping it together:

- *Invitations:* Include details of any special dress or period costume expected of guests.
- *Transportation to the event:* Transport guests in a manner that will get them in the mood for what's to come.
- *Décor:* Really focus on the entrance(s) to set the tone; for very large events (500 guests or more), place large props well above eye level.
- *Atmospheric touches:* Use fog, lighting, soundscaping, and/or scents to help create a mood.
- *Food and beverage menus:* Carry the theme through with any ethnic cuisine and food presentation, including the color scheme, fabric print for linens, tableware, buffet displays, and so on.
- *Music and entertainment:* Select appropriate musicians or entertainers for the event or, at least, get the band to dress in costume, in the spirit of the event.
- *A "script" for the event:* Who says what, when? Toasts, announcements, and award presentations can all be written with the theme in mind. This is often the most overlooked of all event planning activities, as the caterer assumes the hosts are taking care of it. Don't assume anything! Ask the clients what they have in mind and how you can assist.
- *Costumes:* Themed costumes for staff and/or guests make the event especially fun.

Often, the event itself dictates the theme, whether it's a party for a particular holiday, a birthday (ask about the guest of honor's hobbies, favorite foods, job, etc.), an anniversary, or another lifetime milestone. But when it doesn't, the off-premise caterer should be a fountain of ideas for interesting themes to fit any situation. Eclectic Events

International, mentioned earlier in this chapter, lists dozens of "Themes for Thought" on its website, www.eclecticeventsintl.com/themes.asp. Themes come from everywhere. Consider these sources:

- Popular books (classics or current bestsellers) and movies
- Regional foods and themes: the New England clambake, the Wild West barbecue and square dance, the California Surfin' party
- Heritage events: Kwanzaa, Cinco de Mayo, Obon, Chinese New Year, Bastille Day, Santa Lucia/Festival of Lights
- Historic periods: Roaring '20s, Fabulous '50s, Groovy '60s, ancient Greece or Egypt
- Local costume shops
- Venues with built-in themes—museums, historical sites, etc.

Before you get carried away with any theme, however, you must be certain that it fits the client's original needs and purpose, including the budget and the guest demographics. These additional tips involve logistics that can enhance a theme or make it less practical:

- Consider accessibility by cars, motor coaches, horse-drawn carriages, boats/yachts.
- Consider the flow of guests within the space, and allow plenty of room for the props.
- Always have a backup plan in case of inclement weather.
- Find out whether there are scheduling conflicts with competing events.

You can find hundreds of theme ideas on the Internet. Try www.party411.com or www.themepartiesnmore.com. Popular magazines are also excellent sources of theme ideas. *Bon Appétit*, *Sunset*, and *Wine Spectator* are full of ideas that can be adapted for off-premise events; when *Vanity Fair* highlights a star-studded party, take a look beyond the smiling celebrities in the photos for design and décor possibilities. Travel magazines are also great sources of inspiration.

If there is a downside to theme parties, it is that planning and executing them is time-consuming and labor-intensive, requiring total immersion for the caterer. You would be well advised to charge accordingly for these services. This includes time spent on research and development; time spent meeting with clients; and the cost of the costumes, props, décor, and all the other "extra" elements, as well as employees' time to round them up. This expense is over and above the costs of food, beverages, tables, chairs, linens, china, glassware, flatware, and staffing. The good news is that if a particular theme works well for you with one group, it can be used again with others.

Kosher Catering

The term *kosher* is so widely used that it has gained a place in American slang to mean "appropriate, legitimate, or proper." When it comes to dining, kosher food is defined as food that meets Jewish dietary laws, or *kashrut*. This means it must meet very strict guidelines that adhere to Jewish law, or *halacha*.

Kosher is not a cooking style, and referring to a dish, no matter how traditional, as "Jewish" or "kosher-style" does not mean it is kosher. It must be properly prepared in order to be kosher. The kosher food laws are rather extensive. Some are derived directly from the Bible, others through rabbinic interpretations over the centuries. There are even "degrees" of kosher, some liberal and others very conservative. The most conservative, known as *glatt kosher*, requires a certified rabbi to be present during the food preparation and service.

In true kosher preparation, meat and dairy products cannot be served together and must be prepared in separate kitchens. In commercial kosher businesses, this means completely separate cooking equipment, refrigeration and freezers, smallwares, plate service, and so on. In addition, the dishes and utensils in a kosher kitchen cannot be washed together.

As you might imagine, these requirements present some challenges for off-premise caterers, although they are not impossible to meet with some planning.

These are some of the basic kosher food rules:

- According to the Torah, cloven-hoofed, cud-chewing mammals are kosher. These are animals that "double-digest" their food—that is, it goes from the stomach back into the mouth, where it is chewed a second time before being swallowed and digested. Cattle, deer, sheep, and goats are kosher. Pigs and rabbits are not. (Important note: Animals killed for sport are not considered kosher.)

- In the United States, only certain birds are considered kosher, including chicken, duck, goose, and turkey.

- Poultry and meat animals must be slaughtered under strict and humane guidelines (called *shechita*, which means "without pain") by people who are trained and qualified to do this. When the animal is dead, another team of experts examines the carcass to ensure that the animal was without illness, abnormalities, or anything else considered "unsanitary." (The individuals who do this are called *mashgiach*.) In particular, they look at the lungs to be sure that they are "pure"—if not, or if other questionable conditions exist, the meat cannot be used. All blood, nerves, and most of the fat is removed from the carcass.

- For beef, only the front quarter of the animal can be used; nothing below the middle portion of the carcass can be used.
- For fish or seafood to be kosher, it must have fins and easily removable scales. Tuna, carp, and herring are kosher, but only if they have been prepared by a kosher fishmonger with kosher knives and machines. In most cases, the scales must still be present on the fish for it to be considered saleable to a kosher consumer.
- Shellfish—clams, lobster, shrimp—is not kosher. Shellfish is considered the "garbage fish of the sea" and is never kosher, no matter how it is caught or prepared.
- Fish and meat cannot be served on the same plate, but can be served at the same meal on different plates.
- Milk and meat or poultry cannot be served together; it's permissible to serve fish with milk, however.
- Fruits and vegetables are permitted but must be inspected for pests. No organic produce can be kosher.
- Grape products, including wines, made by non-Jews cannot be consumed. All wine must be certified as kosher.

There are many other rules to be followed for a food item to be considered kosher. A few of the stricter rules are not universal, so the particulars must be discussed with a Jewish family before preparing for their event.

To make identification easier for consumers, kosher foods are often identified by a kashrut certification symbol on packaging. It is generally indicated by an identifiable symbol that includes the letter *K*, or by the word *pareve*, which means the food is "neutral," neither dairy nor meat product.

The Bar or Bat Mitzvah

A *bar mitzvah* is a ceremony and celebration usually performed in a temple or synagogue on the Sabbath (in Jewish culture, Saturday) near the date of a Jewish boy's 13th birthday. In the Jewish tradition, this is when he becomes a Bar Mitzvah, or "son of commandment," celebrating the beginning of adulthood. For a girl, the celebration is called a *bat mitzvah* or *bas mitzvah*, and she can be 12 years of age.

This is a major event in a young person's life. The key word to describe foods served for such an event, hosted by the child's parents, is "abundant"! And the menu must be selected to please both the teen and the adults. Some sample menus are shown in Exhibit 13.2.

EXHIBIT 13.2 Sample Kosher Meals

Brunch Buffet–Dairy Menu
Cheese Blintzes with Sour Cream, Warm Apples,
Strawberries, and Fruit Toppings
or
Blueberry Blintz Soufflé
or
Spinach Almond Quiche
Poached Salmon Filet
Pineapple-Papaya Salsa and Cucumber Dill Sauce
Apricot Noodle Kugel
Grilled Seasonal Vegetables
Roman Salad with Caesar Dressing
Challah Knot Rolls with Herbed Butter
Chocolate Hazelnut Torte
or
Assortment of Petite Sweets
Iced Juices
Fresh Orange Juice, Apple Juice, and Cranberry Juice
Coffee and Tea Service
Rich, Full-Bodied Coffee (regular and decaf)
Selection of Herbal Teas

Formal Served Lunch or Dinner–Meat Menu
Spinach Almond Salad with Grated Egg and Toasted Almonds
Honey-Mustard Dressing
Beef Tenderloin Garnished with a Handmade Sage Potato Chip Wild Mushroom Glacé
Herbed Mashed Potatoes
with Parvé Margarine
Sweet Pepper Green Beans
or
Seasonal Baby Vegetables
Specialty Rolls
Served with Parvé Herbed Spread
Phyllo Tulip Cups
Filled with Parvé Chocolate Mousse
On a Plating of Wild Raspberry Sauce
Iced Soft Drinks and Cucumber Ice Water
Coffee and Tea Service

Rich, Full-Bodied Coffees (regular and decaf)
Selection of Herbal Teas

(Source: Courtesy of Maxine Turner, Cuisine Unlimited Catering and Special Events, Salt Lake City, Utah.)

Today's bar mitzvahs are exciting events. Evening events can be quite lavish and are generally theme-oriented. Some feature deejays who play high-energy dance tunes to get everybody onto the dance floor, video games, laser lights, fog machines, roving video cameras that capture guests and flash their images on a big screen, and various themes, depending on what is popular with kids at the time.

It's easy for the off-premise caterer to get caught up in the party planning for these occasions, but don't forget that they are the culmination of some serious religious study by the young people who are the guests of honor. In many cases, they have performed a charitable project as part of their responsibilities—ask about it, and you can perhaps use it as a jumping-off point for a theme.

In addition to visiting the websites we mentioned, if you plan to cater for a Jewish clientele, you might subscribe to one of the following publications:

- *Joy of Kosher with Jamie Geller*
- *Kashrus*
- *Kosher Spirit*

The websites of Mitzvah Chic (by Gail Greenberg, who also has a book by the same name) and Jewish Link are also helpful. The latter contains links to information about traditional music, art, and much more, in addition to kashrut expertise.

Weddings and Receptions

The amount of information available on weddings and receptions has grown astronomically, primarily due to wedding-related television shows and Internet websites like those of The Knot and The Wedding Channel.

There is good news and bad news about this wealth of information. The bad news is that caterers, bridal couples, and their parents can be totally overwhelmed and overloaded by all they can find. The good news is that, with patience and persistence, a good off-premise caterer can help sort through the clutter and aim the bewildered wedding party in the right direction for a terrific celebration that represents the couple's hopes and wishes and fits their budget too.

Weddings can be big business for off-premise caterers, and some are known specifically for their wedding expertise. For most of us, weddings occupy the weekends and corporate events are mainly held during the week. It's a profitable niche, but you have to be the right kind of person for this peculiar type of stress—infinitely patient, very understanding, and knowledgeable about the many wedding traditions and etiquette.

Some caterers have wedding planners on staff or choose to take wedding planning classes, just to become familiar with all the pomp and ritual. There are numerous online certification courses.

This kind of background is important because today's brides are looking for one-of-a-kind venues, complete with exotic foods for their once-in-a-lifetime fantasy day—and, often, they can afford it. They expect first-class "hand-holding" (attention to every detail), explicit time lines, production values, food tastings, cutting-edge or elegant venue choices, and streamlined flowcharts.

We classify the three major potential "negatives" about a wedding as bad food, bad music, and a bad flow of events. Successful weddings have layouts that flow smoothly; the movement of the wedding party and guests is very important. A wedding can quickly turn into a disaster when things don't go as planned. Most mishaps are predictable and/or preventable, but timing is critical and every activity must be planned in advance. Caterers also need to know how to handle simple but inevitable timing-related situations: What if the guests arrive early at the reception? What if the bride and groom arrive incredibly late? What if the relatives change the itinerary altogether, before the newlyweds even get there? What if the florists or musicians don't show up on time?

Most of these situations can be handled by meeting with family members and vendors in advance to ensure a smooth flow. If a wedding planner is not involved, it is often up to the caterer to orchestrate a full rehearsal in advance, with all key players in attendance and every detail checked and double-checked. Communication is the key to ensuring a great wedding day experience for everyone involved, so the off-premise caterer must understand that the time spent with bridal couples and their families will far exceed the amount of time spent in planning a corporate event.

Additionally, it is important for caterers to consider what a hectic time it is for the members of the wedding party. In planning for the wedding, think about the small but significant steps you can take to make things a little easier for the bride and groom, their attendants, and family members. Include a complimentary light meal while the wedding participants are dressing—nothing that would stain the wedding gown, of course—perhaps tea sandwiches and fruit, to refresh them and keep them from being famished. Make sure that everyone in the wedding party has directions to all events and a copy of the time line.

Wedding Time Lines and Traditions

Wedding plans begin with the engagement. Normally, the bride's family determines the number of guests but should consult with the groom's family before determining this number. Usually, only close friends and family members are invited. Business acquaintances are not invited unless the wedding is to be extremely large.

The caterer should be able to assist a couple in suggesting sites, not only for the wedding and reception, but also for engagement parties and the rehearsal dinner. Younger couples may never have planned a catered event before, and their parents may be only slightly more experienced in this area. They will usually welcome—and expect—your ideas for interesting locations or your professional opinion of venues they are already considering. They might rely on you for suggestions about music, photography, vows, flowers, the wedding cake, and even the knife to cut it with. They may inquire about an officiant to perform the ceremony. Many off-premise caterers assume the role of wedding consultant, handling myriad details for the bride. Just be sure that your fees reflect this labor-intensive role. It is one thing to cater a reception and quite another to plan a full wedding weekend for a busy bride.

Even in these modern times, there is an incredible amount of tradition associated with weddings. Do not expect your clients to know about all these customs! You should become familiar with wedding protocol for all types of ceremonies and with basic etiquette issues, to assist couples and their families with the actual ceremonies.

There are dozens of, shall we say, interesting situations today. The parents of the bride are divorced, may or may not have remarried others, and may or may not be speaking to one another. People may want their children and friends—or even their pets—to be part of the ceremony. The bride and groom may practice different faiths and wish to incorporate both. And what about same-sex marriages, or commitment ceremonies? Caterers who know how to handle these delicate circumstances further demonstrate their value to prospective clients.

The Wedding Reception

Of course, very little is "typical" when it comes to the modern wedding. People get married as they skydive, scuba dive, or stand barefoot on the beach.

No matter what the setting, they still need to eat. Budget-minded couples may decide not to have a full meal for guests after the wedding, opting instead for nice hors d'oeuvres, cake, and sparkling wine. However, the traditional, more formal receptions still include a cocktail time with hors d'oeuvres and drinks, during which guests mingle and socialize (while the posed wedding party photos are being taken). The main meal is served when the bride and groom join the reception, sometimes preceded by a "first dance" and a Champagne toast. The proper toasting sequence is:

1. The best man toasts the bride and groom.
2. The groom toasts the bride and her family.
3. The fathers toast the bride and groom.
4. The bride and groom toast each other.

If the couple has selected an expensive premium Champagne for the toast (rather than a nice-but-less-pricey sparkling wine), it is best to do the toasting before the meal, so the guests are better able to appreciate it. We've seen half-full glasses of incredible bubbly sitting untouched on tables at the end of an evening because the toast was done at the same time as the cake cutting, near the end of the reception. Serve the good stuff first—and if you're using the less expensive sparklers, the toast can be delayed until after dinner with the wedding cake, when taste buds are saturated and most guests are full. For receptions where Champagne is served only for the toast, it is best to save the toast until the time of the cake cutting, so that guests will be less likely to go to the bar for refills and be refused additional Champagne.

Off-premise caterers are frequently asked to place party favors on guest tables, provide a separate gift table (although most guests do not bring wedding gifts to the reception and it is considered poor etiquette to do so), and provide an escort table on which seating cards can be placed.

The main meal can be a seated, served meal; a buffet; or an arrangement of food stations—or it may contain elements of all of these. There can be food stations during the cocktail reception, for example, then a preset first course, followed by a buffet. Again, think "flow"—what will keep the guests happy, interested, and involved in the festivities? When the meal is finished, we have found it's best to offer dancing before the cake cutting. This allows guests a chance to move around after the meal and ensures that they stay in the spirit of the event.

Wedding Cakes

If the Champagne toast is not done before the meal, it should be done immediately before the wedding cake is cut. The bride and groom cut the first piece of wedding cake

together, using a special, decorated cake knife. The cake table setup is especially important for the caterer, who should provide a plate, napkin, and two forks for the couple to
use. Here's how it's supposed to go: First, the bride feeds a bite of cake to the groom,
and then the groom feeds a bite of cake to the bride. This symbolizes their willingness
to share each other's lives. After this, the catering staff cuts and serves the rest of the
cake to the guests. A nice additional touch is to serve fresh fruits or another, lighter
dessert on the same plate as the cake. This creates a more visually interesting plate, satisfies those guests who choose not to eat wedding cake, and generates a bit of additional
profit for the caterer.

In past years, the top layer of the cake was saved and frozen for the couple to eat
on their first-year anniversary, although some eat it on their first-month "anniversary."
While you may still be asked by some families to box up the top layer, it is more modern
to offer a fresh cake—a small replica of the original—for the couple's first anniversary,
free of charge. A fresh cake surely tastes better than one that has been frozen for a year!
Make sure that this is part of your discussion with the couple, as well as your agreement
with the pastry chef.

At some receptions, there is a groom's cake in addition to the wedding cake.
(Historically, the groom's cake was the actual wedding cake, but today it is a classy alternative, often a chocolate or spice cake, to the wedding cake.)

Many off-premise caterers employ their own in-house pastry chefs who produce
wedding cakes. If you don't, you should align yourself with one or more pastry chefs
at bakeries known for their top-quality wedding cake designs. Today's wedding cakes
can practically leap off the table—they are edible works of art and can be designed to
reflect the couple's professions, hobbies, or whimsical personalities. We've seen them
made of Krispy Kreme doughnuts, cupcakes, cannolis, and mini-creampuffs, to name a
few. So much is going on in this field that it's impossible to do justice to the topic here.
We suggest visiting the websites of the following companies for fantastic wedding cake
ideas and photos: Ana Paz Cakes, Mike's Amazing Cakes, and Sylvia Weinstock Cakes.

Some caterers ask the bakery for a referral fee, and others receive a wholesale price for
the cake and then charge the client the retail price. Some charge a cake-cutting fee, in
addition to charging for the cake itself. When ordering wedding cakes, couples should
be prepared to provide the following information to the caterer or pastry chef:

- The number of expected guests
- The desired color and flavor of icing and trim

- The flavor of the filling and the cake
- What kind of cake-topper they wish to have (figurines, marzipan sculptures, flowers, etc.)
- The particular style of cake they like, if any (flowers, rolled fondant icing, fresh fruit as garnish, etc.)
- What they want done with any leftover cake at the reception

As the caterer, you will be asked for your advice, so you should be able to refer the couple to the websites of any pastry chef you recommend. In your own selection of vendors, it's important to sample the cakes. Are they flavorful, attractive, and moist? The most frequent complaint about wedding cakes overall is that they are "dry." The couple should also be encouraged to sample the cake selections. Pastry chefs who offer various flavors—carrot cakes, mocha, white chocolate, liqueurs, and fresh fruits—are always in demand. Our current favorite is lavender lemon!

As the caterer, if you are not at all involved in the cake order, you should at least have the contact information for the pastry chef, so that if the cake does not arrive on time, you or your event supervisor can find him or her without disturbing the bridal couple or their families.

If the cake is to be decorated with fresh flowers, it is smart to rely on the florist who is hired for the wedding to supply them rather than the pastry chef. This ensures that the flowers at the reception are all fresh and color coordinated.

Delivery times and other details must be coordinated between the pastry chef, the couple, and the off-premise caterer to avoid confusion and losses.

Final Reception Details

After the cake cutting, dancing usually resumes. Traditionally, as the event drew to a close, the bride would toss her bouquet to the single women in attendance and the groom would remove a symbolic garter from the bride's leg and toss it to the eligible bachelors. Today, however, many couples choose to eschew these traditions altogether or to replace them with alternatives.

As the bridal couple departs, whether from the church or reception site, guests frequently throw birdseed, flower petals, confetti, streamers, or lavender buds—there are many options. Every facility—even outdoor locations, like city parks—has rules about what can (and cannot) be tossed, and caterers must absolutely know these regulations. Some facilities do not permit any items at all to be tossed. If birdseed or flower petals are thrown, the off-premise caterer should immediately make sure that they are swept up to prevent people from slipping.

At the end of the reception, off-premise caterers should have the following items clean, packed, and ready for the couple or family to take with them:

- Any leftover foods or wedding cake, as prearranged
- Toasting goblets, cake knives, and any other accessories provided by the couple for use at the reception
- The guest book and pen in their original boxes

Almost every off-premise caterer now requires weddings to be paid for in this manner: 50 percent of the cost at the time the event is booked, and 50 percent five days in advance of the ceremony. This leaves the couple and their families free to enjoy their special day without anyone having to carry cash or remember to hand over a credit card. The caterer also keeps a credit card number on file, in case there are additional last-minute charges for alcohol, staff overtime, extra guests, and so on. Of course, these should be included on an updated invoice and sent electronically to the clients, so they are not surprised by additional charges on their credit card statement.

Working with Wedding Planners

When caterers work with wedding planners who are not part of their company, care must be taken to make sure that the responsibilities of each are clearly outlined, particularly when planning large, elaborate weddings. Like caterers, some wedding planners are better than others. The best ones are absolute godsends—professional, well organized, and competent. They allow you and your staff more time to devote to what you do well: providing excellent food and service.

Many wedding planners not only charge the bride for their time, but also expect some form of referral fee or commission from the catering company. Ethically, the wedding planner is required to inform the bridal couple about this fee. A planner who accepts such a fee is also, technically, liable if the caterer (or any other supplier) does not live up to the clients' expectations.

Like caterers, wedding planners are obligated to provide the best possible service at the best possible price. It can be a good working relationship because a wedding planner can relieve the caterer of so many time-intensive details—from creating place cards and placing them on tables, to negotiating contracts with other vendors. Wedding planners will also be familiar with formalwear options and availability, a topic not covered in this chapter.

In terms of your overall business, a good wedding consultant will bring you prequalified clients, which also saves you time and can increase your profitability. When things go wrong, as they sometimes do, a competent planner will work with you to correct the situation, and under no circumstances would a planner tell a harried bride about near misses and minor mishaps.

What a professional wedding consultant expects from you is the ability to be a team player in the wedding preparations. This means being helpful, responding to requests in a timely manner, and keeping your ego in check. After all, weddings are a true team effort. And the real stars are the bride and groom—not the planner or the caterer.

Today's Trends

As bridal couples become increasingly knowledgeable and sophisticated, caterers who want their business must keep up with current trends. Here are just a few that we have observed.

Green Weddings. "Eco-friendly" is the watchword for today's weddings, and there is so much to choose from that "green" can even be the overall wedding theme. Some couples choose an outdoor location—on the banks of a river, at a botanical garden—or they select a nonprofit organization, such as a museum or gallery, where their venue fee is a donation. In selecting a site, one goal is to minimize fuel consumption by ensuring that guests don't have to drive far to get there; the ceremony and reception can be held in the same place.

Invitations can be made of recycled paper with soy- or vegetable-based inks. The bride can wear a gown that is a family heirloom or purchase a vintage or "worn once" gown instead of a new one. If candles are used, they should be soy- or beeswax-based. The wine and foods served can all be organic and/or locally produced. Guests might be asked to make charitable donations in lieu of giving wedding gifts.

These are just a few of dozens of ideas to craft a wedding celebration that adds another *R*—romance—to the phrase "reduce, reuse, recycle." There are plenty of additional resources online. The Wedding Planning Institute now offers a Green Wedding Planner Certificate.

Commitment Ceremonies. Gay, lesbian, and transgender couples are able to legally marry in some states. In other states, they often declare their intention to be in a committed relationship with their partner with a commitment ceremony. This celebration can be as formal or informal as any other wedding. The ceremony can be religious or secular, the guest list large or small. As in a wedding, the couple exchanges vows and rings, and a reception usually follows. Again, it can be by-the-book traditional—cake cutting, Champagne toasting, bouquet tossing—or as casual as a picnic or barbecue for friends and family following the ceremony.

The websites for Two Brides and Two Grooms are great places to start for ideas. There is also wedding planning software, called My Gay Wedding Companion, available for commitment ceremonies and GLBT weddings.

Other Trends and Ideas. We've rounded up a smattering of other wedding-related ideas, as follows:

- Allow couples to place family photos around the reception room to personalize the setting. Wedding photos of parents, grandparents, and other relatives work well, along with photos of the bridal couple from infancy on. If the photos can be rounded up well in advance, a videographer can use them to create a custom video montage, set to music.

- Rent a photo booth, where guests at the reception can duck in for a few moments and emerge with shots to paste into an album for the couple; guests can write a personal note next to the photo.

- Afterglow stations are hot at receptions. These include espresso, cappuccino, and other coffee drinks, along with cognacs, cordials, and liqueurs.

- In lieu of party favors, the couple may make a donation in guests' names to favorite charities.

- Bathroom baskets packed attractively with the necessary essentials for restrooms and bridal party dressing rooms show that all details have been covered.

- Laser-printed menus cost little, yet they add a classy, professional touch.

- Destination weddings will never go out of style. But for the couple who can't afford to take everyone to their favorite Greek island or Hawaiian resort, why not make their dream destination into a theme for the reception?

- Smart caterers learn all they can about the customs and cultures of couples who are from foreign lands or who want to include their family heritage in their celebration.

- A food tasting prior to a wedding is a great way to spend time with the bridal couple, learning about their wants, needs, and desires, as well as an excellent opportunity to up-sell to more elegant food and services.
- Thanks to Martha Stewart and others, more brides seem to want long banquet tables that seat scores of guests, rather than the typical 60- or 72-inch rounds. A 66-inch round is becoming increasingly popular; it seats ten guests a bit more comfortably than the 60-inch table but takes up less room than a 72-inch table.

High-end wedding planning has become a celebrity industry. At this writing, the hottest wedding designers are Preston Bailey and David Tutera; the latter is best known for his television show, *My Fair Wedding with David Tutera*. You'll have fun checking out their sites for inspiration.

 # Summary

This chapter proves that there is a lot more to off-premise catering than food preparation and service. Your clients often rely on you for other aspects of event planning and, as a group, these are known as *accessory services*.

The chapter begins with a discussion about hiring musicians, from how to determine the style of music and the size of the band or orchestra, to what should be included in their contract. Contracts for florists are also necessary. The relationship between caterer and florist is so critical that some off-premise caterers have their own floral departments. Guidelines for how to use floral arrangements and what to do with them at the end of an event are included.

Technology enables photographers, videographers, audiovisual experts, and lighting designers to add panache to all types of catered events. Lighting can set the mood, and the correct A/V components allow everyone to hear and see the action. Candid shots taken on-site, or preedited video montages, can be shown on screens to delight the crowd. These elements must be thoroughly discussed and rehearsed, however, because there is no room for error at a live event. The exciting options of fireworks and/or laser light shows are also mentioned in the chapter.

Arranging such courtesies as ground transportation and valet parking are part of an off-premise caterer's role in making guests feel welcome and comfortable. In some cases, they can be tied into the theme of an event. Theme parties will always be popular—but they work only if they meet the client's needs and budget and fit the types of guests who will attend. In order to succeed, a theme also must be carried through many aspects of the event, from the initial invitation to the food and décor. This chapter offers many sources for theme ideas.

Kosher catering involves extensive knowledge of the Jewish food laws, which are summarized in this chapter along with a discussion of bar and bat mitzvah celebrations.

We also take a quick walk through basic wedding and reception protocol, although we must note once again that today's brides and grooms are less likely to follow tradition and more likely to want their own personal touches incorporated into their special day. We recommend that all off-premise caterers who don't have a wedding planner on staff spend time taking a wedding planning course, to become familiar with the many options.

The more you cater, the more you read, and the more events you attend as a guest yourself, the better you will become at building your knowledge of themes, services, and vendors to help you make these events a reality.

📖 Study Questions

1. Make your case for the way you would charge for providing accessory services as an off-premise caterer. Your options are listed on pages 456–457. If you would handle charges for different services differently, explain why.

2. Interview two local bands or two local florists about how they work with caterers, what they charge, and what their contracts include. Ask what advice they have for off-premise caterers to improve their working relationships with vendors.

3. Create a bar or bat mitzvah menu for 70 guests based on kosher foods you can obtain locally. Mention where you will get each item and include prices.

4. Think of one "extra" that a caterer could offer to a couple, free of charge, to make things go more smoothly at a large wedding or commitment ceremony.

5. Look online for details of a high-dollar celebrity wedding. Then do your best to recreate it on a budget. Detail your findings in a short report.

Budgeting, Accounting, and Financial Management

14

Technology has made it easier than ever to keep the financial records necessary for an off-premise catering company. However, any computer software is only as good as the accuracy of the data you input—and your ability to interpret and use the results to improve your business practices and increase your profit.

QuickBooks is just one example of a program that can be used to track your financial affairs. We have found it is worth the cost, as well as the investment of time required to learn how to use it. In addition, most catering companies find they require the services of a bookkeeper and, at tax time, a Certified Public Accountant (CPA). What you can accomplish with these people and tools is the subject of this chapter. In addition to offering tips on money management and controlling costs, it provides a brief introduction to the following:

- The components and preparation of a budget
- Cash budgets versus revenue budgets
- Keeping accounting records
- Computing your cost of sales
- Reading and analyzing financial statements
- Selecting banks and credit card processors

We tell new caterers, "If you think organizational skills are required to put a wedding together, just wait until you try doing your first-year taxes!" Off-premise caterers who understand the financial aspects of their business will definitely increase their chances of success in this challenging field. They need to know how to prepare budgets, produce accounting records, analyze financial reports, implement cost control techniques, deal with banks, and limit tax liabilities, as well as understand how computers and software programs can assist them.

Successful caterers know how the revenues and expenses from catered events flow through the business records and end up as profits or losses. They understand the difference between "profit" and "cash." Caterers who fail to understand their business "by the numbers" will simply be more likely to fail over time. So, in addition to knowing these basics—and even if you plan to hire an accountant—we suggest that you also take an accounting course or two. Another excellent resource for the business owner or manager is *Streetwise Finance and Accounting: How to Keep Your Books and Manage Your Finances without an MBA, CPA, or Ph.D.*, by Suzanne Caplan (Avon, MA: Adams Media Corporation, 2000). It is still in print and widely available. A more recently updated resource is *Finance and Accounting for Nonfinancial Managers: All the Basics You Need to Know*, by William G. Droms and Jay O. Wright (New York: Basic Books, 2010). This is the sixth edition of this very handy guide, highly recommended by accountants we know who work with entrepreneurs.

In addition, there are small business networking groups and Small Business Administration (SBA) offices in most major cities. Take advantage of their expertise to improve your own financial skills.

Preparing a Budget

No one should even consider starting an off-premise catering operation without first preparing a budget to determine the feasibility of the business venture. Off-premise caterers have lost millions of dollars by not first projecting their sales and then relating these sales to actual overhead expenses. Together, these steps form a basic budget.

A *budget* is a plan for operating a business expressed in financial terms. It includes sales and expenses, which are projections based on whatever information is available to you: past performance, current prices, future forecasts, and the like.

One of the most common mistakes made by a new caterer is committing to large overhead expenses (such as rent, utilities, and equipment financing) without first determining how these expenses will relate to the projected sales. This caterer takes on large financial obligations, assuming that large sales will follow. When these sales fail to appear or materialize more slowly than the caterer expected, the expenses exceed revenues, and the business often has no chance to catch up.

For example, a start-up off-premise caterer with no guaranteed sales or previous experience would probably be foolish to take on a $5,000 monthly lease and a $1,500 monthly payment for equipment financing. As a general rule, these two expenses should never exceed 10 percent of monthly sales, which means in this case that the caterer would need to average monthly sales of $65,000. A more realistic amount would be $1,000 per month for these expenses as the required revenues would be significantly less and obviously more achievable.

Today, a realistic guideline for the budgeting process is that a catering company that maintains a 38 percent food cost, 30 percent labor cost, and 20 percent fixed cost can expect a profit of about 12 percent.

For the purpose of illustrating basic accounting principles, we've created a fictitious caterer, whose business is aptly named Hypothetical Catering Company. This person is starting a small off-premise catering business from a small kitchen equipped with basic kitchen equipment and utensils. The caterer pays an annual rent of $12,000 ($1,000 a month), is financing the business with personal savings, and plans to rent the necessary front-of-house equipment from a local rental company. All examples and exhibits in this chapter refer to this fictitious company, and readers are cautioned at this point not to use these exhibits and examples as absolutes. They are not. Nor should readers assume that the various revenues, expenses, and profits are the exact figures to be emulated by all off-premise caterers. Again, they are not. Every off-premise caterer operates differently. The purpose of our example is simply to relate financial theory to reality.

The first step in developing a budget is to project sales based on past performance and projected future performance. Obviously, start-up caterers will have no past performance to evaluate, so they must make "educated guesstimates" about their projected sales. When estimating upcoming sales, it is better to err on the conservative side. Your projections should be based on your own best estimates of the following:

- Number of events you expect to cater

- Average selling price of each event

- Seasonal variations

- National and local economic indicators

- Competitive factors
- Industry trends

If you still have absolutely no idea what sales might be, start with the 10 percent figure mentioned in our discussion of Hypothetical Catering Company—that is, when you know what your rent and the payment on your equipment purchase loan or lease agreement must be, and you know they should be 10 percent of your monthly sales amount, then you can easily determine what that sales figure should be.

$$\text{Monthly rent} + \text{Monthly equipment purchase or rental}$$
$$\text{payment} \times 10 = \text{Total monthly sales target}$$

When you make these projections for a full year, as you should, you must consider that some months will be better than others. For instance, a start-up off-premise caterer who will focus on outdoor events in the southern United States will generate more sales in the cooler months (those with more pleasant weather) and fewer sales in the scorching-hot months. This caterer, who projects $180,000 in first-year sales, could realistically have these monthly sales projections:

January	$1,500 (first month in business)
February	3,600
March	9,000 (pleasant weather conditions)
April	7,200
May	12,600
June	7,200 (warmer months begin)
July	3,600
August	5,400
September	9,300
October	19,800 (weather begins to cool down)
November	28,000 (reputation is building)
December	72,000 (excellent holiday season)
First year total	$179,200

Why is it necessary to project sales on a monthly basis? Isn't it adequate to simply project them for the year? The answer is no! Bills must be paid monthly, no matter what the profit for a particular month, and a start-up business must plan accordingly to have enough operating capital (cash) on hand. In our example, it is more than likely that Hypothetical Catering Company will lose money for more months than it makes money but will generate a profit by year's end nonetheless. In those months of overall loss, the business will be unable to pay its expenses from revenues; therefore, operating capital (cash) will be needed. A detailed discussion of this subject follows later in this chapter.

The next step in preparing a budget is to estimate expenses. The four main expense categories are:

- Cost of sales (food cost; also called *cost of goods sold*)
- Payroll and related costs
- Direct operating expenses
- Administrative and general expenses

There is a detailed discussion of these expense categories in the section in this chapter on the Chart of Accounts (page 509). For now, we offer a brief definition and description of each of them.

Cost of Sales. Also referred to as "Cost of Goods Sold," this is estimated by reviewing past performance results for this category, as well as two factors:

- Your menu pricing strategy, which means what you will charge for each item. This figure should always include a percentage of profit.
- Current prices of raw materials and ingredients.

For example, an off-premise caterer whose overall pricing strategy is to triple the basic cost of the food should achieve a 33⅓ percent cost of sales, as depicted here:

Food cost for dinner is $5 \times 3 = \$15$ (per person)

$5 divided by \$15 is the cost of sales percentage $= 33⅓$ percent

Here are a few realistic markup factors and their associated food cost percentages:

Markup Factor	Projected Food Cost/Cost of Sales
5	20%
4	25%
3.5	28%
3	$33\frac{1}{3}\%$

Catering Software

There are several brands of computer software on the market to help small businesses determine what their prices and expenses should be. Off-premise caterers should research them and take advantage of them to help with the all-important financial functions of their company, as well as menu development, inventory control, payroll, and more.

Most catering software is designed for at least one of these business areas:

- *Sales and service:* These types of programs focus on keeping you organized as a manager. They keep track of bookings and changes to those bookings (and eliminate accidental double bookings), maintain customer and vendor databases, and provide "trace file" functions that automatically remind the caterer to confirm guest counts, finalize menus, obtain deposits from clients, and ask about new business from a client who hasn't recently been "active." The software also contains templates of contracts, letters, and other documents that can be customized for your business or a particular situation. Some include management of social media and other marketing functions.

- *Back-of-house management:* These programs can help a caterer make sufficient staffing assignments, day to day or before an event; track accessory services; and keep vendor and supplier records. The programs contain customizable forms for various functions or departments of the company, as well as layout or design features that can be used to plan parties, weddings, and other special events.

- *Human resources:* These programs enable a caterer to schedule staff and keep hiring information on file and can be used with time-tracking systems to record hours worked.

- *Revenue and cash flow:* Features of these programs include cost and profit analyses, menu management, development and pricing functions, and bookkeeping features that enable the caterer to manage Accounts Receivable.

While today's off-premise caterer cannot do business without software, we would caution you to use it in tandem with your own unique knowledge of your products, people, and location. For instance, don't rely too heavily on the software's pricing program without taking into consideration local market conditions that affect prices but are not reflected in the software.

If you're going to purchase software, invest the time necessary to learn how to use it—not just the basics, but how to get the most out of it. If that means paying for key staff members to learn as well, it is a wise investment. Ask about the availability of such training, and customer support functions, before you buy.

On this list, we have included only software applications that have been designed for catering and event management. There are others, of course, but here's a start:

>Caterease
>CaterPro
>CaterTrax
>CaterWare
>CookenPro Commercial
>EventMaster Plus!
>ReServe Interactive

Payroll and Related Costs. Payroll taxes, unemployment taxes, and other costs directly related to payroll vary according to local, state, and federal laws. Unlike the cost of sales, which can vary based on the caterer's business volume, payroll costs have some components that are fixed and others that are variable. For instance, most caterers employ one or more employees on a permanent basis, who come to work and must be paid regardless of the level of business. These people's paychecks are essentially "fixed payroll." Successful caterers know that the fewer employees in this category, the better. When business drops off in slower seasons, these employees must still be paid, and a large fixed payroll can quickly erode profits and create huge losses. So every off-premise caterer should strive to keep payroll costs in check by keeping permanent employees at a minimum, staffing events with part-timers who work only when needed. These are "variable payroll" costs, and they should make up the bulk of your payroll expense.

Ideally, payroll and related costs as a percentage of sales should stay constant rather than fluctuate as sales increase or decrease from month to month. Off-premise caterers generally operate with payroll and related labor costs of about 30 percent. Hypothetical Catering Company often hires additional staff for parties. This additional staff, including related costs, is 10 percent of total revenue.

Direct Operating Expenses. These include the costs of doing daily business, from such expenses as supplies, to transportation, utilities, and advertising. Of course, they vary greatly among businesses. Within this category, some operating expenses are fixed; others are variable.

Administrative and General Expenses. These may seem like operating expenses, but they are classified differently. They are the office expenses of your business—the costs of things like phone and Internet service, insurance, repairs and maintenance to the building, and so on. Again, these amounts vary greatly, depending on the company.

In both of these categories, costs should be kept at a minimum to attain maximum profitability. A complete explanation of operating and administrative expenses follows later in this chapter, but for our budgeting illustration, we'll assume our fictitious caterer tries to keep both administrative and general expenses at $750 per month.

Armed with all this knowledge, it is now possible for us to complete an annual budget by month for our Hypothetical Catering Company. The annual totals for each category are at the bottom of the table.

Revenue	Cost of Sales 30%	Payroll Fixed 20%	Payroll Variable 10%	Operating Expenses 5%	Administrative & General 15%	Profit/ (Loss) 20%
$1,500	$450	$3,000	$150	$750	$2,250	($5,100)
3,600	1,080	3,000	360	750	2,250	(3,840)
9,000	2,700	3,000	900	750	2,250	(600)
7,200	2,160	3,000	720	750	2,250	(1,680)
12,600	3,780	3,000	1,260	750	2,250	1,560
7,200	2,160	3,000	720	750	2,250	(1,680)
3,600	1,080	3,000	360	750	2,250	(3,840)
5,400	1,620	3,000	540	750	2,250	(2,760)
9,300	2,790	3,000	930	750	2,250	(420)
19,800	5,940	3,000	1,980	750	2,250	5,880
28,800	8,640	3,000	2,880	750	2,250	11,280
72,000	21,600	3,000	7,200	750	2,250	37,200
$180,000	$54,000	$36,000	$18,000	$9,000	$27,000	$36,000

In this example, it is interesting to note that most of the profit is made in December, which means that, in effect, there is negative cash flow during the rest of the year. Hypothetical Catering Company's owner would be unable to extract any cash from the business until the end of the year, unless he or she was able to receive large advance deposits on future business, which is quite unlikely in the case of a first-year caterer.

It is also apparent that, on a monthly basis, this caterer does not generate a profit until monthly sales reach at least $10,000. This is the break-even point, which is discussed later in this chapter.

Is $36,000 an acceptable profit for a first-year caterer? This depends entirely on the caterer. Is Hypothetical Catering Company a part-time or full-time venture? Was this caterer unhappily employed for a number of years, and is this person now just happy to be on his or her own? What are the caterer's other financial obligations? Are there savings from which to draw until the business becomes more successful?

Creation of a budget is also the first step in controlling costs. You will use it, every week or every month, to compare actual expenses to what you have budgeted. It can help you see clearly whether any of your overhead expenses are creeping up and need to be reexamined or trimmed.

Start-Up Expenses

As pointed out earlier in this text, the best way to start an off-premise catering business is by utilizing an existing foodservice facility that operates for other purposes, such as a restaurant, church, club, or hotel. However, there are some instances in which an individual may wish to rent a commissary to use exclusively for off-premise catering.

How much will this cost? There are many factors that will affect this calculation, so our estimate for a 2,000-square-foot commissary shows a range of figures. These are annual figures for a business with projected gross annual sales between $400,000 and $1,000,000 per year:

Advance rent and security deposits	$3,000–5,000
Equipment and fixtures	50,000–100,000
Leasehold improvements	10,000–20,000
Licenses and permits	1,000–2,000

Marketing expenses	1,000–10,000
Utility and phone deposits	500–1,000
Accounting and legal services	1,000–2,000
Preopening payroll	2,000–5,000
Supplies and uniforms	1,000–2,500
Prepaid insurance	2,000–5,000
Miscellaneous other expenses	1,000–3,000
Total start-up cost range	$72,500–155,500

These figures are simple, rough estimates of what it might cost to lease and set up a catering commissary. Each situation will be different, and ours for this book is strictly hypothetical. The figures are not meant for use as anything other than examples for the discussion within this text.

Cash Budgets

We've talked about estimating income and estimating expenses, but neither of these estimates accounts for cash flow. They simply record revenues and expenses and do not take into account when the actual cash is received.

A *cash budget* accounts for the actual flow of cash in and out of the catering business. Income from a catered event is recorded on the day the event occurs, but for the same event the cash flow could be different.

For example, assume that Hypothetical Catering Company books a party for March 15, with a total price for the event of $1,000. This caterer requires a $250 deposit, which is received on January 15. Another $250 is paid on February 15, and the balance is paid on the day of the event. In this particular situation, cash is received during three months of the year, yet the sale (revenue) is not recorded until March 15. This is one way in which cash flow differs from basic budgeting.

A second budgeting difference occurs on the expense side. The off-premise caterer purchases food and supplies on credit and does not need to pay for them until the 10th of the following month. In this example, suppose that the food and supplies that must be bought for the event will cost the caterer $250. However, this caterer need not pay for them until the 10th of the following month.

What other factors separate income and expense budgets from cash budgets? Prepaid expenses, such as insurance fees and utility deposits, are accounted for differently. Many off-premise caterers finance their insurance premiums, paying anywhere from one-fourth to one-half of the policy's premium amount in advance, then financing the rest over a 6- to 10-month period. In the case of a $3,000 annual insurance policy, the payment will show up on the income and expense budget as a monthly expense of $250 for all 12 months of the year. However, in the cash flow budget, it must be recorded the way the caterer chooses to pay it. The actual cash flow could be a big payment of $1,000 on January 1, and the remaining $2,000 in 10 payments of $200 over the next 10 months. The cash budget would show this as follows:

Month	"Outward" Cash Flow
January	$1,000
February–November	$200
December	None

Another major difference between cash and revenue budgeting occurs with the purchase of major equipment and fixtures. Based on our example of start-up costs, let's say Hypothetical Catering Company needs $50,000 worth of equipment to get started. For cash budgeting purposes, assume that half this amount can be paid in advance and the remaining balance is to be financed over three years.

The cash flow statement would show outward cash flow of $25,000 in January, and equal amounts of outward cash flow during the next 36 months for the remaining $25,000 that was financed, plus interest charges.

However, the income and expense budget would show different figures—equal to the amounts that can be depreciated under federal and state laws. (For an understanding of depreciation and the rules pertaining to it, an off-premise caterer should definitely seek the professional advice of a CPA and an attorney.) Assume for now that the law allows this caterer to depreciate the equipment over a five-year period. In that case, the monthly depreciation amount would be the price of the equipment ($50,000) divided by its "useful life" (60 months), which equals $833.33 per month. The income and expense budget would show a cost of $833.33 per month for equipment.

Start-up off-premise caterers must project their cash flows annually, with the first year of operation being the most important. Now let's take the example (with first-year sales expected to be $180,000) and determine the cash needs for Hypothetical Catering Company, using a basic cash budget system that projects cash receipts and payments on a monthly basis.

The cash receipts include:

Cash sales

Collection of accounts receivable

Advance deposits for future parties

The cash payments include:

Food purchases (cost of sales)

Payroll and related expenses

Direct operating expenses

Administrative and general expenses

Owner's draw (amount of money the owner takes from the business)

Prepaid expenses (such as insurance)

Start-up costs

In order to produce a cash flow statement, some assumptions must be made:

- That all clients pay advance deposits equal to one-half the total bill during the month prior to the party; all remaining balances are due the day of the party.

- That the cost of goods sold (cost of sales) and operating expenses are paid in the month following the event.

- That administrative and general expenses, and payroll and related expenses, are paid in the same month as the event.

- That our caterer does have a $3,000 insurance policy and is paying it off with one-third ($1,000) in January and the rest in ten equal monthly payments of $200 from February through November. (Any interest charges for not paying the policy in full are included in the $3,000 total.)

Our example does not include any start-up expenses, but these can vary significantly—from zero to six-figure amounts. To keep it simple, this example addresses cash flow from operations. Let's take a look at the books:

January Cash Receipts

Revenue	$1,500 (all of the month's sales revenue)
Advance deposits	1,800 (half of February's sales revenue)
Total receipts	$3,300

January Cash Expenses

Cost of goods sold	-0- (all on credit, to be paid in February)
Operating expenses	-0- (all on credit, to be paid in February)
Payroll	$3,150
Administrative and general	3,000 (adjusted for prepaid insurance)*
Total disbursements	$6,150

*This figure was determined by increasing the monthly $2,250 administrative and general expense by $750 because it was necessary to prepay $1,000 of the insurance premium. Therefore, the cash disbursement was $750 more than the budgeted amount.

Cash Balance at End of Month (January)

Receipts	$3,300
Disbursements	6,150
Cash balance at end of month	($2,850)

So in January, the records indicate a loss. However, things don't look so bad from a cash flow standpoint because Hypothetical Catering Company received some advance deposits and did not have to pay some major expenses (cost of goods sold and operating expenses) until February.

This brings up an important point: Set up payment terms with your suppliers so that your large expenses are not all due at the same time, allowing cash flow to be more evenly distributed. Stagger the biggest expense items—typically rent, food costs, and payroll—to the extent that this is possible.

Now let's see how the cash flow situation is in February:

February Cash Receipts

Revenue	$1,800
Advance deposits	4,500 (half of March's sales revenue)
Total receipts	$6,300

February Cash Expenses

Cost of goods sold for January	$450
Operating expenses for January	750
Payroll	3,360
Administrative and general	2,200*
Total disbursements	$6,760

*This month, administrative and general expenses were $50 less than the budgeted amount.

Cash increase during February	($460)
Cash balance at beginning of month	(2,850)
Cash balance at end of month	($3,310)

If you'd like to practice, just continue this exercise throughout the year and project the positive and negative cash flows for the remaining ten months.

The point is that it's very important to understand the inherent differences between cash flow accounting—which keeps track of cash as it flows in and out of the business—and your income and expense accounting, which is a true measure of the profitability of a business. Both are important. However, without positive cash flow, you will be unable to remain in business.

The Break-Even Point

All off-premise caterers must know their *break-even point*—that is, the amount of revenue necessary for the business to "break even," posting neither profit nor loss. At the break-even point, revenue equals expenses.

To calculate a break-even point, costs must be divided into two types: fixed and variable. *Fixed costs* are a specific dollar amount, while *variable costs* are a percentage of revenue because they will go up or down, depending on how busy you are. Referring to our Hypothetical Catering Company, we can separate these costs as follows:

Variable Costs

Cost of goods sold	30% of revenues
Payroll (for part-timers)	10% of revenues
Total monthly variable costs	40% of revenues

Fixed Costs

Fixed monthly payroll (for employees)	$3,000
Operating expenses	750
Administrative and general expenses	2,250
Total monthly fixed costs	$6,000

There are a number of methods for determining the break-even point, some of which are extremely sophisticated, using techniques with names like *regression analysis*. In this case, though, simplicity is the key. One formula that can be used is:

Fixed costs ÷ Contribution margin = Break-even point

The contribution margin is the difference between 1 and the variable costs. In this case, it would be:

1 − 40% = 60%, or .60

(1.0 − .40 = .60)

Using this formula, our break-even point can be calculated as follows:

$6,000 (fixed costs) ÷ .60 (contribution margin) = $10,000

The break-even point for this caterer for any given month is $10,000. This figure can be verified by taking a look back at the projected profit and loss chart we made for Hypothetical Catering Company for the year. The financial projections for months in which sales are less than $10,000 show losses; those with sales over $10,000 show profits.

The break-even point is really just a target at which to aim. It gives you some indication of the level of revenue it will take to turn a profit. Potential investors and bankers will ask for this information as well. It's also important to note that your break-even point can change over time, so you should recalculate it a couple of times a year. Costs tend to inch up, and the break-even point will reflect this. In addition to controlling costs, you may have to consider raising prices if your projections show that, month after month, you're not meeting the break-even point.

Accounting for Revenue and Expenses

The purpose of this section is to introduce you to basic accounting for restaurants and caterers. While most of your accounting can be accomplished with a bookkeeping software program, you still need to understand what you're putting into the system and why. The basics are easy to learn and can quickly be taught to a qualified staff member.

Knowing how to do the books does not eliminate the need for a CPA, particularly for year-end tax preparation, but it does provide a structure for documenting daily revenues and expenses, and for producing the records a CPA will require to handle your tax needs. This can save thousands of dollars in expensive accounting fees.

Perhaps the most critical requirement of a good accounting system is that records be kept on a daily basis and always input into the computer on a timely basis. When small business owners don't keep their financial records up-to-date, nothing good can come of it—bills and/or taxes are not paid on time, and penalties and/or interest charges may be levied.

The end results of all record keeping for a particular time period are the Income Statement and the Balance Sheet. These two documents show an off-premise caterer the company's financial status for that time period. The Income Statement shows the net profit or net loss. The Balance Sheet is essentially a snapshot of the financial status of the business as of a particular date. We will look more closely at both of these documents shortly.

Accounting Terminology

An accounting system is the method you use to record various financial transactions—sales, expenses, and so forth. Basic accounting components allow the caterer to prepare *Income Statements* (also called *Profit and Loss Statements*) and *Balance Sheets* by simply recording totals and major figures from these categories.

In this part of the chapter, we have included very brief descriptions of some of the common terms you will see and hear in the field of accounting. It is by no means a complete list—just the basics to get you started.

Accounts Payable.   These are your outstanding bills, amounts that you owe to your suppliers, landlord, utility companies, and so on.

Accounts Receivable. These are the amounts owed to you, by clients whom you have billed for their events and so on.

Assets and Liabilities. Items you own are assets, even if you have not fully paid for them. Liabilities are debts, the amounts you owe for everything from lease payments to employee payroll. A commercial range is an asset; the $2,000 you still owe on it is a liability.

Sales and Cash Receipts. As the name suggests, these are the various categories of revenues and cash receipts, as well as any service charges, sales taxes, and gratuities. Examples of revenue and cash receipts include:

Advance deposits

Food sales

Labor charges

Beverages, setups, mixers, and wine corkage fees

Rentals and equipment

Flowers and décor

Music and entertainment

Parking and valet services

Photography and video

Service charges

Gratuities

Sales taxes

Total amounts paid

Many of these must be recorded only when the caterer actually provides or subcontracts for these services—for music, valet services, floral design, photography, and so on. When the clients directly pay these vendors, there is no need for a caterer to record the transactions since they do not affect the financial affairs of the catering business.

The source documents for these figures to be input or "posted" into your system are the invoices provided to clients, and receipts for any advance deposits they have paid. Exhibit 14.1 shows a sample invoice for an off-premise event.

EXHIBIT 14.1 Sample Invoice for Off-Premise Catering and Related Services

January 15, 20____
(Date of Invoice)

(Name of Client)
(Address of Client)

INVOICE FOR OFF-PREMISE CATERING SERVICES ON JANUARY 15

30 DINNERS AT $15 PP	$450
30 BEVERAGE SETUPS, MIXERS, ICE AT $2 PP	60
STAFFING	200
FLORAL DÉCOR	100
RENTAL EQUIPMENT	400
TOTAL PRICE	$1,210
20% SERVICE CHARGE	242
6% STATE SALES TAX (VARIES BY STATE)	87.12
TOTAL CHARGE FOR EVENT	$1,539.12
LESS: ADVANCE DEPOSIT PAID	(600.00)
BALANCE DUE	$939.12

NOTES

1. In this example, sales tax is charged on the service charge, which is the law in most states.
2. It is highly recommended that off-premise caterers be paid in full no later than the day or night of the event, rather than extending credit. Even the largest corporations have ways to pay for things if required. Astute caterers will advise all clients that they require payment in full upon the completion of the event.
3. One way to do this easily, without disturbing the client on the night of the event, is to submit an invoice in advance of the event and ask the client to bring a check in that amount. (Some caterers require payment in full prior to the day of a wedding reception. This is a much smoother procedure than disturbing a bride or her parent near the end of a wedding reception to write a check.) Additional charges for extra guests or other unexpected costs can be invoiced.
4. Invoices may be prepared on preprinted invoice forms, or simply on the caterer's letterhead paper. It is highly recommended that invoices be prenumbered for control purposes, to ensure that all invoices are accounted for and reconciled to cash receipts.
5. Math and other errors in invoices can be extremely costly and embarrassing. It is difficult to go back to a client one month after the party and ask for additional money due to an invoice mistake. Overcharges can be embarrassing and can give some clients the impression that the off-premise caterer is deliberately overcharging.
6. In the preceding example, state sales tax was charged on the service charge. What about charging sales tax on tips that the client pays? In most states, sales tax on gratuities need not be charged only when the following conditions are met:

   - The gratuity or tip is 100 percent voluntary.
   - All of the gratuity is distributed to employees.
   - These two conditions are stated in the contract.

Chart of Accounts. All sources of revenue and expense are recorded with a *Chart of Accounts*. Each type of account has a number, which is assigned by you or your bookkeeper or CPA, enabling you to track income and outgo by category. Continuity is important to be able to categorize and organize your finances from month to month, and the Chart of Accounts makes each category easier to compare. Exhibit 14.2, created for this book by Cuisine Unlimited Catering and Special Events, is a sample of categories in a basic Chart of Accounts for an off-premise catering company. Any Chart of Accounts will require customization based on your business model.

EXHIBIT 14.2 Chart of Accounts

Account Number	Account	Type of Account
1000	Operating Account	Bank
1200	Accounts Receivable	Accounts Receivable
1300	Inventory–Food	Other Current Asset
1310	Inventory–Beverage	Other Current Asset
1320	Prepaid Expenses	Other Current Asset
1330	Security Deposit	Other Current Asset
1340	Undeposited Funds	Other Current Asset
1400	Fixed Assets	Fixed Asset
1410	Building Improvements	Fixed Asset
1420	Furniture, Fixtures, Equipment	Fixed Asset
1430	Accumulated Depreciation	Fixed Asset
2000	Accounts Payable	Accounts Payable
2010	Credit Card Payable	Credit Card
2100	Payroll Liabilities	Other Current Liability
2112	Accrued Payroll	Other Current Liability
2114	Federal Unemployment–FUTA	Other Current Liability
2116	Federal Withholding	Other Current Liability
2118	IRA/401K Liability	Other Current Liability
2120	Medicare	Other Current Liability
2122	Social Security	Other Current Liability
2124	State Unemployment–SUI	Other Current Liability
2126	State Withholding	Other Current Liability
2200	Sales Tax Payable	Other Current Liability
2400	Notes Payable	Other Current Liability
2500	Gift Certificates	Other Current Liability
2600	Vehicle Loan	Long-Term Liability

(Continued)

EXHIBIT 14.2 Chart of Accounts (*Continued*)

CATERING INCOME

4010	Food Income	Income
4020	Beverage Income	Income
4030	Music and Entertainment Income	Income
4040	Rental Income	Income
4050	Service Fee	Income
4060	Delivery Fee	Income
4070	Server Income	Income

OTHER INCOME

4100	Event Change Fee	Income

CATERING COST OF GOODS

5010	Food Cost	Cost of Goods Sold
5020	Beverage Cost	Cost of Goods Sold
5030	Music and Entertainment Cost	Cost of Goods Sold
5040	Rental Cost	Cost of Goods Sold
5050	Venue Costs	Cost of Goods Sold
5060	Kitchen Wages	Cost of Goods Sold
5070	Server Wages	Cost of Goods Sold

VEHICLE COSTS

5110	Fuel and Mileage	Cost of Goods Sold
5120	Fuel Surcharge (a negative number, which helps offset costs)	Cost of Goods Sold
5130	Vehicle Insurance	Cost of Goods Sold
5132	Vehicle License and Registration	Cost of Goods Sold
5134	Vehicle Repairs and Maintenance	Cost of Goods Sold

VARIABLE EXPENSES

6010	Advertising and Promotion	Expense
6020	Credit Card Fees	Expense
6030	Cleaning and Janitorial	Expense
6040	Professional Fees	Expense
6042	Accounting	Expense
6044	Consulting	Expense
6046	Legal	Expense
6050	Postage and Delivery	Expense
6060	Repairs and Maintenance	Expense

6062	Catering Equipment	Expense
6064	Kitchen Equipment	Expense
6066	Office Equipment	Expense
6070	Smallwares	Expense
6080	Supplies	Expense
6090	Uniforms	Expense
6090	Travel and Entertainment	Expense
6092	Business Meals/Entertainment	Expense
6094	Travel	Expense

FIXED COSTS

6100	Bank Service Charges	Expense
6110	Depreciation	Expense
6120	Dues and Subscriptions	Expense
6130	Leased Equipment	Expense
6140	Liability Insurance	Expense
6150	Licenses and Permits	Expense
6160	Loan Finance	Expense
6170	Payroll Expense	Expense
6172	Health and Dental Insurance	Expense
6174	Recruitment	Expense
6176	Payroll Tax Expense	Expense
6178	Payroll Service	Expense
6180	Salaries and Wages	Expense
6182	Owner/Manager Salary	Expense
6184	Office/Administration	Expense
6186	Sales	Expense
6190	Worker's Compensation Insurance	Expense
6200	Occupancy Expenses	Expense
6242	Cell Phones	Expense
6244	Natural Gas	Expense
6246	Electricity	Expense
6248	Internet	Expense
6250	Building Rent	Expense
6252	Security/Alarm System	Expense
6254	Telephone (land line)	Expense
6256	Waste Removal/Rendering	Expense
6258	Water/Sewer	Expense

(*Source:* Courtesy of Cuisine Unlimited Catering and Special Events, Salt Lake City, Utah.)

Petty Cash. This is the small amount of cash a company keeps on hand to be used for small, miscellaneous expenses. A last-minute purchase at the supermarket on the way to an event site is an example of a petty cash expense. There is nothing "petty" about keeping good records of your petty cash. Although these expenses are not large amounts, they add up quickly, and petty cash can be the least secure of your finances, easily pilfered if you don't keep an eye on it. Petty cash is not meant to pay for major purchases.

Off-premise caterers wishing to establish a petty cash fund should first write and cash a check, made payable to "Cash," for the amount of the fund. Most such funds range from $200 to $1,000, depending on the size of the business and the expected uses. Petty cash should always be kept separate from your personal cash.

Off-premise caterers should retain receipts for all petty cash purchases, and the total value of these receipts, added to the remaining cash in the fund, must always equal the total amount of the fund. For example, if your petty cash fund is $500 and there is $300 in cash in the petty cash box, there should be $200 worth of receipts.

Once the petty cash fund is depleted to a point where it should be replenished, the receipts are input into your accounting system and a replenishment check is written that totals the exact amount of the receipts. No matter how small, the goal is to keep a running summary of all petty cash purchases, with a total for each type of expense. The fund should always be replenished at the end of each accounting period to ensure that all expenses are accounted for in the same period. It also must be emphasized that all petty cash receipts must be marked "Paid" once they have been reimbursed from the petty cash fund to prevent fraudulent reuse at later times by a dishonest individual.

Whenever petty cash is handled by employees other than the company owner, it is our belief that only one person should have access to the petty cash fund, which is kept secure at all times. This individual signs a receipt for the money upon withdrawing it. The fund must be available at all times for an audit or spot check, and it must contain cash and receipts equal to the designated amount of the fund. Shortages are the responsibility of the person in charge of the fund.

Advance Deposits. Deposits are an important part of booking weddings, parties, and other events, and it is critical to keep track of which clients have paid which amounts in advance for their events, including the date the deposit is paid and the date of the event. This ensures that they receive proper credit for what they have paid up front when their final invoice is being prepared.

When you prepare a Balance Sheet, the total amount of advance deposits is listed under "Liabilities" because the off-premise caterer has yet to perform the necessary service and is "liable," so to speak, for performance.

Occasionally, clients forfeit an advance deposit. In this case, the amount is still a "liability" if it is to be used for a future event. However, if it has truly been forfeited, a deposit amount is shown as "Other Income" on the financial statement.

Cash Disbursements. Every check that is written on any of your business accounts must be recorded. You are dispersing cash, so the process is known as *cash disbursement*. Who are you paying, and for what? As your bookkeeper pays the bills, which come in as invoices from suppliers, these invoices should be checked for accuracy. Did you actually receive, and accept, the merchandise? Some companies process invoices daily; most do it weekly or twice a month. There is no reason to pay bills any sooner than they are due. The invoices are typically filed under the vendor or supplier's name until they are due for payment. At the end of the month, all invoices from each supplier are totaled and compared to the monthly statement you receive from that supplier. If there are discrepancies, the sooner you discuss them with your vendors, the better your relationships with them will be.

Payroll. *Payroll* is the amount you pay employees, or the list of who gets paid and how much. We suggest hiring a payroll company for the preparation of workers' paychecks, federal and state payroll tax reports, and individual earnings records. This work is very detailed and time-consuming and can often be more efficiently handled by firms that specialize in this type of work. Their prices are surprisingly reasonable; many offer to pay the penalty if they make a mistake or pay your payroll taxes late. A simple Internet search for "payroll services" will give you plenty to choose from.

Income Statement Summary

The *Income Statement Summary* is a worksheet used to summarize and calculate certain expenses that you will use to prepare an Income Statement for the accounting period. (An accounting period is usually either one month or three months.) Most expense amounts can simply be transferred "as is" from Cash Disbursements to the Income Statement; however, some expenses—things like cost of goods sold, payroll and related expenses, and prepaid insurance—require some intermediate calculations before they can be part of an Income Statement.

Accounting software typically performs these calculations automatically, but it's still important to understand where the figures come from and why the calculations are necessary. So let's examine these calculations in greater detail.

Cost of Goods Sold Calculation

In catering, *Cost of Goods Sold* means your food costs. The basic formula for computing Cost of Goods Sold (or cost of sales) is:

> The value of your beginning inventory
> plus (+) purchases
> less (−) the value of your ending inventory
> equals (=) Cost of Goods Sold

How do you get the inventory figures? As a caterer, you take inventory by counting everything you have in stock for the type of inventory you are doing (dishes, food, equipment, etc.) and then calculate the value of that inventory. This may be done weekly, monthly, quarterly, or annually. Exhibit 14.3 is a sample inventory page.

Most inventories are very long forms, with enough pages to list all the items to be inventoried or counted. Each of these pages is extended and totaled. *Extension* means multiplying the number of units of an item by the unit cost. The figures are totaled by adding all the extensions on each page. Once each page is totaled, a *grand total* (or *total inventory value*) is obtained by adding all the individual page totals. The grand total is posted to the Income Statement Summary.

The ending inventory for one month becomes the beginning inventory for the following month. For example, the inventory taken on January 31 is both the ending inventory for January and the beginning inventory for February.

Taking inventory is time-consuming, and for many off-premise caterers whose businesses and inventories are small, the time could be better spent in other areas. But for any business that needs to keep a very careful eye on costs, the inventory process is essential.

At this juncture, let's assume that our Hypothetical Catering Company took an inventory at the end of January and calculated an inventory value of $200. How does this figure relate to the cost of sales calculation on the Income Statement Summary?

Income Statement Summary Calculations—January

Beginning inventory for January	$0000
Food purchases for January	559
Less (−) ending inventory for January	(200)
Cost of food sales for January	$359

EXHIBIT 14.3 Sample Inventory Page

Location: Dry Storage   Date of Inventory: _____

Item Description	Item Code	Unit Size	Cost	Quantity	Total Value
Pasta—Bowtie	5309547	Case	$15.29	1	$15.29
Pasta—Spaghetti	5309540	Case	$14.25	2	$28.50
Rice—Basmati	400254	Lb	$1.47	8	$11.76
				TOTAL	$55.55

Source: Courtesy of Cuisine Unlimited Catering and Special Events, Salt Lake City, Utah.

Income Statement Summary Calculations—February

Beginning inventory for February	$200
Food purchases for February	914
Less (−) ending inventory for February	(300)
Cost of food sales for February	$814

Prepaid Expense Calculations

Off-premise caterers frequently prepay bills for insurance and other major expenses. They may pay their total annual insurance premium in January, for instance, but because the insurance is in effect for the whole year, this expense should be spread out over the entire 12-month period to present the most realistic picture of the company's finances. If it were "charged" in total on January's books, this would totally distort the financial results by overstating the January loss and either understating losses or overstating profits in future months. This topic was addressed earlier in the "Cash Budgets" section of this chapter. The correct calculation would be:

Total cost for insurance for year	$3,000
Expense per month (divided by 12)	$250

Please note, however, that even with this calculation of the true monthly expense, you can choose to handle the actual payment of the expense a little differently. Our fictitious caterer made a $1,000 insurance payment in January, one-third of the total amount due. Then, the remaining balance is paid off $200 at a time, which is shown (through November) as a $200 disbursement.

There may be other calculations unique to particular off-premise caterers that can be done on the Income Statement Summary. Once these are complete, work can begin on preparing the Income Statement.

Payroll and Related Expense Calculations

An Income Statement Summary also includes what a caterer pays for labor in a certain time period, which includes not only the workers' wages, but also the benefits and related taxes that are paid as an employer. Here is the formula:

> Gross wages
> plus (+) employer's share of Social Security (FICA)
> plus (+) federal and state unemployment taxes
> plus (+) cost of any other employee benefits
> equals (=) Payroll and Related Expenses

Let's use this formula to calculate the payroll costs for January, using Hypothetical Catering Company's figures:

Gross wages	$2,740
plus (+) FICA (7.65%)	210
plus (+) unemployment taxes	100
plus (+) Workers' Comp insurance	100
Total payroll and related costs	$3,150

The Income Statement

A properly prepared *Income Statement* is also commonly referred to as a *Profit and Loss Statement* (P&L) because it depicts a company's profit or loss, as well as other key numbers, for a particular period. The period may be a month, a quarter, or a year. Completing this statement is an excellent way to measure the financial health of an operation. Exhibit 14.4 is a sample Income Statement for a full year for Hypothetical Catering Company. Note that it is organized based on the Chart of Accounts.

EXHIBIT 14.4 Sample Income Statement

Year ending December 21, 20___

Account Number	Account	Amount
CATERING INCOME		
4010	Food Income	$140,000
4020	Beverage Income	12,000
4030	Music and Entertainment Income	8,000
4040	Rental Income	5,000
4050	Service Fee	4,000
4060	Delivery Fee	3,000
4070	Server Income	8,000
		$180,000
OTHER INCOME		
4100	Event Change Fee	0
CATERING COST OF GOODS		
5010	Food Cost	$40,600
5020	Beverage Cost	3,600
5030	Music and Entertainment Cost	6,400
5040	Rental Cost	3,000
5050	Venue Costs	400
5060	Kitchen Wages (variable payroll)12,000	
5070	Server Wages (variable payroll)	3,500
		$69,500
	GROSS MARGIN	**$110,500**
VEHICLE COSTS		
5110	Fuel and Mileage	$950
5120	Fuel Surcharge	(700)
5130	Vehicle Insurance	
5132	Vehicle License and Registration	350
5134	Vehicle Repairs and Maintenance	1,500
		$2,100
DIRECT OPERATING EXPENSES		
6010	Advertising and Promotion	$1,500
6020	Credit Card Fees	1,200
6030	Cleaning and Janitorial	600
		(Continued)

EXHIBIT 14.4 Sample Income Statement (*Continued*)

6040	Professional Fees	
6042	Accounting	350
6044	Consulting	0
6046	Legal	0
6050	Postage and Delivery	420
6060	Repairs and Maintenance	
6062	Catering Equipment	500
6064	Kitchen Equipment	850
6066	Office Equipment	150
6070	Smallwares	400
6080	Supplies	600
6090	Uniforms	120
6090	Travel and Entertainment	
6092	Business Meals/Entertainment	210
6094	Travel	0
		$6,900

TOTAL DIRECT OPERATING EXPENSES   **$9,000**

GENERAL AND ADMINISTRATIVE

6100	Bank Service Charges	$120
6110	Depreciation	0
6120	Dues and Subscriptions	60
6130	Leased Equipment	3,600
6140	Liability Insurance	3,000
6150	Licenses and Permits	0
6160	Loan Finance	0
6170	Payroll Expense	0
6172	Health and Dental Insurance	0
6174	Recruitment	0
6176	Payroll Tax Expense	2,000
6178	Payroll Service	0
6180	Salaries and Wages	
6182	Owner/Manager Salary	30,000
6184	Office/Administration	0
6186	Sales	0
6190	Workers' Compensation Insurance	1,200
6200	Occupancy Expenses	0
6242	Cell Phones	680
6244	Natural Gas	1,800
6246	Electricity	3,000
6248	Internet	360

6250	Building Rent	18,000
6252	Security/Alarm System	0
6254	Telephone (land line)	960
6256	Waste Removal/Rendering	420
6258	Water/Sewer	300
TOTAL GENERAL & ADMINISTRATIVE		**$65,500**

Source: Courtesy of Cuisine Unlimited Catering and Special Events, Salt Lake City, Utah.

The Balance Sheet

A Balance Sheet should be prepared annually, at least, as it will be required for federal income tax purposes. Off-premise caterers should be familiar with Balance Sheets to gain a clearer picture of their business. Whereas an Income Statement shows the revenue and expenses of a company for a certain period of time, a *Balance Sheet* shows a company's assets, liabilities, and net worth—as we mentioned, it is a snapshot of its financial condition. When total liabilities are deducted from total assets, the resulting figure is the net worth of the company on that specific date.

Assets are items of value owned by the business. For an off-premise caterer, assets include:

- Cash
- Amounts due from clients (your Accounts Receivable)
- Food and other types of inventory
- Prepaid expenses (such as insurance)
- Fixed assets (land, buildings, improvements to a building, vehicles, major kitchen and operating equipment)

Accumulated depreciation on the fixed assets is deducted from their value, a task best left to your accountant. *Accumulated depreciation* is the total of all depreciation charged to the business for income tax purposes. The laws governing how this is done, and how much depreciation is allowed over a certain time period, are strict and thorough.

Liabilities are the caterer's financial obligations. These include:

- Outstanding loans
- Advance deposits from customers (for events yet to occur)

- Amounts owed to vendors (your Accounts Payable)
- Accrued payroll (amounts owed to employees as of a certain date)
- Sales taxes paid to local and state governments

The difference between the amounts of assets and liabilities is called *equity*.

A simple example of the Balance Sheet for Hypothetical Catering Company at the end of its first year of operation could be as follows:

Balance Sheet
Hypothetical Catering Company
for the Period Ending December 31, 20__

Current Assets	
Cash	
In the Bank	5,000
In Savings	2,000
Total Cash	$7,000
Accounts Receivable	
Due from Clients	1,000
Total Accounts Receivable	$1,000
Inventories	
Food	500
Total Inventories	$500
Prepaid Expenses	-0-
Total Current Assets	$8,500
Fixed Assets	-0-
Total Assets	**$8,500**
Liabilities and Equity	
Current Liabilities	
Accounts Payable	1,000
Accrued Payroll	500
Advance Deposits from Clients	1,000
Total Current Liabilities	$2,500
Long-Term Liabilities	-0-
Total Liabilities	$2,500
Equity	$6,000
Total Liabilities and Equity	**$8,500**

Analyzing Financial Statements

In addition to knowing where to put the numbers on financial statements, a caterer must also understand how to analyze the data on the Income Statement, Balance Sheet, and other financial records, so they will be useful for making good management decisions. In fact, the primary reason your financial reports must be accurate and timely is so that they can be of maximum use to you.

Analyzing Income Statements

Income Statements should include year-to-date figures, which are essentially totals of the results for the year. These totals help you make sense of the month-to-month fluctuations in revenues and costs and can be easily compared with year-to-date figures for prior years to see how the business is growing (or not). You can also compare year-to-date totals with the amounts you have budgeted to see whether you are meeting your budget projections.

Percentage comparisons are done for revenues and expenses to see how well the caterer is controlling expenses. Percentage comparisons are handy because they take into account fluctuations in revenues. For example, the Cost of Goods Sold figure for food one month might be $1,000, and the following month, $2,000. Does this mean that food costs are rising and becoming excessive? Not necessarily! It depends on the amount of food revenues. If food costs are budgeted to be about 33 percent of sales and sales for these two months are $3,000 and $6,000, respectively, then things look fine. However, if sales in the second month are only $5,000, this means that food cost has jumped to 40 percent of sales, and the caterer needs to investigate and perhaps take corrective action.

The formula for calculating a food cost percentage, for example, is as follows:

$$\frac{\text{Cost of Goods Sold}}{\text{Food Sales}} = \text{Food Cost as a Percentage}$$

Another way to compare is to look at a particular month, the same month in the previous year, and the month immediately before it. (Example: May 2012, May 2011, and April 2011.) With the three sets of figures in front of you, check them carefully. Are sales increasing or decreasing from the prior year and/or the prior month? How do they compare with budgeted amounts? If sales are up from the prior periods, were prices raised or were more guests served?

Yet another comparison is to divide total sales during a period by the number of guests served to determine a *check average*. Restaurants do this frequently to determine spending patterns (an average amount spent per guest), as well as how well their servers are selling "extras" like desserts, drinks, and appetizers to increase the check average.

The *payroll percentage* is another key. This is computed by dividing food, payroll, and related costs by food revenues to come up with a percentage. Seasonal operators will see large variances in their payroll percentages between busy and slow seasons. Many off-premise caterers experience large swings in monthly revenues, which will affect this percentage greatly if key staff members are kept on the payroll during the slow season.

Prime cost is the term used for the combined cost of food and payroll. Many operators use this as a guideline. They realize that if their food costs are high, then their payroll costs must be low, or vice versa. An off-premise caterer who operates with a 40 percent food cost will not stay in business long with a 40 percent labor cost. The total of 80 percent prime cost is simply too high to generate a profit. Successful off-premise caterers operate with prime costs in the range of 40 to 65 percent.

It is tempting to analyze only the food and labor costs since these are your biggest expenses in the catering business. But don't neglect direct operating costs and administrative costs, which should be compared in the same manner. You need to know if any of these expenses are too high or too low, and if so, what changes can be made to adjust them.

Of course, the most important figure is the net profit or loss amount. When people talk about a business's "bottom line," this is it—and, for many, it represents the true measure of success. How much did a business earn after all expenses were paid?

And how much is "enough?" The answer depends on the individual caterer. In general, profit percentages for off-premise caterers are greater than those reported by restaurants. But profits also vary greatly from month to month for caterers with highly seasonal businesses. During slow periods, losses are common; during peak seasons, profits are generous. It takes a hardy and committed businessperson to ride the financial roller coaster.

Analyzing Balance Sheets

Balance Sheets for off-premise caterers also reveal operational successes and failures. Let's look over several of the figures on a typical Balance Sheet, and consider what they might indicate about your business.

The first place to check is the cash in the operational (business checking) account. Is there enough to pay all the bills on time? If there is more than enough, excess cash should be deposited into interest-bearing accounts to generate a little more income. Is there too little? If so, is the Accounts Receivable amount high (meaning that clients are not paying you on time) or are your payment terms too lenient? Other common reasons for too little cash are:

- The business is not profitable in the long run.
- The owners are withdrawing too much cash from the business.
- Inventories are too high.
- The business is experiencing one of its seasonal fluctuations.

Some caterers who experience seasonal cash fluctuations obtain lines of credit from their banks from which to draw during slow seasons; they pay the money back when business improves. Others borrow money in the form of loans. Still others, who are well established and know that during certain seasons there will be a lack of cash, can ask their clients for larger advance deposits for events during those times. This is very effective because the caterer doesn't have to pay any interest expense, but it may (in some cases) require giving the clients a slight discount on the events in exchange for the higher deposits.

Accounts Receivable should be practically nonexistent or, at least, kept to a minimum. Many businesses "age" their Accounts Receivable by separating them into time frames:

- Current (due and payable within 30 days)
- Less than 30 days past due
- 31–60 days past due
- 61–120 days past due
- More than 120 days past due

The longer accounts are past due, the less likely you'll be able to collect them, so astute caterers will not allow their accounts to become past due. Of course, there are always those rare and unpleasant situations when a check bounces or a caterer is duped into granting credit before realizing the debt will be almost impossible to collect. Some off-premise caterers establish a reserve account for this type of situation by expensing small amounts each month to the operation as "bad debt" expense. This transaction does not involve cash. It is nothing more than a paper entry, charging a small expense against profits each month and making an offsetting charge to a reserve account or bad debt account. By doing this, caterers can prevent a bad debt from distorting a particular month's financial statement. A CPA can tell you more about this procedure and its impact on a company's federal income taxes.

Food inventory turnover is determined by dividing the Food Cost of Goods Sold for the month by the end-of-month food inventory value. If Hypothetical Catering Company has $10,000 of Food Cost of Goods Sold for a month and the ending food inventory for the same month is valued at $1,000, this caterer's food inventory turnover is 10 ($10,000 divided by $1,000). The higher the food inventory turnover figure, the better—as long as there are sufficient amounts of foods on hand with which to operate efficiently. Restaurants operate with inventory turnovers of 3 to 5, but most off-premise caterers should have higher turnovers. Astute off-premise caterers monitor their inventory contents and promote or discount items that have been in stock for long periods of time—as long as they are still fresh, of course.

It is well understood among experienced off-premise caterers and restaurateurs that low inventories help reduce theft and pilferage. Thieves are more likely to steal from large inventories, thinking that a disappearance is less likely to be noticed, than from smaller inventories.

Another Balance Sheet analysis compares current assets to current liabilities. This comparison is known as the business's *current ratio*. A ratio of two-to-one, in which current assets are twice as large as current liabilities, is considered good. For off-premise caterers, a current ratio of one-to-one is also acceptable because inventories and receivables are generally low, meaning a large portion of the current assets consists of cash.

Controlling Costs

Controlling costs is a daily function of all successful off-premise caterers. These business owners operate with their eyes wide open, always looking for waste, inefficiency, and other problems that can adversely affect profitability. Smart caterers recommend these hands-on measures:

- Consider an active "green initiative" that will create cost savings on utilities, paper usage, fuel for vehicles, and more.
- Check trash cans for product that has been discarded accidentally. You'd be surprised at how much flatware and other items are carelessly tossed!

- Count all rental equipment before and after each event.

- Learn to schedule intelligently. Schedule just enough staff to complete the job accurately and on time: not too few people so that everyone needs to rush, and not too many so that people are standing around waiting for something to do.

- Monitor utility costs. Turn appliances and lights off when not in use or install timers or motion detectors on lights in some rooms.

- Buy labor-saving devices (computers, kitchen equipment) that will reduce daily payroll expenses. Portable electric time clocks can be purchased for off-premise events.

- Inspect all areas for safety hazards and correct them promptly.

- Carefully examine each operating cost and administrative and general cost at least quarterly to determine if there are any savings that can be made.

- Get three bids on the various forms of insurance your company has each year.

- Involve the staff in safety and cost-saving measures by encouraging and rewarding their ideas and suggestions.

It is a discouraging reality that some losses could be the result of theft or fraud. Experts say that the conditions that prompt a worker to embezzle are need, failure of conscience, and opportunity. As an employer, you can't do anything about the first two, but you certainly can minimize the opportunity. Simply being present at all events, watching and working alongside your employees, will do wonders to prevent problems and reduce costs overall.

In addition to hands-on techniques, there are several types of forms that caterers have developed to suit their own needs for projecting, analyzing, and controlling costs. Many of them are computerized. Now we will examine three types of forms that can be very effective tools for projecting and controlling costs.

Managing Money

In your catering career, you will no doubt have to deal with banks and bankers. In so doing, it is wise to adhere to a few simple but important rules. We've numbered them to make them easier to refer back to if necessary.

1. Pay all bills on time. Never pay bills early unless there is a cash discount offered for early payment. There is clearly no advantage to early payment and definitely

a disadvantage when money paid early could possibly be earning interest in an interest-bearing account.

2. Place any excess cash (that is, whatever is not needed for day-to-day operations) into interest-bearing accounts. There is no reason not to take advantage of every opportunity to generate additional income. Off-premise caterers should pay particular attention to this during very busy times of year, like Christmas, when money can pile up quickly in general accounts.

3. Do not extend credit to clients. Off-premise caterers are in the catering business, not in the banking business to offer short-term loans. Caterers dealing with large corporations and organizations that take 30 to 60 days to process invoices should develop the practice of billing early (in advance of an event) for the estimated amount of the party or at least a large percentage of the expected total due, and ask that the bills be paid in full prior to the day or night of the event. Any remaining smaller balances can be invoiced after the event.

4. Collect what is owed you promptly and professionally. Off-premise caterers are no different than other small businesses—they hate the uncomfortable task of approaching a client or vendor who owes them money and asking for it. You don't have to be rude to make your case.

5. Never write a check when there are insufficient funds in the bank to cover it. It is almost always better to approach creditors first and tell them of your financial difficulties, with a plan in mind for exactly how you intend to pay the bills. A good rule for a checking account is that the balance on any given day should average no less than 30 percent of the total amount of the checks written during the month. For example, if you write $10,000 worth of checks during the month, you should maintain an average balance of $3,000 in your business checking account at all times.

6. All checking accounts must be *reconciled* (balanced) once a month, immediately upon receipt of the bank statement(s). Any delay can result in compounding of errors and undue hardship in trying to unravel the financial disarray. Errors made by customers and banks can result in embarrassment when a supplier returns a check because of insufficient funds. One of the worst things a caterer can do is to let bank statements accumulate and then try to reconcile many months at one time.

7. Most banking is done online today, and catering companies are no exception. The bank can make the company's bank statements available online to multiple

people—the owners and the bookkeeper, for example—and also can restrict access to some online banking functions for some people. It is an important safeguard to limit the people who have access to bank accounts, while still allowing those who need to see the information (bookkeeper, CPA) to do so.

8. In catering companies with two or more owners, two signatures should be required on checks that exceed a certain dollar amount. Moreover, one owner should be responsible for approving the invoices; the other owner should sign the checks.

9. Bank deposits should be made on a daily basis. As soon as money is received, it should be deposited. It is not a good policy to pay bills directly from cash receipts. Payment by check, or from the petty cash fund, leaves a better audit trail.

10. When you are setting up your bank accounts, inquire about a line of credit. It can be very helpful when cash flow becomes a problem during slow time periods.

11. Make it your goal to set aside a small percentage of every event's profit in a rainy day fund.

 Payment Policies

Invoices for purchases should be paid when they are due. There is generally no advantage to paying bills early unless the supplier offers a discount for doing so. On the other hand, become known for paying bills late and you will be faced with higher prices, strained relationships, and possibly poorer-quality products from suppliers, as well as late payment fees and interest charges. Slow payers lose their negotiating edge since suppliers offer their best prices to good customers who pay on time.

The unfortunate reality of this type of business is that most off-premise caterers will, at one time or another, be faced with a cash shortage and find themselves unable to pay certain invoices when due. Preventing this problem is why a business line of credit and/or a rainy day fund are worth having. If you do not have one of these, however, don't ignore the problem and wait for suppliers to call. It is far better to talk with them, inform them of the difficulties, and develop a suitable payment plan. Honesty and a sincere effort to pay promptly will maintain good supplier relationships—and remedy that feeling of dread every time the phone rings.

(Continued)

Astute off-premise caterers know that when they make large purchases for equipment and large food orders, it is advantageous to first negotiate the price, and then negotiate the terms for payment. Most suppliers, eager to conclude a sale, will offer better terms once the price is agreed upon because they wish to ensure that the sale is made.

An interesting way to deal with suppliers is an arrangement by which a caterer opens an account with a new purveyor, and the purveyor is not paid for any merchandise for 30 days. After the 30 days are up, the caterer pays the supplier each week for any invoices more than 30 days old. Many suppliers like this arrangement because they can expect a check each and every week.

Whenever possible, purchases should be paid for by check. Frequently, off-premise caterers need cash to pay for emergency purchases or to pay suppliers who accept only cash. Petty cash funds are the answer to such cash-payment situations, as discussed earlier in this chapter.

Selecting a Bank

Off-premise caterers should shop for a bank the same way they shop for other vendors and suppliers, and place their primary business accounts with a bank that can make the largest overall contribution to the business, even if it is not conveniently located. When searching, caterers should ask the advice of other business owners and suppliers and look for a bank that understands the foodservice industry—not all of them do.

The banking industry in recent years has changed drastically. Many banks have closed or merged, and those that remain have scrambled to restore profit levels. Unfortunately for customers, this has meant tightening up on loan terms and raising all types of fees, from credit card interest rates to late payment penalties. The so-called free checking account is often free only if you maintain a hefty minimum balance.

As a small business, decide which services you need from a bank and then comparison shop. It isn't as easy as it sounds as most major banks have at least a half-dozen different types of accounts to choose from. Some "bundle" their services for a flat monthly fee; others allow you to choose individual services and pay only for those. Start by analyzing the terms for their business credit cards and the online banking services they offer. Some allow you to transfer money between branches, send custom invoices, and apply for loans, all online. Be sure to consider credit unions as well as banks in your search for the right fit.

Caterers must also feel comfortable as individuals when dealing with the bank and the bankers. Most bank branches have at least one person who serves as a liaison for small businesses, and it is smart to establish a personal relationship with that person. At some point, a problem or need will arise and you will need advice, money, or some other special service from the bank. It is far better to deal with an individual at that bank with whom you have established a relationship than to hunt for someone and have to explain your situation.

Bob Seiwert, senior vice president of the American Banking Association, suggests getting to know at least two people at your local bank branch and starting those conversations long before you actually need to borrow money.

And finally, because banking industry closures are expected to continue, you will want to be sure that yours has deposit insurance from the Federal Deposit Insurance Corporation (FDIC).

Loan Applications

When off-premise caterers need to borrow money, they should first look to the financial institution where they keep their general, payroll, and other checking accounts. The chief problem with many banks is that they have very conservative lending practices, particularly for foodservice businesses. In recent years, since Wall Street's financial meltdown, the terms have gotten even tougher.

When you apply for a loan, good accounting work is mandatory and copies of your company's bank statements should be provided along with the actual loan request. Off-premise caterers should provide accurate and realistic figures and should be prepared to answer bankers' inquiries about these figures. Astute bankers know that it is a sure sign that someone is not on top of his or her business when they ask a question and the loan applicant responds with, "I need to find out from my accountant and get back to you."

Those who need assistance in completing loan applications and financial projections can contact local offices of the SBA (www.sba.gov). We'll talk more about the SBA in a moment.

The Service Corps of Retired Executives (SCORE) is another organization whose business expertise can be tapped for a small fee, or even at no cost in some cases. The SBA and SCORE can also assist with such decisions as what type of business you want yours to be—sole proprietorship, corporation, limited liability partnership, or another type—and how to write your business plan. A third place to go for expert assistance is a Small Business Development Center (SBDC). There are about 900 of them in the United States, federally funded and often affiliated with college campuses.

Lenders consider the following factors when making loan determinations:

- *Company History:* Experience in catering, special skills, business reputation, integrity, and willingness to pay back the loan promptly. In our experience, it helps to be extremely well prepared before making the loan request, including having a realistic business plan to accompany the financial documents.

- *Capacity:* The realistic ability of the applicant to pay back the loan with interest. To prove this, you must show projected Income Statements, Balance Sheets, and Cash Flow Statements for three to five years.

- *Capital:* The cash that the borrowers already have available to them. Loans to off-premise caterers must be personally guaranteed by the owner. If you are the owner, you must decide which of your personal assets (if any) you are willing to risk.

- *Collateral:* The assets that could be sold for cash if necessary to finance the business. Since foodservice equipment depreciates quickly and has no particular value to lenders, many banks require that personal property be put up as collateral, which will be seized if the loan is not paid back. Examples of personal property are home equity and personal savings accounts.

Prudent lenders will look at the first year's financial statements (for someone already in business) and may ask to see projections for the next three years of operation. They won't lend you a bundle—the maximum sum will most likely be 8 to 10 percent of the business's total revenue. For example, an off-premise caterer who projects $750,000 in business during the next three years could perhaps obtain a loan for $60,000 to $75,000, with payback terms over the next three years.

SBA-guaranteed loans may be granted to entrepreneurs who cannot qualify for commercial loans. These loans offer an extended payment schedule of seven to eight years, but they have a reputation for being difficult to obtain and involving lots of paperwork. Some banks have an SBA loan guarantee department.

Aside from applying for bank loans and SBA loans, off-premise caterers may look to credit unions, private investor groups, limited partnerships, and even friends and family members to help finance their start-up businesses. We must caution, however, that borrowing should be kept at an absolute minimum to maximize profits and cash flow. It is difficult and stressful to start out a business saddled with obligations of monthly debts and/or high interest to repay.

Credit Card Processing Services

As their businesses grow, most caterers find they must eventually accept credit card payments for their services. It's a convenience for the client, but can be a rather expensive proposition for the caterers because credit card companies charge a processing fee that varies from 2 percent to as much as 7 percent or more. And it's amazing how a credit card processor with an advertised fee of 2.5 percent can quickly double it with "special charges"—transactions fees, monthly fees, and miscellaneous other fees. If you do a certain dollar amount of credit card business per month or if your personal credit rating is high, the company might discount the rate.

You must apply for credit card processing capability at a bank (known in this case as a *merchant bank*) or a third-party processing company. Of course, there are application fees too. The company might ask to visit your commissary and might take a photograph of it, to prove that you are doing business at that location. Or the company might ask you to provide the photo, along with business licenses and financial documents (tax records, bank statements, etc.)

Some merchant banks require that you have an account there to process credit card payments. One aspect of credit card processing that makes business owners squeamish is that you're allowing someone access to your account—bank employees will be depositing payments but also deducting fees and/or charge-backs. The agreement between your company and the bank probably allows the bank to put a hold on at least part of your account. Be sure that these are terms you can agree to before signing up; they might be negotiable.

You will want to ask how quickly the money is posted to your account after a credit card transaction is made, and if the fees are higher when the credit card information is taken by phone instead of by "swiping" the card.

Third-party processors often offer package deals that include software and equipment, "everything you need" to start accepting credit cards. What they might not emphasize is that you are locking yourself into a multiyear contract and leasing these components at a much higher price than what you could purchase them for on your own.

When you've started taking credit cards, you will want to check the monthly statements you receive from the company to be sure that you're not being hit with unnecessary charges.

The cost of this "convenience" should also be taken into consideration when setting your prices. A gross margin of 2 to 7 percent on each event is very significant and must be included in the pricing structure or you end up losing a small percentage on every transaction paid for by credit card.

Caterers who choose not to accept credit cards on a regular basis but find themselves in need of credit card processing occasionally to book a client should take a look at www.paypal.com, which offers credit card processing at fairly modest fees.

Federal Taxes

What would business be like in the United States if there were no federal taxes? Most likely, almost all businesses would be more profitable and, certainly, would require less paperwork. However, taxes are a way of life, and business owners face what many believe is more than their fair share. The major tax laws that affect off-premise caterers relate to payment of:

- Federal income taxes (both corporate and personal)
- Social Security (also known as the *Federal Insurance Contributions Act, FICA*)
- Medicare taxes (MICA)
- Federal unemployment taxes (FUTA)

There are also a number of state and local taxes on sales, payroll, income, and so on. These change often, so there is no substitute for the services of a good Certified Public Accountant (CPA) to assist you with them. This text is meant only as an overview of the touchy topic of taxes; it contains general information that is relevant at the moment, as we're writing this. For federal tax questions and forms, the Internal Revenue Service (IRS) website (www.irs.gov) is a gold mine of information.

Most off-premise caterers are incorporated and must file a corporate income tax return at the end of the year. A year means either a calendar year or a fiscal year. If based on a calendar year, the tax return is normally due no later than March 15 of the following year. Ask your CPA for clarification.

It is imperative to report income and expenses properly on the income tax form! Overstatements of expenses and/or understatements of income can ultimately ruin a successful business. The penalties for errors and omissions are substantial, and the cost for professional tax preparation assistance is small compared to the consequences of preparing the report incorrectly. This is serious business, involving interest, penalties, and even prison terms in some cases, if the IRS decides that information was given fraudulently to avoid paying taxes.

However, there is nothing wrong with taking full advantage of the legal deductions allowed by the tax laws. Here are a few of the tax deductions that catering businesses often overlook:

- Employers' payments for educational expenses—either their own or their staff members' attendance at classes and seminars
- Magazines, books, CDs, and DVDs related to business skills
- Bank and/or credit bureau service charges and fees
- Gifts to vendors and clients
- Casual (part-time) labor and tips
- Casualty and theft losses
- Home office expenses
- Commuting miles between home and work
- Business-related computer services charged to personal accounts and/or credit cards
- Parking, meters, tolls, and cab fares related to business
- Postage
- Participation in, or attendance at, trade shows
- Telephone calls away from the business
- Contributions to SEP and Keogh accounts (self-employed retirement plans)

Your CPA can surely add to this list as well. As you prepare for year-end taxes, it is time to take a hard look at your expected profit. If it is high, that is a mixed blessing in terms of taxes. If your profits are higher than expected, consider taking these steps:

- Purchasing equipment and/or stockpiling nonperishable inventory
- Paying vendors in advance on accounts due
- Delaying client billing until the beginning of the next accounting period

If your profits are lower than expected, consider taking these steps:

- Arranging with key vendors to delay payment until the beginning of the next accounting year
- Reducing your own pay as company owner for a month or two
- Asking key clients for larger advance deposits

Being tax-savvy and taking these steps can improve your profits and show your banker improved results.

Tax Withholding

Employers are required to pay one-half of the Social Security (FICA) and Medicare (MICA) taxes for their employees. The other half is withheld from employees' paychecks by you, as their employer, and paid quarterly to the IRS. The maximum wage base for payment of Social Security tax is $106,800; however, all wages are subject to the Medicare tax.

Like any other self-employed person, off-premise caterers must also pay the full amount (both the employer's and the employee's halves) of Social Security and Medicare taxes on their own wages that they receive from the catering firm. You may be able to reduce the amount of Social Security tax you pay if you are married and your spouse happens to work outside the business and pay FICA at that job.

Off-premise caterers are also required to pay federal unemployment insurance (FUTA) for their staff, as well as state unemployment tax. Amounts of the state taxes vary among the states; normally, the amount of federal unemployment tax is reduced by the amount paid to the state.

What happens to the money you withhold from employees' paychecks for FICA, Medicare, and FUTA? There are very specific federal rules about this, with which your CPA will be familiar. These monies must be deposited at certain intervals into banks; then the banks forward the money to the U.S. Treasury. Sometimes a business owner who is short on cash may be tempted to use these withheld wages for business expenses, postponing the federal deposit until cash flow improves. We know business owners who have been jailed for this and/or whose companies have been shut down for not making their federal payments. It is a violation of federal law, and the penalties are severe. We hear business owners say that although the IRS will allow delinquent taxpayers to negotiate payment plans for what they owe, it is better to borrow money to keep the taxes current than to have to deal with the IRS when they fall behind. In our view, this is true.

Summary

Delicious food, impeccable service, and flawless event planning must generate profit for your company—and the better you understand the financial workings of your business, the more likely that is to happen. This chapter touches on the basics, and the best advice contained herein might be to take a separate accounting course. Even if you will not be doing the books yourself, you will need to be able to interpret financial data to make many everyday business decisions. This means monitoring not only sales volume, but also the expenses that affect the company's overall profitability.

In this chapter, the would-be off-premise caterer learns about preparing a budget, calculating start-up expenses, and determining the business's cash flow, month to month. The chapter includes the formula for determining a break-even point, and explains common accounting terminology. The Chart of Accounts is introduced and the various types of accounts are described. Sample Income Statements and Balance Sheets are provided and explained.

Other practical financial considerations are also part of the chapter, from tips on selecting accounting software for catering firms, to guidelines for choosing a bank and credit card processor and managing money with an eye on fraud prevention. The chapter ends with a brief discussion of federal taxes and the importance of calculating them correctly and paying them on time.

Study Questions

1. Why is a deposit for a future event accounted for as a liability?
2. How is it possible for a business to have a net loss in a month but maintain positive cash flow?
3. What is a Chart of Accounts, and why does your business need one?
4. Describe one more way to control costs that is not listed on pages 524–525.
5. What is the difference between an Income Statement and a Balance Sheet?

Index